Limnological Modeling

Limnological Modeling

A case Study of River Suswa

– Authors –

D. R. Khanna

R. Bhutiani

2018

Daya Publishing House®

A Division of

Astral International Pvt. Ltd.

New Delhi - 110 002

First Published, 2007
Reprinted, 2018

ISBN: 978-81-7035-449-9 (Hardbound)

Publisher's note:

Every possible effort has been made to ensure that the information contained in this book is accurate at the time of going to press, and the publisher and author cannot accept responsibility for any errors or omissions, however caused. No responsibility for loss or damage occasioned to any person acting, or refraining from action, as a result of the material in this publication can be accepted by the editor, the publisher or the author. The Publisher is not associated with any product or vendor mentioned in the book. The contents of this work are intended to further general scientific research, understanding and discussion only. Readers should consult with a specialist where appropriate.

Every effort has been made to trace the owners of copyright material used in this book, if any. The author and the publisher will be grateful for any omission brought to their notice for acknowledgement in the future editions of the book.

Published by : **Daya Publishing House**®
A Division of
Astral International Pvt. Ltd.
– ISO 9001:2008 Certified Company –
4736/23, Ansari Road, Darya Ganj
New Delhi-110 002
Ph. 011-43549197, 23278134
E-mail: info@astralint.com
Website: www.astralint.com

Abbreviations

AAS	Atomic Absorption Spectrophotometer
BGLB	Brilliant Green Lactose Bile Broth
BMKBM	Beck Modified Khanna Bhutiani Model
BOD	Biochemical Oxygen Demand
Ca/Mg	Total Hardness
CFU	Colony Forming Unit
COD	Chemical Oxygen Demand
DECS	Delaware Estuary Comprehensive Study Model
DO	Dissolved Oxygen
DOC	Dissolved Oxygen Concentration
DOSAG	Dissolved Oxygen Sag Model
EBT	Eriochrome Black T
EDTA	Ethylene di-amine Tetra Acetic Acid
Eh	Oxidation Reduction Potential
Free CO_2	Free Carbon Dioxide
HCL	Hollow Cathode Lamp

HPC	Heterotrophic Plate Count
JTU	Jackson's Turbidity Unit
K	Conductivity
MB	McConkey's Broth
MFT	Membrane Filter Technique
MPN	Most Probable Number
MTFT	Multiple Tube Fermentation Technique
NAM	Nutrient Agar Medium
NGRBAA	Neo-peptone Glucose Rose Bengal Aureomycin Agar
PA	Phenolphthalein Alkalinity
pH	Hydrogen Ion Concentration
QUAL II	River Quality Model
r	Coefficient Correlation
rH_2	Oxidation Reduction Index
SD	Standard Deviation
SPC	Standard Plate Count
TS	Total Solids
TA	Total Alkalinity
TCD	Temperature Control Device
TMDL	Total Maximum Daily Loadings
USEPA	United States Environmental Protection Agency

Preface

Water as a natural resource has been a primary concern of man throughout his existence. We receive fresh water from the rivers, lakes, Ponds etc. but we also dump our wastes in these water bodies, which have created the problem of water pollution. The quality and quantity of drinking water is decreasing day by day, the main cause is water pollution. Increasing population is one of the main reasons of deterioration in quality of water. Hence it becomes a great challenge to provide the clean and safe drinking water for both rural and urban population throughout the World. Because failing to provide safe drinking water may adversely affect the progress of country Therefore, it becomes essential to understand water quality and methods to control water pollution.

Seeing the mounting public pressure of water bodies the need to protect it from pollution is essential, where mathematical modeling is the best alternative as accepted by the decision makers. Today mathematical modeling has become integral component of water quality and management programs. Mathematical modeling is a good modern test whether the process is understood.

Why the mathematical modeling? What advantages are there for the efforts expanded? The advantage lies in the fact that the processes involved are dynamic–that is they are not constant with time. The use of systems analysis and mathematical modeling for formulating and solving river pollution problem is of relatively recent vintage and has not been used widely during the last three decades.

Various models regarding the complex biological, ecological and physiological solutions have been developed so far and a variety of mathematical techniques have been employed to solve these models.

This book Limnological Modeling is a case study of river Suswa and consists of various methods to analyze physico-chemical, biological and microbiological parameters, besides these methods this book consists models to predict the river quality in terms of Dissolve Oxygen (DO) and Biochemical Oxygen Demand (BOD).

All the models developed so far regarding DO–BOD interaction, uses light intensity, but in cloudy day or in monsoon season when light intensity is zero our model provides good results. Other part of the book deals with the data requirement to assess water quality, the approaches to, and applications to limnological modeling.

We are indebted to the Head, Department of Zoology and Environmental Sciences, Gurukula Kangri Vishwavidyalaya, Haridwar, for encouraging us from time to time and for providing the laboratory facilities for this work Acknowledgement is also made to M/s Daya Publishing House, New Delhi for publishing this book.

D.R. Khanna

R. Bhutiani

Contents

Chapter 1

Introduction

"आपोहिष्ठा मयोभुवस्ता न अर्जेदघातन महें रणांम चक्षसे"

-यजु0 11/50

Which means,

Water is an elixir of life; it is the source of energy, governs the evolution and function of the universe on the earth.

Throughout history water has been considered a natural resource critical to human survival. Being a natural resource it has been a primary concern of man throughout his existence. Human history can, infact, be written in terms of interactions and interrelations between human and water (Biswas, 1970).

Fresh water resources are finite and exist in a closed system. Only a tiny fraction of the water which covers the earth is of use to humanity-97 percent is salt water, filling the oceans and seas.Of the remainder, 99 percent is out of reach, frozen up in icecaps and glacier, or buried deep underground. We depend on what is left in rivers, lakes and accessible aquifers to quench our thirst, wash away our wastes, water our crops and, increasingly, to power our industries.

Water has been used for several purposes like drinking, bathing, irrigation, fisheries, industrial processes, transportation and wastes disposal etc. Therefore it is not difficult to realize why civilization and habitats often developed along the banks of several strategically important rivers. Human survival and welfare generally depended on regular availability and control of water.

In most parts of the world, fresh water resources are overstrained. Industrial wastes, sewage and agricultural runoff overload rivers and lakes with chemicals, wastes and nutrients, consequently poisoning water supplies.

On a global scale, total water abundance is not the problem; the problem is water's availability in the right place at the right time in the right form.

Today, with the rapid increase in population, unplanned urbanization, over exploitation etc. for different purposes, the quality of water has been deteriorating at an alarming rate, which ultimately results in depletion of aquatic biota. In many developing countries, governments are having difficulty, coping with fecal contamination of drinking water, the degradation of fresh water resources, and hazardous waste pollution. Many cities seem unable to control and reduce the dumping of raw sewage and garbage into rivers and drainage canals, or stop the growth of mountains of solid wastes from households and industries.

The easy availability of fresh water is a major problem as 80 per cent of our rivers are polluted due to industrial and domestic discharges. With increasing pollution problem availability of fresh water is decreasing at a greater rate. Today very rare or no river has been spared from industrial discharge, this untreated industrial discharge increases the water pollutants. Presence of high values of parameters such as BOD, acidity, alkalinity, hardness, heavy metal etc. makes the water unfit for human consumption.

The consequences of these activities have been the expensive contamination of thousands of private and public water sources. Often when water is contaminated, there are no biological indications to indicate any change in water quality. Thus, people may continue to drink contaminated water until they fall ill. A contaminated water supply may only be noticed when an entire population becomes affected by an epidemic.

Today with the unthoughtful use of water, many countries located in arid and semiarid regions have started facing the problem of water crisis, as total global population is increasing. On one hand due to increasing population, water requirement is steadily increasing and on the other hand per capita water available is declining steadily since the total amount of freshwater available is limited. Most of the cities of India are facing water crisis and availability of freshwater for humans is becoming a dream. If this trend continues then in the next fifty years there may be possibility of a world war, *i.e.*, the war on water, and whole of our world would become desert where availability of water will not be an easy job.

Discharges of pollutants can degrade the quality of water, and hence adversely affect the water's beneficial uses as well as the health of its aquatic ecosystem. To manage the quality of natural water bodies that are subject to pollutant inputs, one must be able to predict the degradation in quality that results from those inputs. Many models have been developed to assist managers in making these predictions. Before investments are made to improve or protect water quality, it is prudent to predict, to the best of one's ability–*i.e.* the water quality improvement–associated with each alternative water quality management decision. Admittedly these predictions will not be perfect since future pollutant loads and water quantities are unknown. Since any prediction model will always be a simplification of reality, and the parameter values of any water quality model will likely be uncertain, there will always be uncertainty associated with any model prediction.

Seeing the mounting public pressure at water bodies the need to protect it from pollution is essential where mathematical modeling is the best alternative as accepted by the decision-makers.

The use of systems analysis and mathematical modeling for formulating and solving river pollution problem is of relatively recent vintage and has been used widely during the last three decades.

Let us take as a premise fact that river water quality is never in a steady-state situation nor can its behavior be completely determined. The system is therefore intrinsically dynamic and uncertain. Therefore any models that are to be developed must at least be accommodated with this premise, although that would not preclude simplifying assumptions. The water quality model should be usable for optimizing data collection, for setting up a monitoring network, for siting potable water intakes and ascertaining the concentration of the pollution sources.

Moreover when formulating the water quality model it is to be assumed that there would be deforestation, the areas would be inundated and that humus would be removed. If these actions do not take place then for the time of decomposition the actual organic matter content will be higher than the computed value whereas the DO content will decrease and odour and taste producing substances may appear in the water.

The requirement of river monitoring was for both a biological and a physico-chemical monitor. These have different though complementary functions.

The limnological models can be used to conduct numerical experiments, test hypotheses, and help understand the response of river limnology. A mathematical model is representation of physical stream. It acts as a bridge between study of mathematics and application of mathematics in limnology and other fields.

Suswa is a spring fed river with which people of Raiwala are sentimentally attached. It has been deteriorated considerably due to increased human interference in several ways *viz.* bathing, dumping of domestic wastes, sewage discharge, excessive fishing etc. All these human activities have not only affected adversely the river water quality and its biota, but have also increased the unsuitability of water for social and economic purposes.

It is quite essential that the natural environment of the river should be conducive to the extent that the fish may thrive, grow and reproduce to the best, but various human activities change the physico-chemical characteristics, which directly affects the flora and fauna of the water.

Because freshwater resources are the lifelines of a community, it is essential that communities get involved and work together to ensure they have continuous clean sources.

The Suswa water is utilized for a variety of purposes. The study on this river is scanty. So, this study will therefore be useful in determining its suitability for different purposes in this region. Hence, the present study deals with the riverine ecological factors of the river Suswa at Raiwala.

"Water flows from high in the mountains, water run deeps the earth, miraculously, water comes to us, and sustain all life."

Thich Nhat Hanh

Physio-geographical Features of Raiwala and Description of Sampling Stations

Raiwala is a town in district Dehradun (30º 16′N latitude and 78º 00′E longitude). The town Raiwala is situated on the right bank of the river Suswa at the foothills of the Shivalik Himalayas. The town has a total population of approx. 50,000 people and is surrounded by Hardwar, Rishikesh and Dehradun (Figure 1.1). Raiwala is mainly famous for its cantonment area.

Raiwala is situated at an altitude of approximately 370 meters form sea level. The location of Raiwala on globe is on latitude 30º 00′ N and longitude 78º 16′ E. (Figure 1.1). Suswa is a spring fed river. It originates from Ramgarh (Dehradun) and after passing a total distance of approximately 36 kilometers from reserve forest and as well as from places habitat by human beings it merges into river Ganga at Gohri range forest.

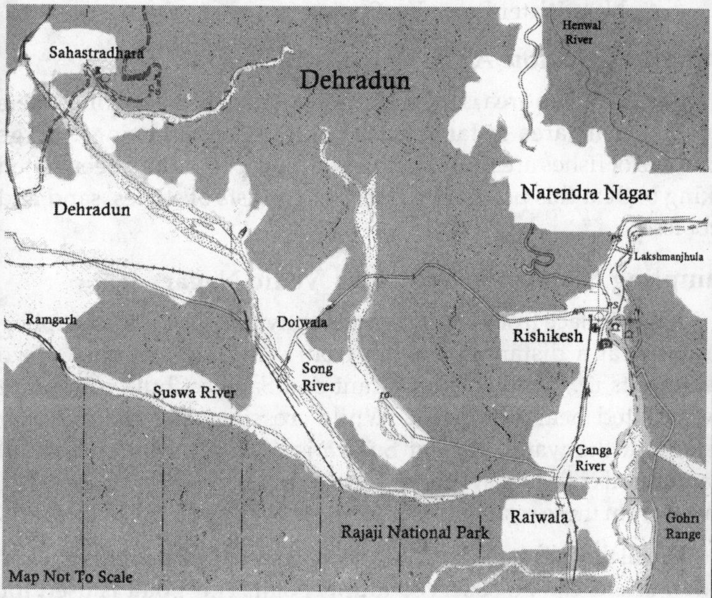

Figure 1.1: Map Showing River Suswa

The Raiwala citizens utilize the Suswa water for a variety of purposes, so at some places it receives town effluents and other wastes. These wastes change the physico-chemical characteristics of this river. Besides this, it adversely affects the ecology of fishes residing there. Immediately after crossing Raiwala, the Suswa river assimilates into the Ganga hence, it was considered desirable to examine the aquatic ecology of the Suswa at Raiwala (Dehradun).

Sampling Stations

Following four sampling stations were selected for this study (for the analysis of physico-chemical, biological and microbiological parameters), which are located at a stretch of 5.5 kms. (Plates 1.1–1.4).

1. Satyanarayan Area
2. Upstream Vedic Nagar
3. Down stream Vedic Nagar
4. Near Water Pumping Station

Sampling Station A: Satyanarayan Area

Satyanarayan area is the first area where river Suswa first enters Raiwala. This area is far from habitat of human beings. Large numbers of fishes are found in this site. Few people had been noted taking bath at this point. The riverbed consists of stones, sand and pebbles.

Sampling Station B: Upstream Vedic Nagar

It is the place from where human activities start. This sampling station is at a distance of 2 km from sampling station A. Two restaurants *i.e.,* Midway restaurant and Sanjha Chula restaurant are situated near this point. While crossing near the midway restaurant the water of river Suswa is diverted through a small channel and collected in field of restaurant for boating purpose. The wastes from these restaurants also mix in to river Suswa at this spot.

On all the 365 days of the year, fecal matter, waste clothes, food materials etc. can be observed at this point. This point is used for bathing and washing purposes also. The riverbed consists of pebbles and sand.

Plate 1.1: Sampling Station A (Satyanarayan Area)

Plate 1.2: Sampling Station B (Upstream Vedic Nagar)

Plate 1.3: Sampling Station C (Downstream Vedic Nagar)

Plate 1.4: Sampling Station D (Near Water Pumping Station)

Sampling Station C: Downstream Vedic Nagar

This sampling station is between Satyanarayan area and water pumping station of Raiwala. The sampling station is at a distance of 1.5 km from sampling station B. While crossing from this station the water of Suswa is diverted through various small channels to agricultural fields for irrigation purpose. Occasionally bathing and washing activities can be seen at this point. At this sampling station riverbed consists of stones and sand.

Sampling Station D: Near Water Pumping Station

This sampling station is situated at a distance of 2 km from sampling station C. River water is diverted to agricultural land by means of small channels while crossing this sampling station. Here width and depth of river decreases as compared to other sampling stations. No bathing and washing activities are seen at this sampling station during the course of study. At this sampling station Suswa flows with slow speed. The riverbed consists of stones and sand.

Purpose of the Study

The Suswa water is utilized for a variety of purposes. The study on this river is scanty. So this study will therefore be useful in determining its suitability for various purposes in this region.

1. As the river assimilates into Ganges, it was considered desirable to examine the aquatic ecology of the Suswa at Raiwala.
2. The interesting part of the study was to demonstrate changes in water quality, taking into account the representative water quality characteristics of the Suswa as well as the intended use of water.
3. To study effect of rapid natural variations.
4. The use of mathematical models lead to an increased capability for defining and evaluating possible alternatives and provides for a wider range of options at every level of decision-making.

Chapter 2

Review of Literature

It is a universal truth that life cannot exist without water. Today we are going fast towards the way of success. Although man is touching the height of perfection yet on other side he is the prime amuse for the explosion of the planet and its water resources. The very first criteria, *i.e.*, standard criteria for drinking water was reported in the literature in 1921, when United States published USPH standard for drinking water, but it specified only bacteriological parameters.

The physico-chemical characteristics of water and the dependence of all life processes on these factors makes it desirable to take water as an environment. Physico-chemical features such as dissolved solids, dissolved oxygen; turbidity, temperature, hardness etc mainly influence productivity of water.

According to Hutchinson (1957), a skillful limnologist can probably learn more about the nature of a lake from a series of oxygen determination than from any other kind of chemical data. The physico-chemical factors directly influence the aquatic biota. Therefore, it attracted several biologists who made commendable contribution on the biological aspect of water bodies.

Fresh water lakes and streams together cover about 0.20 per cent of the earth's surface and have a volume of 2.04 per cent × 10^5 Km^3 [Lickens, 1961]. A close analysis of literature in Indian context tells that a good quantity of valuable data is available on lentic systems in comparison to that of stream and rivers owing to the difficulties in the methodologies to be adopted in river system.

The need to define the quality of water has developed with the increasing demand for water, which is suitable for specific uses and confirms to a desired quality. The most fundamental need is for water suitable for drinking, personal hygiene and food preparation and that poses no risk to human health. Increasing development and its associated industrialization has, in addition, introduced the need for water quality with specific physical, chemical or biological characteristics.

Accurate assessment of water quality, whether in relation to the requirements of intended water uses or in order to determine the impacts of an activity on the water resource (such as water disposal or abstraction) depends on the results generated by specific monitoring activities which define the physical, chemical and/or biological condition of the resource.

Several workers both from India and abroad studied various aspects of water quality. Marsh (1907) examined the impact of industrial waste on fish. Kofoid (1908) studied the plankton of river Illinois. Birge and Judey (1911) worked on physico-chemical and biological characteristics of lake Wiscosin. Allen (1920) studied plankton of the San Joaquin river and its tributaries in California. Richardson (1921) reported various changes in the composition of bottom and shore fauna of Illinois river and its connecting lakes. Atkin and Harris (1924) observed seasonal changes and the Heleoplankton of fresh water ponds. Galtsoff (1924) studied the limnology of upper Mississippi. Clarke (1924) analyzed the composition of the river and lake waters of United States. Greenfield (1925) observed the chemical and biological parameters of Illinois river. Eddy (1934) studied the fresh water plankton communities of Illinois river. Garner *et al.* (1936) made a survey on chemical and biological characteristics of river Holme. Alexander *et al.* (1935) made a survey of the river Tees. Chandler (1940) made limnological studies of western lake Erie. Welch (1948) published book on limnological methods. Berner (1951) made a study about the limnology of the lower Missouri river. Griffith (1955) analyzed the plankton yield in relation to certain physico-chemical parameters of lake Michigen. Thomas (1958) made a study on Mississippi and Churchill rivers. Oliff (1959) analyzes the hydrobiology of Tugela River. Holden and Green (1960) studied the hydrology and plankton of river Sokoto. Peenak (1962) investigated quantitative zooplankton sampling in littoral vegetation areas. Dorris (1963) studied the limnology of the middle Mississippi.

Hynes (1970) studied the ecology of running water. Needham and Needham (1972) gave a guide to study fresh water biology. Robinson and Kaller (1976) made a comparative study on the water characteristics of four northern-west Virginia rivers. Crayton and Sommerfield (1979) works on the composition and abundance of phytoplankton in tributaries of the lower Colorado River. Whitton (1983) studied the ecology of a number of European rivers.

In India, the first work on hydrology and hydrobiology was of a pond in Indian Museum compound at Calcutta by Pruthi (1933), he studied the bionomics of fresh waters of India. Ghosuddin (1934) made a study of the algal flora of the river Mossi. Ganpati and Chacko (1951) made an investigation on the river Godavari and examined the effects of paper mill pollution at Rajahmundry. Chacko and Srinivasan (1955) studied the hydrobiology of the major rivers of Madras State of South India. Chakarbarty *et al.* (1959) made a survey on the plankton and physico-chemical conditions of the Jamuna River at Allahabad. Singh (1960) studied the Chlorophyceae of Kumaon. Zafer (1964) make studies on the ecology of algae in certain fishpond in Hyderabad. Rao and Govind (1964) carried out the hydrobiology of Tungbhadra reservoir. Baloni and Sarkar (1965) made some observation on pollution of river Yamuna at Okhla water works intake Delhi. Saxena *et al.* (1966) observed pollution of the Ganga near Kanpur. Venkateshvarlu and Jayanti (1968) study the hydrobiology of river Sabarmati to evaluate water quality. Agarwal *et al.* (1976) analyzed the hydrobiology of river Ganga at Varanasi. Kant and Anand (1978) investigated the inter-relationship of phytoplankton and physical parameters in Mansar lake of Jammu.

Badola and Singh (1981) works on hydrobiology of river Alaknanda. Tirath and Bhargava (1982) study the water quality of Gomti River. Raina *et al.* (1984) made pollution study of river Jhelum. Chattopadhya *et al.* (1984) made a study on the pollution status of river Ganga at Kanpur. Bhowmick and Singh (1985) worked on the phytoplanktonic population in relation to physico-chemical factors of river Ganga. Nautiyal (1990) explained the ecology of the Ganga river system in the upland of Garhwal Himalayan environment. Mir and Kachroo (1990) studied limnological studies on Kashmir lakes VIII dynamics of Phytoplankton in Dal Lake. Bhatnagar and Garg (1990) worked on qualitative and quantitative analysis of micro fungi colonizing leaf litter or *Oryza sativa*. Pathak (1991) studied some aspects of ecology of river Sarju and Gomti of the Kumaon Himalayas. Singh (1991) published a book "Advances in Limnology". Babu & Manoharachary (1992) studied the extra aquatic fungi associated with two polluted water bodies. Sarkar and Chaudhary (1993) studied fungi of wastewater environment in relation to pollution of river Hooghly. Joshi *et al.* (1993) evaluated the physico-chemical characteristics of river Bhagirathi in the uplands of Garhwal Himalayas. Saxena and Chauhan (1993) observed the physico-chemical aspects of pollution in river Yamuna at Agra. Khanna (1993) reported the pollution aspects of river Ganga at Hardwar. Khanna *et al.* (1993) studied about the plankton ecology of river Ganga at Chandi Ghat, Hardwar. Pandey *et al.* (1993) studied on the physico-chemical quality of water of river Kosi at Purnia. Chopra & Patrick (1994) studied the effect of domestic sewage on self-purification of Ganga water at Rishikesh. Khulbe *et al.* (1995) worked on ecological study on water molds of some rivers of Kumaon Himalayas Dwivedi *et al.* (1995) made a limnological investigation in relation to fish production of two ponds of Patna. Chopra & Rehman (1995) made a study on self-purification of physico-chemical properties of Ganga canal water at Jwalapur, Hardwar. Joshi *et al.* (1996) did a study of planktonic and benthic components of three selected tributaries of river Ganga between Devprayag and Rishikesh. Joshi (1996) studied the hydro biological profile of river Sutlej in its middle stretch in western Himalayas. Khanna *et al.* (1997) investigated population of green algae in relation to physico-chemical factors of river Ganga. Jindal and Ghezta (1998) reported pollution status of water bodies of Chandigarh. Kaur and Khulbe (1998) studied occurrence, distribution and ecology of water Molds in Nanak Sagar reservoir. Singh & Ahmed (1998) worked on comparative study of the phytoplankton of river Ganga and pond of patna. Sharma and Pande (1998) investigated the pollution status of Ramganga river at Moradabad. Khanna *et al.* (1999) studied correlation between abiotic factors and planktonic population in river Ganga at Rishikesh (U.P). Khanna and Singh (1999) observed diurnal variation in microbial ecology of Narkewala pond at Ferupur, Hardwar. Khanna *et al.* (1999) studied fishes and their ecology of the river Suswa at Raiwala, Dehradun. Badola & Badola (1999) gave observations on destructive fishing methods and recommendations to protect fish fauna in Garhwal Himalayas. Chugh (2000) studied the seasonal variation in microbial ecology of river Ganga at Hardwar. Khanna *et al.* (2000) observed 20 genera of phytoplanktonic population of a pond they revealed that highest phytoplanktonic population was recorded in winter season while lowest in monsoon season. Jain and Sharma (2000) worked on water quality of Rampur reservoir of Guna district (M.P). Gandhe & Gandhe (2000) worked on occurrence of riverine water molds in relation to hydrogen ion concentration. Gautam *et al.* (2001) made an attempt to explain the pollution sources along the river Ganga from Rishikesh to Haridwar. Khanna *et al.* (2001) studied fluctuation in the population density of Macro-Invertebrates of river Ganga at Pashulok Barrage, Rishikesh. Sharma & Jain (2001) works on diurnal variation in some aspects of limnology of Gopalpura tank of district Guna (M.P.). Lazaras and Mishra (2002) worked on physico-chemical components of Machna river water and related fish ecology at Betul (MP). Mahajan *et al.* (2002) made an attempt to present the results of physico-chemical and biological investigations carried out on the river Kunda. Patel *et al.* (2002) studied on hydro biological observations of Virla reservoir at Khargone. Sukumaran (2002) worked on coliform bacteria (an index of aquatic pollution). Basu and Mitra (2002) studied on pollution of river Damodar at Burdwan with special reference to metals, COD and pH. Jhajhria (2002) recognized 11 genera of zooplankton and 19 genera of phytoplankton during limnobiotic studies of Shekhawat pond, Jodhpur. Kumar & Sharma (2002) studied the water quality of river Krishni (Part-I physico-chemical characteristics). Kumar & Sharma (2002) studied the water quality of river Krishni (Part-II Biological characteristics and bio indicators). Fokmare and Musaddiq (2002) investigated the quality of Kapshi Lake and Purna river waters to evaluate their suitability for drinking purposes. Srivastava and Patil (2002) made an attempt for the assessment of pollution in river Tapti in Khandesh plain region. Kala & Sharma (2002) worked on effect of physico-chemical factors on phytoplankton population.

Raghavendra and Hosmani (2002) worked on hydrobiology of Mandakally Lake. Shanthi *et al.* (2002) deals with the ecological studies of lake Singanallur with reference to physico-chemical characteristics and water pollution. Sedamkar and Angadi (2002) studied primary productivity of two fresh water bodies of Gulbarga. Abraham *et al.* (2002) studied the distribution of hydrographic parameters and heavy metal ions in river Periyar. Mruthunjaya and Hosmani (2002) worked on comparative account of physico-chemical parameters, enzymatic activity and plankton population in three water bodies of Mysore city. Ahmed & Begum (2002) conducted study to assess the bacteriological quality of water sample in hill stream of Khanapara during different seasons. Naz *et al.* (2002) studied aquatic fungi as indicator organism. Khanna and Bhutiani (2003) worked on limnological characteristics of river Ganga at Hardwar. Kaur & Joshi (2003) describes seasonal variation in some physico-chemical parameters of river Ganga. Monichan and Sharma (2003) study on distribution status of fish fauna in Etawah district U.P. Khanna and Bhutiani (2003) worked on limnological status of Satikund pond at Hardwar and they observed that phytoplanktonic concentration was dominated by diatoms and recorded 3 genera of zooplankton. Shaikh and Yeragi (2003) studied the bio diversity of plankton in Tansa river of Thane district. Patnaik and Nayak (2003) studied the diurnal variation of some physico-chemical properties of Gopalpur coastal waters of Orissa during monsoon period. Prasad and Singh (2003) studied the composition, abundance and distribution of phytoplankton and zoo benthos in a tropical water body. Sivakumar *et al.* (2003) studied on water quality of the river Ambarampalayam. Selvaraj *et al.* (2003) studied on hydrology and fish species diversity of Thamiraparani River in Kanyakumari district. Arjariya (2003) studied the physico-chemical profile and plankton diversity of Ranital lake. Jena *et al.* (2003) studied on water quality parameters around Sagar Island. Maruthanayagam *et al.* (2003) studies the qualitative analysis of zooplankton population of pond indicators and reported occurrence of 21 species during both summer and rainy season. Subramanyam and Kumar (2003) worked on evaluation of water quality of lake by pollution index method. Chatterjee and Raziuddin (2003) worked on physico-chemical parameters of loco tank, a reservoir in Asansol town. Prasad (2003) studied the physico-chemical and bacteriological quality and evaluate the suitability of ground water for drinking purpose.

Parashar *et al.* (2003) assessed the impact of collective bathing and increased organic load on quality of Ganga canal water downstream from Har-ki-Pauri. Khanna and Bhutiani (2004) worked on fish and their ecology of river Ganga at Gohri Ghat, Garhwal.

Other important contributions of Indian fresh water are those by Zafer (1959, 1966, 1968, 1986), Verma (1967), Vasisht and Dhir (1970), Kaul (1977), Munawar (1970), Sreeniwasan (1970, 1974), Unni (1982, 1983,), Adoni (1975,1985), Seenaya and Zafar (1979), Awatramani (1980), Rao and Shrivastava (1981), Varshney (1981), Nayak *et al.* (1982), Sehgal (1983), Jayadevi (1985), Rao *et al.* (1988), Siddiqui (1990), Pandey *et al.* (1993), Chandrashekhar and Kodarkar (1994), Kodarkar (1994), Jayachandran *et al.*(1995) and Choubey (1997).

Jhingran (1975) published a book on fish and fisheries of India. Mathur (1982) published a laboratory manual for water and wastewater testing. Shrivastava (1986) published a book on fishes of eastern Uttar Pradesh. Das (1989) published a handbook on limnology and water pollution. Khanna & Singh (2002) published a book on pond fish ecology & economics.

Seeing the mounting public pressure at water bodies the need to protect it from pollution is essential where mathematical modeling is the best alternative as accepted by the decision makers.

In looking over the many papers in the literature, it becomes obvious that system analysis is alive and well, and that it is being used wisely in water pollution control and does indeed greatly help in making rational decisions in water quality management.

Stimulated by the need to control pollution of the major sources of fresh water supply and to ensure protection of public health, sanitary engineers were probably among the first to examine quantitatively the physico–chemical and biological response of streams to loading of nutrients, either natural or man-induced. Among the first models in water management was the Delaware Estuary comprehensive (DECS) study model, formulated by Thomann (1963) and his associates for the Federal water Pollution Control Administration in the United States.

In the late 1960s the mounting public pressure in the developing countries for control of pollution stimulated investment in a host of special studies to find the best alternative ways of protecting the aquatic environment. The computer and computer science, especially mathematical modeling were stressed by zealous practitioners of the modeling art as aids to decision makers. Encouraged by even the modest success of the DECS experience and a few others, governmental agencies began to invest heavily in the new technology (Orlob, 1983).

During this period the comparatively simple Streeter-Phelps model of dissolved oxygen concentration (DOC) and biochemical oxygen demand (DO-BOD) appeared in a variety of computerized forms. The model DOSAG developed by the Texas water development board (1970) solved the steady state problem for a multi segment river system, providing flexibility in dealing with variable de-oxygenation coefficients, QUAL I, also produced for the Texas agency (Masch and Associate, 1970) simulated stream temperature as well as DO and BOD, allowing temperature adjustment in rate coefficients to be made internally during simulation. An extended version, QUAL II, produced for the United states environmental Protection Agency (USEPA), (Water Resources Engineers, Inc., 1973) included the capability to stimulate more complex stream systems for both steady and unsteady flow and to evaluate the impact of nutrient loading on the oxygen resources of the stream. Ecological interactions including photosynthesis and primary productivity have been the subjects of the most recent work on deterministic modeling of streams (Kelly 1975, Stehfest 1977).

Several workers have done important studies regarding mathematical modeling of water quality. Johnson (1996) worked on geochemical model of water quality in pit lake in oxidized Tuff. Jokiel and Loucks (1998) worked on water quality predictions and management. Chapman (1998) studied the water quality monitoring. Hanna *et al.* (1999) studied the results of simulated temperature control device operations on in reservoir and discharge water temperature using CE-QUAL-W2. McBean *et al.* (1999) described the "weight of evidence" approach, essential for consideration of intrinsic remediation as a means of protecting exposure risks in the environment.. Schumann *et al.* (2000) worked on the application of a geographic information system for conceptual rainfall-runoff modeling. Crowder and Diplas (2000) works on two-dimensional hydrodynamic models at scales of ecological importance. Rutherford *et al.* (2000) modified a computer model for epilithic algae and grazer biomass in streams to better predict the effects of temperature. Asaeda *et al.* (2000) developed a model to illustrate the annual lifecycle and the decomposition process of *Potamogeton pectinates*. Comin *et al.* (2000) edited a book on limnology and aquatic birds: Monitoring, modeling and management. Asaeda and Karunaratne (2000) developed a dynamic model to stimulate the growth dynamics of a monospecific stand of *Phragmites australis* in fresh water ecosystems. Viney *et al.* (2000) presented conceptual model of nutrient mobilization and transport applicable at large catchments scale. Akan *et al.* (2000) studied the modeling storm water run of quantity & quality from marine dry-docks. Vogler and Scherfig (2000) works on modeling BOD removal in constructed wetlands with mixing cell method. Bale (2000) described the construction and application of a numerical model representing mercury transformations and bioavailability in the aquatic environment of clear lake. Olsen *et al.* (2000) studied the distribution of phytoplankton in Eglwis Nynydd, a water supply reservoir in Wales using 3D Numerical modeling. Pinault *et al.* (2001) studied on inverse modeling of the hydrological and the hydro chemical behavior of hydro systems. Krishna *et al.* (2001) studies the prediction of treatment concentration for the reduction of COD of the effluents of pesticide plant using LOGIT model.

Asaeda *et al.* (2001) developed a numerical model incorporating phytoplankton, submerged macrophytes, *Potamogeton pectinatus* L., their decomposition process and resulting nutrient dynamics in overlying water. Saito *et al.* (2001) investigated the effects on the reservoir food web of a new temperature control device (TCD) on the dam of Shasta Lake.

Bartholow *et al.* (2001) studied the simulated limnological effects of the Shasta lake temperature control device. Saito *et al.* (2001) worked on inter disciplinary modeling to assess ecosystem effects of reservoir operations. Asaeda *et al.* (2001) studied the control of algal blooms in reservoirs with a curtain. Jha *et al.* (2001) worked on two-dimensional river modeling using finite element technique. Chandramouli and Raman (2001) works on multi reservoir modeling with dynamic programming and neural networks.

Gelda *et al.* (2001) worked on probabilistic model of ammonia and toxicity status for urban lake. Meixner. (2002) worked on multi criteria parameters estimation for models of stream chemical composition. Brezonic and Stadelmann (2002) studied the analysis and predictive models of storm water run off volumes, loads and pollutant concentration from watersheds in the twin cities metropolitan area. Gangji *et al.* (2002) worked on sediment and metals modeling in Shallow River. Chau and Jiang (2002) developed and implement the three-dimensional pollutant transport model for Pearl river Estuary. Clark and Sivaganesen (2002) worked on predicting chlorine residuals in drinking water. Juang and Shao (2002) worked on a simplified equilibrium model for sorption of heavy metal ions from aqueous solutions on chito–san; Karunaratne and Asaeda (2002) studied mathematical modeling as a tool in aquatic ecosystem management. Naito *et al.* (2002) worked on application of an ecosystem model for aquatic ecological risk assessment of chemicals for a Japanese lake. Chapra (2003) worked on engineering water quality models and TMDLs. Blois *et al.* (2003) presented the concept of robustness and applied to a model for the analysis of the impacts of spatially distributed policy measures on the surface water quality on a river basin scale. Son and Fujino (2003) proposed a model of the development of a periphyton community in a stream under the influence of nutrients and light. Li and Fleming (2003) developed a three dimensional mathematical model for free surface flow based on the Reynolds's–averaged Navier-stokes equation in a sigma co-ordinate system. Wang *et al.* (2003) developed a model to study the phosphorous release across sediment –water interface. Radwan *et al.* (2004) described the sensitivity and uncertainty for river quality modeling.

Keinath and Wanielista (1975) published a book on mathematical modeling for water pollution control processes. Morley (1979) published a book on mathematical modeling in water and wastewater treatment. Stiff (1980) edited the book on River pollution control. Orlob (1983) edited the book, mathematical modeling of water quality, Streams lakes and reservoir. Thomann and Muller (1987) published a book on principles of surface water quality modeling and controls. Canter (1996) wrote a book on environmental impact assessment. Schnoor (1996) published a book on environmental modeling

Giordano *et al.* (1997) published a book on a first course in mathematical modeling. Biswas (1998) edited a book on water resources. Kapur (2000) published a book on mathematical modeling.

Chapter 3
Materials

Sampling Programmes and Analysis

Bearing in mind the river characteristics, and the water quality requirements, the following routine sampling and analysis programmes were devised:

Number of Sites

Four.

Collection of samples

Monthly [Between 15th – 20th of each month].

Time of Sample Collection

Between 7 A.M. to 10.00 A.M.

On Site Analysis

Dissolved oxygen, free CO_2, temperature, pH and velocity

Analysis Within 24 Hours of Sampling

COD & all physico-chemical, biological parameters taken under study.

Analysis within Fifteen Days of Sampling

All heavy metals.

Application of Data in Mathematical Modeling

After completion of analytical work.

Material

It is an old axiom that the result of any testing method can be no better than the sample on which it is performed. Because of the increasing importance placed on verifying the accuracy and representativeness of data, greater emphasis is placed on proper sample collection, tracking and preservation techniques.

For the study of limnological status of river Suswa, water samples were collected monthly from different sampling stations *i.e.*, (A) Satyanarayan area, (B) Upstream Vedic nagar, (C) Down stream Vedic nagar and (D) Near water pumping station, during April 2002 to March 2004 in morning hours (from 7.00 a.m. to 10.00 am) (Figure 3.1).

Chemicals

The chemicals used in the present investigation were of analytical grade and were supplied by E. Merck India, S.D fine chemicals and B.D.H., India.

Instruments

Following instruments were used during the study

Sl.No.	*Name of Instruments*	*Make/Manufactured by*
1.	BOD incubator	Tasco
2.	Laminar bench	Yorco
3.	Spectrophotometer	Besto
4.	Electronic balance	Roy Electronic
5.	Conductivity meter	Tasco Chipset
6.	Jackson turbidity meter (flame)	-
7.	Vertical auto clave	Tasco
8.	COD Assembly	-
9.	Atomic absorption spectrophotometer	Shimadzu
10.	Hot plate	Sunvic
11.	Hot air oven	Modern Scientifics

Figure 3.1: Flow Diagram of Working Procedure

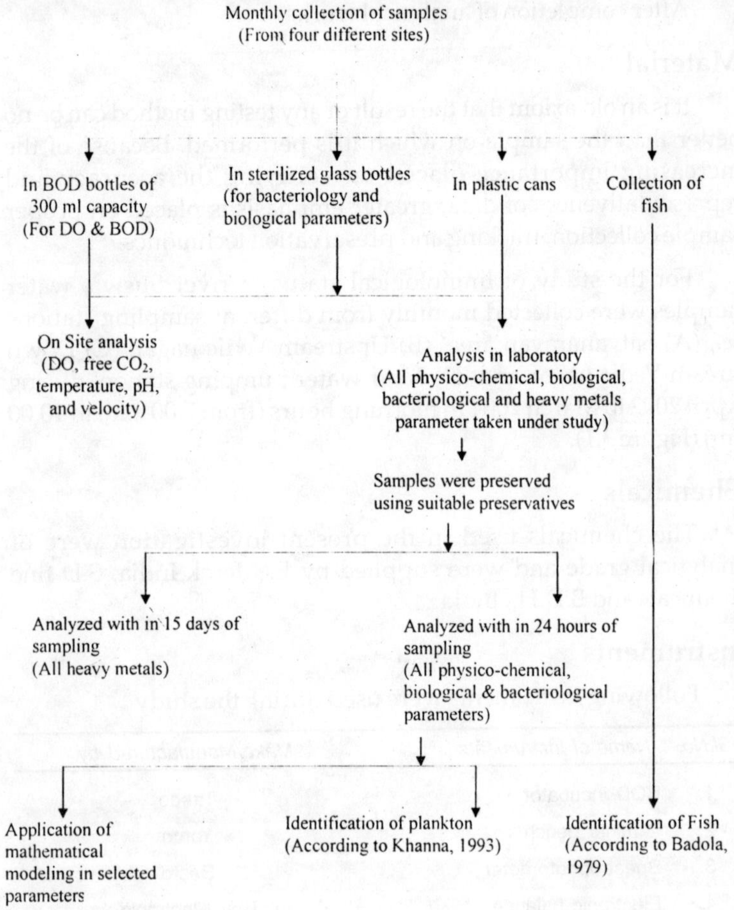

Sl.No.	Name of Instruments	Make/Manufactured by
12.	Microscope	-
13.	Plankton collection net	-
14.	Sedgwick rafter counting cell	-
15.	Mantle heater	A.J. Enterprises
16.	pH meter	Tasco
17.	Electronic colony counter	Blue Line
18.	Refrigerator	Godrej

Glasswares

All the glasswares used were of corning grade, manufactured by Borosil India Ltd.

Sampling Method

(A) Cleaning and Sterilization of Glasswares

All the glasswares and jerricans were cleaned or washed with soda and chromic acid and rinsed with double distilled water 2-3 times.

(*i*) Sample Bottles

300-ml capacity BOD bottles made of borosil were used for sample collection. They were washed with washing soda and chromic acid and rinsed with tap water followed by distilled water; the neck and stopper were wrapped with butter paper with the help of rubber band. The bottles were then sterilized in an autoclave at 15 lbs. pressure (121°C) for 15-25 minutes.

(*ii*) Pipettes

Pipettes of different volume size were washed and fitted with cotton plug at the upper end; these were then wrapped in butter paper and sterilized in an autoclave at 15-lbs./inch^2 pressure at 121°C for 15-20 minutes.

(*iii*) Petri Dishes

Petri dishes were washed with washing soda and chromic acid wrapped in butter paper and then sterilized in a hot air oven at 160-180 °C for 2-3 hours.

(*iv*) Test Tubes

Borosil test tubes were washed and then plugged with non-absorbent cotton wool, these were arranged in test tube racks and sterilization was done in an autoclave at 15-lbs./inch^2 pressure at 121°C for 15-20 minutes.

(*v*) Other Glasswares

Such as conical flasks, beakers, measuring cylinders etc. were washed carefully and then sterilized in hot air oven at 160-180°C for 2-3 hours.

(B) Collection of Samples

(i) For Determination of the Parameters

Conductivity, turbidity, total solids, pH (hydrogen ion concentration), COD, oxidation reduction index (rH_2), oxidation reduction potential (Eh), free CO_2, acidity, total alkalinity, total hardness Ca/Mg, chlorides, phosphates, lead, copper, iron, manganese, zinc, cobalt, calcium and magnesium. Samples were taken from 2 feet below the surface water by keeping and opening jerricans below the surface water. Caps of cans were removed after dipping the can and also closed in the water after filling up of can.

(ii) For Dissolved Oxygen/Biochemical Oxygen Demand

Samples were collected in sterilized 300 ml capacity BOD bottles. The bottles were filled completely with sample water up to the rim and stopper was placed inside water only avoiding any kind of air bubble inside it. DO was immediately fixed by adding 2 ml each of alkaline potassium iodide and manganese sulphate ($MnSO_4$) at sampling spot. While the sample for BOD was incubated for 5 days in BOD incubator at 20°C.

(iii) Sampling for Bacteriological Analysis

For determination of bacteriological parameters, cleaned and sterilized sampling tubes were used. Tubes were dipped inside water with its neck downward up to 6 inches below water surface and then its mouth was opened under water against the flow. Tube was not filled completely and about 10% of the volume of the tube was kept empty. It was closed immediately to avoid contamination of sample; the neck and the stopper were wrapped by butter paper with the help of rubber band.

(iv) Sampling for Biological Analysis

For biological analysis of water, samples were collected with the help of plankton net attached with a collection tube at the base of net. For this a known amount of water was filtered through the plankton collection net and sample was collected inside collection tube. The sample was then transferred in sterilized tube of 50 ml capacity and preserved by adding one drop of lugol's solution or formaldehyde solution.

(C) Reagents Preparation

(i) Potassium Hydrogen Phthalate Buffer

Dissolve 10.2 gm of potassium hydrogen phthalate in distilled water to prepare 1000 ml of buffer.

(ii) Phosphate Buffer

Dissolve 3.4 gm of KH_2PO_4 and 4.45 gm of $Na_2HPO_4.2H_2O$ in distilled water to prepare 1000 ml of buffer.

(iii) Borax Buffer

Dissolve 3.81 gm of $Na_2B_4O_7 10H_2O$ in distilled water to prepare 1000 ml of buffer.

Besides these buffers of pH ready buffers of pH value are also available in the market.

(iv) Potassium Dichromate Solution 0.025N

Dissolve 12.259 gm of dried A.R. grade $K_2Cr_2O_7$ in distilled water to make one liter of solution. Dilute it 10 times to make 0.025N $K_2Cr_2O_7$ solution.

(v) Ferrous Ammonium Sulphate (0.01N)

Dissolve 39.2 gm of Fe $(NH_4)_2 (SO_4)_2 6H_2O$ in distilled water, adding 20 ml of concentrated H_2SO_4 to make 1 liter of solution. Dilute it 10 times to make 0.01 N Fe $(NH_4)_2 (SO_4)_2 6H_2O$ solution.

(vi) Ferroin Indicator

Dissolve 1.485 gm of 1,10–Phenonthroline and 0.695 gm of ferrous sulphate ($FeSO_4 7H_2O$) in distilled water to make 100ml of solution.

(vii) Sulfuric Acid

H_2SO_4 Concentrated (sp. gr.1.84)

(viii) Mercuric Sulphate

$HgSO_4$ Solid.

(ix) Silver Sulphate

Ag_2SO_4 Solid

(x) Sodium Thiosulphate (0.025N):

Dissolve 24.82 gm of $Na_2S_2O_3.5H_2O$ in boiled distilled water to make final volume to one liter. A pellet of NaOH or 0.4 gm borax was added as stabilizer. This is 0.1 stock N solution. Dilute 0.1N stock solution 4 times with boiled distilled water to prepare 0.025N solution. Keep it in brown glass stopper bottle.

(*xi*) Alkali Iodide Azide Solution

(a) Dissolve 500 gm of NaOH or 700 gm of KOH and 150 gm of KI in distilled water to makes one liter of solution.

(b) Dissolve 10 gm of NaN_2 in 40 ml of distilled water mix both (a) and (b) solution.

(*xii*) Manganous Sulphate Solution

Dissolve 100 gm of $MnSO_4.4H_2O$ in 200 ml of boiled distilled water and filter.

(*xiii*) Starch Solution

Dissolve 1 gm of starch in 100 ml of warm distilled water and adds a few drops of formaldehyde solution

(*xiv*) Sodium Hydroxide, (0.05N)

Dissolve 40 gm of NaOH in one liter boiled CO_2 free distilled water to prepare 1N NaOH stock solution. Dilute 50 ml of 1N NaOH stock solution to 1 liter distilled water. Standardized the solution using $H_2 SO_4$.

(*xv*) Phenolphthalein Indicator

Dissolve 0.5 gm of phenolphthalein in 50ml of 95% ethanol and add 50 ml of distilled water. Add slowly 0.05N CO_2 free NaOH until solution turns faintly pink.

(*xvi*) Methyl orange Indicator

Dissolve 0.5 gm methyl orange in 100 ml of distilled water.

(*xvii*) Hydrochloric Acid (0.1N)

Dilute 12N concentrate HCl (sp.gr.1.18) to 12 times (8.34–100ml) to prepare 1.0N HCl. It is further diluted ten times to make 0.1N HCl (100–1000ml).

(*xviii*) EDTA Solution (0.01M)

Dissolve 3.723 gm of di-sodium salt of EDTA in distilled water to prepare one liter of solution.

(xix) Buffer Solution

(a) Dissolve 16.9 gm of ammonium chloride (NH_4Cl) in 143 ml of concentrated ammonium hydroxide (NH_4OH).

(b) Dissolve 1.179 gm of disodium EDTA and 0.78 gm of $MgSO_4.7H_2O$ in 50 ml distilled water.

Mix (a) and (b) solution and make final volume to 250 ml using distilled water.

(xx) Eriochrome Black-T indicator

Mix 0.5 gm of EBT with 100 gm of NaCl (A.R) and grind.

(xxi) Sodium Hydroxide Solution (1N)

Dissolve 40 gm of NaOH in one liter distilled water.

(xxii) Murexide indicator

Mix 0.2 gm of ammonium purpurate with 100 gm NaCl and grind.

(xxiii) Silver Nitrate, (0.02N)

Dissolve 3.40 gm of dried $AgNO_3$ (A.R) in distilled water to make one liter of solution and kept in dark bottle.

(xxiv) Potassium Chromate (5%)

Dissolve 5 gm of K_2CrO_4 in 100 ml of distilled water.

(xxv) Ammonium Molybdate Solution

(a) Dissolve 25.0 gm of ammonium molybdate in 175 ml distilled water.

(b) Add 280 ml of Concentrated H_2SO_4 to 400 ml of distilled water and cool.

Mix (a) and (b) solution and dilute to 1 liter.

(xxvi) Stannous Chloride

Dissolve 2.5 gm of stannous chloride in 100ml glycerol by heating on water bath for rapid dissolution.

(xxvii) Standard Phosphate Solution

Dissolve 4.388 gm dried anhydrous potassium hydrogen phosphate K_2HPO_4 in distilled water and make up the volume to 1 liter, dilute this solution 100 times (10–1000ml). This is standard phosphate solution containing 10 mg P/L (1 ml = 0.01 mg P).

(*xxviii*) Crystal Violet

(a) Dissolve 2 g. of crystal violet in 20ml. of 95% ethyl alcohol.

(b) Dissolve 0.8 g. of ammonium oxalate in 80-ml. of distilled water.

Mix the two solutions (a and b).

(*xxix*) Gram's Iodine

Dissolve 1 g. of iodine and 2 g. of KI in 300 ml. of distilled water.

(*xx*) Ethyl Alcohol, 95% or Acetone alcohol (1 : 1).

(*xxi*) Safranin, 0.5%

Preparation of Lugol's Solution

Dissolve 10gm of KI and 5 gm of iodine crystals in 20 ml of distilled water and then add 50 ml distilled water in which 5 gm anhydrous sodium acetate has been dissolved.

Apparatus and Material for Microbiological Analysis

(A) Fermentation tubes (50ml)

(B) Durham's vials

(C) Pipettes (sterilized)

(D) Inoculation loop

(E) Incubator

(F) Petri–plates

(G) Conical flasks

(H) Spirit lamp

(I) Autoclave

(J) Laminar bench

(K) Water bath/oven

(L) Culture tubes

(M) Colony counter

Composition of MacConkey's Broth (MB)

Bile salts	5.0 gm
Peptone	20.0 gm
Lactose	10.0 gm

NaCl	5.0 gm
Bromocresol purple or neutral red	1.0 ml
Distilled water	1.0 liter
Final pH	7.4 ± 0.2

Neutral red indicator is prepared by dissolving 0.1 g methyl red indicator in 300ml ethyl alcohol and 200 ml of distilled water.

Composition of the Brilliant Green Lactose Bile Broth (BGLB)

Peptone	10.0 gm
Lactose	10.0 gm
Ox gall	20.0 gm
Brilliant green	0.0133 gm
Distilled water	1.0 liter
pH	7.2 ± 0.2

Composition of Nutrient Agar Medium (NAM)

Beef extract	3.0 gm
Peptone	5.0 gm
Glucose	1.0 gm
Agar-agar	15.0 gm
Distilled water	1.0 liter
pH	6.8 ± 0.2

Composition of Neo-peptone-Glucose rose Bengal Aureomycin agar (NPGRBAA)

Neopeptone	5.0 gm
Glucose	10.0 gm
Rose Bengal solution	3.5 ml
Agar	20.0 gm
Distilled water	1.0 liter
Final pH	6.50 ± 0.2

Prepare rose bengal solution by dissolving 1gm rose bengal dye in 100ml distilled water.

Analytical Methods

Samples were analyzed for the following parameters:

Physico-chemical Parameters

(*a*) Velocity
(*b*) Water temperature
(*c*) Conductivity
(*d*) Turbidity
(*e*) Total Solids (T.S)
(*f*) pH
(*g*) BOD
(*h*) COD
(*i*) DO
(*j*) Oxidation reduction index (rH_2)
(*k*) Oxidation reduction potential (Eh)
(*l*) Free CO_2
(*m*) Acidity
(*n*) Total alkalinity
(*o*) Total hardness (Ca/Mg)
(*p*) Chlorides
(*q*) Phosphates

Metallic Parameters

(*a*) Lead
(*b*) Copper
(*c*) Iron
(*d*) Manganese
(*f*) Zinc
(*g*) Cobalt
(*h*) Calcium
(*i*) Magnesium

Biological Parameters

(a) Plankton

(*i*) Zoo plankton

(*ii*) Phytoplankton

(b) Bacteriological

(*i*) MPN

(*ii*) HPC (Identification of bacteria)

(*iii*) Aquatic fungi (Qualitative and quantitative)

(b) Fish

(iv) Mathematical Modeling of few parameters

Chapter 4
Methodology

The samples for different parameters were analyzed with the help of the procedures described by Welch (1948), Mathur (1982), Trivedi and Goel (1984), APHA (1998). Plankton were identified according to Khanna (1993). The Fish were identified according to Jhingran (1975), Badola (1979), Shrivastava (1986) and Das (1989), and Mathematical modeling was done according to Beck (1974), Giordono *et al.* (1997) and Ruther ford *et al.* (2000).

Velocity

The speed of water current was measured by the surface float method. The rate of flow of the uppermost stratum of the water in the river was measured by releasing the pre-weighted light piece of wood in different portions of the river. The time taken by the wood piece to cover a known distance was calculated by the given formula:

$$V = d/t$$

where,

V = velocity (meter/second)

d = distance (meter)

t = time (second)

Temperature

Centigrade calibrated thermometers were used to record the temperature of surface water for measuring water temperature. Thermometer was dipped into water up to a desirable depth for 5-7 minutes and reading was taken. Thermometer should not be taken out of water body while taking reading.

Conductivity

Conductivity, K, is a measure of the ability of an aqueous solution to carry an electric current. This ability depends on the presence of ions; on their total concentration, mobility, and valence; and on the temperature of measurement.

Conductivity of the sample was observed with the help of conductivity meter having a conductance cell-containing electrode of platinum coated with Pt. Black Carbon.

Turbidity

Clarity of water is important in producing product destined for human consumption and in many manufacturing operations. The clarity of a natural body of water is an important determinant of its condition and productivity.

Turbidity in water is caused by suspended and colloidal matter such as clay, silt, finely divided organic and inorganic matter, plankton and other microscopic organisms. Turbidity is an expression of the optical property that causes light to be scattered and absorbed rather than transmitted with no change in direction or flux level through the sample. The turbidity of water was measured with the help of Jackson's Candle turbidity meter. It consists of three parts (a) Candle (b) Holder (c) Calibrated glass tube.

Procedure

Collected samples were shaked thoroughly in jerricans and were slowly transferred into calibrated glass tube of Jackson's Candle turbidimeter until the flame of the candle disappears and the light path was noted in centimeters (measured from inside the bottom of the glass tube). The reading (cm) was then converted in to Jackson turbidity unit (JTU) using conversion table.

Total Solids

Solids refer to matter suspended or dissolved in water or wastewater. Solids may affect water or effluent quality adversely in a number of ways.

Total Solid is a term applied to the material residue left in a vessel after evaporation of a sample and its subsequent drying in an oven at a defined temperature.

Procedure

A 50ml washed and dried beaker was taken and weighted. 20ml of unfiltered sample was taken in that beaker and sample was evaporated over hot plate/water bath and then dried in an oven at 105 ± 1°C for one hour. The final weight of the beaker was taken after drying of sample.

Calculation

$$\text{Total solid, mg/l} = \frac{A - B \times 1000 \times 1000}{V}$$

where,

A = Final weight of beaker in gm

B = Initial weight of beaker in gm

V = Volume of sample taken in ml

pH (Hydrogen ion concentration)

Measurement of pH is one of the most important and frequently used tests in water chemistry. pH is the hydrogen ion activity or concentration in the given water sample. pH equal to negatively $\log_{10}$ of hydrogen ion concentration

$$pH = -\log_{10}(H^+)$$

pH as defined by Sorenson (1909) is $-\log_{10}(H^+)$; it is the "intensity" factor of acidity. pH of water sample was measured by the use of pH strips, but the accurate method is the electrometric method. The sample was analyzed with the help of electronic digital pH meter consisting of a reference and indicator eletrode.

Procedure

Calibrate the electrode system against standard buffer solution of known pH. Rinse the electrode using distilled water now dip the electrode in sample water and note the reading on digital screen.

Biochemical Oxygen Demand (BOD)

The biochemical oxygen demand (BOD) determination is an empirical test in which standardized laboratory procedures are used to determine the relative oxygen requirement of wastewater effluents, and polluted waters.

The test measure the molecular oxygen utilized during a specified incubation period for the biochemical degradation of organic matter (carbonaceous demand) and the oxygen used to oxidize inorganic material such as sulfides and ferrous ions. In other words biological oxygen demand, (BOD) represents the amount of oxygen required for the microbial decomposition of the organic matter in the water. The BOD procedure, which is used extensively in monitoring water quality and biodegradation of waste material, is designed to determine how much oxygen microorganisms consume during oxidation of the organic matter in the sample.

Principle

The principle of the method involves, measuring the difference of the oxygen concentration between the sample and after incubating it for 5 days at 20°C.

Procedure

Samples were collected in two BOD bottles of 300 ml capacity from each site. One set of the bottle were kept in BOD incubator at 20°C for 5 days and the DO constant was determined in another set immediately. After the compilation of 5 days incubation, the DO of first set was determined and BOD was calculated by means of given formula:

Calculation

$$BOD, mg/l = (D_o - D_5)$$

where,

D_o = Initial DO in the sample

D_5 = DO after five days incubation

Chemical Oxygen Demand (COD)

Chemical oxygen demand (COD) is defined as the amount of specified oxidant that reacts with the sample under controlled conditions.

COD is widely used to characterize the organic strength of wastewater and pollution of natural waters. It is the measure of oxygen consumed during the oxidation of the oxidizable organic matter by a strong oxidizing agent.

Principle

The sample is refluxed with $K_2Cr_2O_7$ and H_2SO_4 in presence of mercuric sulphate, to neutralize the effect of chlorides and silver sulphate, which acts as a catalyst. Excess potassium dichromate ($K_2Cr_2O_7$) is titrated against ferrous ammonium sulphate using ferroin as an indicator. The amount of $K_2Cr_2O_7$ used is proportional to the oxidizable organic matter present in the sample.

Procedure

20 ml of Sample was taken in a 250 ml capacity COD flask; slowly add 10 ml of $K_2Cr_2O_7$ and a pinch of $HgSO_4$ and Ag_2SO_4 were added (In case COD is expected more than 50 ppm add 10 ml of 0.25 N $K_2Cr_2O_7$). Add slowly 30 ml of concentrated H_2SO_4 and reflux condenser was connected to the COD flask, reflux for 2 hours on hot plate. Now remove the flask, cooled and make the final volume to 140 ml in flask using distilled water, take suitable amount of sample in conical flask add 2-3 drops of ferroin indicator and titrate against 0.01N ferrous ammonium sulphate.

Run a blank with distilled water using same quantity of chemicals.

Calculation

$$\text{COD, mg/l} = \frac{(B-A) \times \text{N of Ferrous ammonium Sulphate} \times 1000 \times 8}{\text{ml of sample}}$$

where,

A= ml of titrant with sample

B= ml of titrant with blank

Dissolved Oxygen (DO)

Dissolved oxygen (DO) level in natural water and wastewater depend on the physical, chemical and biochemical activities in the water body. The analysis for DO is a key test in water pollution and waste treatment process control.

DO is the measure of oxygen concentration present in a given water sample. The concentration of oxygen reflects whether the process undergoing is aerobic or anaerobic.

Principle

The manganous sulphate reacts with the alkali (KOH, NaOH) to form a white precipitate of manganous hydroxide, which in the presence of oxygen, gets oxidized to a brown colour compound. In the strong acid medium manganic ions are reduced by iodide ions which get converted into iodine equivalent to the original concentration of oxygen in the sample. The iodine can be titrated against thiosulphate using starch as an indicator.

Certain oxidizing and reducing materials may effectively interfere with the determination of oxygen by converting iodide ions to iodine or vice-versa. The azide modification removes the interference substance specially nitrite, which is destroyed by sodium azide (NaN_2). That's why azide modification method is used to determine dissolved oxygen instead of wrinkler's iodometric method.

Procedure

Fill sample water in 300 ml capacity BOD bottle up to the rim and stopper is placed inside water body avoiding any kind of air bubble inside it. Add 2 ml each of $MnSO_4$ and alkaline iodide azide solution using separate pipettes. A precipitate was appeared. The bottle was kept for some time after mixing thoroughly. At this stage the DO was fixed 2 ml of Concentrated H_2SO_4 was added to dissolve the precipitate by shaking it. The part or whole of the content was titrated against sodium thio-sulphate using starch as an indicator. At end point blue colour changes to colourless.

Calculation

When whole contents have been titrated

$$\text{Dissolved oxygen, (mg/l)} = \frac{(\text{ml} \times \text{N}) \text{ of titrant} \times 1000 \times 8}{V_1 - V}$$

When only a part of content has been titrated

$$\text{Dissolved Oxygen, (mg/l)} = \frac{(\text{ml} \times \text{N}) \text{ of titrant} \times 1000 \times 8}{V_2 \left(\frac{V_1 - V}{V_1} \right)}$$

where,

V_1 = Volume of sample bottle after placing stopper (300 ml)

V_2 = Volume of part of the contents titrated

V = Volume of $MnSO_4$ and KI added (4 ml)

Oxidation Reduction Potential (Eh)

A substance which losses electrons is oxidized and the substance, which gains, is reduced. When a platinum electrode is immersed in such a system, a potential is developed on it depending upon the ratio of oxidized and reduced states, is called as redox potential. A solution containing an excess of the reduced state will be oxidized after losing its electrons to platinum; while if solution contains more oxidized state will be reduced, after taking the electrons from the platinum electrode. This potential can be measured by using a reference electrode.

Eh was determined indirectly from the equation based on pH of water sample, *i.e.*,

$$Eh = Eo - 0.058 \text{ pH} + 0.0145 \times \log pO_2$$

where,

Eo = Standard electrode potential was determined directly from Figure 4.1.

pO_2 = Partial oxygen pressure of water system = dissolved oxygen.

Figure 4.1: Standard Electrode Potential

Oxidation Reduction Index (rH_2)

It was calculated by the equation:

$$rH_2 = \frac{Eh}{0.029} + 2pH$$

Free Carbon Dioxide (CO_2)

Surface water normally contain less than 10 mg free carbon dioxide (CO_2) per liter while some groundwater may easily exceed that concentration. The CO_2 content of water may contribute significantly to Corrosion.

Principle

Free CO_2 reacts with sodium carbonate or sodium hydroxide to form sodium bicarbonate. Completion of the reaction is indicated potentiometrically or by the development of the pink colour characteristic of phenolpthalein indicator at the equivalent pH of 8.3. At this pH all the free CO_2 is converted into bicarbonates.

Procedure

Take 100 ml of sample in a conical flask and add 2-3 drops of phenolphthalein indicator if sample remained colorless titrate it against 0.05N NaOH. Pink colour appeared at the end point.

Calculation

$$\text{Carbon dioxide } (CO_2), \text{mg/l} = \frac{(\text{ml} \times \text{N}) \text{ of NaOH} \times 1000 \times 44}{\text{ml of sample}}$$

Acidity

Acidity of water is its capacity to neutralize a strong base and is mostly due to the presence of strong minerals acids, weak acids, (Carbonic, acetic acids) and the salts of strong acids and weak bases (*e.g.*, Ferrous sulphate, aluminium sulphate etc.). These salts on hydrolysis produce a strong acid and metal hydroxide, which are sparingly soluble thus producing the acidity.

Acids contribute to corrosiveness and influence chemical reaction rates, chemical speciation and biological processes. The measurement also reflects a change in the quality of the source water.

Procedure

Take 100 ml of colourless sample in a conical flask and add 2-3 drops of methyl orange indicator, if solution turns yellow methyl orange acidity is absent. If solution turns pink titrate it against 0.05N NaOH until colour changes to yellow. Now add few drops of phenolpthalein indicator and titrate against 0.05N NaOH at end point solution turns pink.

Calculation

$$\begin{array}{l}\text{Methyl orange acidity} \\ \text{mg/l as } CaCO_3\end{array} = \frac{(\text{A} \times \text{N}) \text{ of NaOH} \times 1000 \times 50}{\text{ml of sample}}$$

$$\begin{array}{l}\text{Phenolphthalein acidity} \\ \text{mg/l as } CaCO_3\end{array} = \frac{(\text{B} \times \text{N}) \text{ of NaOH} \times 1000 \times 50}{\text{ml of sample}}$$

$$\begin{array}{l}\text{Total acidity to pH 8.3} \\ \text{mg/l as } CaCO_3\end{array} = \frac{(\text{A} + \text{B}) \text{ N of NaOH} \times 1000 \times 50}{\text{ml of sample}}$$

where,

A = Volume of NaOH used with methyl orange in titrating the sample to pH 3.7

B = Volume of NaOH used with phenolphthalein in titrating the sample from pH 3.7 to pH 8.3

Total Alkalinity

Alkalinity of water is its acid–neutralizing capacity. It is the sum of all the titrable bases.

Principle

Total alkalinity, carbonates and bicarbonates can be estimated by titrating the sample with a strong acid (HCL or H_2SO_4), first to pH 8.3 using phenolphthalein as an indicator and then further to pH between 4.2 and 5.4 with methyl orange.

Procedure

Take100 ml of sample in a conical flask and add 2 drops of phenolphthalein indicator, if solution remain colourless then phenolphthalein alkalinity (PA) = 0 *i.e.*, absent and total alkalinity was determined, if solution turns pink, titrate it against 0.1 N HCl until color disappears this is phenolphthalein alkalinity (PA). Add 2-3 drops of methyl orange indicator to the same sample and titrate against 0.1N HCl until yellow color changes to pink at the end point this is total alkalinity (TA).

Calculation

$$\text{PA as } CaCO_3 \text{ mg/l} = \frac{(A \times N) \text{ of HCl} \times 1000 \times 50}{\text{Volume of sample (ml)}}$$

$$\text{TA as } CaCO_3 \text{ mg/l} = \frac{(B \times N) \text{ of HCl} \times 1000 \times 50}{\text{Volume of sample (ml)}}$$

where,

A = ml of HCl used with only phenolphthalein

B = ml of total HCl used with phenolphthalein and methyl orange

Total Hardness

Water hardness was understood to be a measure of the capacity of water to precipitate soap. Soap is precipitated chiefly by the calcium and magnesium ions present.

Principle

If a small amount of dye such as Eriochrome black T [EBT] is added to an aqueous solution containing calcium and magnesium ions at a pH of 10.0 ± 0.1, the solution becomes wine red. If EDTA is added as a titrant, the calcium and magnesium will be complexed and solution turn from wine red to blue, marking the end point of titration.

Procedure

Take 100 ml of sample in a conical flask and add a pinch of EBT indicator and one ml of buffer solution, the solution turns wine red, titrate it against EDTA until wine red color change to blue.

Calculation

$$\text{Hardness as mg/l, } CaCO_3 = \frac{\text{ml EDTA used} \times 1000}{\text{ml of sample}}$$

Calcium

Calcium is one of the most abundant substances of the natural water. Calcium is necessary in plant and animal nutrition and is an essential component of bones, shells and plant structures.

Principle

When EDTA is added to the water containing both calcium and magnesium, it combines first with the calcium. Calcium can be directly determined, with EDTA, when the pH is made sufficiently high that the magnesium is largely precipitated as the hydroxide and an indicator is used that combine with calcium only.

Procedure

Take 50 ml of sample in a conical flask and add 20ml of 1N NaOH solution, add a pinch of murexide indicator, solution turn pink, titrate it against EDTA until pink colour change to purple this is end point.

Calculation

$$\text{Calcium, mg/l} = \frac{A \times 400.8}{\text{ml of sample}}$$

where,

A = volume of EDTA used.

Magnesium

Magnesium is an essential element in chlorophyll and in red blood cells. Some salts of magnesium are toxic by ingestion or inhalation.

Magnesium had been estimated by subtracting the calcium hardness from total hardness.

Calculation

$$Mg^{++}\text{, mg/l} = (\text{Total hardness}-\text{Calcium hardness}) \times 0.244$$

Chlorides

The chloride concentration is higher in wastewater than in raw water because sodium chloride (NaCl) is a common article of diet and passes unchanged through the digestive system.

Principle

Silver nitrate reacts with chloride to form very slightly soluble white precipitate of AgCl. At the end point when all the chlorides get precipitated, free silver ions react with chromate to form silver chromate of reddish brown colour.

Procedure

Take 50 ml of sample in a conical flask and add 2 ml of potassium chromate to it, titrate the solution against silver nitrate until persistent red tinge appears.

Calculation

$$\text{Chloride, mg/l} = \frac{(\text{ml} \times \text{N}) \text{ of } AgNO_3 \times 1000 \times 35.5}{\text{ml of sample}}$$

Phosphates

Phosphorus occurs in natural water and in wastewater almost solely as phosphates. Phosphorus is essential to the growth of organisms and can be the nutrient that limits the primary productivity of a body of water. The quality criteria for phosphorus in water are only to check nuisance growth of algae and process of eutrophication.

Principle

All the form of phosphorus, whether dissolved or particulate are converted to inorganic forms (Phosphates) after digestion of oxidation of the sample.

Procedure

50 ml of sample was taken in a flask followed by the addition of acid ammonium molybdate solution (2ml) and add 4-5 drops of $SnCl_2$ solution. A blue colour appears the same procedure was run with a blank (distilled water) sample for comparison. Both (Sample and blank) were then kept on white paper, followed by the addition of standard phosphate solution to the blank drop by drop with the help of graduated pipette (1ml) until the colour of blank reached at equivalent to the sample, at the end point. The ml of standard phosphate used was placed in the equation to get the amount of phosphates.

Calculation

Phosphates, mg/l = ml of solution used × 0.01 × 20

Metallic

Heavy metals of water samples were analyzed using atomic absorption spectrophotometer (AAS).

Principle of AAS

Atomic absorption spectrophotometer (AAS) uses the hollow cathode lamp (HCl). The hollow cathode lamp gives off light characteristics to the elemental wavelength being measured. Thus, the light absorbed measures the atomic density. In other words it is based on the measurement of the decrease in light intensity from a source (hollow cathode lamp) when it passes through a vapour layer of the atoms of the analytic element.

Method for Using AAS

In AAS, a sample is aspired into a flame and automized and a light beam is directed through the flame, into a monochromater and onto a detector that measures the amount of light absorbed by the automized element in the flame. Each metal has its own characteristic wavelength. A source lamp composed of that element is used. The amount of energy of the characteristic wavelength absorbed in the flame is proportional to the concentration of element in the sample.

The instrument was calibrated, for each metal to be detected, with known standard. After calibration and programming, the prepared samples were aspirated to the flame. Zero was set with double distilled water before each determination. Results were displayed in μgm/l from which the actual concentration in water samples was calculated. It was the total content of water sample, which was expressed in mg/l (ppm).

Biological Examination

Plankton

The term 'plankton' refers to those microscopic aquatic forms having little or no resistance to currents and living free floating and suspended in natural water. The phytoplankton (microscopic algae) occurs as unicellular, colonial, or filamentous forms. The Zooplankton in fresh water comprises principally protozoan, rotifers, cladocerans and copepods.

Collection of Plankton

The plankton of river water was collected by fine plankton collection net. A known amount of water was filtered through plankton collection net and concentrated in desired quantity inside collection tube. The sample was preserved in Lugol's solution.

Procedure

1 ml of concentrate was taken and placed in sedgwick rafter counting cell a glass slip was placed over it avoiding any kind of bubble. Applying the following formula did counting of the organisms:

Calculation

$$\text{Plankton/l} = \frac{(a \times 1000)\,C}{L}$$

where

a = Average number of plankton in one small counting chamber of Sedgwick rafter counting cell

C = ml. of plankton concentrate

l = Volume of original water filtered in liter.

Bacteriological Examination

Most Probable Number (MPN)

Coliforms are defined as facultative anaerobic, gram-negative non-spore forming rods that ferment lactose with gas, formation within 48 hr. at 35°C.

Two techniques are available for the estimation of most probable numbers *i.e.*, multiple tube fermentation technique (MTFT) and the membrane filter technique (MFT). Out of this multiple tube fermentation technique has been used to enumerate positive presumptive and confirmed coliform tests. Results of the test are expressed as the most probable number (MPN), since the count is based on statistical analysis of sets of tube in a series of serial dilution. MPN is by definition is related to a sample volume of 100ml.

Procedure

Several dilution of the sample up to 1:1000 was required. 5 fermentation tubes were filled with 9 ml broth for each dilution. Durham's vials were put inside the tube in an inverted position and tubes were plugged with cotton and sterilized in an autoclave. All the dilutions were shaked vigorously before moving the sample to fermentation tubes. Separate pipettes were used for each dilution and sample. Fermentation tubes were shaked gently. Tubes were incubated for 48 hrs at a temperature of 35°C-37°C for gas production. The tubes were recorded as positive (P) showing the gas production in Durham's vials, even a tiny bubble should be recorded as positive. The tubes showing positive results are now subjected to confirmatory test. Negative tubes were incubated for further 24 hrs to confirm the test.

10 ml BGLB broth and inverted Durham's vial were taken in fermentation tubes. The number of tubes should be equal to the all-positive tube in presumptive test. Gently shake the positive tube. With the help of inoculation loop one loopful of liquid was transferred

to tubes having BGLB. These tubes were incubated for 48 hrs at 35–37°C.

The tubes were recorded positive showing gas production. The numbers of positive tubes were put in MPN table and then in the formula to calculate MPN/100ml.

Calculation

$$\text{MPN/100ml} = \frac{\text{MPN table value} \times 10}{\text{Starting value}}$$

Heterotrophic Plate Count (HPC)

The heterotrophic plate count (HPC), formally known as the standard plate count (SPC), is a procedure for estimating the live heterotrophic bacteria in water.

On a solid medium, counting of organisms depends upon the fact that living cells will produce sufficient progeny to form a colony visible to naked eyes. Colonies may arise from pairs, chains, clusters, or single cells all of which are included in the term "Colony-forming units" (CFU).

Preparation of Serial Dilution

Five culture tubes were filled with 9 ml distilled water, plugged with cotton and sterilized in an autoclave the sample was shaked vigorously and 1ml liquor was transferred to the first tube, now 1ml water from first tube was again transferred to 2nd tube and so on. Separate pipettes were used for each transfer. The dilutions were 1:10, 1:100, 1:1000,1:10000 and so on.

Procedure

1ml of sample from selected dilutions were transferred in to sterilized petriplates by opening them gently. Now 15-20ml of NAM was slowly poured in these plates the temperature of NAM should be about 45°C. Sample and NAM were mixed gently by rotating the plates. When medium solidifies plates were incubated at 37 ± 2°C temperature for 48 hours in an inverted position. The colonies were counted after 48 hours by colony counter and colony forming unit (CFU)/ml was calculated.

Calculation

$$CFU/ml = \frac{\text{Colonies counted}}{\text{Dilution factor}}$$

Aquatic Fungi

Aquatic fungi are found wherever non living organic matter occurs, although some species are pathnogenic and other are parasitic, unpolluted stream water has relatively large number of species representing the true aquatic fungi (species possessing flagellated zoospores and gametes) aquatic hypomycetes and soil fungi.

Procedure

1ml of sample from selected dilutions were transferred in to sterilized Petri plates by opening them gently. Now 15-20ml of Rose Bengal media was slowly poured in these plates the temperature of media should be about 45°C. Sample and media were mixed gently by rotating the plates. When medium solidifies plates were incubated at 27 ± 2°C temperature for 48 hours in an inverted position.

The colonies were counted after 2-3 days by colony counter and colony forming unit (CFU) / ml was calculated.

Calculation

$$CFU/ml = \frac{\text{Colonies counted}}{\text{Dilution factor}}$$

Isolation and Identification of Bacterial Culture

Isolation of Bacteria

Two methods were used to isolating bacteria are (i) pour plate and (ii) streak plate method.

Pour Plate Method

In this method 5 or 6 culture tubes containing 9 ml distilled water, were sterilized after plugging for serial dilution. The sample was vigorously shaken and 1 ml water was transferred to the first culture tube. Now 1 ml water from first tube was again transferred to 2nd test tube and so on. Separate pipettes were used for each transfer. The dilution were 1:10, 1:100, 1:1000, 1:10000, and so on.

3 pairs of borosil petri dishes were sterilized in an oven. Now 1 ml of liquid from last 3 dilutions was transferred to the petri dishes by opening them gently. 15-20 ml medium was poured into these plates. The temperature of NAM should be about 45°C. Both water sample and medium were mixed by gently rotating the plate. When medium became solidify the plate were inverted and incubated at 37 ± 2°C temperature for 48 hours.

Streak Method

From these poured plates, individual colony was transferred with the help of sterilized loop (by incineration), on another media plate and streaked. These plates were incubated for further 48 hours at 37 °C ± 2, for identification of pure colony.

Identification of Bacteria

Incubation Temperature

Each isolated colony was incubated at below 20° C (Psycrophilic), 20-45° C (Mesophilic), and 45°C and above (Thermophilic).

Gram Staining

Individual isolated colony was stained by Gram stain and differentiated in Gram positive and Gram negative.

Principle

Gram staining is a method of differential staining, which employs two stains to distinguish usually morphologically similar but different species of bacteria. The technique involves staining of bacteria by crystal violet (primary stain) safranin or basic fuchsin (counter stain). The bacteria retaining the primary stain are called gram-positive, while the bacteria yielding out the primary stain by alcohol washing and retaining the counter stain are called gram-negative.

Procedure

1. Prepare a suspension of bacterial colony in sterile 0.85% NaCl (Saline) to disperse the bacterial-cells.
2. Take a slide and mark an area on it by a glass marking pencil.

3. Prepare a smear of the bacterial suspension in the area marked on the glass slide. Air-dry and fix the smear by very slight heating.
4. Pour the crystal violet primary stain on it and allow reacting for 1-2 minutes. Wash the slide with water to remove the excess stain.
5. Put Gram's iodine solution on the smear and keep for about a minute.
6. Wash the slide with 95% alcohol or acetone alcohol till the last traces of the colour come out.
7. Wash the slide with water and stain with safranin for about 30 sec.-1 minute.
8. Give the final washing with water, air dry and observe under a high power microscope preferably with an oil immersion lens.
9. The bacteria showing violet colour are gram-positive, while the bacteria showing red or pink colour and gram-negative.

Aerobic, Facultative Anerobic or Anaerobic

Individual culture was inoculated in sterilized liquid. Soyacasien digest medium (Hi-Media) and by the growth pattern, differentiation was established whether they are aerobic, Facultative, anerobic or Anaerobic Cultures.

Motility

Culture was mounted on grooved slide and motility of the microorganisms was observed under light microscope.

Fermentation

Isolated bacteria were further check for its fermenting nature, *i.e.*, growth with gas and acid production in Mac-Conkeys Broth medium.

Several dilution of the sample for Suswa water was prepared. Dilutions above than 1:1000 are required. 5 fermentation tubes for each dilution were filled with 9 ml. of broth and one Durham's vial was put in each tube in inverted condition. Now all the tubes were plugged with cotton and sterilized in autoclave. All the dilutions were shaked vigorously before moving the sample to fermentation tube. Separate sterilized pipettes were used for different dilutions as well as samples. Fermentation tubes were gently shaked. Now these tubes were incubated at 35-37°C temperature for 48 hours. All the tubes were examined after 48 hours for gas production.

The tube, showing gas production in Durham's tube, were recorded as positive.(+ve). Even a tiny bubble should be recorded as positive. The tubes not showing gas or acids production are noted as negative (– ve).

Mathematical Modeling

It seems that Streeter and Phelps used mathematical models, for the first time about eight decades ago, their study refers to independent variables called the 'time of flow'. However, in many practical applications of their work it is assumed that the velocity of river flow is time-invariant. This means that the independent variable time of flow is tentamount to the independent variable of distance along the stream. So the implications of proposing a steady-state model for the description of DO-BOD interaction are mainly the assumptions that concentrations of DO & BOD, *i.e.*, the value of DO and the flow rate of the river are the same at every point along the river. This makes the model inferior in as much as the real situation is concerned. There after a number of models were suggested to study the problem and for an excellent discussion on various models, one may refer to Masch and Associates (1970), Vogler and Scherfig (2000), Moley (1979), Orlob (1983).

Indeed the interaction between DO and BOD is a complex process which depends upon the several important factors for any given river system, Beck (1974) has given a detailed discussion of processess governing DO-BOD interaction our model is based upon black box model, which is used to obtain input/output relationships between upstream and downstream DO, BOD given by Beck (1974). Our model largely motivated by a case study of river CAM (Beck, 1974), encompases the parameters $\lambda_1, \lambda_2, U_1$ and e_1 (see below).

Precisely, we have used the following model to study DO and BOD concentration in Suswa river:

$$\text{DO: } \lambda_1(S) = C_1\lambda_1(S-1) + C_2U_1(S-1) + C_3e_1(S)$$

$$\text{BOD: } \lambda_2(S) = C_4\lambda_1(S-1) + C_5U_1(S-1) - C_6e_1(S)$$

where,

1. λ_1 (S): Value of DO (mg/l) to be obtained in particular season
2. λ_2 (S): Value of BOD (mg/l) to be obtained in particular season
3. λ_1 (S-1): DO/BOD observation of same place in previous season
4. U_1 (S-1): DO/BOD observation of upstream in previous season
5. e_1 (S): f (SD), errors of possibility
6. C_1, C_2, C_3, C_4, C_5 and C_6 are constants with the following values:

$$C_1 = 0.715 \qquad C_4 = 0.751$$
$$C_2 = 0.174 \qquad C_5 = 0.102$$
$$C_3 = 0.554 \qquad C_6 = 0.313$$

For details of these constants, one may refer to Beck's model (1974). This model will be called Beck modified Khanna Bhutiani model (BMKBM) throughout this work.

Statistical Analysis of the Data

The data for all physico-chemical and biological parameters were collected and data were analyzed for calculating mean, standard deviation of each parameter and correlation as per Goel (1999) with the help of computer on Microsoft excel.

$$\text{Mean } \{x\} = \frac{\Sigma X}{N}$$

where,

X = Individual reading of parameter

Σ X = Total of all readings for parameter.

N = Number of samples.

Standard Deviation(SD or σ)

$$SD = \sqrt{\frac{\Sigma (X - \bar{x})^2}{n - 1}}$$

where,

X = Individual reading of parameter

$\bar{x}$ = Mean Σ X

n = Number of samples.

Coefficient of Correlation (r)

$$r = \frac{\Sigma\,(X - \bar{x})\,(Y - \bar{y})}{\sqrt{\Sigma\,(X - \bar{x})^2\;\Sigma(Y - \bar{y})^2}}$$

where,

X = Individual reading of 1st parameter

$\bar{x}$ = Mean of Σ X

Y = Individual reading of 2nd parameter

$\bar{y}$ = Mean of Σ Y

Chapter 5

Observations

Physico-chemical Parameters

Physico-chemical parameters impart a major role in the determination of the quality of any water body. The river is a dynamic state with respect to its geological age and geo-chemical characteristics. The activities of human beings upset this dynamic state, resulting in deterioration of aquatic environment. So the measurement of physico-chemical parameters is the best way to observe the water quality. The physico–chemical parameters of the river Suswa studied at Raiwala were Water temperature (°C), conductivity (siemens/cm), turbidity (JTU), total solids (mg/l), velocity (m/s), pH, BOD (mg/l), COD (mg/l), dissolved oxygen (mg/l), oxidation reduction index (rH2), oxidation reduction potential (Eh), free CO_2 (mg/l), acidity (mg/l), alkalinity (mg/l), total hardness (mg/l), chlorides (mg/l), magnesium (mg/l), phosphates (mg/l), calcium (mg/l) and Heavy metals (a) lead (b) copper (c) iron (d) manganese (e) zinc (f) cobalt. The observations were made during April 2002 to March 2003 and April 2003–March 2004 are presented in the Table 5A.1 to 5A.8 and their interrelationship in the Figure 5A.1 to 5A.40.

Sampling Station A (Satyanarayan Area)

The physico-chemical and heavy metals parameters of sampling station A are presented in Table 5A.1-5A.2 and Figure 5A.1-5A.10.

Table: 5 A.1: Seasonal Variations in Physico-chemical Parameters of River Suswa at Sampling Station A (2002-2004)

Physico-chemical Parameters	*2002-2003*				*2003-2004*			
	Summer	*Monsoon*	*Winter*	*Average*	*Summer*	*Monsoon*	*Winter*	*Average*
Temperature (ºC)	22.91±2.21	23.90±3.29	20.00±0.81	22.27±2.02	23.41±1.91	24.91±1.56	19.62±1.31	22.64±2.72
Conductivity (Siemens/cm)	0.023±0.01	0.021±0.009	0.019±0.002	0.21±0.002	0.085±0.123	0.020±0.007	0.017±0.002	0.04±0.03
Turbidity (JTU)	0.0±0.00	25.0±3.00	0.00±0.000	8.33±14.43	0.0±0.00	30±9.00	0.0±0.00	10.00±17.32
Total Solids mg/l)	791.63±337.06	1125.00±78.71	752.08±286.29	889.58±204.83	750.0±288.67	754.16±283.94	750.0±288.67	751.0±2.40
Velocity (m/s)	0.25±0.07	0.34±0.07	0.22±0.05	0.27±0.06	0.29±0.03	0.26±0.04	0.23±0.07	0.26±0.03
pH	7.33±0.22	7.70±0.28	7.32±0.11	7.45±0.21	7.38±0.15	7.54±0.21	7.35±0.12	7.42±0.10
BOD (mg/l)	0.52±0.21	0.67±0.27	0.73±0.43	0.64±0.10	0.60±0.24	0.83±0.41	0.62±0.25	0.68±0.12
COD (mg/l)	2.05±0.22	1.90±0.07	3.10±0.57	2.35±0.65	2.75±0.11	3.90±0.12	3.70±0.16	3.45±0.61
DO (mg/l)	8.08±0.22	8.23±0.50	8.35±1.62	8.22±0.13	8.37±0.34	7.52±1.38	8.33±0.63	8.07±0.47
Oxidation Reduction Index (rH_2)	28.75±0.26	28.90±0.16	28.35±0.22	28.66±0.28	28.41±0.36	28.10±0.29	27.92±0.10	28.14±0.24
Oxidation Reduction Potential (Eh)	0.36±0.03	0.36±0.02	0.38±0.00	0.36±0.01	0.40±0.01	0.42±0.00	0.38±0.00	0.40±0.02
Free CO_2 (mg/l)	3.23±2.26	4.10±2.08	2.0±1.16	3.11±1.05	2.10±0.71	3.00±1.50	1.52±0.16	2.20±0.74
Acidity (mg/l)	51.04±24.41	53.33±11.05	57.33±21.59	53.90±3.18	67.91±21.88	46.87±7.94	57.62±11.79	57.46±10.52
Alkalinity (mg/l)	260.83±45.48	249.16±19.50	256.66±3.04	255.55±5.91	284.16±45.75	319.58±35.39	263.75±8.53	289.16±28.24
Total hardness (mg/l)	235.83±22.82	226.99±14.29	249.49±9.46	237.43±11.33	245.66±3.79	242.74±27.41	239.50±16.66	242.46±3.33
Chlorides (mg/l)	16.86±3.51	19.41±3.55	16.79±1.95	17.68±1.49	16.62±2.44	20.09±6.,06	16.09±1.74	17.60±2.17
Magnesium (mg/l)	40.85±3.83	39.94±3.99	45.83±2.04	42.20±3.17	45.83±5.32	39.24±1.77	48.67±3.10	44.58±4.83
Phosphates (mg/l)	0.03±0.00	0.11±0.02	0.09±0.06	0.07±0.04	0.02±0.07	0.15±0.03	0.01±0.03	0.06±0.07
Calcium (mg/l)	55.67±6.52	61.00±4.60	61.60±3.33	59.42±3.26	64.81±11.85	69.61±16.59	57.5±2.88	63.97±6.09

± = Standard deviation.

Table 5 A.2: Seasonal Variations in Metallic Parameters of River Suswa at Sampling Station A (2002-2004)

Metallic Parameters	*2002-2003*				*2003-2004*			
	Summer	*Monsoon*	*Winter*	*Average*	*Summer*	*Monsoon*	*Winter*	*Average*
Lead (Pb) (mg/l)	0.066± 0.008	0.068± 0.008	0.068± 0.004	0.067± .001	0.064± 0.004	0.07± 0.006	0.062± 0.011	0.064± 0.005
Iron (Fe) (rng/l)	5.35± 0.70	5.28± 0.28	5.68± 0.64	5.43± 0.21	4.92± 0.33	5.55± 0.40	5.78± 0.59	5.41± 0.44
Manganese (Mn) (mg/l)	0.003± 0.001	0.003± 0.001	0.002± 0.001	0.002± 0.0005	0.003± 0.001	0.004± 0.007	0.004± 0.001	0.003± 0.0005
Zinc (Zn) mg/l)	3.89± 0.11	3.47± 0.29	3.22± 0.06	3.52± 0.33	3.85± 0.13	3.45± 0.44	3.81± 0.13	3.70± 0.22
Cobalt (Ca) (mg/l)	0.008± 0.012	0.009± 0.011	0.002± 0.0008	0.006± 0.003	0.009± 0.015	0.009± 0.011	0.001± 0.0003	0.006± 0.004
Copper(Cu) (mg/l)	0.017± 0.001	0.018± 0.002	0.017± 0.001	0.017±.0005	0.018± 0.003	0.016± 0.002	0.016± 0.0005	0.05± 0.001

± = Standard deviation.

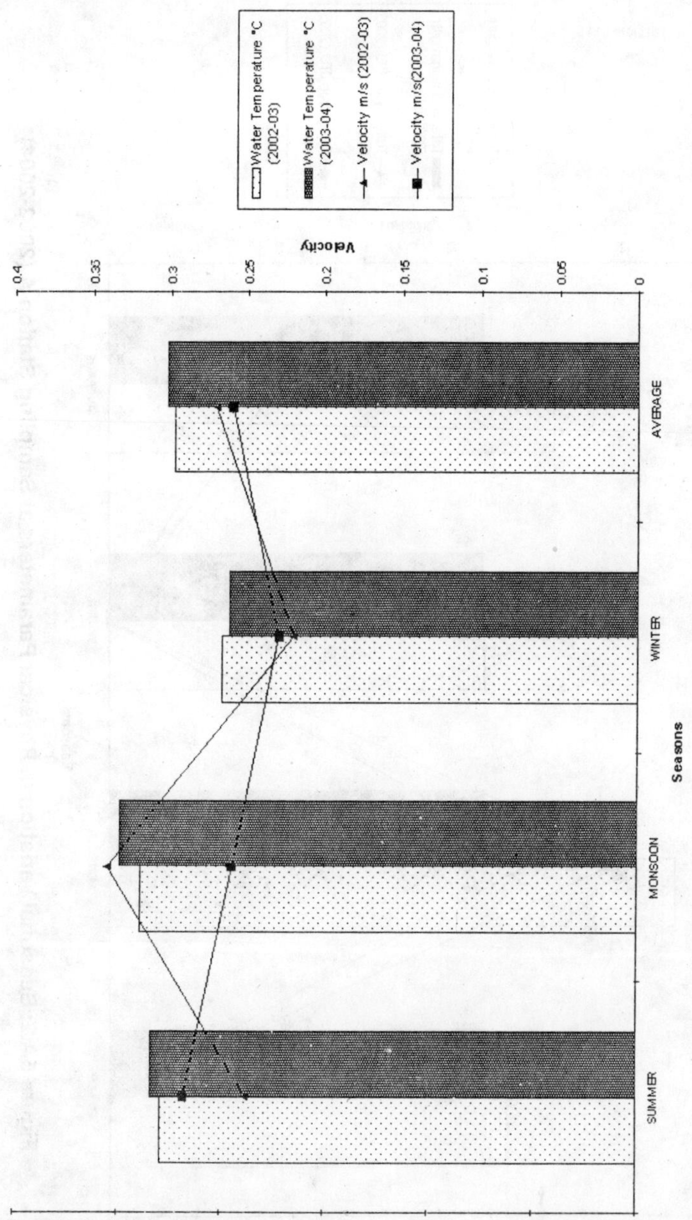

Figure 5A.1: Seasonal Variation in Physical Parameters at Sampling Station A (2002-2004)

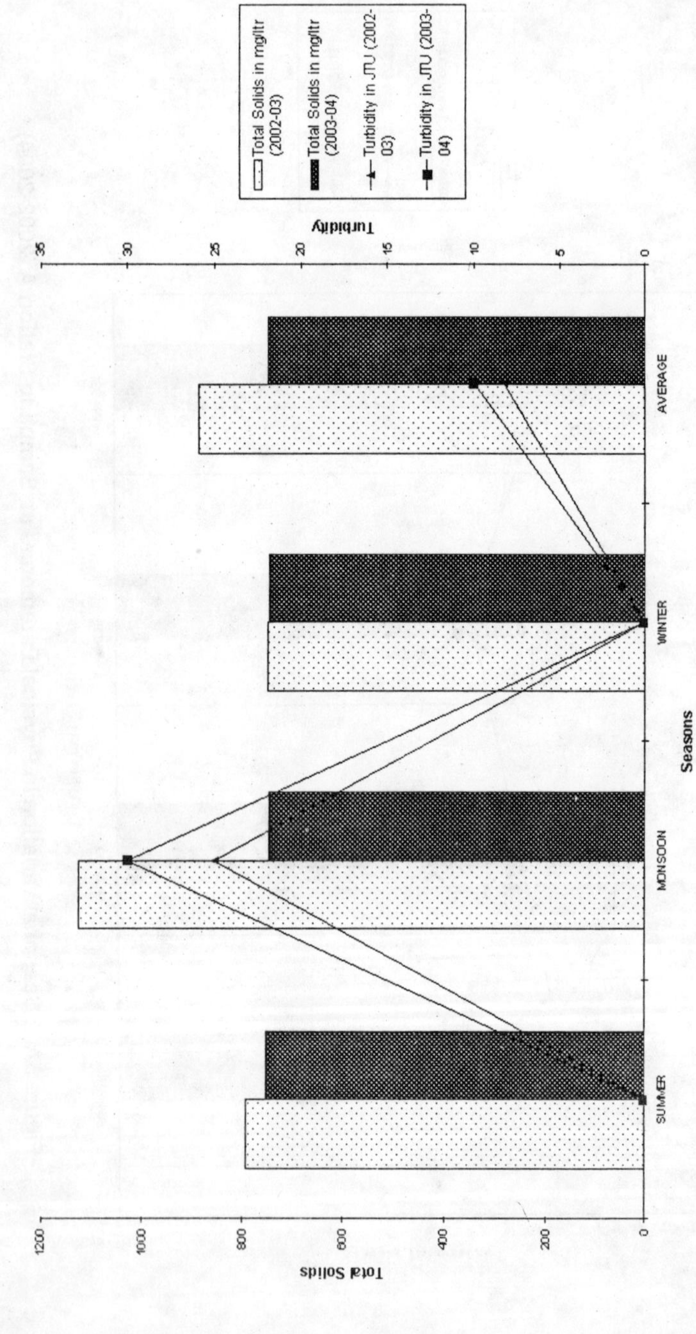

Figure 5A.2: Seasonal Variation in Physical Parameters at Sampling Station A (2002-2004)

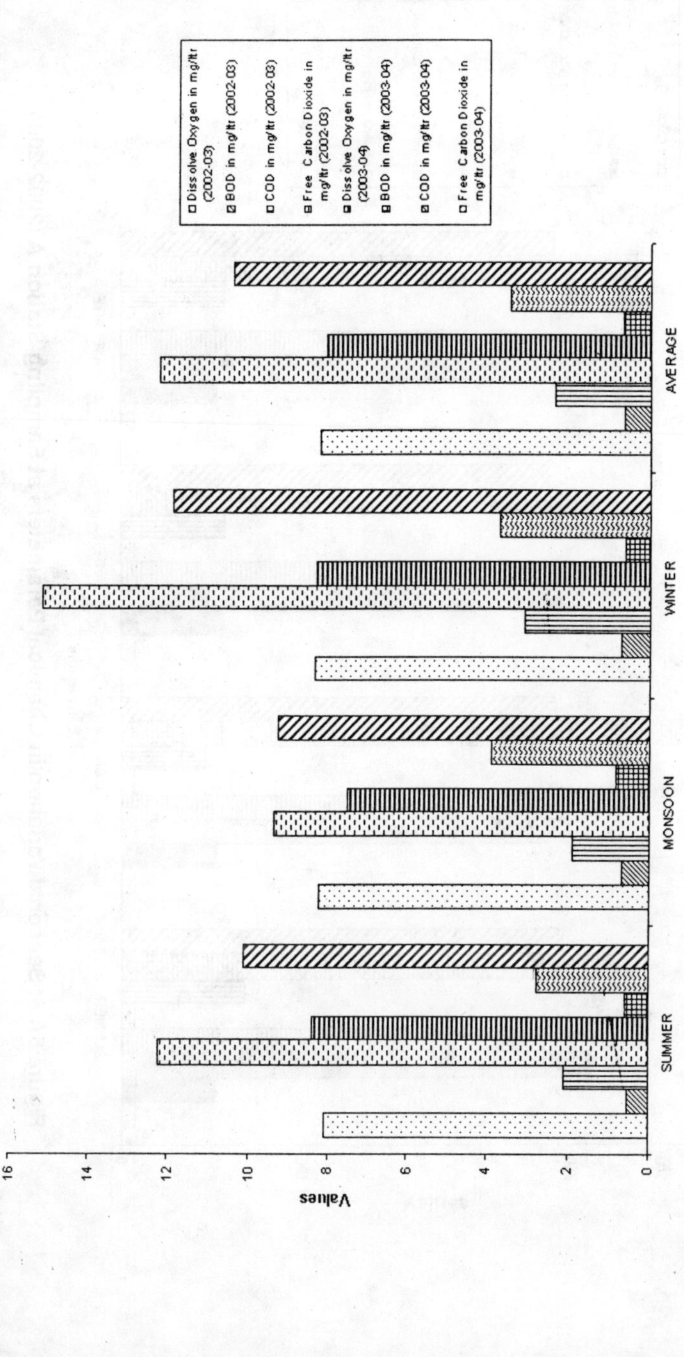

Figure 5A.3: Seasonal Variation in Chemical Parameters at Sampling Station A (2002-2004)

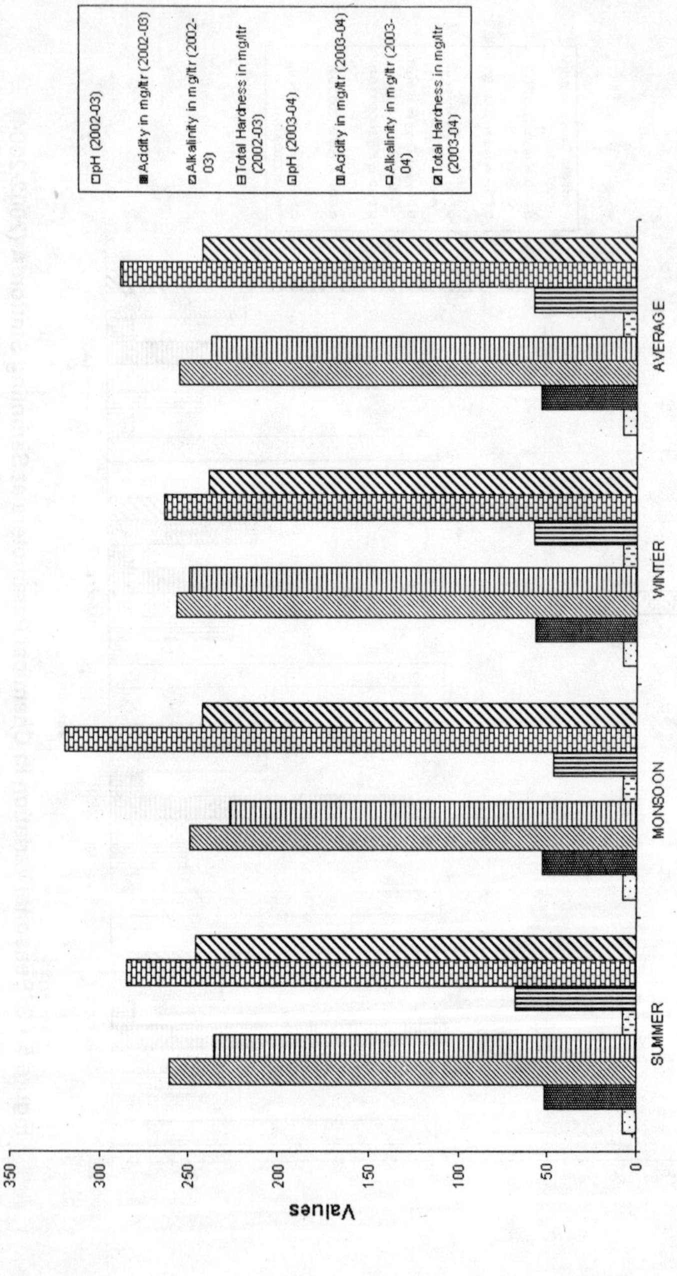

Figure 5A.4: Seasonal Variation in Chemical Parameters at Sampling Station A (2002-2004)

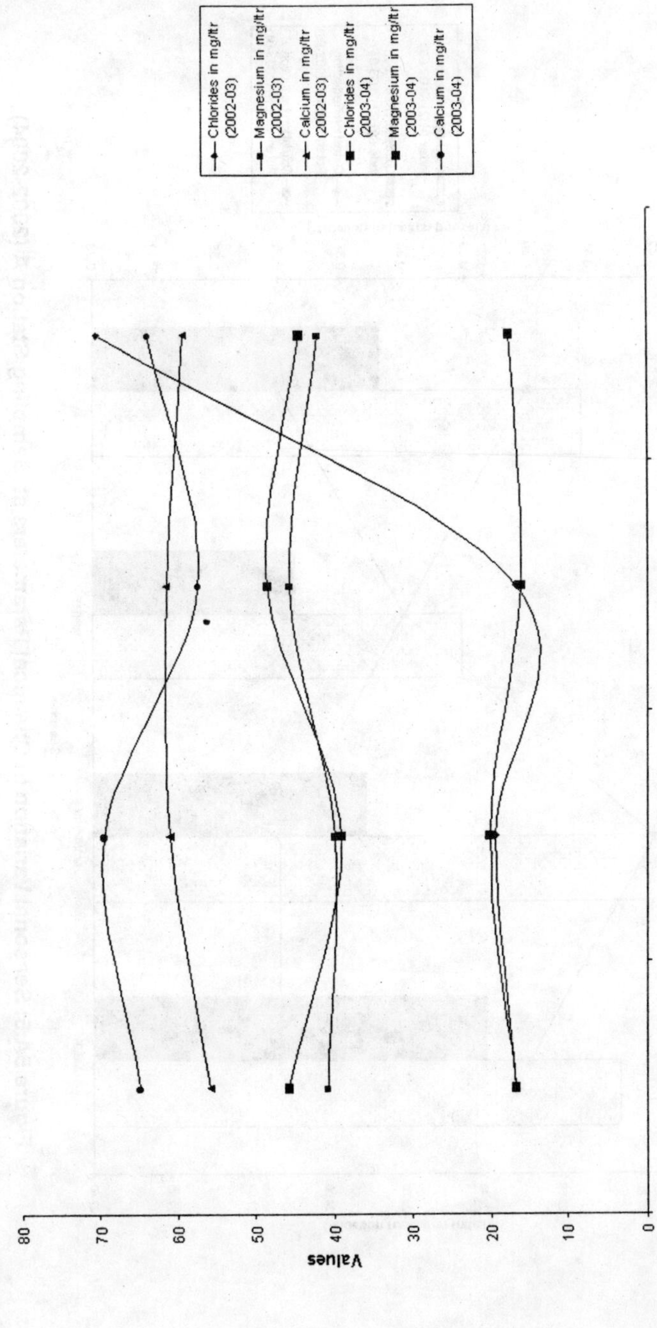

Figure 5A.5: Seasonal Variation in Chemical Parameters at Sampling Station A (2002-2004)

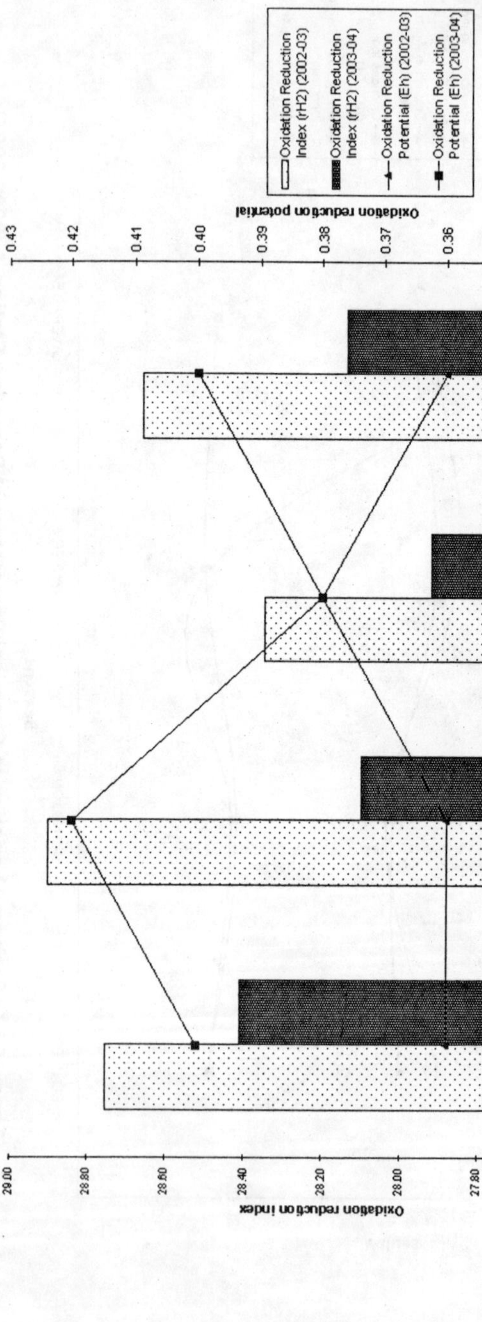

Figure 5A.6: Seasonal Variation in Chemical Parameters at Sampling Station A (2002-2004)

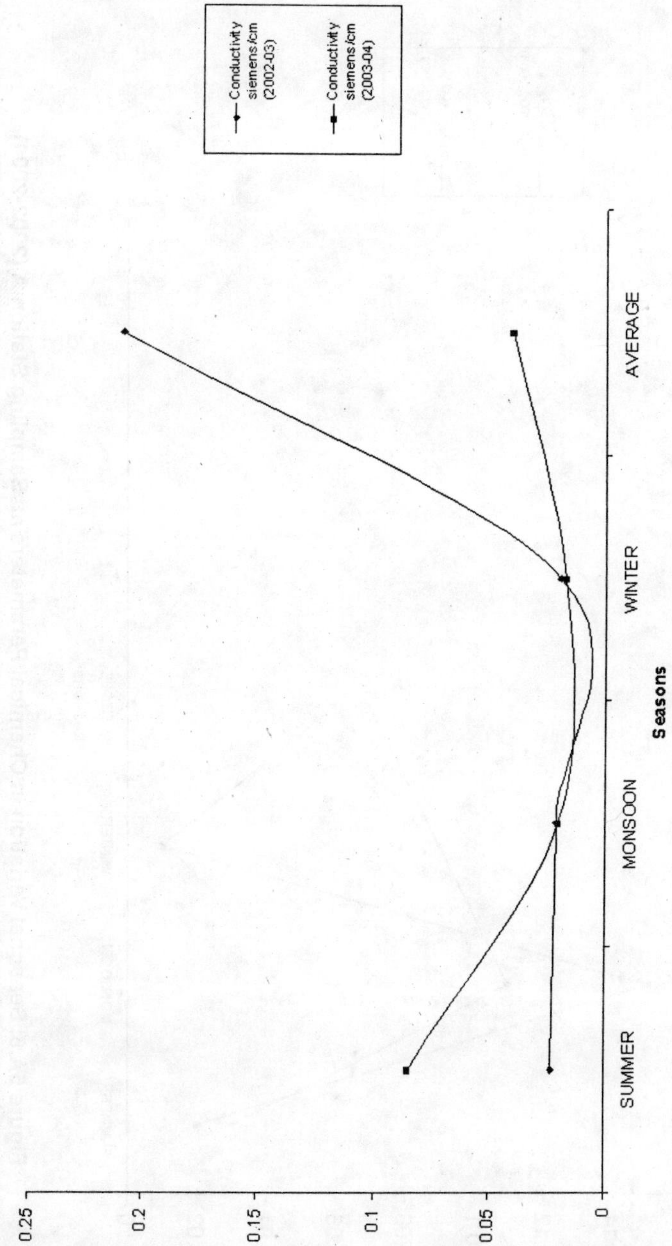

Figure 5A.7: Seasonal Variation in Chemical Parameters at Sampling Station A (2002-2004)

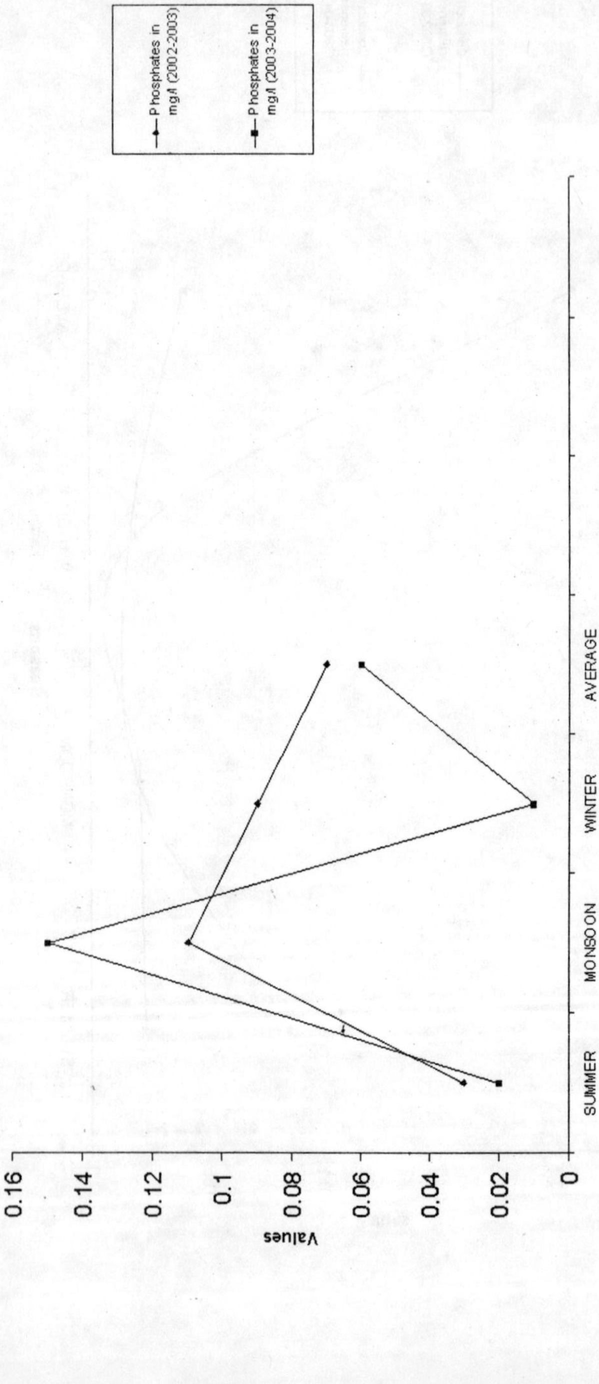

Figure 5A.8: Seasonal Variation in Chemical Parameters at Sampling Station A (2002-2004)

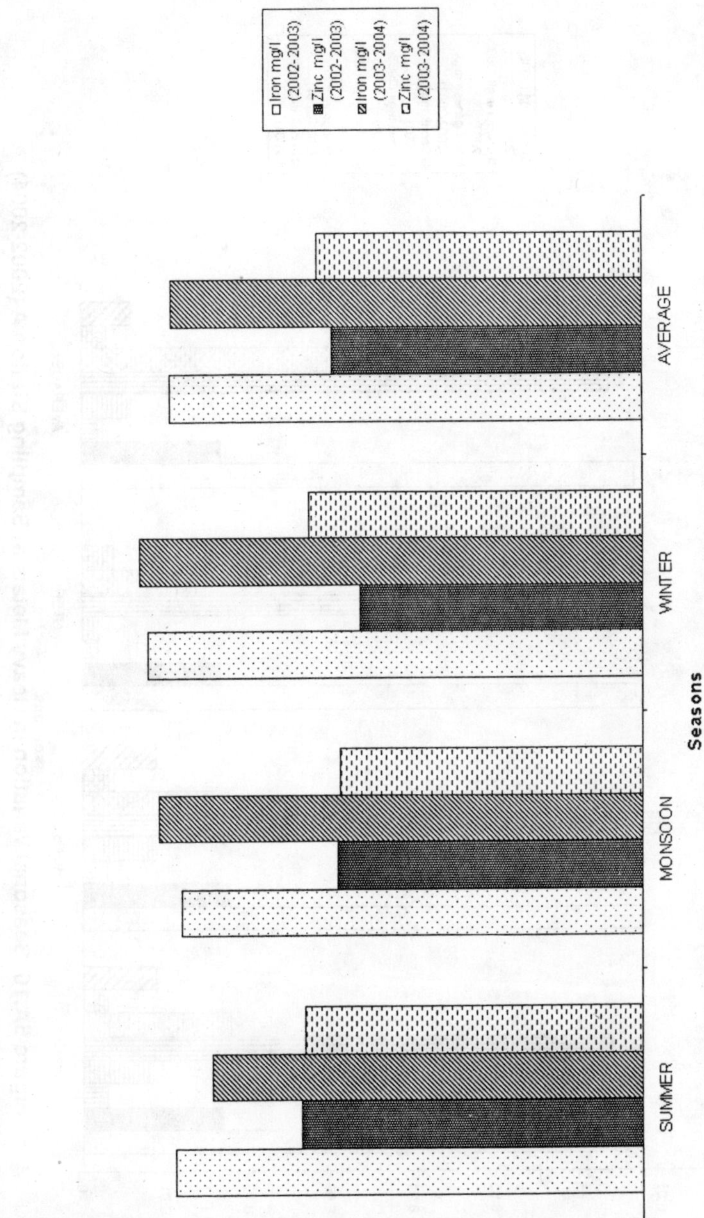

Figure 5A.9: Seasonal Variation in Heavy Metals at Sampling Station A (2002-2004)

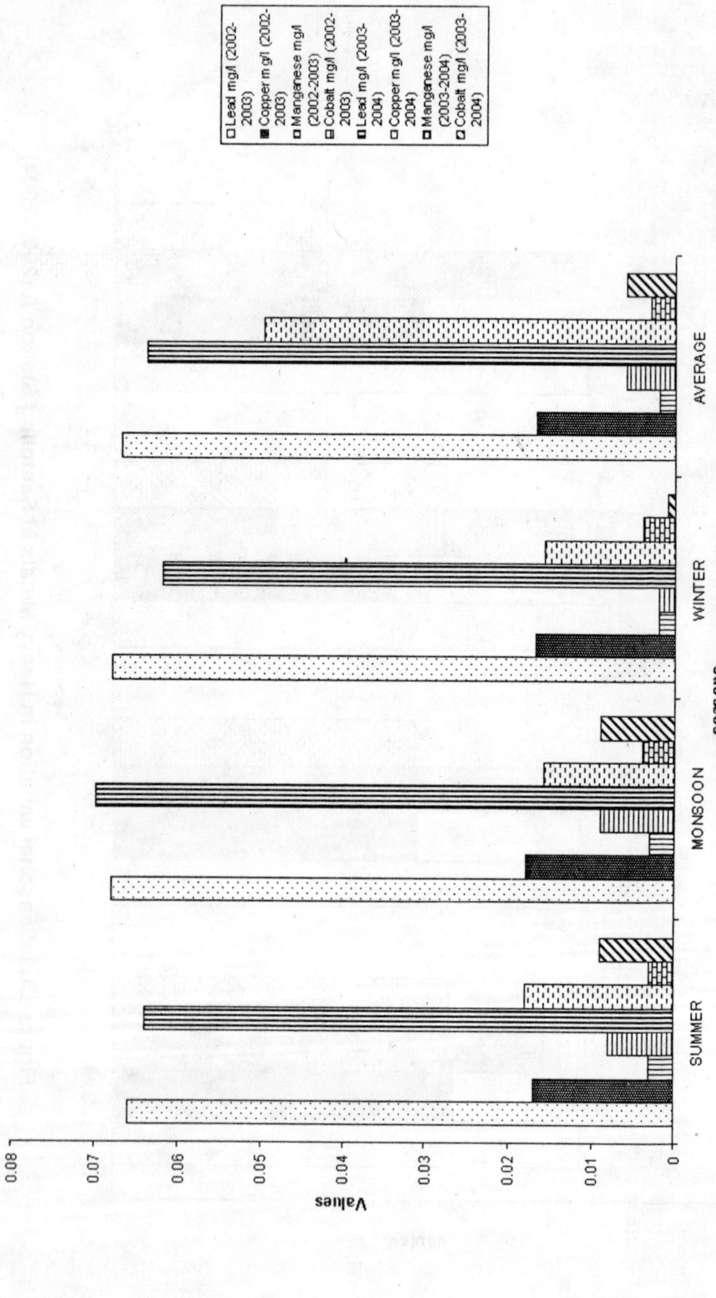

Figure 5A.10: Seasonal Variation in Heavy Metals at Sampling Station A (2002-2004)

Water Temperature

The water temperature of river Suswa at this sampling station was observed to be lowest in winter season (2003–2004) 19.62 °C ± 1.31 which goes highest up to 24.91 °C ± 1.56 in monsoon season (2003–2004). The annual average recorded for first year (2002–2003) was 22.27 °C ± 2.02 and for second year (2003–2004) it was calculated to be 22.64 °C ± 2.72.

Conductivity

The maximum value of conductivity of river Suswa at this sampling station was observed in summer season of 2003–2004, 0.085 siemens/cm ± 0.12. The value was found decreasing from summer to winter during both the years. The minimum value was observed in winter season of 2003–2004, 0.017 siemens/cm ± 0.002. The annual average observed for the first year (2002–2003) was 0.21 siemens/cm ± 0.00 and for second year (2003–2004) was 0.04- siemens/cm ± 0.03.

Turbidity

The turbidity of water at this spot was observed as 0.00 JTU ± 0.00 in summer and winter season, which goes up in monsoon season. The turbidity in monsoon season during (2002–2003) was recorded, as 25.0 JTU ± 3.0 while it was observed as30.00 JTU ± 9.00 in monsoon season of 2003–2004. The annual average for the first year (2002–2003) was recorded as 8.33 JTU ± 14.43 and for the second year (2003–2004) it was observed as 10.00 JTU ± 17.32.

Total Solids

The total solids of river Suswa at this sampling station was recorded to be lowest in 2003–2004 winter season, 750 mg/l ± 288.67, which goes highest up to 1125.0 mg/l ± 78.71 in 2002–2003 monsoon season. The annual average calculated for first year (2002–2003) was 889.58mg/l ± 204.83 and second year (2003–2004) was 751.0 mg/l ± 2.40.

Velocity

The velocity at this sampling station of river Suswa was noted to be minimum in winter season of 2002–2003,0.22 m/sec ± 0.05, which goes maximum up to 0.34m/sec ± 0.07 in monsoon season of 2002–2003.The annual average calculated for first year (2002–2003) was 0.27 m/sec ± 0.06 and second year (2003–2004) was 0.26 m/sec ± 0.03.

pH (Hydrogen ion concentration)

The minimum value of pH at this sampling station was noted in winter season (2002–2003), 7.32 ± 0.11 and maximum 7.70 ± 0.28 in monsoon season (2002–2003). The annual average calculated for first year (2002–2003) was 7.45 ± 0.21 and for the second year (2003–2004) was 7.42 ± 0.10.

Biochemical Oxygen Demand (BOD)

The maximum value of Biochemical Oxygen Demand of river Suswa at this sampling station was noted in monsoon season (2003–2004), 0.83 mg/l ± 0.41 and minimum in summer season (2002–2003), 0.52 mg/l ± 0.21. The annual average calculated for first year (2002–2003) was 0.64 mg/l ± 0.10 and second year (2003–2004) was 0.68 mg/l ± 0.12.

Chemical Oxygen Demand (COD)

The chemical oxygen demand (COD) of river Suswa at this sampling station was observed to be least in monsoon season (2002–2003), 1.90 mg/l ± 0.07, which goes highest up to 3.90 mg/l ± 0.12 in monsoon season (2003–2004) The annual average calculated for first year (2002–2003) was 2.35 mg/l ± 0.65 and second year (2003–2004) was 3.45 mg/l ± 0.61.

Dissolved Oxygen

The Dissolved oxygen of river Suswa at this sampling station was recorded to be minimum in monsoon season (2003–2004), 7.52 mg/l ± 1.38, which goes maximum up to 8.37 mg/l ± 0.34 in summer season (2003–2004). The annual average calculated for first year (2002–2003) was 8.22 mg/l ± 0.13 and second year (2003–2004) was 8.07 mg/l ± 0.47.

Oxidation Reduction Index (rH_2)

The Oxidation Reduction Index (rH_2) of river Suswa at this sampling station was observed to be least in monsoon season (2003–2004), 28.10 ± 0.29, which goes highest up to 28.90 ± 0.16 in monsoon season (2002–2003). The annual average calculated for first year (2002–2003) was 28.66 ± 0.28 and second year (2003–2004) was 28.14 ± 0.24.

Oxidation Reduction Potential (Eh)

The maximum value of Oxidation Reduction Potential (Eh) of river Suswa at this sampling station was observed in monsoon season (2003–2004), 0.42 ± 0.00, and minimum in summer season (2002–2003), 0.36 ± 0.03 The annual average calculated for first year (2002–2003) was 0.36 ± 0.01 and for second year (2003–2004) was 0.40 ± 0.02.

Free Carbon Dioxide

The free carbon dioxide of river Suswa at this sampling station was observed to be lowest in winter season (2003–2004), 1.52 mg/l ± 0.16, which goes highest up to 4.10 mg/l ± 2.08 in monsoon season (2002–2003). The annual average calculated for first year (2002–2003) was 3.11mg/l ± 1.55 and second year (2003–2004) was 2.20 mg/l ± 0.74.

Acidity

The acidity of river Suswa at this sampling station was observed to be least in summer season (2002–2003), 51.04 mg/l ± 24.41, which goes highest up to 67.91 mg/l ± 21.88 in summer season (2003–2004). The annual average calculated for first year (2002–2003) was 53.90 mg/l ± 3.18 and second year (2003–2004) was 57.46 mg/l ± 10.52.

Alkalinity

The minimum value of alkalinity at Satyanarayan Area was noted in monsoon season (2002–2003), 249.16 mg/l ± 19.50, which goes highest up to 319.58 mg/l ± 35.39 in monsoon season (2003–2004). The annual average calculated for first year (2002–2003) was 255.55 mg/l ± 5.91 and second year (2003–2004) was 289.16 mg/l ± 28.24.

Total Hardness

The total hardness of river Suswa at this sampling station was observed to be least in monsoon season (2002–2003), 226.99 mg/l ± 14.29, which goes highest up to 249.49 mg/l ± 9.46 in winter season (2002–2003). The annual average calculated for first year (2002–2003) was 237.43 mg/l ± 11.33 and second year (2003–2004) was 242.46 mg/l ± 3.33.

Chloride

The chloride in water of river Suswa at this sampling station was observed to be least in winter season (2003–2004), 16.09 mg/l ± 1.74, which goes highest up to 20.09 mg/l ± 6.06 in monsoon season (2003–2004) The annual average calculated for first year (2002–2003) was 17.68 mg/l ± 1.49 and second year (2003–2004) was 17.60 mg/l ± 2.17.

Magnesium

The Magnesium of river Suswa at Satyanarayan Area was observed maximum in winter season (2003–2004), 48.67 mg/l ± 3.10, and minimum in monsoon season (2003–2004), 39.24 mg/l ± 1.77.The annual average calculated for first year (2002–2003) was 42.20 mg/l ± 3.17 and second year (2003–2004) was 44.58 mg/l ± 4.83.

Phosphates

The Phosphates of river Suswa at this sampling station was observed minimum in winter season (2003–2004), 0.01 mg/l ± 0.03, which goes maximum up to 0.15 mg/l ± 0.03 in monsoon season (2003–2004) The annual average calculated for first year (2002–2003) was 0.07 mg/l ± 0.04 and second year (2003–2004) was 0.06 mg/l ± 0.07.

Calcium

The maximum amount of calcium of river Suswa at this sampling station was observed in monsoon season (2003–2004), 69.61 mg/l ± 16.59, and minimum in summer season (2002–2003) 55.67 mg/l ± 6.52. The annual average calculated for first year (2002–2003) was 59.42 mg/l ± 3.26 and second year (2003–2004) was 63.97 mg/l ± 6.09.

Metallic Parameters

Lead (Pb)

The minimum concentration of Lead at this sampling station of river Suswa was recorded in winter season (2003–2004), 0.062 mg/l ± 0.011, which goes maximum up to 0.07mg/l ± 0.006 in monsoon season (2003–2004). The annual average calculated for first year

(2002–2003) was 0.067 mg/l ± 0.001 and second year (2003–2004) was calculated as 0.064 mg/l ± 0.005.

Copper (Cu)

At this sampling station of river Suswa the copper was recorded to be lowest in winter season (2003–2004), 0.016 mg/l ± 0.0005 which goes highest up to 0.018 mg/l l ± 0.002 in monsoon season (2002–2003). The annual average observed for the first year (2002–2003) was 0.017 mg/l ± 0.0005 and second year (2003–2004) was 0.05 mg/l ± 0.001.

Iron (Fe)

The maximum concentration of Iron at this sampling station of river Suswa was recorded in winter season (2003–2004), 5.78 mg/l ± 0.59, while its minimum concentration was observed in summer season (2003–2004), 4.92 mg/l ± 0.33. The annual average observed for the first year (2002–2003) was 5.43mg/l ± 0.21 and second year (2003–2004) was5.43mg/l ± 0.44.

Manganese (Mn)

The manganese of this sampling station was found maximum in monsoon season (2003–2004), 0.004 mg/l ± 0.001 while minimum in winter season (2002–2003), 0.002 mg/l ± 0.001. The annual average for the first year (2002–2003) was observed as 0.002 mg/l ± 0.0005 while for the second year (2003–2004) it was observed as 0.003 mg/l ± 0.005.

Zinc (Zn)

At this spot the Zinc was recorded to be minimum in winter season (2002–2003) 3.22 mg/l ± 0.06, which goes maximum up to 3.89 mg/l ± 0.11 in summer season (2002–2003). The annual average calculated for the first year (2002–2003) was 3.52 mg/l ± 0.33 and second year (2003–2004) was 3.70 mg/l ± 0.22.

Cobalt (Co)

At this spot the Cobalt was recorded to be minimum in winter season (2003–2004), 0.001 mg/l ± 0.0003, which goes maximum up to 0.009 mg/l ± 0.01 in monsoon season (2002–2003). The annual average calculated for the first year (2002–2003) was 0.006 mg/l ± 0.003 and second year (2003–2004) was 0.006 mg/l ± 0.004.

Sampling Station B (Upstream Vedic Nagar)

The physico-chemical and heavy metals parameters of sampling station B are presented in Table 5A.3-5A.4 and Figure 5A.11–5A.20.

Water Temperature

The water temperature of river Suswa at this sampling station was observed to be lowest in winter season (2003–2004), 19.12 ºC ± 1.65 that goes highest up to 25.25 ºC ± 0.95 in monsoon season (2002–2003). The annual average recorded for first year (2002–2003), 23.17 ºC ± 2.57 and for second year (2003–2004) it was calculated 22.46 ºC ± 2.93.

Conductivity

The maximum value of conductivity of river Suswa at this sampling station was observed in summer season of 2003–2004, 0.029 siemens/cm ± . 0.008 The minimum value was observed in summer season of 2002–2003, 0.014 siemens/cm ± 0.009.The annual average observed for the first year (2002–2003) was 0.017 siemens/cm ± 0.003 and for second year (2003–2004) was 0.23 siemens/cm ± 0.005.

Turbidity

The turbidity of water at this spot was observed as 0.00 JTU ± 0.00 in summer and winter season, which goes up in monsoon season. The turbidity in monsoon season during (2002–2003) was recorded, as 25.0 JTU ± 6.0 while it was observed as35.00 JTU ± 0.00 in monsoon season of 2003–2004. The annual average for the first year (2002–2003) was recorded as 8.33 JTU ± 14.43 and for the second year 2003–2004 it was observed as 11.66 JTU ± 20.20.

Total Solids

The total solids of river Suswa at this sampling station was recorded to be lowest in 2003–2004 winter season, 500.00 mg/l ± 0.00, which goes highest up to 1000.0 mg/l ± 408.24 in 2002–2003 monsoon season. The annual average calculated for first year (2002–2003) was 958.5 mg/l ± 72.16 and second year (2003–2004) was 791.66 mg/l ± 260.20.

Velocity

The velocity at this sampling station of river Suswa was noted to be minimum in summer season of (2002–2003), 0.29 m/sec

Table 5 A.3: Seasonal Variations in Physico Chemical Parameters of River Suswa at Sampling Station B (2002-2004)

Physico-chemical	*2002-2003*				*2003-2004*			
Parameters	*Summer*	*Monsoon*	*Winter*	*Average*	*Summer*	*Monsoon*	*Winter*	*Average*
Temperature (°C)	23.99±2.38	25.25±0.95	20.29±1.20	23.17±2.57	23.70±2.22	24.58±1.03	19.12±1.65	22.46±2.93
Conductivity (Siemens/cm)	0.014±0.009	0.017±0.012	0.021±0.003	0.017±0.003	0.029±0.008	0.020±0.010	0.020±0.003	0.23±0.005
Turbidity (JTU)	0±0.00	25.0±6.00	0.00	8.33±14.43	0.00	35±0.00	0.00	11.66±20.20
Total Solids (mg/l)	1000±0.00	1000.0±408.24	875±478.71	958.5±72.16	1000±408.24	875.0±250.0	500.0±0.00	791.66±260.20
Velocity (m/s)	0.29±0.058	0.33±0.097	0.33±0.053	0.31±0.02	0.35±0.100	0.38±0.099	0.33±0.06	0.35±0.02
pH	7.38±0.19	7.46±0.10	7.21±0.26	7.35±0.12	7.24±0.108	7.30±0.09	7.37±0.22	7.30±0.06
BOD (mg/l)	0.69±0.50	0.74±0.72	0.73±0.98	0.72±0.02	0.87±0.49	0.89±0.15	0.57±0.22	0.77±0.17
COD (mg/l)	3.25±0.23	3.00±0.00	2.95±0.31	3.06±0.16	3.35±0.53	3.55±0.11	2.10±0.09	3.00±0.78
DO (mg/l)	7.93±0.84	8.25±0.93	9.11±0.77	8.43±0.61	8.55±0.29	7.05±0.58	8.53±0.48	8.04±0.86
Oxidation Reduction Index (rH_2)	28.26±0.44	28.49±0.18	27.77±0.27	28.17±0.36	28.80±0.00	28.27±0.20	26.85±0.54	27.97±1.00
Oxidation Reduction Potential (Eh)	0.40±0.003	0.38±0.01	0.36±0.02	0.38±0.02	0.39±0.01	0.40±0.02	0.36±0.06	0.38±0.02
Free CO_2 (mg/l)	2.93±0.96	5.07±1.77	1.25±0.62	3.08±1.91	3.0±1.18	4.86±1.80	1.11±4.40	2.99±1.87
Acidity (mg/l)	44.58±8.53	49.50±10.09	58.74±6.54	50.94±7.18	54.95±24.45	45.83±4.35	53.95±8.18	51.57±5.00
Alkalinity (mg/l)	241.24±33.86	267.91±52.65	253.74±3.15	254.29±13.34	267.70±38.23	306.66±52.29	263.12±15.46	279.16±23.92
Total hardness (mg/l)	231.08±16.38	219.00±19.02	236.33±20.54	228.80±8.88	250.62±6.01	245.49±29.86	243.45±7.91	246.52±3.69
Chlorides (mg/l)	21.09±5.91	19.97±5.03	16.80±1.47	19.28±2.22	15.70±0.76	24.33±6.58	17.61±1.34	19.21±4.53
Magnesium (mg/l)	38.97±5.69	37.23±3.74	43.19±5.35	39.79±3.06	40.18±6.50	38.75±7.10	39.10±6.16	39.34±0.74
Phosphates (mg/l)	0.03±0.01	0.11±0.00	0.06±0.02	0.06±0.04	0.05±0.03	0.09±0.03	0.05±0.02	0.06±0.02
Calcium (mg/l)	62.12±5.85	59.28±1.35	59.32±5.83	60.24±1.62	57.93±7.84	68.19±13.55	56.06±5.42	60.72±6.53

± = Standard deviation.

Table 5 A 4: Seasonal Variation in Metallic Parameters of River Suswa at Sampling Station B (2002-2004)

Metallic	*2002-2003*				*2003-2004*			
Parameters	*Summer*	*Monsoon*	*Winter*	*Average*	*Summer*	*Monsoon*	*Winter*	*Average*
Lead (Pb) (mg/l)	0.075±0.01	0.081±0.00	0.074±0.02	0.07±0.00	0.073±0.02	0.079±0.03	0.075±0.02	0.071±0.00
Copper (Cu) (mg/l)	0.021±0.00	0.019±0.00	0.023±0.00	0.021±0.002	0.018±0.002	0.023±0.001	0.021±0.003	0.020±0.002
Iron (Fe) (mg/l)	5.50±0.90	5.19±0.37	5.38±0.28	5.35±0.15	6.10±0.16	5.16±0.27	5.88±0.29	5.71±0.49
Manganese (Mn) (mg/l)	0.006±0.001	0.008±0.001	0.007±0.002	0.007±0.001	0.005±0.001	0.003±0.002	0.003±0.001	0.002±0.001
Zinc (Zn) (mg/l)	3.92±0.005	3.72±0.022	3.76±0.031	3.8±0.10	3.81±0.03	3.50±0.03	3.62±0.02	3.64±0.15
Cobalt (Ca) (mg/l)	0.007±0.01	0.009±0.01	0.007±0.03	0.007±0.001	0.07±0.01	0.008±0.00	0.008±0.01	0.028±0.035

± = Standard deviation.

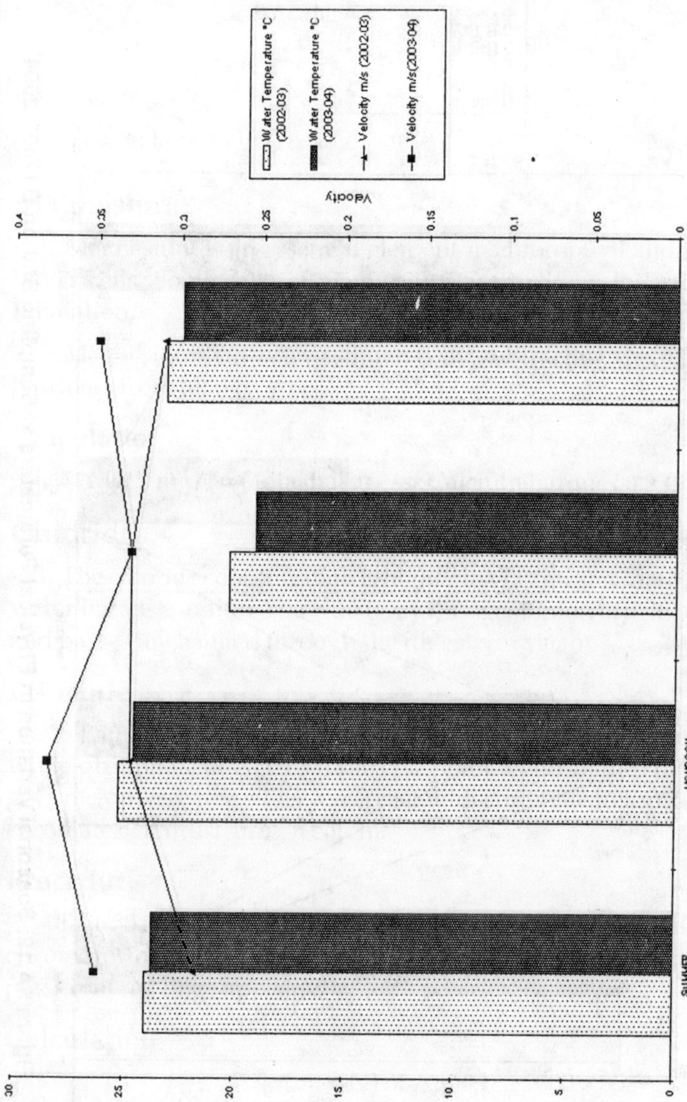

Figure 5A.11: Seasonal Variation in Physical Parameters at Sampling Station B (2002-2004)

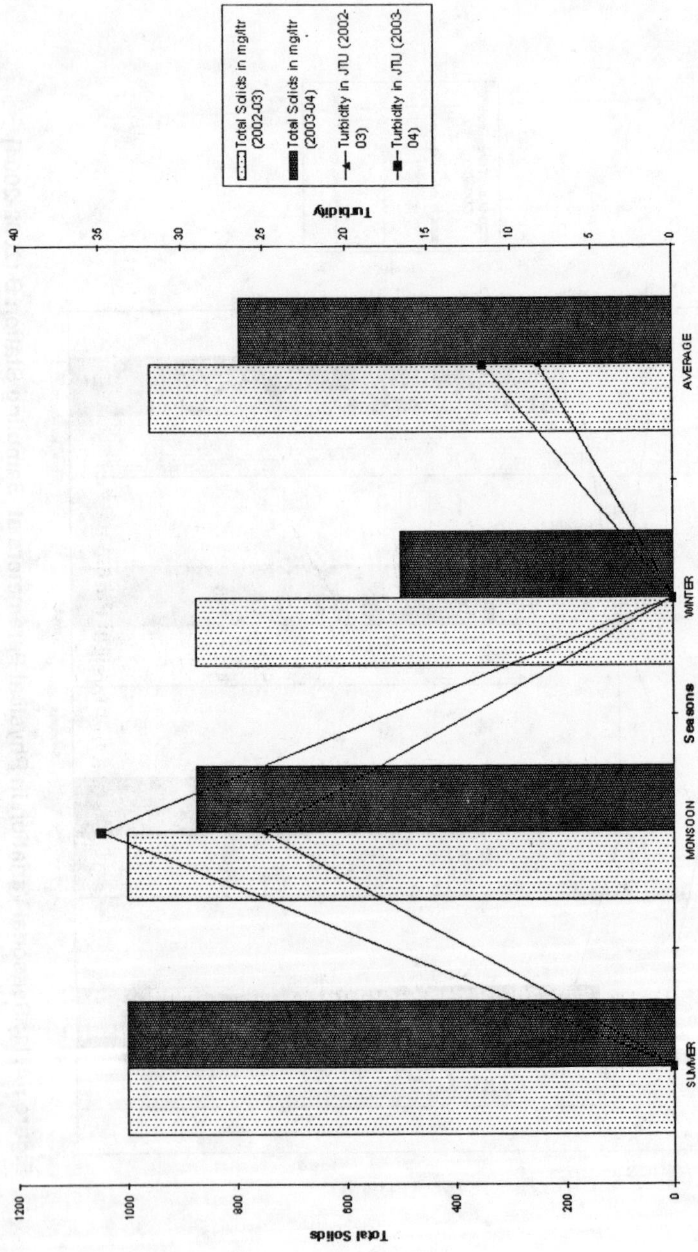

Figure 5A.12: Seasonal Variation in Physical Parameters at Sampling Station B (2002-2004)

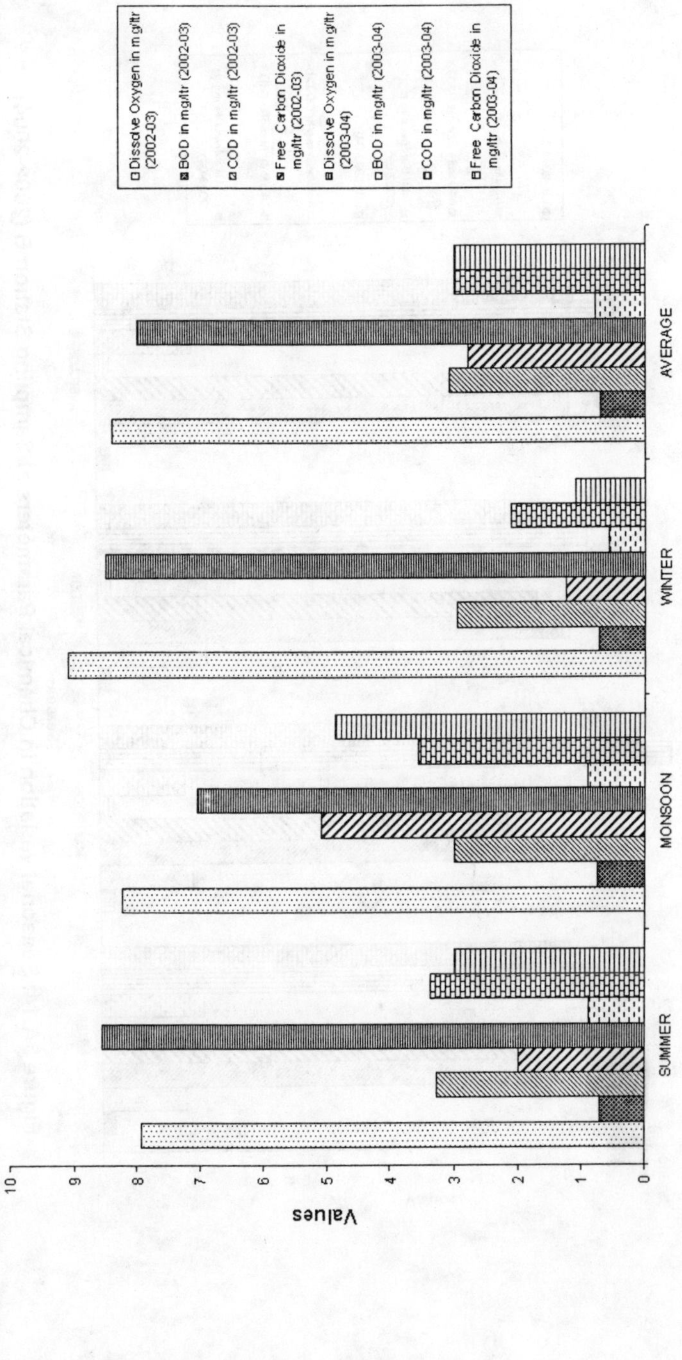

Figure 5A.13: Seasonal Variation in Chemical Parameters at Sampling Station B (2002-2004)

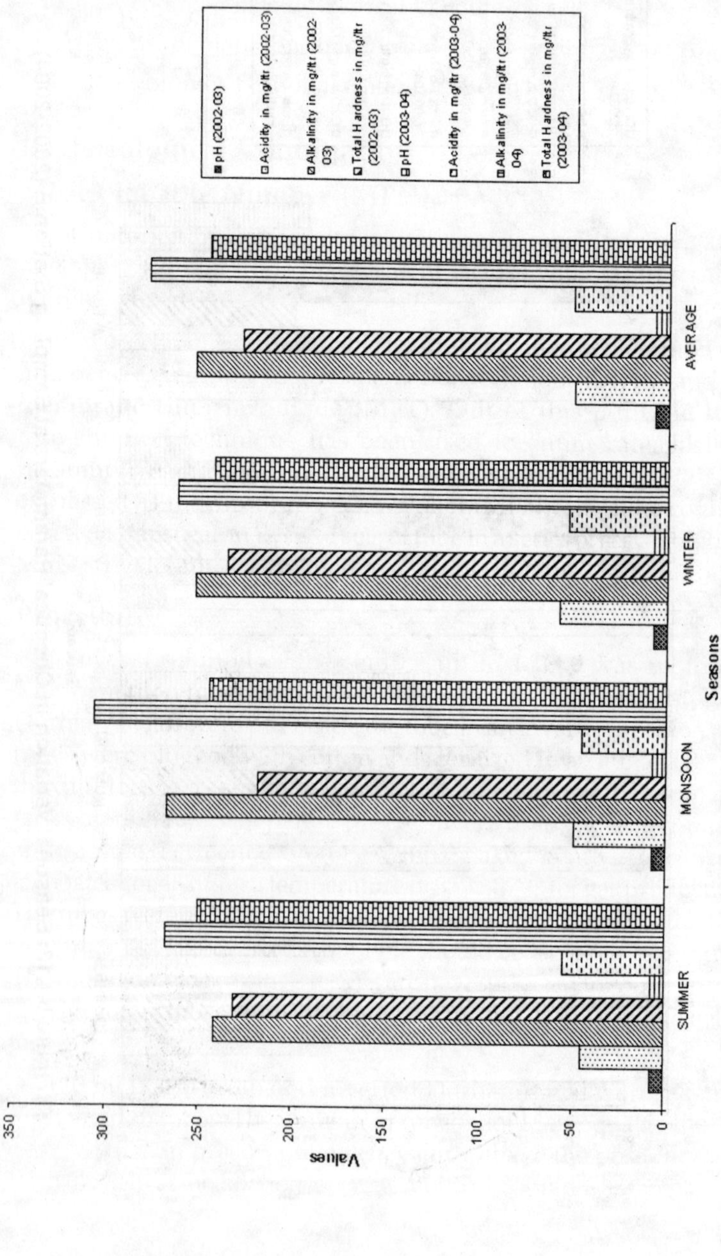

Figure 5A.14: Seasonal Variation in Chemical Parameters at Sampling Station B (2002-2004)

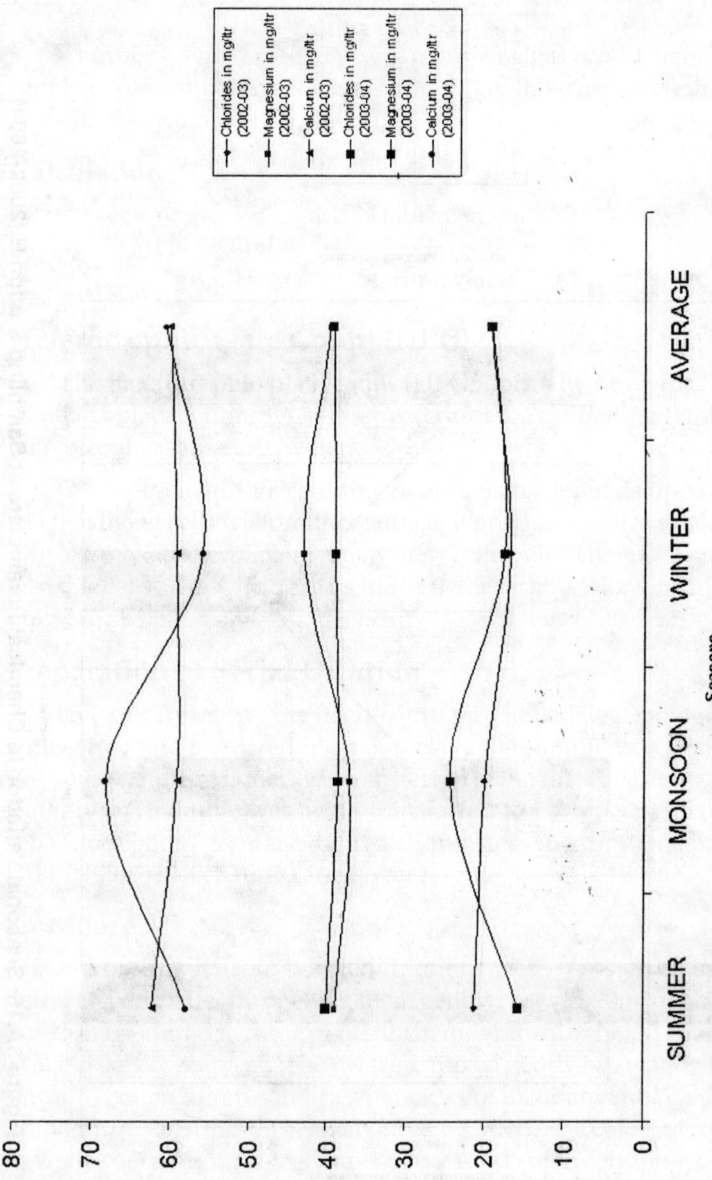

Figure 5A.15: Seasonal Variation in Chemical Parameters at Sampling Station B (2002-2004)

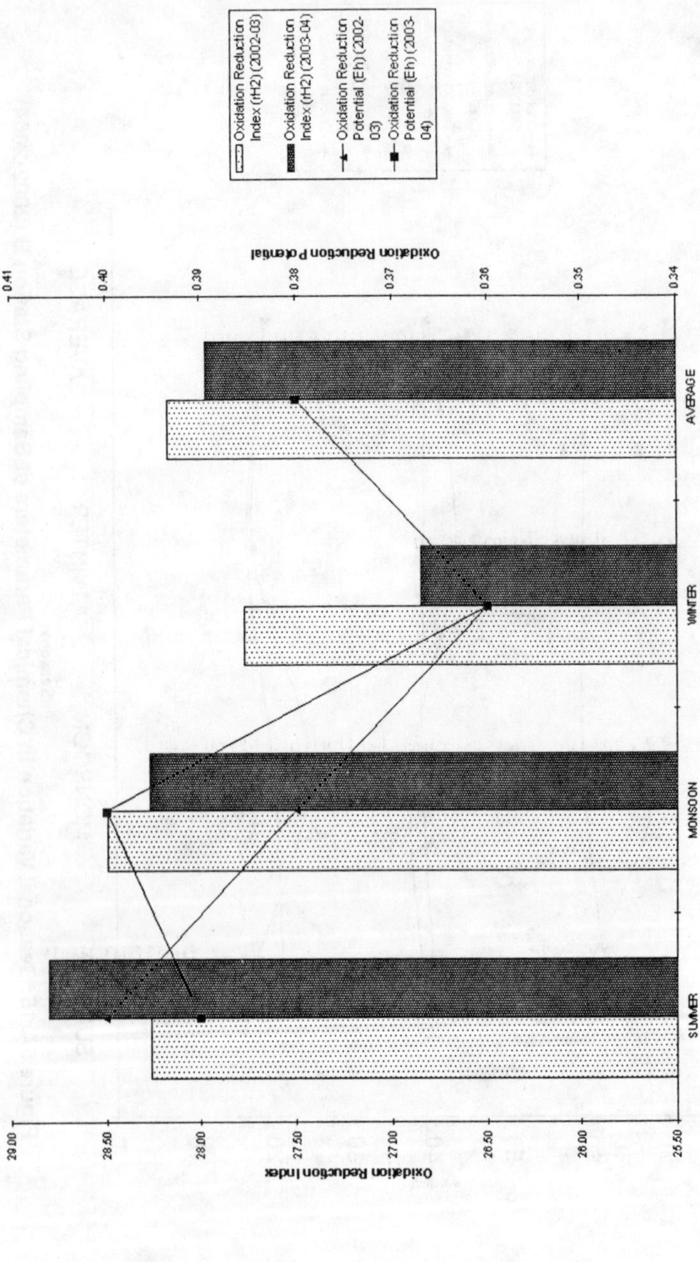

Figure 5A.16: Seasonal Variation in Chemical Parameters at Sampling Station B (2002-2004)

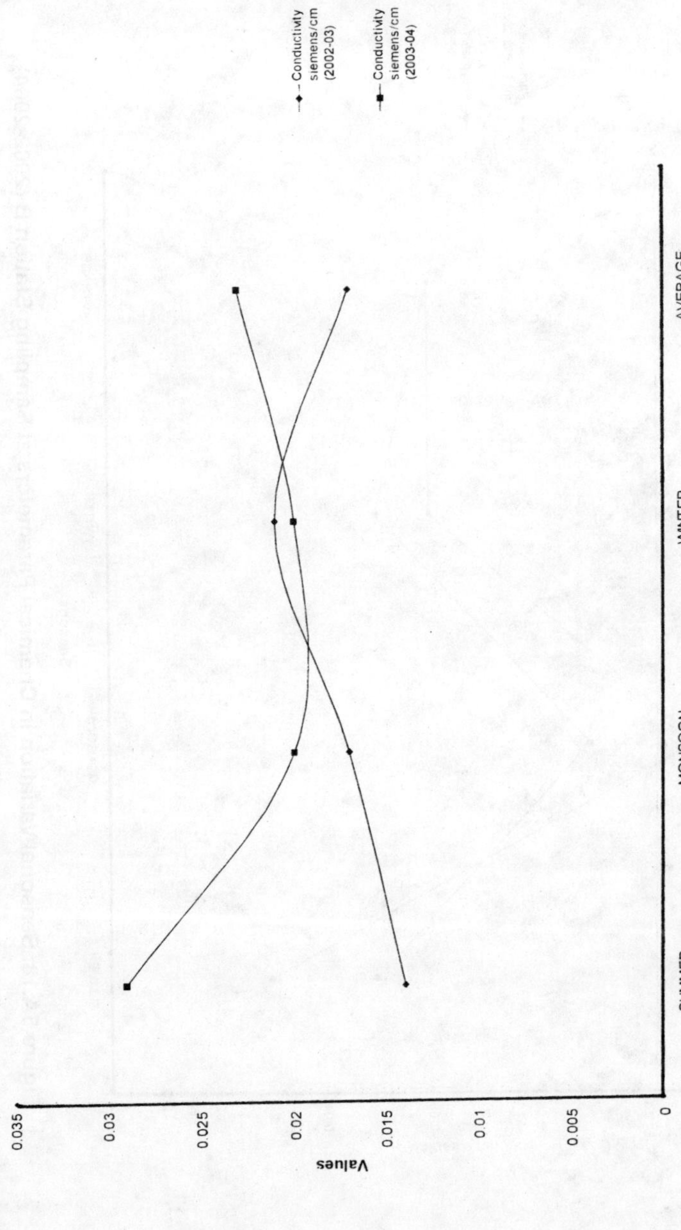

Figure 5A.17: Seasonal Variation in Chemical Parameters at Sampling Station B (2002-2004)

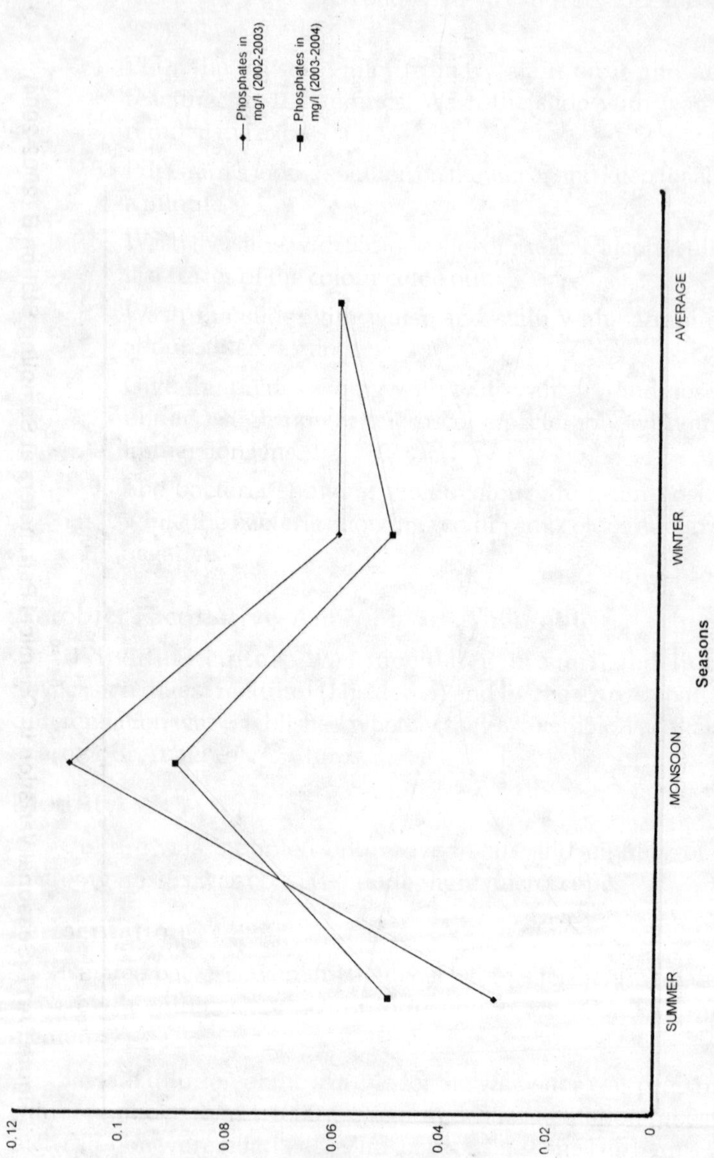

Figure 5A.18: Seasonal Variation in Chemical Parameters at Sampling Station B (2002-2004)

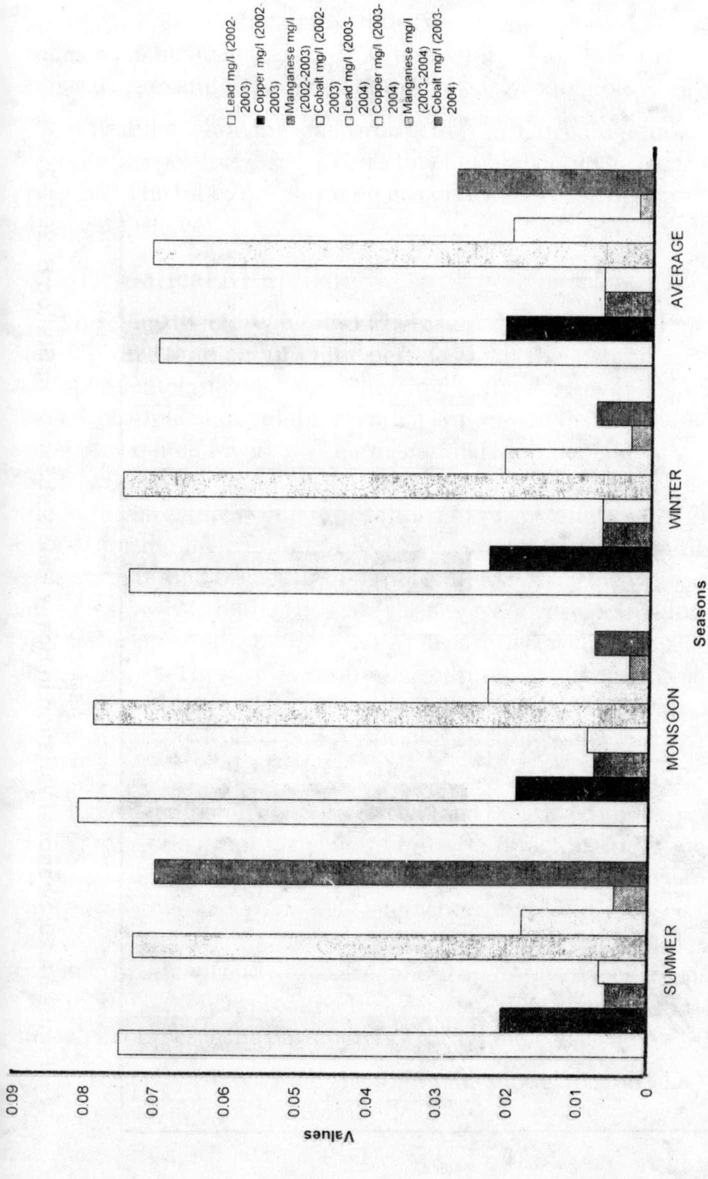

Figure 5A.19: Seasonal Variation in Heavy Metals at Sampling Station B (2002-2004)

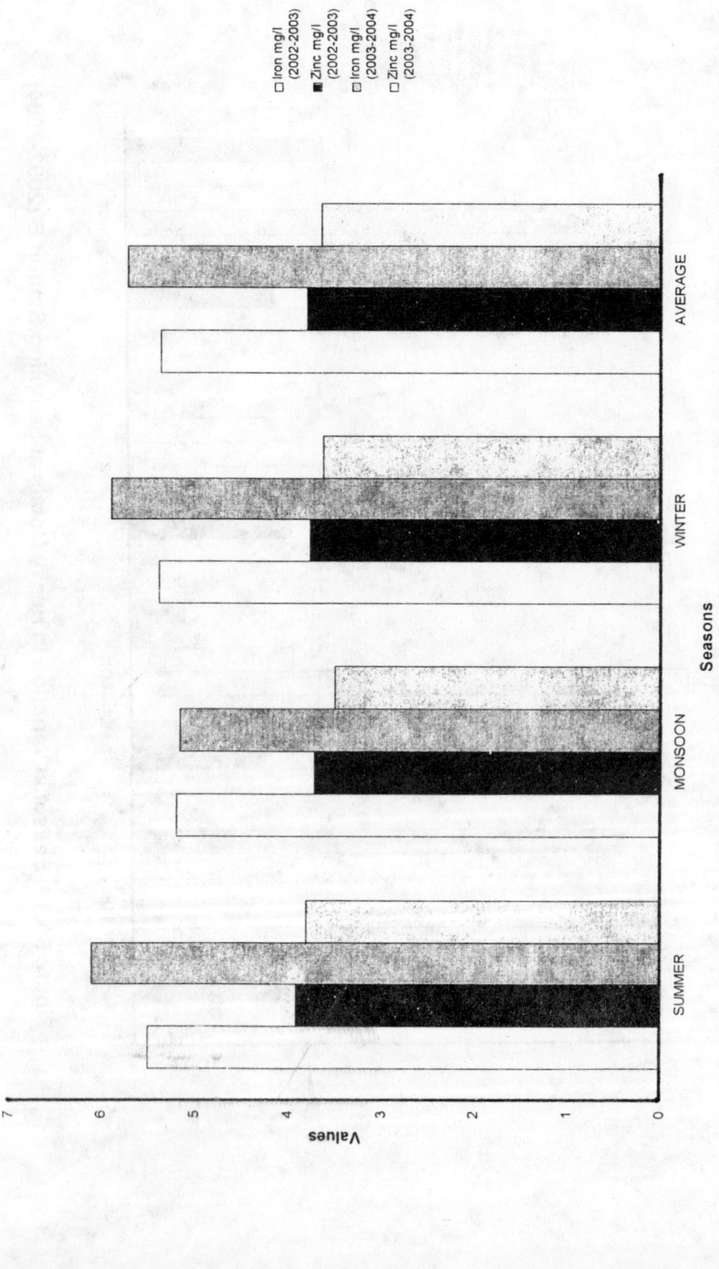

Figure 5A.20: Seasonal Variation in Heavy Metals at Sampling Station B (2002-2004)

± 0.058, which goes maximum up to 0.38m/sec ± 0.099 in monsoon season of 2003–2004.The annual average calculated for first year (2002–2003) was 0.31 m/sec ± 0.02 and second year (2003–2004) was 0.35 m/sec ± 0.02.

pH (Hydrogen ion concentration)

The minimum value of pH at this sampling station was noted in winter season (2002–2003), 7.21 ± 0.26 and maximum 7.46 ± 0.10 in monsoon season (2002–2003). The annual average calculated for first year (2002–2003) was 7.35 ± 0.12 and second year (2003–2004) was 7.30 ± 0.06.

Biochemical Oxygen Demand (BOD)

The maximum value of Biochemical Oxygen Demand of river Suswa at this sampling station was noted in monsoon season (2003–2004), 0.89 mg/l ± 0.15 and minimum in winter season (2003-2003), 0.57 mg/l ± 0.21. The annual average calculated for first year (2002–2003) was 0.72 mg/l ± 0.02 and second year (2003–2004) was 0.77 mg/l ± 0.17.

Chemical Oxygen Demand (COD)

The chemical oxygen demand (COD) of river Suswa at this sampling station was observed to be least in winter season (2003–2004), 2.10 mg/l ± 0.09, which goes highest up to 3.55 mg/l ± 0.11 in monsoon season (2003–2004). The annual average calculated for first year (2002–2003) was 3.06 mg/l ± 0.16 and second year (2003–2004) was 3.00 mg/l ± 0.78.

Dissolved Oxygen

The Dissolved oxygen of river Suswa at this sampling station was recorded to be minimum in monsoon season (2003–2004), 7.05 mg/l ± 0.58, which goes maximum up to 9.11 mg/l ± 0.77 in winter season (2002–2003). The annual average calculated for first year (2002–2003) was 8.43 mg/l ± 0.61 and second year (2003–2004) was 8.04 mg/l ± 0.86.

Oxidation Reduction Index (rH_2)

The Oxidation Reduction Index (rH_2) of river Suswa at this sampling station was observed to be least in winter season (2003–2004), 26.85 ± 0.54, which goes highest up to 28.80 ± 0.00 in summer season (2003–2004) The annual average calculated for first year (2002–2003) was 28.17 ± 0.36 and second year (2003–2004) was 27.97 ± 1.00.

Oxidation Reduction Potential (Eh)

The maximum value of Oxidation Reduction Potential (Eh) of river Suswa at this sampling station was observed in summer season (2002–2003), 0.40 ± 0.003, and minimum in winter season (2002–2003), 0.36 ± 0.02 The annual average calculated for first year (2002–2003) was 0.38 ± 0.02 and for second year (2003–2004) was 0.38 ± 0.02.

Free Carbon Dioxide

The free carbon dioxide of river Suswa at this sampling station was observed to be lowest in winter season (2003–2004), 1.11 mg/l ± 0.40, which goes highest up to 5.07 mg/l ± 1.77 in monsoon season (2002–2003). The annual average calculated for first year (2002–2003) was 3.08 mg/l ± 1.91 and second year (2003–2004) was 2.99 mg/l ± 1.87.

Acidity

The acidity of river Suswa at this sampling station was observed to be least in summer season (2002–2003), 44.58 mg/l ± 8.53, which goes highest up to 58.74 mg/l ± 6.54 in winter season (2002–2003) The annual average calculated for first year (2002–2003) was 50.94 mg/l ± 7.18 and second year (2003–2004) was 51.57 mg/l ± 5.00.

Alkalinity

The minimum value of alkalinity at upstream Vedic nagar was noted in summer season (2002–2003), 241.24 mg/l ± 33.86, which goes highest up to 306.66 mg/l ± 52.29 in monsoon season (2003–2004). The annual average calculated for first year (2002–2003) was 254.29 mg/l ± 13.34 and second year (2003–2004) was 279.16 mg/l ± 23.92.

Total Hardness

The total hardness of river Suswa at this sampling station was observed to be least in monsoon season (2002–2003), 219.00 mg/l ± 19.02, which goes highest up to 250.62 mg/l ± 6.01 in summer season (2003–2004) The annual average calculated for first year (2002–2003) was 228.80 mg/l ± 8.88 and second year (2003–2004) was 246.52 mg/l ± 3.69.

Chloride

The chloride in water of river Suswa at this sampling station was observed to be least in summer season (2003–2004), 15.70 mg/l ± 0.76, which goes highest up to 24.33 mg/l ± 6.58 in monsoon season (2003–2004) The annual average calculated for first year (2002–2003) was 19.28 mg/l ± 2.22 and second year (2003–2004) was 19.21 mg/l ± 4.53.

Magnesium

The Magnesium of river Suswa at upstream Vedic nagar was observed maximum in winter season (2002–2003), 43.19 mg/l ± 5.35, and minimum in monsoon season (2002–2003), 37.23 mg/l ± 3.74.The annual average calculated for first year (2002–2003) was 39.79 mg/l ± 3.06 and second year (2003–2004) was 39.34 mg/l ± 0.74.

Phosphates

The Phosphates of river Suswa at this sampling station was observed minimum in summer season (2002–2003), 0.03 mg/l ± 0.01, which goes maximum up to 0.11 mg/l ± 0.00 in monsoon season (2002–2003) The annual average calculated for first year (2002–2003) was 0.06 mg/l ± 0.04 and second year (2003–2004) was 0.06 mg/l ± 0.02.

Calcium

The maximum amount of calcium of river Suswa at this sampling station was observed in monsoon season (2003–2004), 68.19 mg/l ± 13.55, and minimum in winter season (2003–2004) 56.06 mg/l ± 5.42 The annual average calculated for first year (2002–2003) was 60.24 mg/l ± 1.62 and second year (2003–2004) was 60.72 mg/l ± 6.53.

Metallic Parameters

Lead (Pb)

The minimum concentration of Lead at this sampling station of river Suswa was recorded in summer season (2003–2004), 0.073 mg/l ± 0.02, which goes maximum up to 0.081 mg/l ± 0.001 in monsoon season (2002–2003). The annual average calculated for first year (2002–2003) was 0.07 mg/l ± 0.003 and second year was calculated as 0.07 mg/l ± 0.003.

Copper (Cu)

At this sampling station of river Suswa the copper was recorded to be lowest in summer season (2003–2004), 0.018 mg/l ± 0.002 which goes highest up to 0.023 mg/l ± 0.001 in monsoon season (2003–2004). The annual average observed for the first year (2002–2003) was 0.021 mg/l ± 0.002 and second year (2003–2004) was 0.02 mg/l ± 0.002.

Iron (Fe)

The maximum concentration of Iron at this sampling station of river Suswa was recorded in summer season (2003–2004), 6.10 mg/l ± 0.16, while its minimum concentration was observed in monsoon season (2003–2004), 5.16 mg/l ± 0.27. The annual average observed for the first year (2002–2003) was 5.35 mg/l ± 0.15 and second year (2003–2004) was 5.71 mg/l ± 0.49.

Manganese (Mn)

The manganese of this sampling station was found maximum in monsoon season (2002–2003), 0.008 mg/l ± 0.001 while minimum in winter season (2003–2004), 0.003 mg/l ± 0.001. The annual average for the first year (2002–2003) was observed as 0.007 mg/l ± 0.001 while for the second year (2003–2004) it was observed as 0.002 mg/l ± 0.001.

Zinc (Zn)

At this spot the Zinc was recorded to be minimum in monsoon season (2003–2004) 3.50 mg/l ± 0.03, which goes maximum up to 3.92 mg/l ± 0.005 in summer season (2002–2003). The annual average calculated for the first year (2002–2003) was 3.80 mg/l ± 0.10 and second year (2003–2004) was 3.64 mg/l ± 0.15.

Cobalt (Co)

At this spot the Cobalt was recorded to be minimum in summer season (2002–2003), 0.007 mg/l ± 0.01, which goes maximum up to 0.009 mg/l ± 0.01 in monsoon season (2002–2003). The annual average calculated for the first year (2002–2003) was 0.007 mg/l ± 0.001 and second year (2003–2004) was 0.028 mg/l ± 0.035.

Sampling Station C (Downstream Vedic Nagar)

The physico-chemical and heavy metals parameters of sampling station C are presented in Table 5A.5-5A.6 and Figure 5A.21–5A.30.

Water Temperature

The water temperature of river Suswa at this sampling station was observed to be lowest in winter season (2002–2003) 19.07 ºC ± 0.94 which goes highest up to 25.61 ºC ± 0.76 in monsoon season (2002–2003) The annual average recorded for first year (2002–2003) 22.67 ºC ± 3.32 and for second year (2003–2004) it was calculated 22.80 ºC ± 2.19.

Conductivity

The maximum value of conductivity of river Suswa at this sampling station was observed in summer season of 2003–2004, 0.028 siemens/cm ± . 0.010.The value was found decreasing from summer to winter during both the year. The minimum value was observed in winter season of 2002–2003, 0.016 siemens/cm ± 0.002.The annual average observed for the first year (2002–2003) was 0.02-siemens/cm ± 0.005 and for second year (2003–2004) was 0.02-siemens/cm ± 0.006.

Turbidity

The turbidity of water at this spot observed as 0.00 ± 0.00 in summer and winter season, which goes up in monsoon season. The turbidity in monsoon season during (2002–2003) was recorded as 40.0 JTU ± 5.0 while it was observed as 35.00 JTU ± 3.00 in monsoon season of 2003–2004. The annual average for the first year (2002–2003) was recorded as 13.33 JTU ± 23.09 and for the second year 2003–2004 it was observed as 11.66 JTU ± 20.20.

Total Solids

The total solids of river Suswa at this sampling station was recorded to be lowest in 2003–2004 winter season, 625.00 mg/l ± 250.00, which goes highest up to 1375.0 mg/l ± 478.71 in 2003–2004 monsoon season. The annual average calculated for first year (2002–2003) was 1125.00 mg/l ± 125.00 and second year (2003–2004) was 1000.00 mg/l ± 375.00.

Velocity

The velocity at this sampling station of river Suswa was noted to be minimum in summer season of 2002–2003, 0.27 m/sec ± 0.04, which goes maximum up to 0.35 m/sec ± 0.04 in winter season of 2002–2003.The annual average calculated for first year (2002–2003) was 0.30 m/sec ± 0.04 and second year (2003–2004) was 0.30 m/sec ± 0.04.

pH (Hydrogen Ion Concentration)

The minimum value of pH at this sampling station was noted in winter season (2002–2003), 7.28 ± 0.04 and maximum 7.55 ± 0.26 in monsoon season (2002–2003). The annual average calculated for first year (2002–2003) was 7.37 ± 0.15 and second year (2003–2004) was 7.14 ± 0.03.

Biochemical Oxygen Demand (BOD)

The maximum value of Biochemical Oxygen Demand of river Suswa at this sampling station was noted in monsoon season (2003–2004), 1.13 mg/l ± 0.60 and minimum in winter season (2003–2004), 0.42 mg/l ± 0.08. The annual average calculated for first year (2002–2003) was 0.69 mg/l ± 0.21 and second year (2003–2004) was 0.75 mg/l ± . 0.35.

Chemical Oxygen Demand (COD)

The chemical oxygen demand (COD) of river Suswa at this sampling station was observed to be least in winter season (2003–2004), 1.75 mg/l ± 0.05, which goes highest up to 4.67 mg/l ± 0.50 in monsoon season (2003–2004) The annual average calculated for first year (2002–2003) was 3.30 mg/l ± 0.30 and second year (2003–2004) was 3.14 mg/l ± 1.46.

Dissolved Oxygen

The Dissolved oxygen of river Suswa at this sampling station was recorded to be minimum in monsoon season (2003–2004), 7.00 mg/l ± 1.74, which goes maximum up to 8.97 mg/l ± 0.66 in winter season (2003–2004). The annual average calculated for first year (2002–2003) was 8.14 mg/l ± 0.27 and second year (2003–2004) was 7.96 mg/l ± 0.98.

Table 5A.5: Seasonal variation in physico chemical parameters of River Suswa at Sampling Station C (2002-2004)

Physico-chemical Parameters	*2002-2003*				*2003-2004*			
	Summer	*Monsoon*	*Winter*	*Average*	*Summer*	*Monsoon*	*Winter*	*Average*
Temperature (°C)	23.35±2.59	25.61±0.76	19.07±0.94	22.67±3.32	23.67±1.46	24.87±1.42	20.50±2.08	22.80±2.19
Conductivity (Siemen s/c)	0.026±0.00	0.018±0.007	0.016±0.002	0.02±0.005	0.028±0.010	0.025±0.010	0.018±0.003	0.02±0.006
Turbidity (JTU)	0.00	40.00±5.0	0.0±0.0	13.33±23.09	0.0±0.0	35.00±3.00	0.0±0.0	11.66±20.20
Total Solids (mg/l)	1000±408.24	1250.0±645.49	1125±478.71	1125±125	1000±408.24	1375±478.71	625.0±250.0	1000±375
Velocity (m/s)	0.27±0.04	0.28±0.06	0.35±0.04	0.30±0.04	0.28±0.07	0.35±0.06	0.28±0.06	0.30±0.04
PH	7.28±0.34	7.55±0.26	7.28±0.04	7.37±0.15	7.37±0.08	7.42±0.13	7.44±0.19	7.14±0.03
BOD (mg/l)	0.83±0.36	0.81±0.57	0.45±0.22	0.69±0.21	0.71±0.19	1.13±0.60	0.42±0.08	0.75±0.35
COD (mg/l)	3.50±0.19	3.45±0.16	2.95±0.20	3.30±0.30	3.00±0.00	4.67±0.50	1.75±0.05	3.14±1.46
DO (mg/l)	8.03±0.77	7.94±1.00	8.45±1.39	8.14±0.27	7.92±0.35	7.00±1.74	8.97±0.66	7.96±0.98
Oxidation Reduction Index (rH_2)	28.02±0.15	28.15±0.36	28.21±0.30	28.12±0.09	28.08±0.29	27.85±0.42	27.77±0.10	27.90±0.16
Oxidation Reduction Potential (Eh)	0.37±0.01	0.39±0.03	0.35±0.02	0.37±0.02	0.36±0.02	1.35±0.01	0.39±0.03	0.36±0.02
Free CO_2 (mg/l)	2.10±1.11	5.00±1.50	0.95±0.01	2.68±2.08	3.62±1.50	4.75±2.10	0.59±0.00	2.98±2.15
Acidity (mg/l)	61.66±24.58	52.47±18.55	55.62±12.86	56.58±4.67	60.49±17.13	50.20±9.31	68.93±3.14	59.87±9.38
Alkalinity (mg/l)	285.41±58.93	243.75±18.55	257.49±7.99	262.21±21.22	293.08±41.09	315.83±49.56	273.37±12.20	294.09±21.24
Total hardness (mg/l)	236.83±16.20	232.91±10.61	249.99±11.64	239.91±8.94	252.29±12.20	257.74±21.73	240.75±8.14	250.26±8.67
Chlorides (mg/l)	17.09±1.97	17.29±2.56	16.09±1.39	16.82±0.64	18.17±1.43	21.42±5.04	17.03±1.27	18.87±2.27
Magnesium (mg/l)	42.62±4.38	39.87±5.96	35.50±3.82	39.33±3.59	49.68±8.10	51.00±7.90	38.87±3.24	46.51±6.65
Phosphates (mg/l)	0.03±0.01	0.11±0.01	0.07±0.00	0.07±0.04	0.09±0.01	0.13±0.01	0.03±0.01	0.08±0.05
Calcium (mg/l)	65.26±13.16	64.97±4.67	60.28±2.20	63.50±2.79	59.63±11.49	66.72±17.55	58.75±5.95	61.7±4.36

± = Standard deviation.

Table 5A.6: Seasonal Variations in Metallic Parameters of River Suswa at Sampling Station C (2002-2004)

Metallic Parameters	2002-2003				2003-2004			
	Summer	*Monsoon*	*Winter*	*Average*	*Summer*	*Monsoon*	*Winter*	*Average*
Lead (Pb) (mg/l)	0.074±0.00	0.080±0.002	0.076±0.0007	0.076±0.003	0.075±0.003	0.075±0.002	0.078±0.002	0.076±0.001
Copper (Cu) (mg/l)	0.021±0.00	0.017±0.02	0.024±0.0014	0.020±0.003	0.018±0.01	0.015±0.02	0.022±0.00	0.019±0.003
Iron (Fe) (mg/l)	5.60±0.75	5.75±0.90	5.59±0.80	5.64±0.08	5.51±0.80	5.26±0.75	5.30±0.01	5.35±16.07
Manganese (Mn) (mg/l)	0.004±0.001	0.006±0.001	0.006±0.002	0.005±0.001	0.003±0.001	0.005±0.00	0.008±0.002	0.005±0.016
Zinc (Zn) (mg/l)	3.91±0.006	3.75±0.03	3.66±0.022	3.77±0.12	3.86±0.02	3.74±0.18	3.72±0.02	3.77±0.07
Cobalt (Ca) (mg/l)	0.005±0.001	0.003±0.001	0.007±0.00	0.005±0.002	0.007±0.01	0.008±0.01	0.88±0.010	0.007±0.0005

± = Standard deviation.

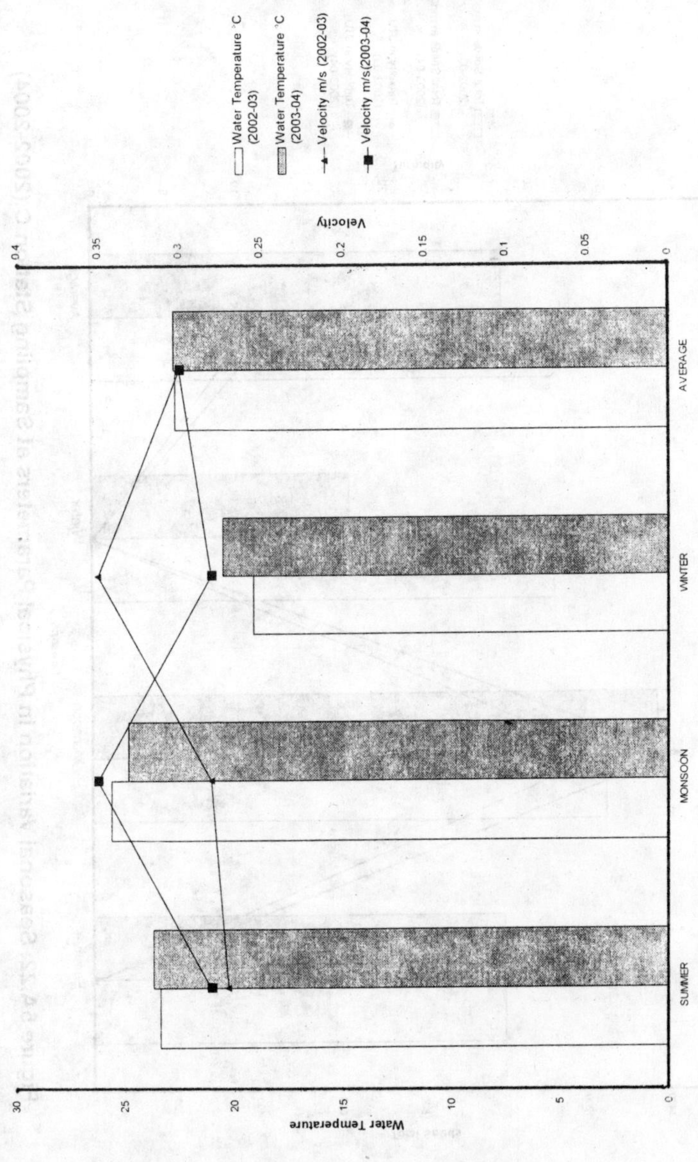

Figure 5A.21: Seasonal Variation in Physical Parameters at Sampling Station C (2002-2004)

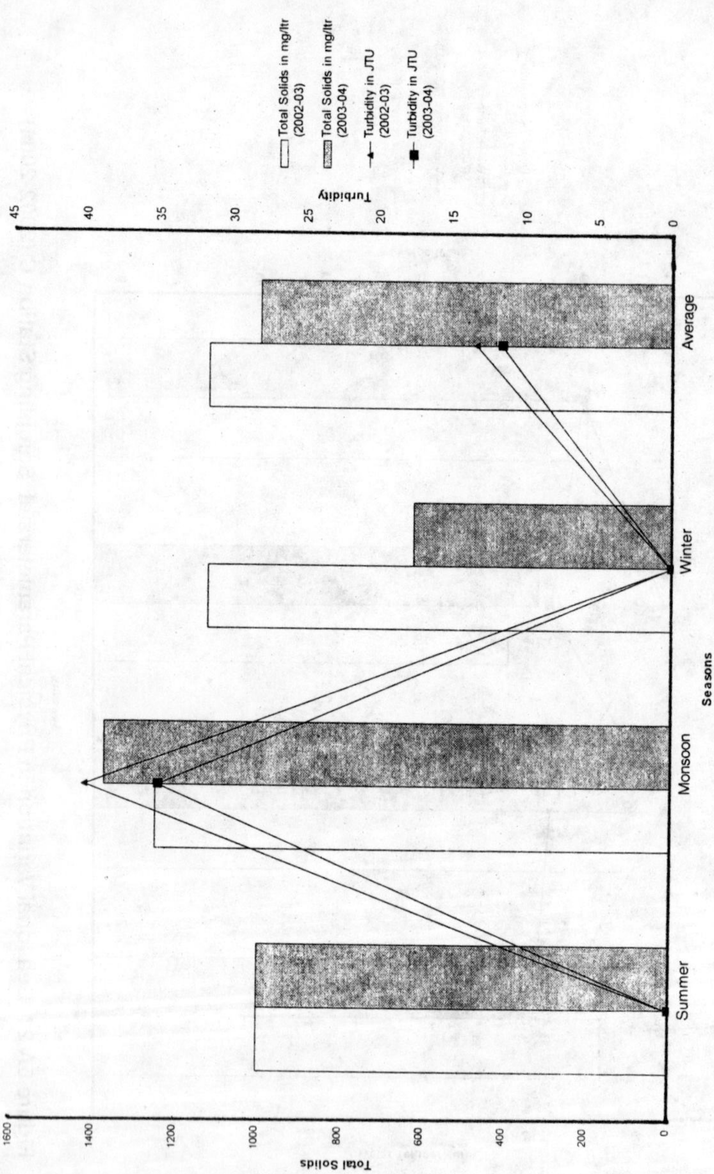

Figure 5A.22: Seasonal Variation in Physical Parameters at Sampling Station C (2002-2004)

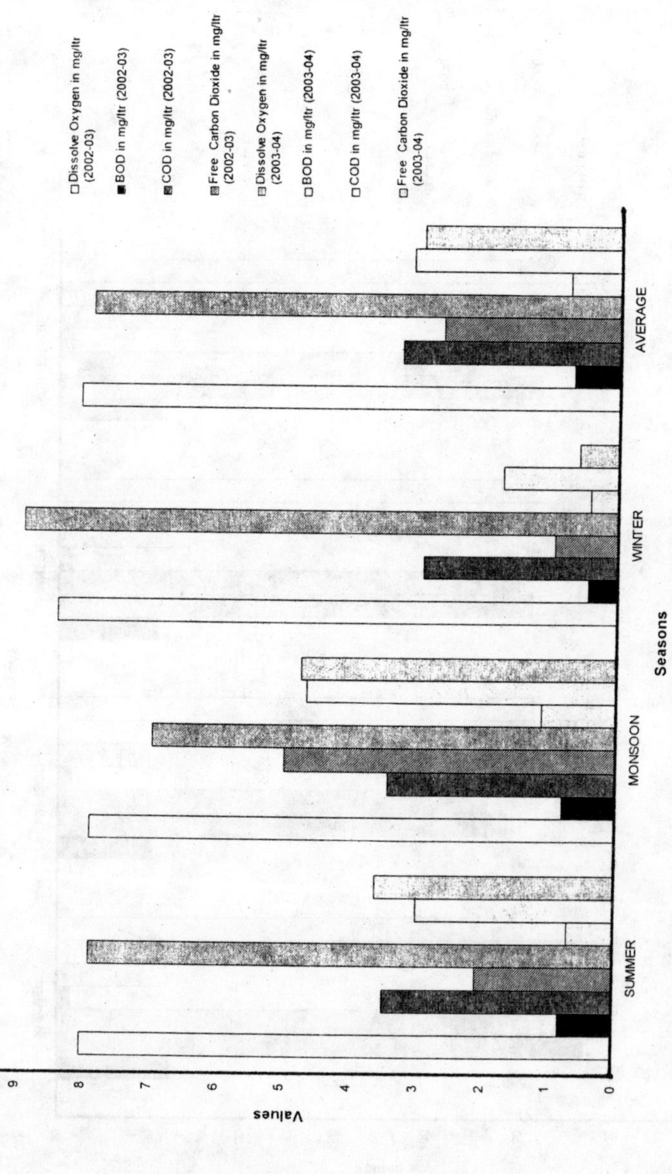

Figure 5A.23: Seasonal Variation in Chemical Parameters at Sampling Station C (2002-2004)

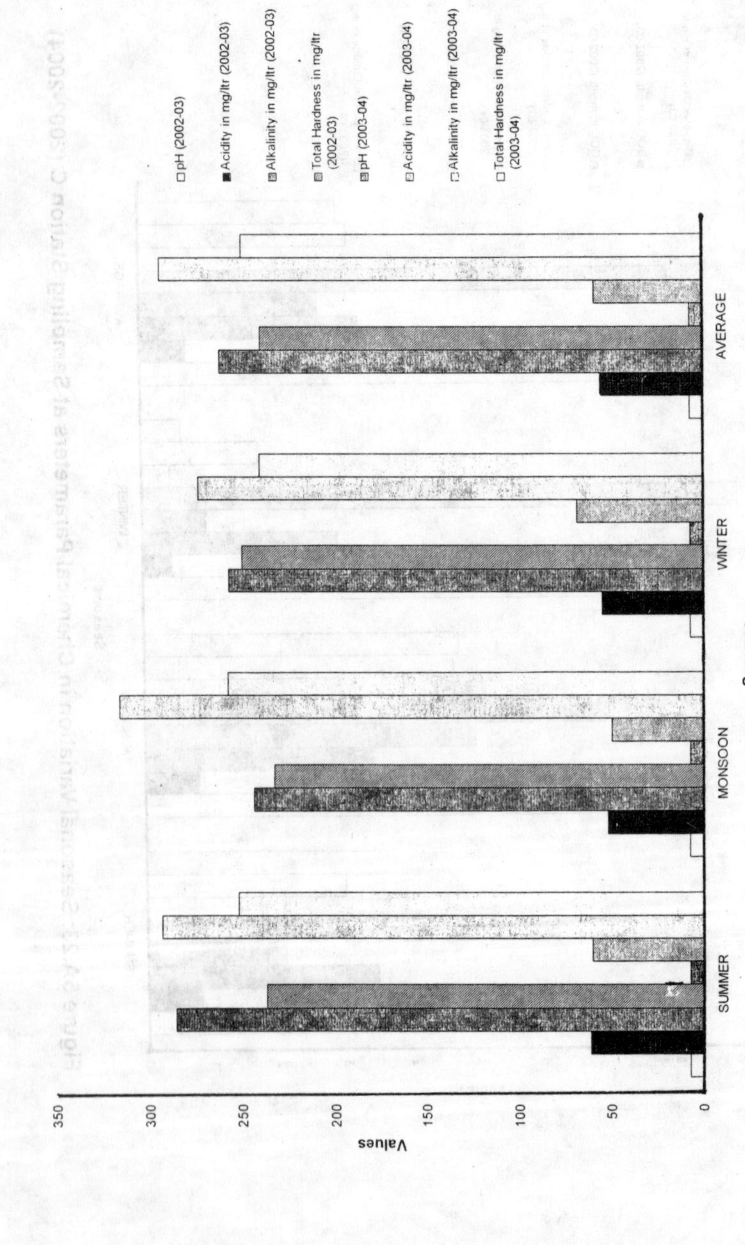

Figure 5A.24: Seasonal Variation in Chemical Parameters at Sampling Station C (2002-2004)

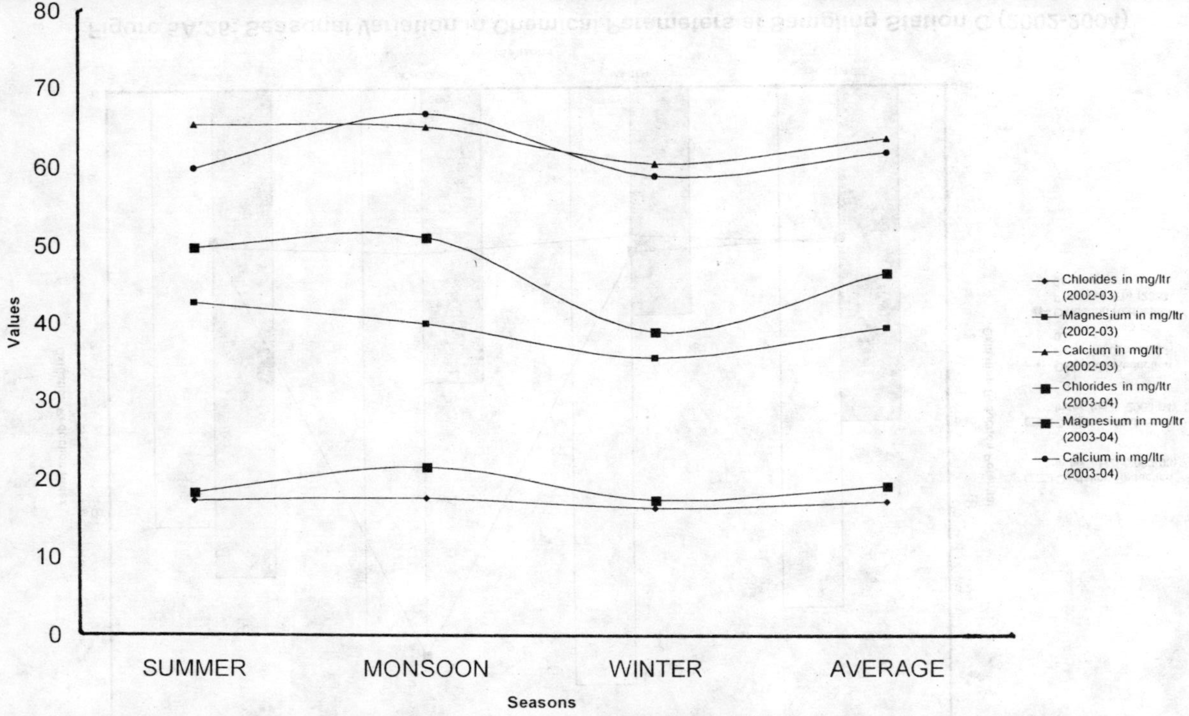

Figure 5A.25: Seasonal Variation in Chemical Parameters at Sampling Station C (2002-2004)

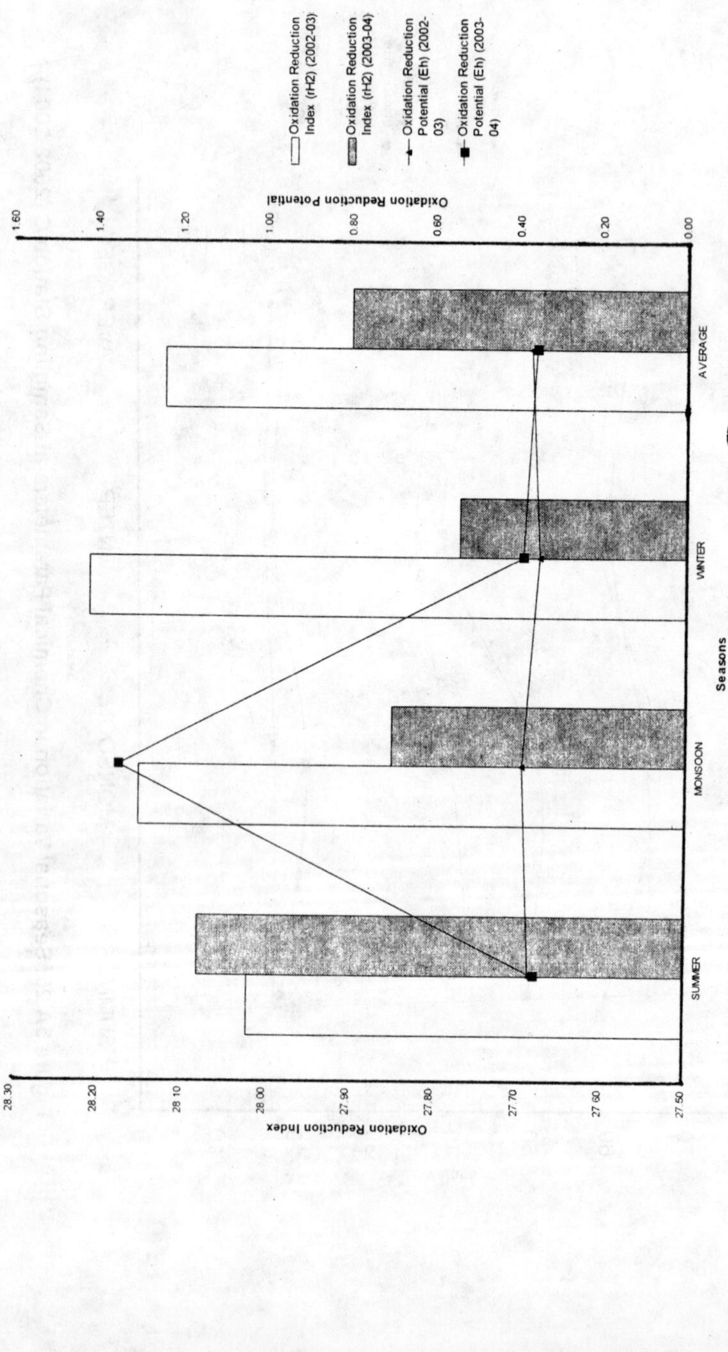

Figure 5A.26: Seasonal Variation in Chemical Parameters at Sampling Station C (2002-2004)

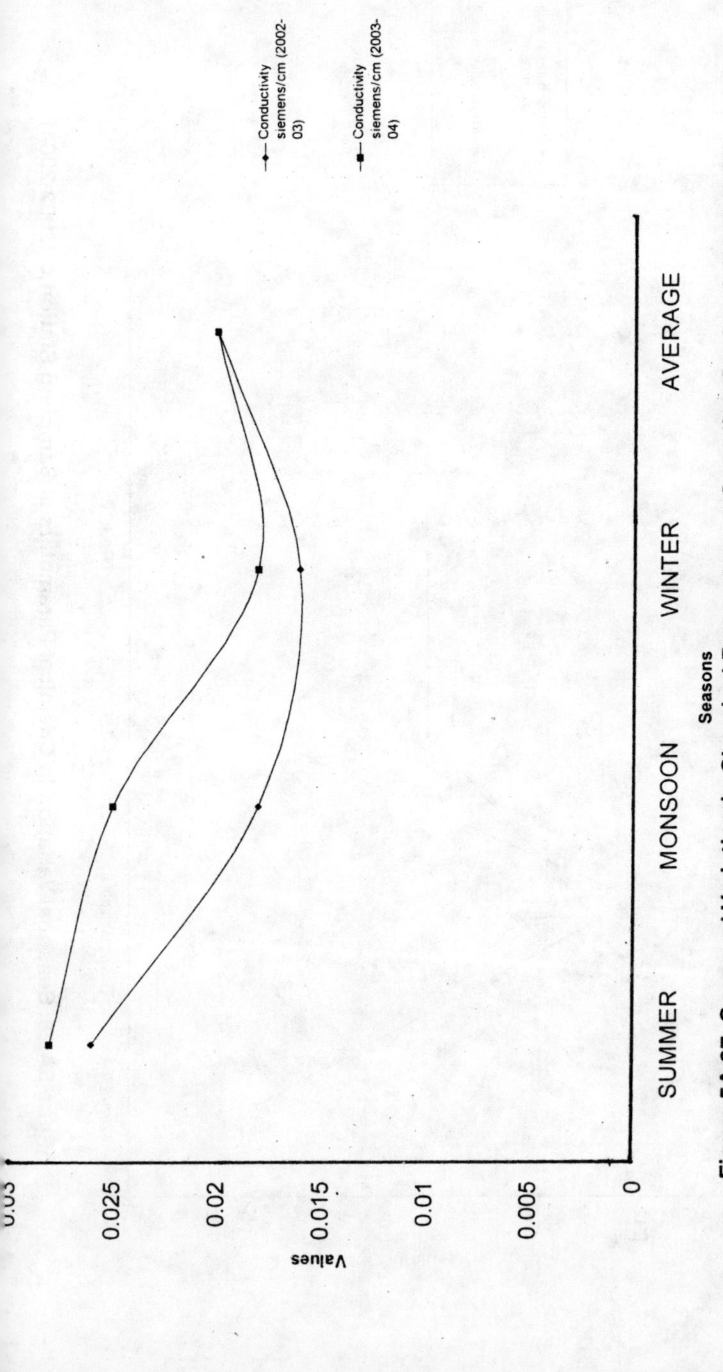

Figure 5A.27: Seasonal Variation in Chemical Parameters at Sampling Station C (2002-2004)

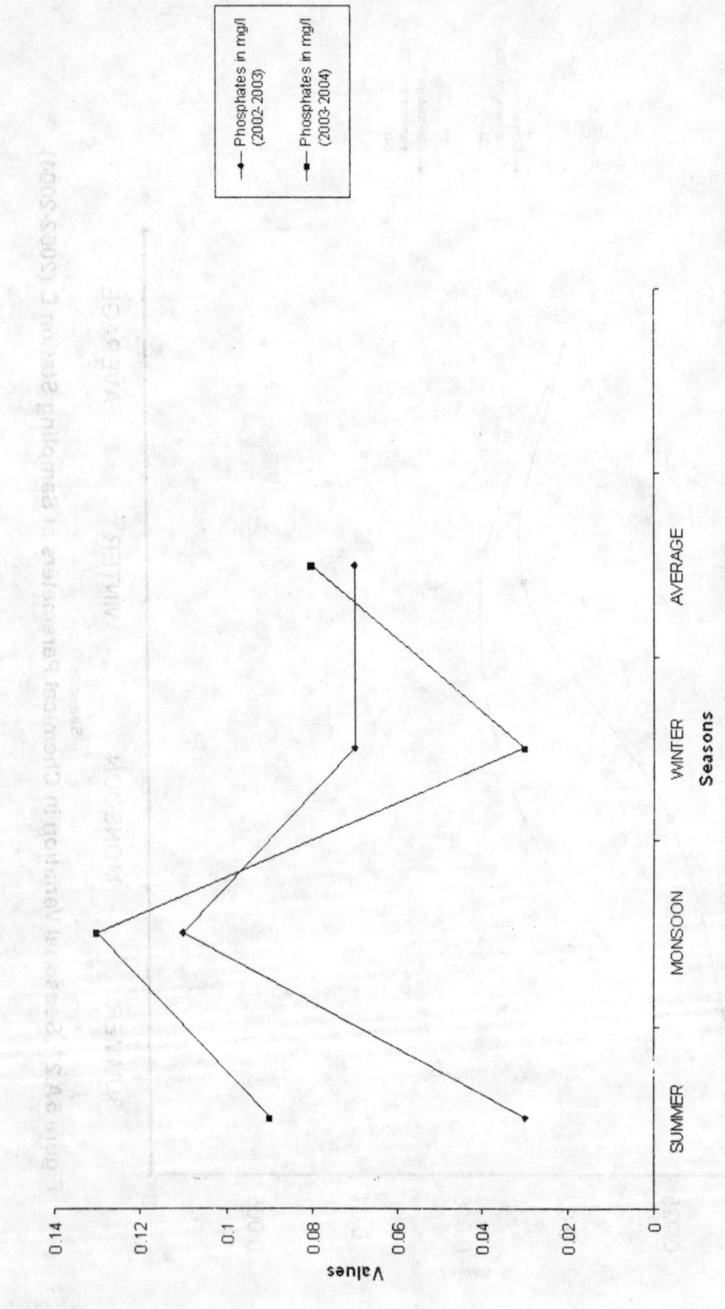

Figure 5A.28: Seasonal Variation in Chemical Parameters at Sampling Station C (2002-2004)

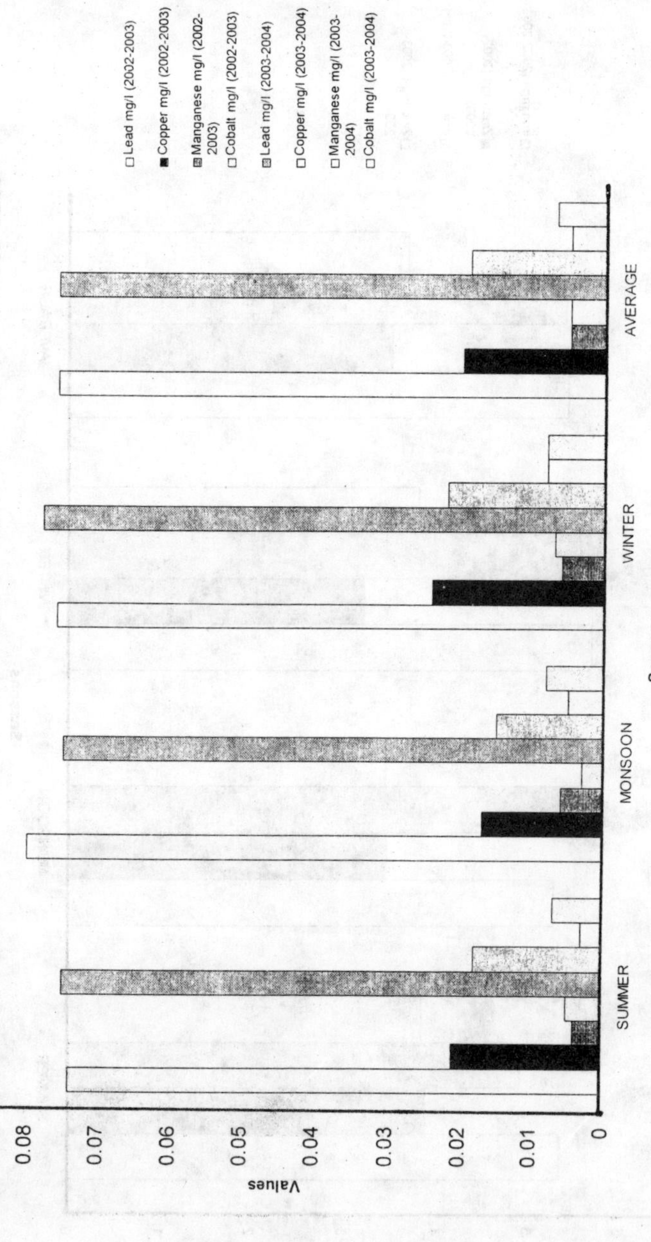

Figure 5A.29: Seasonal Variation in Heavy Metals at Sampling Station C (2002-2004)

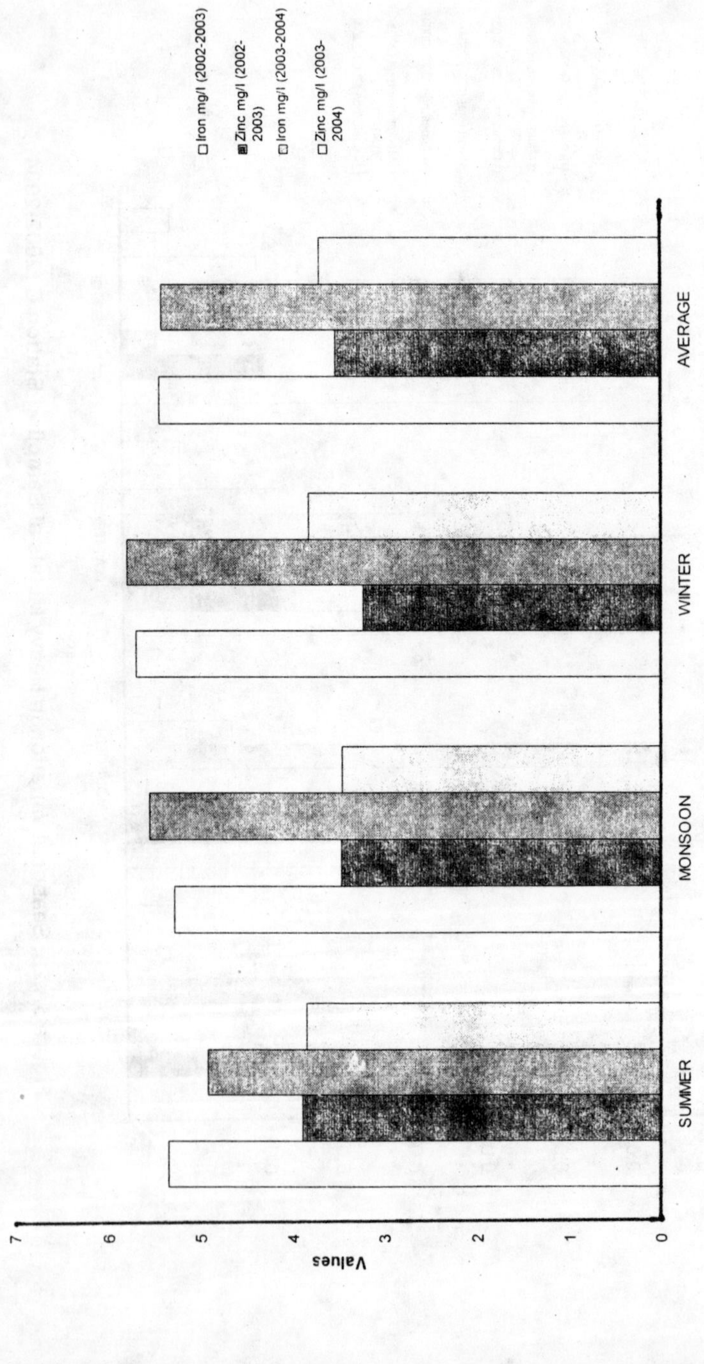

Figure 5A.30: Seasonal Variation in Heavy Metals at Sampling Station C (2002-2004)

Oxidation Reduction Index (rH_2)

The Oxidation Reduction Index (rH_2) of river Suswa at this sampling station was observed to be least in winter season (2003–2004), 27.77 ± 0.10, which goes highest up to 28.21 ± 0.30 in winter season (2002–2003) The annual average calculated for first year (2002–2003) was 28.12 ± 0.09 and second year (2003–2004) was 27.90 ± 0.16.

Oxidation Reduction Potential (Eh)

The maximum value of Oxidation Reduction Potential (Eh) of river Suswa at this sampling station was observed in monsoon season (2003–2004), 1035 ± 0.01, and minimum in winter season (2003–2004), 0.35 ± 0.01 The annual average calculated for first year (2002–2003) was 0.37 ± 0.02 and for second year (2003–2004) was 0.36 ± 0.02.

Free Carbon Dioxide

The free carbon dioxide of river Suswa at this sampling station was observed to be lowest in winter season (2003–2004), 0.59 mg/l ± 0.00, which goes highest up to 5.00 mg/l ± 1.50 in monsoon season (2002–2003). The annual average calculated for first year (2002–2003) was 2.68 mg/l ± 2.08 and second year (2003–2004) was 2.98 mg/l ± 2.15.

Acidity

The acidity of river Suswa at this sampling station was observed to be least in monsoon season (2003–2004), 50.20 mg/l ± 9.31, which goes highest up to 68.93 mg/l ± 3.14 in winter season (2003–2004) The annual average calculated for first year (2002–2003) was 56.58 mg/l ± 4.67 and second year (2003–2004) was 59.87 mg/l ± 9.38.

Alkalinity

The maximum value of alkalinity at downstream Vedic nagar was noted in monsoon season (2003–2004), 315.83 mg/l ± 49.56, which goes minimum up to 243.75 mg/l ± 18.55 in monsoon season (2002–2003). The annual average calculated for first year (2002–2003) was 262.21 mg/l ± 21.22 and second year (2003–2004) was 294.09 mg/l ± 21.24.

Total Hardness

The total hardness of river Suswa at this sampling station was observed to be least in monsoon season (2002–2003), 232.91 mg/l ± 10.61, which goes highest up to 257.74 mg/l ± 21.73 in monsoon season (2003–2004). The annual average calculated for first year (2002–2003) was 239.91 mg/l ± 8.94 and second year (2003–2004) was 250.26 mg/l ± 8.67.

Chloride

The chloride in water of river Suswa at this sampling station was observed to be least in winter season (2003–2004), 16.09 mg/l ± 1.39, which goes highest up to 21.42 mg/l ± 5.04 in monsoon season (2003–2004) The annual average calculated for first year (2002–2003) was 16.82 mg/l ± 0.64 and second year (2003–2004) was 18.87 mg/l ± 2.27.

Magnesium

The Magnesium of river Suswa at Upstream Vedic nagar was observed maximum in monsoon season (2003–2004), 51.00 mg/l ± 7.90, and minimum in winter season (2002–2003), 35.50 mg/l ± 3.82.The annual average calculated for first year (2002–2003) was 39.33 mg/l ± 3.59 and second year (2003–2004) was 46.51 mg/l ± 6.65.

Phosphates

The Phosphates of river Suswa at this sampling station was observed minimum in summer season (2002–2003), 0.03 mg/l ± 0.01, which goes maximum up to 0.13 mg/l ± 0.01 in monsoon season (2003–2004). The annual average calculated for first year (2002–2003) was 0.07 mg/l ± 0.04 and second year (2003–2004) was 0.08 mg/l ± 0.05.

Calcium

The maximum amount of calcium of river Suswa at this sampling station was observed in monsoon season (2003–2004), 66.72 mg/l ± 17.55, and minimum in winter season (2003–2004), 58.75 mg/l ± 5.95. The annual average calculated for first year (2002–2003) was 63.50 mg/l ± 2.79 and second year (2003–2004) was 61.70 mg/l ± 4.36.

Metallic Parameters

Lead (Pb)

The minimum concentration of Lead at this sampling station of river Suswa was recorded in summer season (2002–2003), 0.074 mg/l ± 0.00, which goes maximum up to 0.080mg/l ± 0.002 in monsoon season (2002–2003). The annual average calculated for first year (2002–2003) was 0.076 mg/l ± 0.003 and second year was calculated as 0.076 mg/l ± 0.001.

Copper (Cu)

At this sampling station of river Suswa the copper was recorded to be lowest in monsoon season (2003–2004), 0.015 mg/l l ± 0.02 which goes highest up to 0.022 mg/l l ± 0.00 in winter season (2003–2004). The annual average observed for the first year (2002–2003) was 0.020 mg/l ± 0.003 and second year (2003–2004) was 0.019 mg/l ± 0.003.

Iron (Fe)

The maximum concentration of Iron at this sampling station of river Suswa was recorded in monsoon season (2002–2003), 5.75 mg/l ± 0.90, while its minimum concentration was observed in monsoon season (2003–2004), 5.26 mg/l ± 0.75. The annual average observed for the first year (2002–2003) was 5.64 mg/l ± 0.08 and second year (2003–2004) was 5.35mg/l ± 0.06.

Manganese (Mn)

The manganese of this sampling station was found maximum in winter season (2003–2004), 0.008 mg/l ± 0.002 while minimum in summer season (2003–2004), 0.003 mg/l ± 0.001. The annual average for the first year (2002–2003) was observed as 0.005 mg/l ± 0.001 while for the second year (2003–2004) it was observed as 0.005mg/l ± 0.016.

Zinc (Zn)

At this spot the Zinc was recorded to be minimum in winter season (2002–2003) 3.66 mg/l ± 0.02, which goes maximum up to 3.91 mg/l ± 0.006 in summer season (2002–2003). The annual average calculated for the first year (2002–2003) was 3.77 mg/l ± 0.12 and second year (2003–2004) was 3.77 mg/l ± 0.07.

Cobalt (Co)

At this spot the Cobalt was recorded to be minimum in monsoon season (2002–2003), 0.003 mg/l ± 0.001, which goes maximum up to 0.88 mg/l ± 0.01 in winter season (2003–2004). The annual average calculated for the first year (2002–2003) was 0.005mg/l ± 0.002 and second year (2003–2004) was 0.007 mg/l ± 0.0005.

Sampling Station D (Near Water Pumping Station)

The physico-chemical and heavy metals parameters of sampling station D are presented in Table 5A.7-5A.8 and Figure 5A.31–5A.40.

Water Temperature

The water temperature of river Suswa at this sampling station was observed to be lowest in winter season (2002–2003), 17.70 °C ± 1.11 which goes highest up to 23.95°C ± 1.66 in monsoon season (2003–2004) The annual average recorded for first year (2002–2003) was 21.41°C ± 3.27 and for second year (2003–2004) it was calculated 21.82°C ± 3.57.

Conductivity

The maximum value of conductivity of river Suswa at this sampling station was observed in summer season of 2002–2003, 0.031 siemens/cm ± . 0.008.The value was found decreasing from summer to winter during both the year. The minimum value was observed in winter season of 2002–2003, 0.018 siemens/cm ± 0.004.The annual average observed for the first year (2002–2003) was 0.023 siemens/cm ± 0.007 and for second year (2003–2004) was 0.02 siemens/cm ± 0.004.

Turbidity

The turbidity of water at this spot observed as 0.00 ± 0.00 in summer and winter season, which goes up in monsoon season. The turbidity in monsoon season during (2002–2003) was recorded as 40.00 JTU ± 5.60 while it was observed as 25.00 jTU ± 1.00 in monsoon season of 2003–2004. The annual average for the first year (2002–2003) was recorded as 13.33 JTU ± 23.09 and for the second year 2003–2004 it was observed as 8.33 JTU ± 14.43.

Total Solids

The total solids of river Suswa at this sampling station was recorded to be lowest in 2002–2003 winter season, 625.0 mg/l ±

Table 5 A.7: Seasonal Variations in Physico Chemical Parameters of River Suswa at Sampling Station D (2002-2004)

Physico-chemical	*2002-2003*				*2003-2004*			
Parameters	*Summer*	*Monsoon*	*Winter*	*Average*	*Summer*	*Monsoon*	*Winter*	*Average*
Temperature (°C)	22.62±2.13	23.91±1.32	17.70±1.11	21.41±3.27	23.87±2.78	23.95±1.66	20.0±1.47	21.82±3.57
Conductivity (Siemens/cm)	0.031±0.008	0.020±0.009	0.018±0.004	0.023±0.007	0.023±0.004	0.018±0.003	0.026±0.011	0.02±0.004
Turbidity (JTU)	0.00±0.00	40±5.60	0.00±0.00	13.33±23.09	0.00±0.00	25.00±1.00	0.00±0.00	8.33±14.43
Total Solids (mg/l)	1000±408.24	1125±250.0	625.0±250	916.66±260.2	1375±250	1375±478.71	625±250	1125±433.01
Velocity (m/s)	0.34±0.12	0.36±0.07	0.49±0.08	0.39±0.08	0.42±0.16	0.43±0.05	0.30±0.06	0.38±0.07
pH	7.39±0.30	7.47±0.29	7.19±0.13	7.35±0.14	7.53±0.11	7.49±0.10	7.43±0.18	7.48±0.05
BOD (mg/l)	0.68±0.18	0.50±0.12	0.10±0.29	0.76±0.30	0.87±0.28	0.62±0.17	0.88±0.29	0.79±0.14
COD (mg/l)	2.69±0.31	2.00±0.00	4.57±1.00	3.08±1.33	3.35±0.45	2.95±0.50	3.32±0.41	3.20±0.22
DO (mg/l)	7.97±0.29	7.54±0.62	7.74±1.47	7.75±0.21	7.90±0.36	7.72±0.57	7.49±0.63	7.70±0.20
Oxidation Reduction Index (rH2)	28.21±0.30	28.16±0.53	27.64±3.16	28.0±0.31	28.56±0.24	28.53±0.12	28.28±0.03	28.45±0.15
Oxidation Reduction Potential (Eh)	.0.35±0.006	0.36±0.02	0.35±0.005	0.35±0.005	0.37±0.02	0.39±0.003	0.35±0.016	0.37±0.02
Free CO_2 (mg/l)	3.68±1.00	5.0±2.97	1.11±0.67	3.26±1.97	2.66±0.09	4.78±1.10	0.58±0.01	2.67±2.10
Acidity (mg/l)	64.79±28.35	48.33±16.90	60.55±13.59	57.89±8.54	59.99±21.41	54.16±13.74	73.18±6.85	62.44±9.74
Alkalinity (mg/l)	278.75±49.56	261.25±42.10	255.83±6.16	265.27±11.97	280.58±43.15	308.33±57.97	268.87±14.34	285.92±20.26
Total hardness (mg/l)	233.16±20.78	239.08±26.11	236.99±19.11	236.41±3.00	234.70±13.26	253.24±9.13	242.57±7.42	243.50±9.30
Chlorides (mg/l)	17.82±2.99	21.45±3.84	15.02±1.35	18.09±3.22	17.72±2.25	22.89±4.80	16.35±2.13	18.98±3.44
Magnesium (mg/l)	43.84±3.97	47.51±5.82	53.87±4.17	48.40±5.07	39.82±3.95	45.00±2.88	52.50±1.99	45.77±6.37
Phosphates (mg/l)	0.03±0.01	0.11±0.01	0.02±0.00	0.05±0.04	0.03±0.00	0.07±0.00	0.05±0.02	0.05±0.02
Calcium (mg/l)	64.13±10.73	67.18±5.86	58.27±4.66	63.19±4.52	65.64±6.81	76.89±13.73	54.37±7.73	65.63±11.26

±= Standard deviation.

Table 5A.8: Seasonal Variations in Metallic Parameters of River Suswa at Sampling Station D (2002-2004)

Metallic	*2002-2003*				*2003-2004*			
Parameters	*Summer*	*Monsoon*	*Winter*	*Average*	*Summer*	*Monsoon*	*Winter*	*Average*
Lead (Pb) (mg/l)	0.079±0.001	0.074±0.007	0.075±0.00	0.076±0.002	0.075±0.006	0.077±0.0014	0.076±0.002	0.076±0.001
Copper (Cu) (mg/l)	0.012±0.00	0.016±0.003	0.021±0.002	0.016±0.004	0.014±0.00	0.011±0.002	0.017±0.002	0.014±0.003
Iron (Fe) (mg/l)	5.40±0.01	5.39±0.70	5.43±0.50	5.26±0.25	4.97±0.35	5.52±0.70	5.77±0.62	5.42±0.40
Manganese (Mn) (mg/l)	0.002±0.0015	0.003±0001	0.003±0.00	0.002±0.0005	0.004±0.001	0.004±0.00	0.003±0.002	0.003±0.0005
Zinc (Zn) (mg/l)	3.70±0.006	3.67±0. 023	3.75±0.02	3.70±0.04	3.69±0.005	3.77±0.007	3.73±0.005	3.73±0.04
Cobalt (Ca) (mg/l)	0.007±0.01	0.007±0.03	0.009±0.02	0.007±0.001	0.008±0.01	0.007±0.00	0.008±0.01	0.007±0.0005

±= Standard deviation.

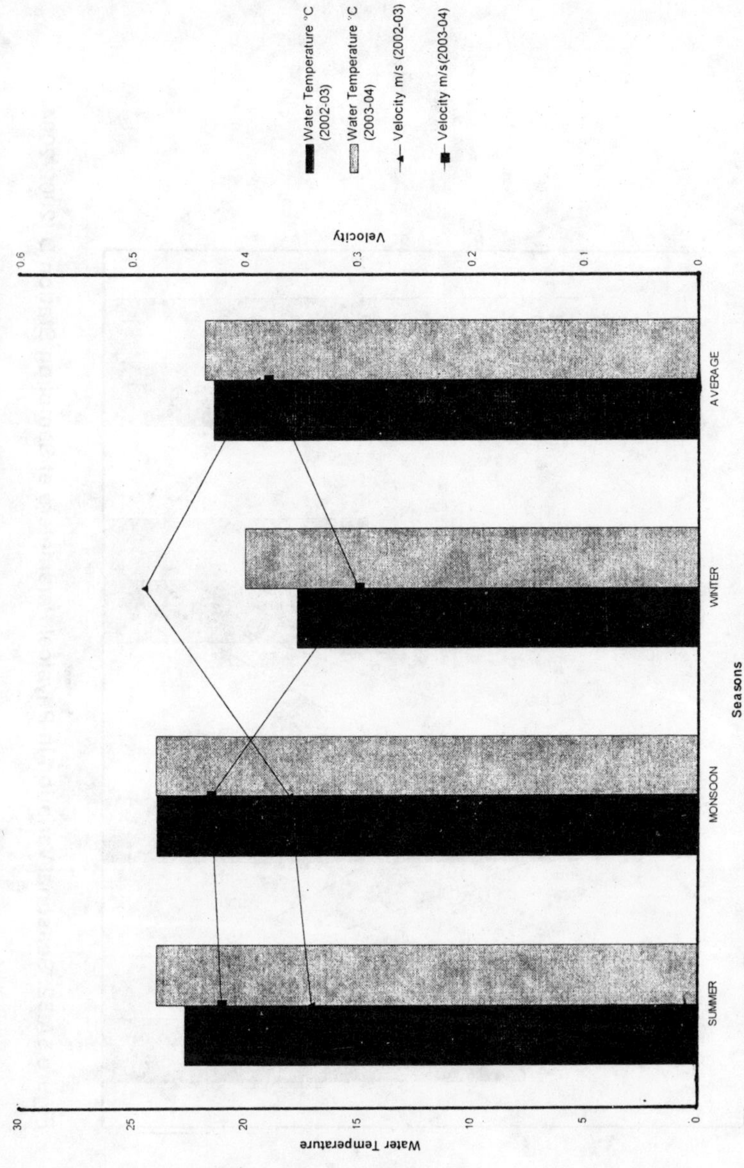

Figure 5A.31: Seasonal Variation in Physical Parameters at Sampling Station D (2002-2004)

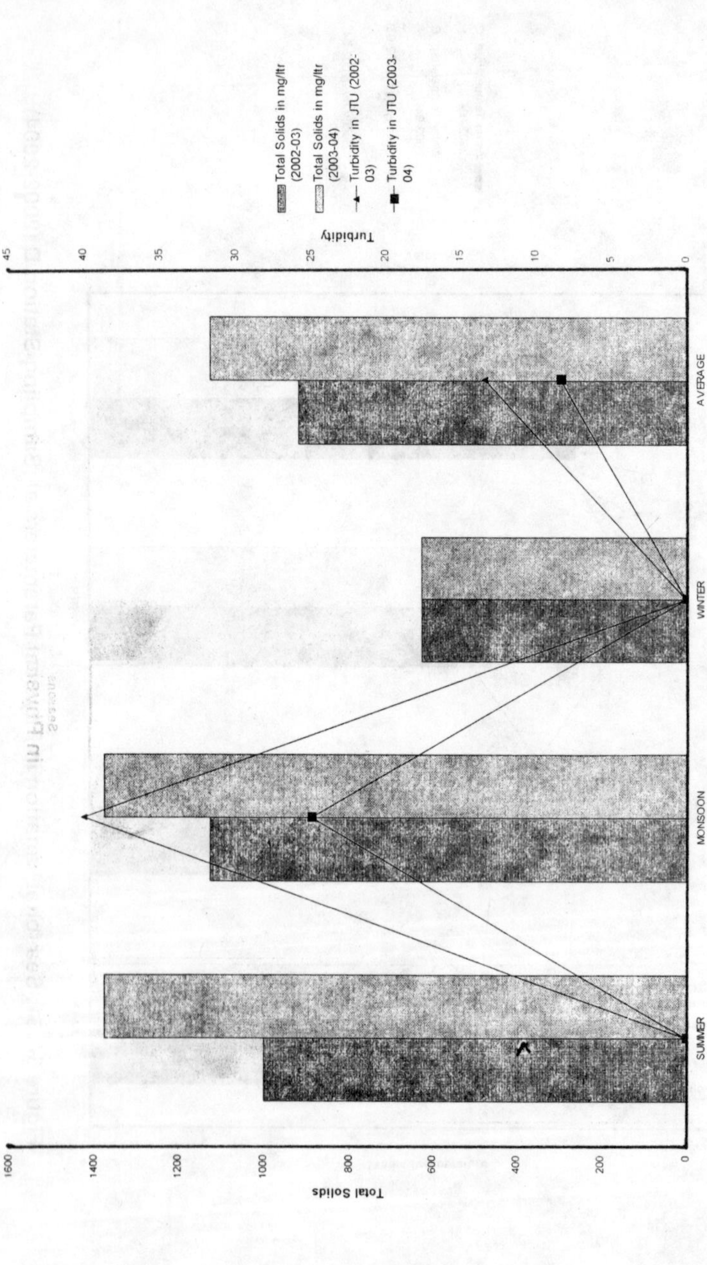

Figure 5A.32: Seasonal Variation in Physical Parameters at Sampling Station D (2002-2004)

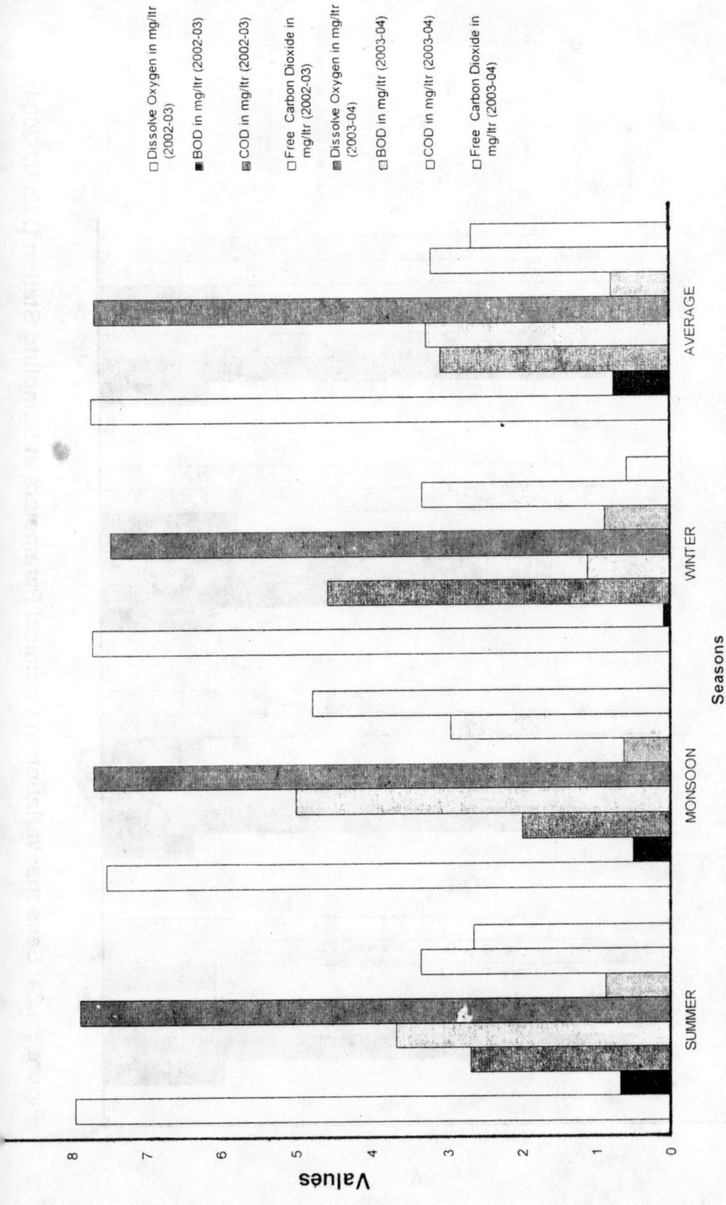

Figure 5A.33: Seasonal Variation in Chemical Parameters at Sampling Station D (2002-2004)

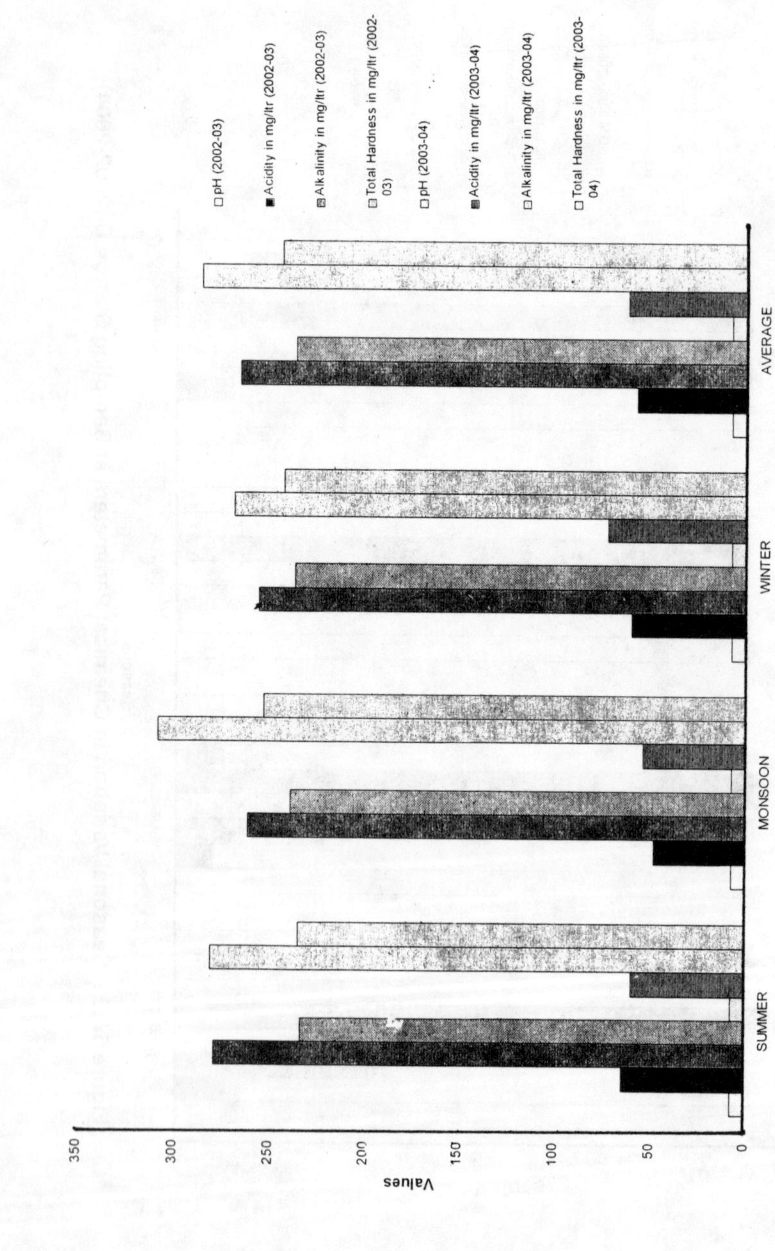

Figure 5A.34: Seasonal Variation in Chemical Parameters at Sampling Station D (2002-2004)

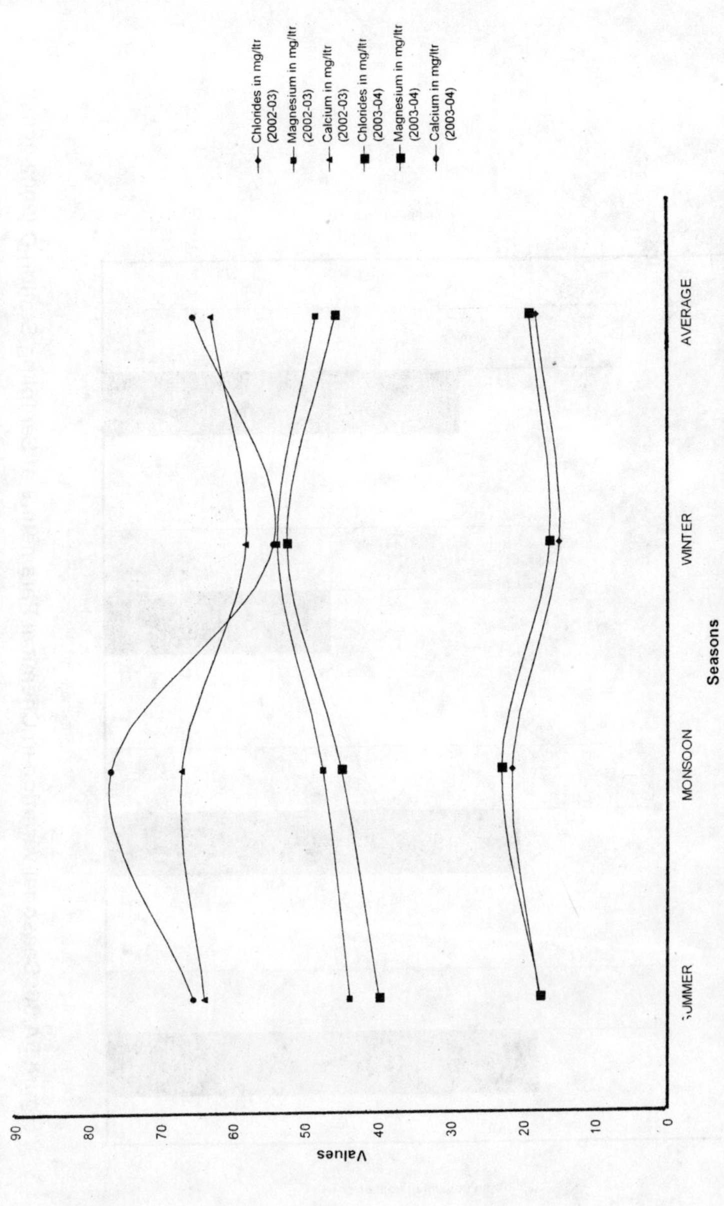

Figure 5A.35: Seasonal Variation in Chemical Parameters at Sampling Station D (2002-2004)

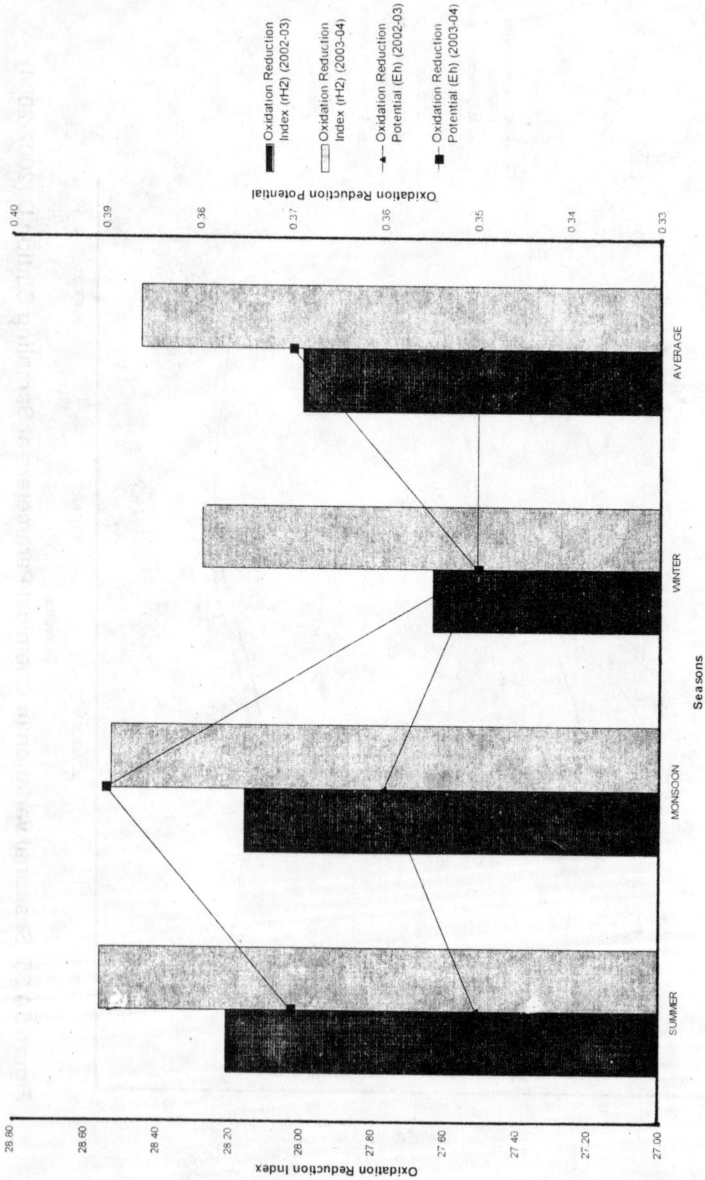

Figure 5A.36: Seasonal Variation in Chemical Parameters at Sampling Station D (2002-2004)

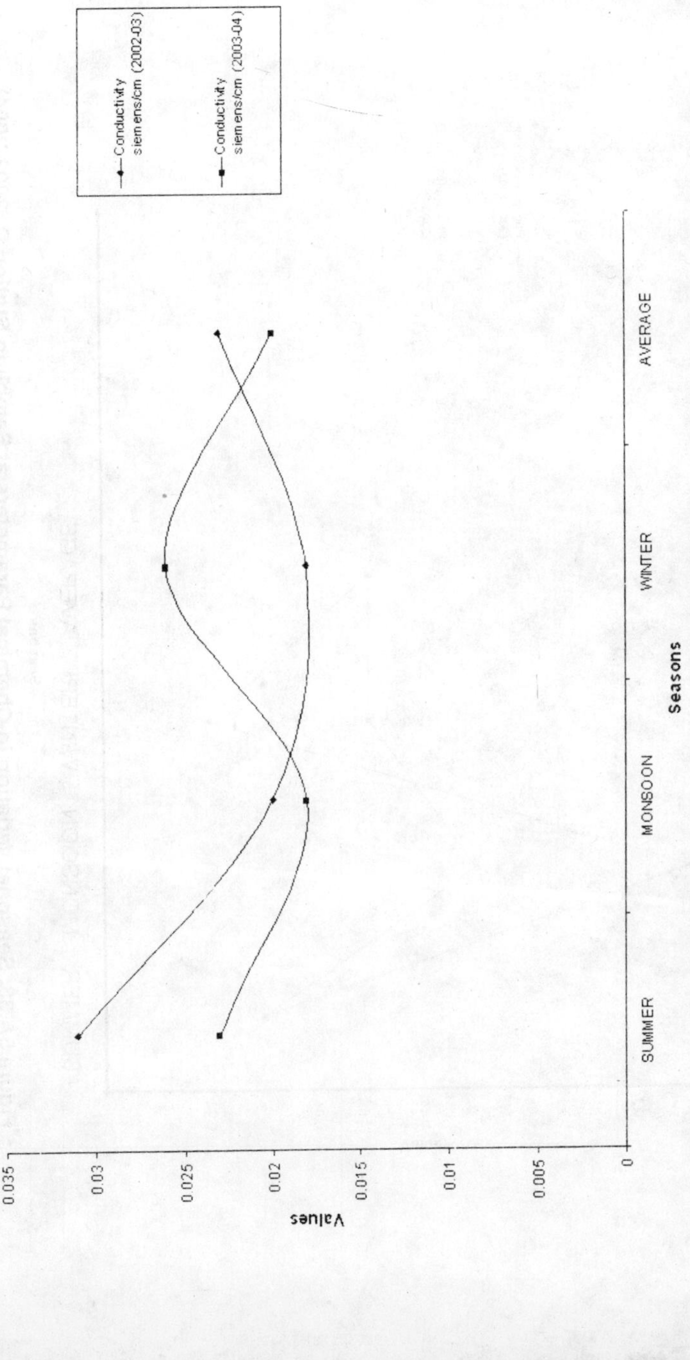

Figure 5A.37: Seasonal Variation in Chemical Parameters at Sampling Station D (2002-2004)

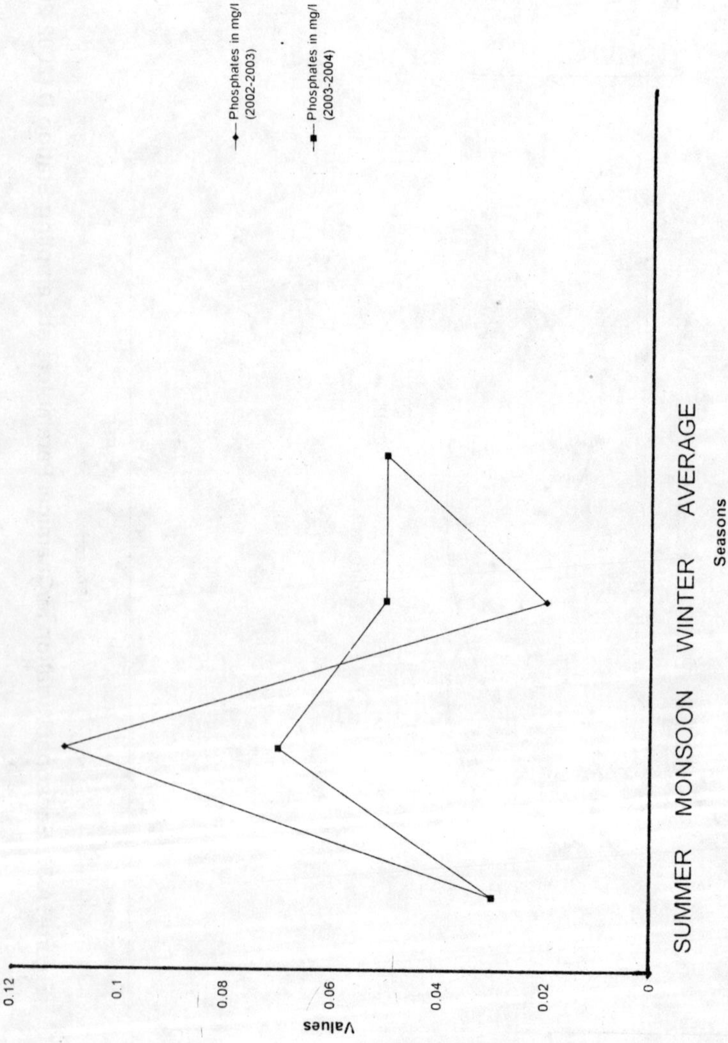

Figure 5A.38: Seasonal Variation in Chemical Parameters at Sampling Station D (2002-2004)

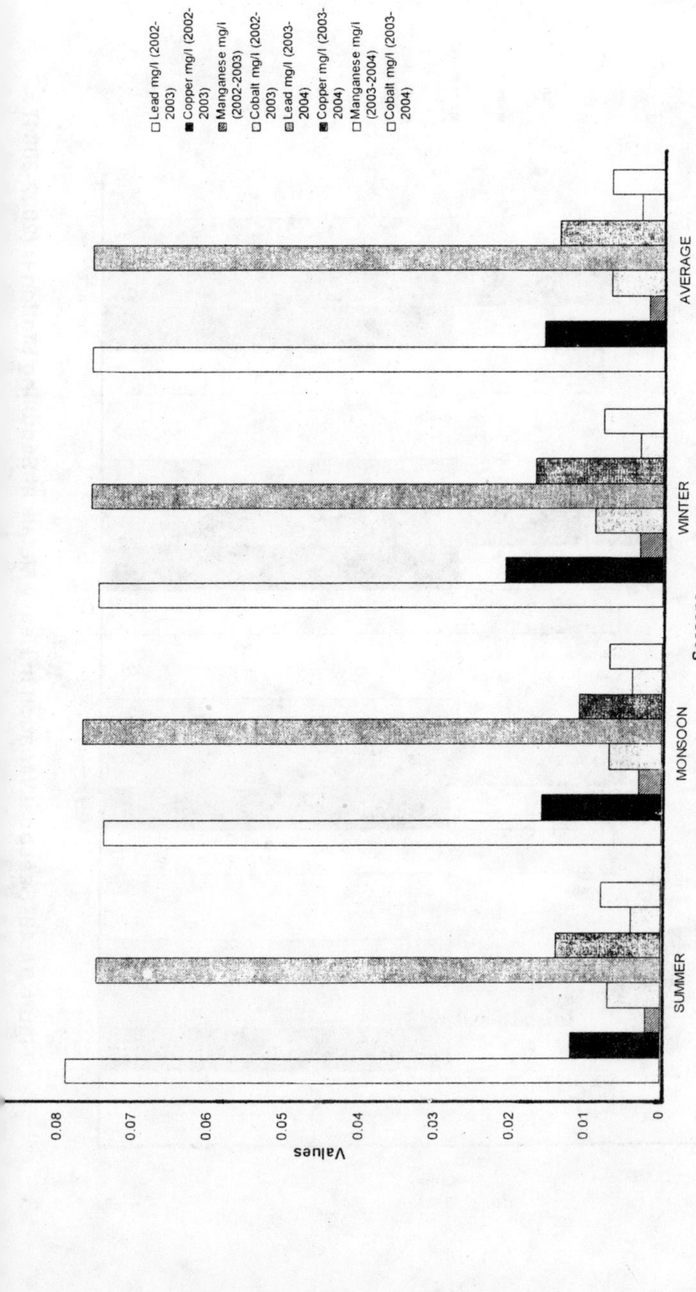

Figure 5A.39: Seasonal Variation in Heavy Metals at Sampling Station D (2002-2004)

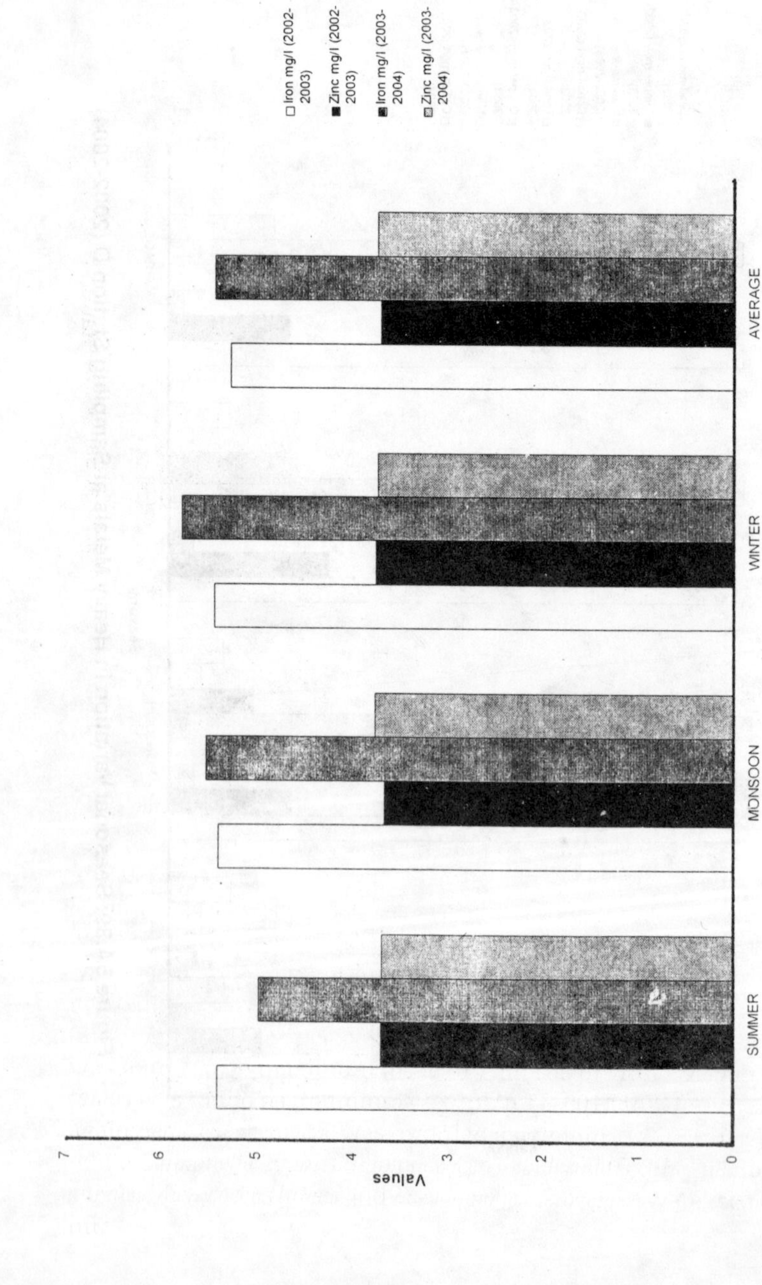

Figure 5A.40: Seasonal Variation in Heavy Metals at Sampling Station D (2002-2004)

250.0, which goes highest up to 1375.0 mg/l ± 478.71 in 2003–2004 monsoon season. The annual average calculated for first year (2002–2003) was 916.66 mg/l ± 260.20 and second year (2003–2004) was 1125.0 mg/l ± 433.01.

Velocity

The velocity at this sampling station of river Suswa was noted to be minimum in winter season of 2003–2004, 0.30 m/sec ± 0.06, which goes maximum up to 0.49m/sec ± 0.08 in winter season of 2002–2003.The annual average calculated for first year (2002–2003) was 0.39 m/sec ± 0.08 and second year (2003–2004) was 0.38 m/sec ± 0.07.

pH (Hydrogen Ion Concentration)

The minimum value of pH at this sampling station was noted in winter season (2002–2003), 7.19 ± 0.13 and maximum 7.53 ± 0.11 in summer season (2003–2004). The annual average calculated for first year (2002–2003) was 7.35 ± 0.14 and second year (2003–2004) was 7.48 ± 0.05.

Biochemical Oxygen Demand (BOD)

The maximum value of Biochemical Oxygen Demand of river Suswa at this sampling station was noted in winter season (2003–2004), 0.88 mg/l ± 0.29 and minimum in monsoon season (2002–2003), 0.10 mg/l ± 0.29. The annual average calculated for first year (2002–2003) was 0.76 mg/l ± 0.30 and second year (2003–2004) was 0.79 mg/l ± 0.14.

Chemical Oxygen Demand (COD)

The chemical oxygen demand (COD) of river Suswa at this sampling station was observed to be least in monsoon season (2002–2003), 2.00 mg/l ± 0.00, which goes highest up to 4.57 mg/l ± 1.00 in winter season (2002–2003) The annual average calculated for first year (2002–2003) was 3.08 mg/l ± 1.33 and second year (2003–2004) was 3.20 mg/l ± 0.22.

Dissolved Oxygen

The Dissolved oxygen of river Suswa at this sampling station was recorded to be minimum in winter season (2003–2004), 7.49 mg/l ± 0.63, which goes maximum up to 7.97 mg/l ± 0.29 in summer season (2002–2003). The annual average calculated for first year (2002–2003) was 7.75 mg/l ± 0.21 and second year (2003–2004) was 7.70 mg/l ± 0.20.

Oxidation Reduction Index (rH_2)

The Oxidation Reduction Index (rH_2) of river Suswa at this sampling station was observed to be least in winter season (2002–2003), 27.64 ± 3.16, which goes highest up to 28.56 ± 0.24 in summer season (2003–2004) The annual average calculated for first year (2002–2003) was 28.0 ± 0.31 and second year (2003–2004) was 28.45 ± 0.15.

Oxidation Reduction Potential (Eh)

The maximum value of Oxidation Reduction Potential (Eh) of river Suswa at this sampling station was observed in monsoon season (2003–2004), 0.39 ± 0.003, and minimum in summer season (2002–2003), 0.35 ± 0.006 The annual average calculated for first year (2002–2003) was 0.35 ± 0.005 and for second year (2003–2004) it was 0.37 ± 0.02.

Free Carbon Dioxide

The free carbon dioxide of river Suswa at this sampling station was observed to be lowest in winter season (2003–2004), 0.58 mg/l ± 0.01, which goes highest up to 5.0 mg/l ± 2.97 in monsoon season (2002–2003). The annual average calculated for first year (2002–2003) was 3.26 mg/l ± 1.97 and second year (2003–2004) was 2.67 mg/l ± 2.10.

Acidity

The acidity of river Suswa at this sampling station was observed to be least in monsoon season (2002–2003), 48.33 mg/l ± 16.90, which goes highest up to 73.18 mg/l ± 6.85 in winter season (2003–2004) The annual average calculated for first year (2002–2003) was 57.89 mg/l ± 8.54 and second year (2003–2004) was 62.44 mg/l ± 9.74.

Alkalinity

The value of alkalinity at this sampling station was noted to be minimum in winter season (2002–2003), 255.83 mg/l ± 6.16, which goes highest up to 308.33 mg/l ± 57.97 in monsoon season (2003–

2004). The annual average calculated for first year (2002–2003) was 265.27 mg/l ± 11.97 and second year (2003–2004) was 285.92 mg/l ± 20.26.

Total Hardness

The total hardness of river Suswa at this sampling station was observed to be least in summer season (2002–2003), 233.16 mg/l ± 20.78, which goes highest up to 253.24 mg/l ± 9.13 in monsoon season (2003–2004) The annual average calculated for first year (2002–2003) was 236.41 mg/l ± 3.00 and second year (2003–2004) was 243.5 mg/l ± 9.30.

Chloride

The chloride in water of river Suswa at this sampling station was observed to be least in winter season (2002–2003), 15.02 mg/l ± 1.35, which goes highest up to 22.89 mg/l ± 4.80 in monsoon season (2003–2004) The annual average calculated for first year (2002–2003) was 18.09 mg/l ± 3.22 and second year (2003–2004) was 18.98 mg/l ± 3.44.

Magnesium

The Magnesium of river Suswa at Upstream Vedic nagar was observed maximum in monsoon season (2002–2003), 53.87 mg/l ± 4.17, and minimum in summer season (2003–2004), 39.82 mg/l ± 3.95.The annual average calculated for first year (2002–2003) was 48.40 mg/l ± 5.07 and second year (2003–2004) was 45.77 mg/l ± 6.37.

Phosphates

The Phosphates of river Suswa at this sampling station was observed minimum in winterseason (2002–2003), 0.02 mg/l ± 0.00, which goes maximum up to 0.11 mg/l ± 0.01 in monsoon season (2002–2003). The annual average calculated for first year (2002–2003) was 0.05 mg/l ± 0.04 and second year (2003–2004) was 0.05 mg/l ± 0.02.

Calcium

The maximum amount of calcium of river Suswa at this sampling station was observed in monsoon season (2003–2004), 76.89 mg/l ± 13.73, and minimum in winter season (2003–2004),

54.37 mg/l ± 7.73. The annual average calculated for first year (2002–2003) was 63.19 mg/l ± 4.52 and for the second year (2003–2004) it was 65.63 mg/l ± 11.26.

Metallic Parameters

Lead (Pb)

At this sampling station of river Suswa the Lead was recorded to be lowest in monsoon season (2002–2003), 0.074 mg/l l ± 0.007 which goes highest up to 0.079 mg/l l ± 0.001 in summer season (2002–2003). The annual average observed for the first year (2002–2003) was 0.076 mg/l ± 0.002 and second year (2003–2004) was 0.076 mg/l ± 0.001.

Copper (Cu)

The minimum concentration of copper at this sampling station of river Suswa was recorded in monsoon season (2003–2004), 0.011 mg/l ± 0.002, which goes maximum up to 0.021 mg/l ± 0.002 in winter season (2002–2003). The annual average calculated for first year (2002–2003) was 0.016 mg/l ± 0.004 and second year was calculated as 0.014 mg/l ± 0.003.

Iron (Fe)

The maximum concentration of Iron at this sampling station of river Suswa was recorded in winter season (2003–2004), 5.77 mg/l ± 0.62, while its minimum concentration was observed in summer season (2003–2004), 4.97 mg/l ± 0.35. The annual average observed for the first year (2002–2003) was 5.26 mg/l ± 0.25 and second year (2003–2004) was 5.42mg/l ± 0.40.

Manganese (Mn)

The manganese of this sampling station was found maximum in monsoon season (2003–2004), 0.004 mg/l ± 0.00 while minimum in summer season (2002–2003), 0.002 mg/l ± 0.0015. The annual average for the first year (2002–2003) was observed as 0.002 mg/l ± 0.0005 while for the second year (2003–2004) it was observed as 0.003 mg/l ± 0.0005.

Zinc (Zn)

At this spot the Zinc was recorded to be minimum in monsoon

season (2002–2003) 3.67 mg/l ± 0.023, which goes maximum up to 3.77 mg/l ± 0.07 in monsoon season (2003–2004). The annual average calculated for the first year (2002–2003) was 3.70 mg/l ± 0.04 and second year (2003–2004) was 3.73 mg/l ± 0.04.

Cobalt (Co)

At this spot the Cobalt was recorded to be minimum in summer season (2002–2003), 0.007 mg/l ± 0.01, which goes maximum up to 0.009 mg/l ± 0.02 in winter season (2002–2003). The annual average calculated for the first year (2002–2003) was 0.007mg/l ± 0.001 and second year (2003–2004) was 0.007 mg/l ± 0.0005.

B) Biological Parameters

Studies on the biological parameters of the river Suswa includes the primary producers like phytoplankton, primary consumers like zooplankton, tertiary consumers like fishes, and bacterial and fungal population. The biological and microbiological parameters of the river Suswa are discussed in the following pages.

Among Zooplankton–Protozoa, Rotifera, Cladocerans and Copepods were found in this study. Further, in phylum: Protozoa–genus: *Arcella* and *Amoeba*; in phylum: Rotifera–genus: *Keratella, Philodima* and *Notholca*, in *phylum: Cladocera*-genus: *Daphnia* and *Bosmina*, in phylum: Copepoda-genus: *Cyclops* were found.

In phytoplankton-Bacillariophyceae, Chlorophyceae and Myxophyceae were observed in this study. Among class Bacillariophyceae (Type Diatoms)–*Achnanthes, Amphora, Cocconeis, Cymbella, Cyclotella, Diatoms, Fragilaria, Frustulia, Gomphonema, Navicula, Nitzschia, Pinnularia* were found. In class C*hlorophyceae–Closterium, Cosmarium, Chlorella, Cladophora, Oedogonium, Schizogonium, Spirogyra, Ulothrix, Zygnema* were found and in class Myxophyceae (Blue green algae)-*Anacystis, Anabena, Oscillatoria* were found at Raiwala.

In Bacteriology-Most probable Number (MPN), Heterotrophic plate count (HPC) and fungal (Plate 5.1-5.7) examination were carried out. Among bacteria in this study at *Raiwala–Salmonella typhii, Streptococcus facecalis, Aerobacter aerogens, Staphylococcus epidermidis, Staphylococcus aureus, Micrococcus luteus, Bacillus subtilis, Escherichia coli, and Pseudomonas aeroginosa* were found while among *Fungus Aspergillus, Penicillium and Fusarium* were recorded.

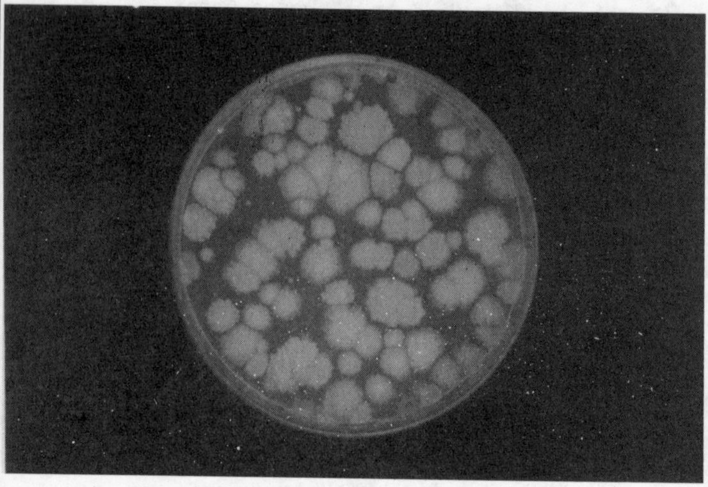

Plate 5.1: Heterotrophic Plate Count (HPC) of Satyanarayan Area

Plate 5.2: Heterotrophic Plate Count (HPC) of Upstream Vedic Nagar

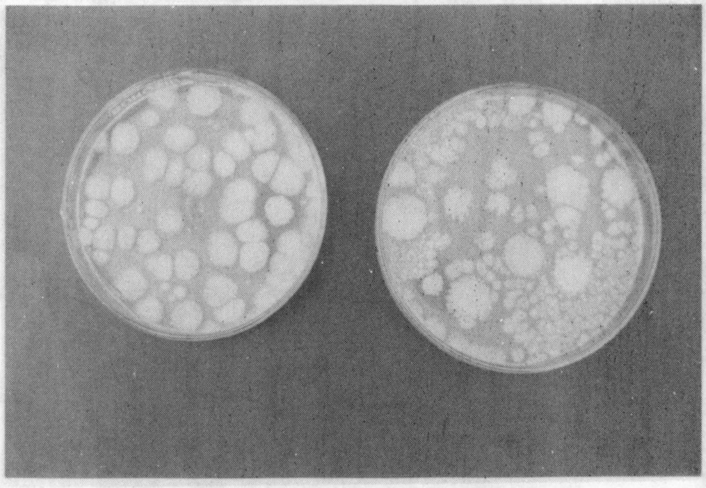

Plate 5.3: Heterotrophic Plate Count (HPC) of Downstream Vedic Nagar

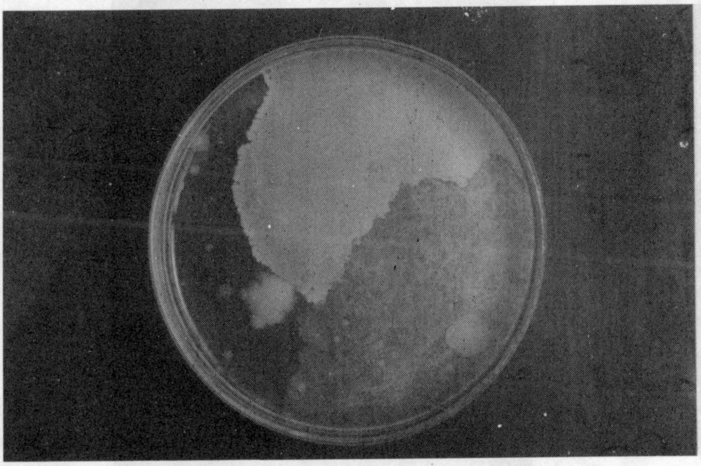

Plate 5.4: Heterotrophic Plate Count (HPC) Near Water Pumping Station

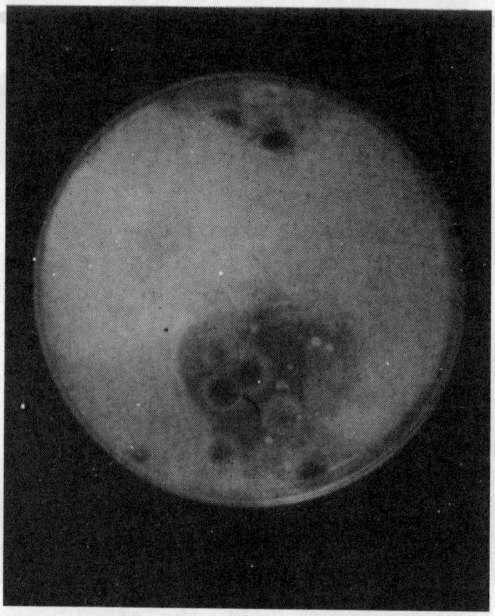

Plate 5.5: Fungus of Upstream Vedic Nagar

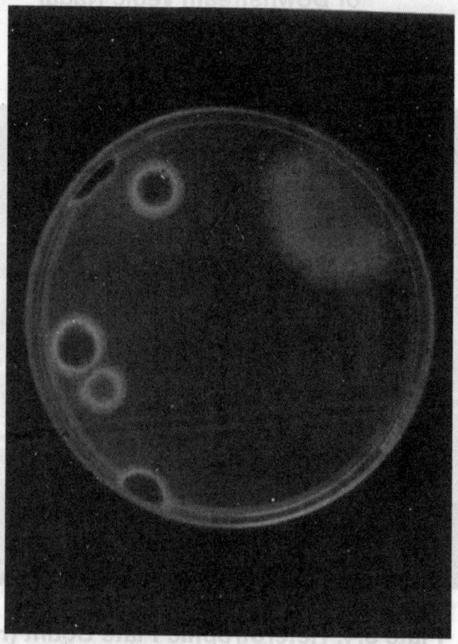

Plate 5.6: Fungus of Downstream Vedic Nagar

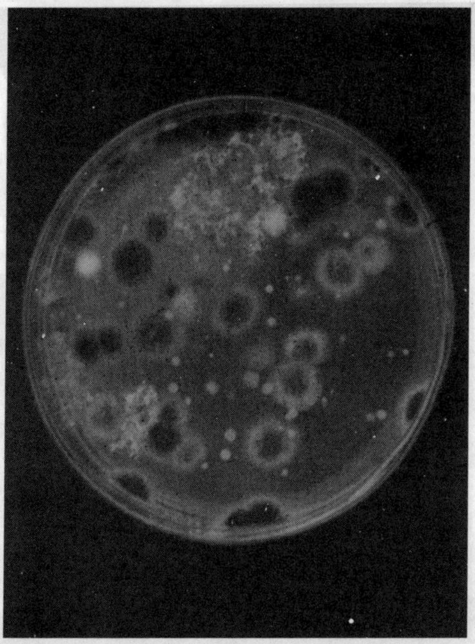

Plate 5.7: Fungus of Near Water Pumping Station

Description of Isolated Bacterial Culture of river Suswa at Raiwala (Plate 5.8)

Salmonella typhii

Salmonella are gram-negative rods about 1-3 µm x 0.5 µm in size. They are motile with peritrichate flagella. These are aerobic and facultatively anaerobic, growing readily on simple media over a range of pH 6-8 and temperature 15-41ºC optimum 37ºC. *Salmonella* ferment glucose, mannitol and maltose, forming acid and gas. An important exception is *S. typhii,* which is an aerogenic. Lactose, Sucrose and salicin are not fermented. They are pathogenic for humans and other animals.

Streptococcus facecalis

Streptococci are gram-positive cocci arranged in chains or pairs. They are part of the normal flora of humans and animals. Some of them are human pathogens. These are non-motile, non-spore forming,

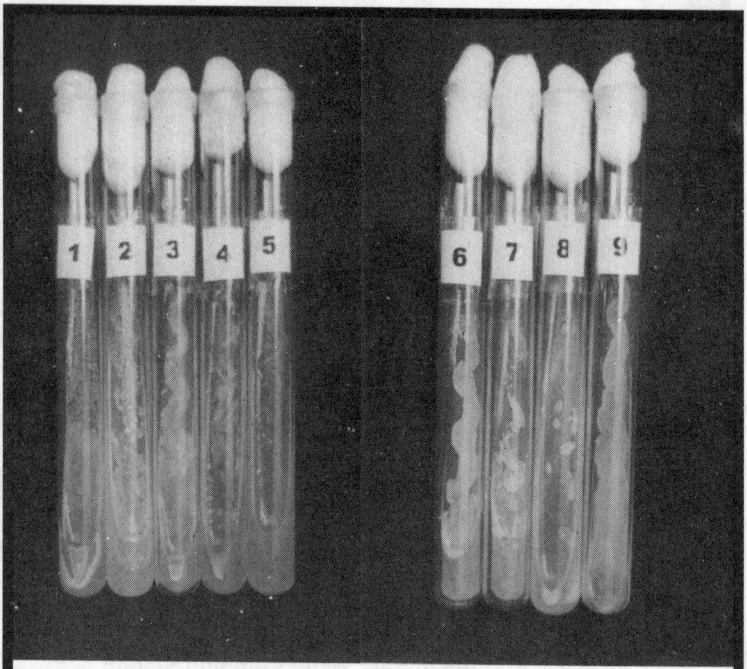

Plate 5.8: Isolated Bacterial Cultures in Slant 1-9

Isolated Bacteria in Slant:

1. *Salmonella typhii*; 2. *Streptococcus facecalis*; 3. *Aerobacter aerogens*; 4. Staphylococcus epidermidis; 5. Staphylococcus aureus; 6. *Micrococcus luteus*; 7. *Bacillus subtilis*; 8. *Escherichia coli*; 9. *Pseudomonas aeroginosa*

aerobic to facultatively anaerobic bacteria. These organisms occur regularly in the mouth and intestine of humans and other animals, in dairy and other food products and in fermenting plant juices.

Aerobacter aerogens

The type species is *A. aerogens*, motile organisms previously placed in this species are now placed in *Enterobacter aerogenes*, and the non-motile organisms have been transferred to *Klebsiella pneumoniae.*

Staphylococcus epidermidis/Staphylococcus aureus

A genus of non-motile, non-spore forming, aerobic to

facultatively anaerobic bacteria containing gram-positive, spherical cells, 0.5 to 1.5 μm in diameter, that occurs in grape like cluster. They are ubiquitous and form the most common cause of localized suppurative lesions in human beings. *Staphylococcus epidermidis* (formally also called *Staphylococcus albus*) containing coagulase negative, mannitol non-fermenting and usually nonpathogenic strains. *Staphylococcus aureus* (formally also called *Staphylococcus pyrogenes*) containing strains giving a positive coagulase test, fermenting mannitol and usually being pathogenic.

Micrococcus luteus

A genus of bacteria (family Micrococcaceae) containing gram-positive, spherical cells that occur in irregular masses, never in packets. Some species are motile or produce motile mutants. These organisms are saprophytic, facultatively parasitic, or parasitic but are not truly pathogenic.

Bacillus subtilis

Sporogenous, rod shaped bacteria, aerobic and consists of aerobic bacilli forming heat resistant spores. They are gram positive but tend to be decolorized easily so as to appear gram variable, or even frankly gram negative. They are generally motile with peritrichous flagella. These are found primarily in soil. A few species are animal pathogens, some species produce antibodies.

Escherichia coli

E. coli is a gram negative, straight rod measuring 1-3 x 0.4–0.7 mm arranged singly or in pairs. It is motile by peritrichate flagella, though some strains may be non motile. Capsules and fimbriae are found in some strains. Spores are not formed. *E.coli* is a parasite living only in the human or animal intestine. Voided in feces it remains viable in the environment only for some days. Detection of *E. coli* in drinking water therefore is taken as evidence of recent pollution with human or animal feces.

Pseudomonas aeruginosa

It is a slender gram-negative bacillus, 1.5–3μm x 0.5μm, actively motile by a polar flagellum. Occasional strains have two or three flagella. It is an obligate aerobe but can grow anaerobically if nitrate is available. The metabolism is oxidative and non fermentive. They occur commonly in soil and in fresh water and marine environment some species are plant pathogens. Other are involved in human infections.

Description of Isolated Fungal Culture of River Suswa at Raiwala (Plate 5.9)

***Aspergillus* sp.**

It is a member of class Ascomycetes, order Aspergillales and family Aspergillaceae. It is chiefly a saprophytic fungus growing on dead and decaying matter. It is popularly called as black mould. It has well developed mycellium made up of loosely interwooven mass of hyaline, bright or pale coloured, extensively branched septate hyphae. In addition to vegetative propogation by fragmentation, it reproduces asexually by conidia produced exogeneously in chains at the tips of conidophores. Sexual reproduction is rare but happens through plasmogamy. Alteration of generations is seen in *Aspergillus*. *Aspergillus oryzae* is employed in making alcohal. *A. niger*, is used in production of citric and other organic acids. A few species are parasitic and cause disease in man, animal and plants. Aspergilloses is disease caused by them. They also occur in human ear and cause Otomycosis, which is spread sometimes while swimming.

***Penicillium* sp.**

The *Penicillium* are commonly known as the green or blue Molds. Usually it grows as saprophyte on decaying fruits and vegetables. Some species are known to grow on forest floors and dampwood and are known to digest hemicelluloses. Some species cause fermentation in cheese. The mycellium is well developed and copiously branched and is composed of colourless, slender tubular and septate hyphae. In addition to vegetative reproduction by fragmentation, slerotium etc. It also commonly reproduces asexually by conidia, which are produced at conidophores. Sexual reproduction is rare but happens by plasmogamy after production of Antheridium and Archegonium. Alteration of generation is seen. *Penicillium* species are known to produce very potent antibiotics like Penicillin, Griesofluvin etc.

***Fusarium* sp.**

It is a member of class Deuteromycetes or fungi imperfecti. In these fungi sexual stage or the perfect stage is unknown. It belongs to order moniliales and family tuberculeriaceae. Many of them live

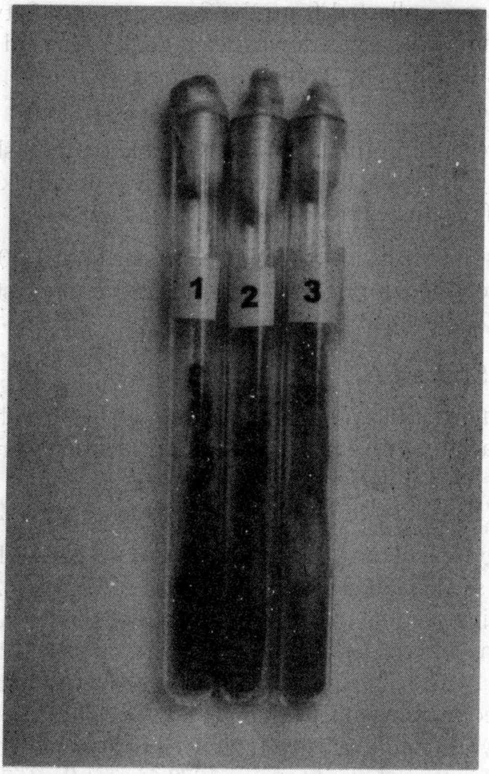

Plate 5.9: Isolated Fungal Cultures in Slant 1-3

Isolated Fungus in Slant:

1. *Aspergillus* species; 2. *Penicillium* species; 3. *Fusarium* species

as parasites of plants and animals. Most of the parasitic species are vascular parasites and are known to cause root rot, stem rot, stem cankere, fruit rot and damping of diseases. Mycellium is extensive, the hyphae are seperate, branched both intercellular and intracellular. When young they may be colourless or with a tinge of pink, purple or yellow and become dark at maturity. They reproduce asexually by three kinds of spores *viz.* microconidia, macroconidia and chlamydospores. They also produce compact resting bodies called selerotia, which serve as storage organs means of penetration and vegetative reproduction.

Fishes

Fishes were collected from the Suswa river at Satyanarayan area, Upstream Vedic nagar, downstream Vedic nagar and near water pumping station. The river contained rich and colourful Ichthyofauna.

As no recent information was available on the fish fauna of Suswa river at Raiwala, the present study was undertaken and the fish fauna of the Suswa river at Raiwala was surveyed.

As a result of fish survey of Suswa river a total of 30 species of fishes were collected during course of study, which are systematically arranged in Table 5B.45.

Sampling Station A

Seasonal Quantitative analysis of plankton at sampling station A (Satyanaran area), revealed that the total planktonic concentration was highest 3605 unit/l ± 1795.34 in winter season of 2003–2004 and lowest (524 unit/l ± 330.92) in monsoon season of 2003–2004.

Both phytoplankton and zooplankton were observed minimum in monsoon season (2003–2004), 496 unit/l ± 257.0 and 28 unit/l ± 5.45 respectively while maximum number of phytoplankton and zooplankton were observed in winter season (2003–2004), 3072 unit/l ± 524.24 and 533 unit/l ± 29.14 respectively. Phytoplankton was observed maximum (3072 unit/l ± 524.24) in winter season of (2003–2004), and minimum (496unit/1 ± 257.0) in monsoon season. The annual average of plankton was 1878.66 unit/l ± 1573.76 (Table 5B.1 and Figure 5B.1 to 5B.2).

ZOOPLANKTON

Rotifera followed by Cladocerans, Protozoa and Copepod dominated the zooplanktonic concentration at this sampling station. The number of protozoa at this sampling station was found maximum (123 unit/l ± 4.94) in winter season of (2003–2004) while minimum (0.00 unit/l ± 0.00) in monsoon season The number of rotifera was found maximum (255 unit/l ± 7.00) in summer season of 2002–2003 and minimum 15 unit/l ± 3.60 in monsoon season of same year (2002–2003) Cladocerans was observed maximum (147 unit/l ± 30.40) during winter season (2003–2004) and minimum (8 unit/l ± 5.65) during monsoon season of second year (2002–2003).

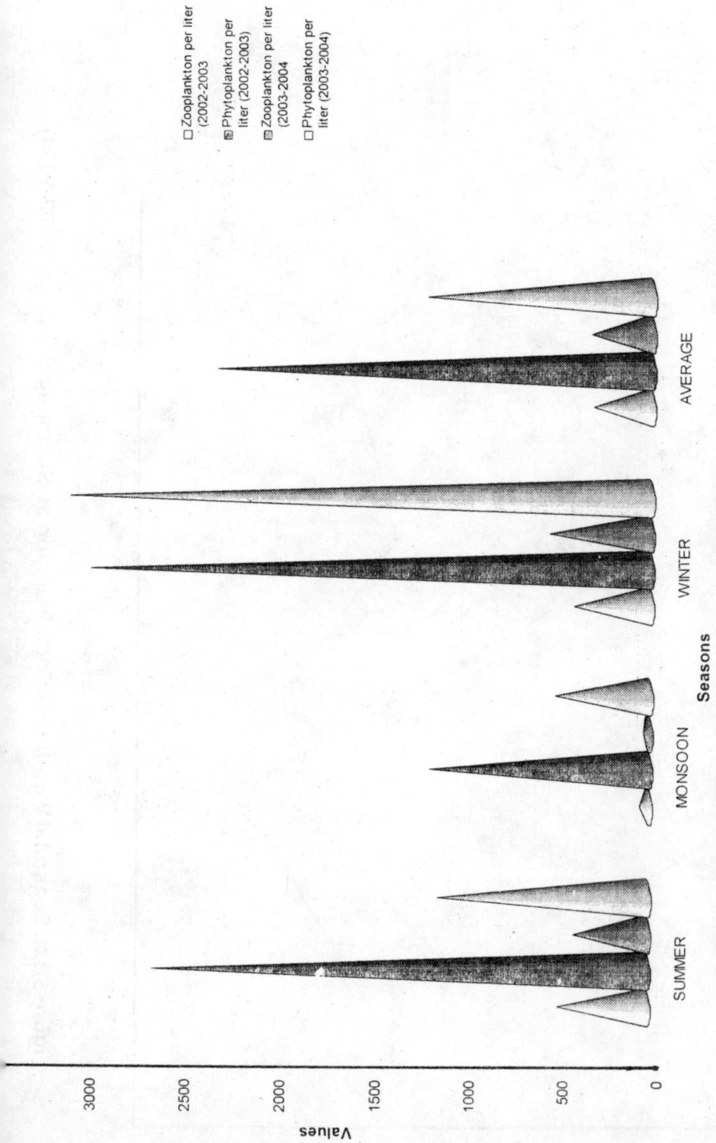

Figure 5B.1: Seasonal Variation in Plankton at Sampling Station A (2002-2004)

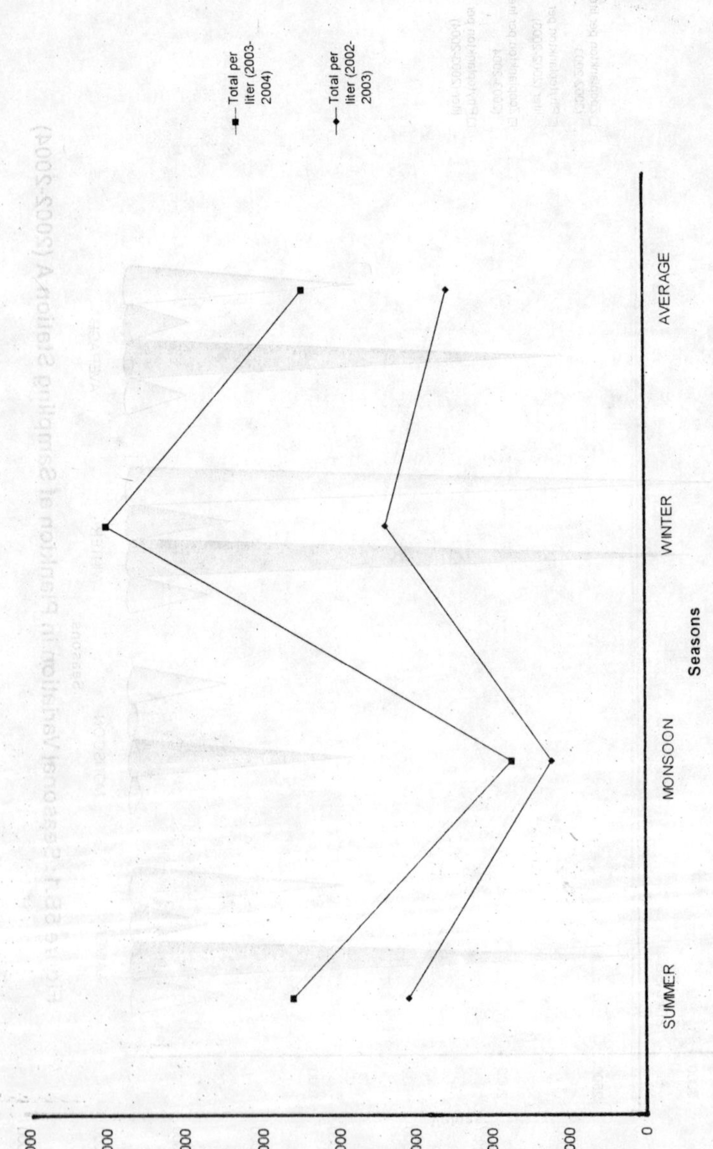

Figure 5B.2: Seasonal Variation in Total Plankton at Sampling Station A (2002-2004)

Copepods were found maximum (108 unit/l ± 8.48) during winter season (2003–2004) and minimum (4 unit/l ± 0.75) during summer season of second year (2003–2004). In total at sampling station A, the highest zooplankton (533 unit/l ± 21.63) was recorded in winter season (2003–2004) and lowest (46 unit/l ± 9.30) in monsoon season of 2002–2003. Table 5B.2 and Figure 5B.3.

Among average value *Daphnia* was found dominating in the zooplankton, 2002–2003 (50.66 unit/l ± 38.27) followed by *Notholca* (44.66unit/l ± 42.09), *Cyclops* (42.33 unit/l ± 19.13), *Philodima* (40 unit/l ± 36.16), *Keratella* (40 unit/l ± 45.43), *Arcella* (35 unit/l ± 31.22), *Amoeba* (31.66 unit/l ± 27.02) and *Bosmina* (19.33 unit/l ± 30.92). While in second year 2003–2004, *Keratella* (48.33 unit/l ± 45.36) was found to be dominating followed by *Daphnia* (47.33 unit/l ± 30.27), *Amoeba* (45.66 unit/l ± 39.70), *Bosmina* (44.66 unit/l ± 43.66), *Philodima* (41.66 unit/l ± 38.83), *Cyclops* (40 unit/l ± 58.92), *Arcella* (36 unit/l ± 31.43) and *Notholca* (25 unit/l ± 17.32). Table 5B.3 and Figure 5B.4.

PHYTOPLANKTON

Among phytoplankton Bacillariophyceae was found dominating in both the years followed by Myxophyceae for first year (2002–2003) and Chlorophyceae in second year (2003–2004). In 2002–2003 Chlorophyceae was found to be least in number and in year 2003 –2004 Myxophyceae was found to be least. Bacillariophyceae was found maximum (1784 unit/l ± 100.29) in winter season (2002–2003) and minimum (462 unit/l ± 33.91) in monsoon season of 2003–2004.Chlorophyceae was found maximum (578 unit/l ± 22.21) in winter season of 2002–2003 and minimum (24 unit ± 8.71) in monsoon season of 2003–2004. Myxophyceae was found to be highest (1310 unit/l ± 59.65) in winter season of 2003–2004 while minimum (250 unit/l ± 21.93) in monsoon season of same year *i.e.*, 2003 –2004 (Table 5B.4 and Figure 5B.5).

Among Bacillariophyceae *Diatoms* was found to be dominating (263.33 unit/l ± 48.56) in 2002–2003 followed by *Gomphonema* (217.33 unit/l ± 94.87), *Achnanthes* (157.0 unit/l ± 106.5), *Fragelaria* (142.66 unit/l ± 79.02), *Amphora* (130.33 unit/l ± 65.57), *Cymbella* (100.66 unit/l ± 55.82), *Frustulia* (76.66 unit/l ± 34.31), *Pinnularia* (74.33 unit/l ± 22.00), *Navicula* (44.00 unit/l ± 24.33), *Cyclotella* (22 unit ± 29.59), *Nitzschia* (12.00 unit/l ± 12.48) and *Cocconeis* (8.66 unit/l

Table: 5B.1: Seasonal variations in Plankton (per liter) of River Suswa at Sampling Station A (2002-2004)

Plankton	*2002-2003*				*2003-2004*			
	Summer	*Monsoon*	*Winter*	*Average*	*Summer*	*Monsoon*	*Winter*	*Average*
Zooplankton	467.00±28.67	46.00±7.42	398.00±18.03	303.61±9.46	391.0±28.0	28.0±5.45	533.0±29.14	317.31±8.95
Phytoplankton	2615±374.55	1162.±377.12	2962±690.02	2295.99±448.89	1116±192.8	496±257	3072±524.24	1190±345.85
Total	3082±1518.86	1208±789.13	3360±1813.02	2550±1170.48	1507±512.65	524±330.92	3605±1795.34	1878.66±1573.76

±= Standard deviation.

Table 5B.2: Quantitative Analysis of Zooplankton (per liter) in Different Seasons of River Suswa at Sampling Station A (2002-2004)

Year	*Seasons*	*Protozoa*	*Rotifera*	*Cladocera*	*Copepod*	*Total*
2002-2003	Summer	102±12.72	255±7.00	65±41.71	45±3.55	467±95.14
	Monsoon	1±0.70	15±.3.60	8±5.65	22±7.85	46±9.03
	Winter	97±4.94	104±14.04	137±19.09	60±9.17	398±31.58
	Average	66.66±56.92	124.66±121.32	70.00±64.64	42.33±19.13	303.65±34.75
2003-2004	Summer	122±15.55	165±31.22	100±35.35	4±0.75	391±68.08
	Monsoon	0±0.00	25.0±7.63	29±0.70	8±1.96	62±13.77
	Winter	123±4.94	155±35.11	147±30.40	108±8.48	533±21.63
	Average	81.66±70.72	115.00±78.10	88.66±64.74	40.0±58.92	325.32±31.06

±= Standard Deviation.

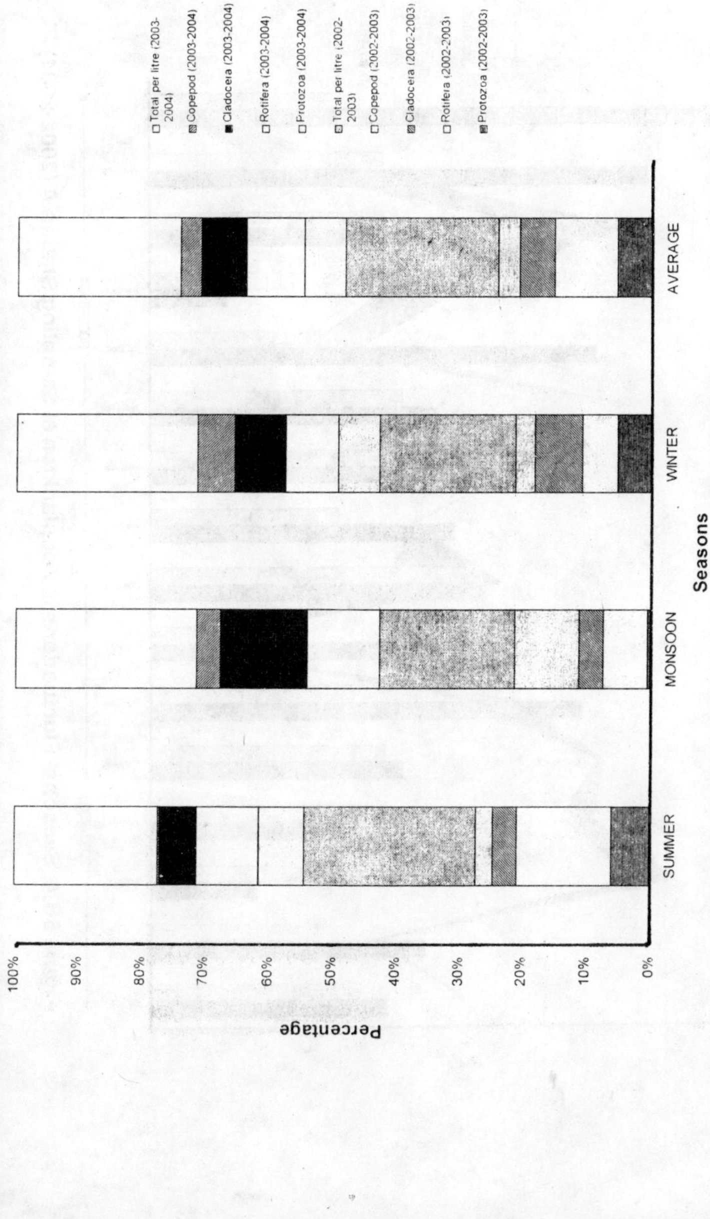

Figure 5B.3: Percentile Fluctuation in Zooplankton at Sampling Station A (2002-2004)

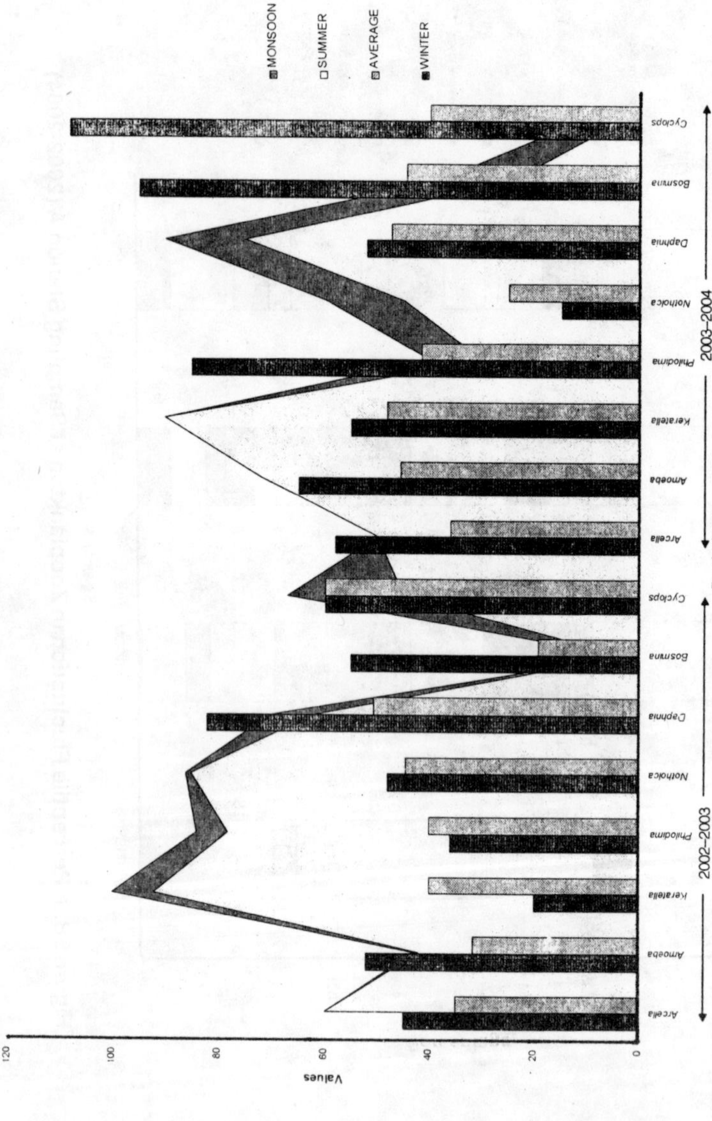

Figure 5B.4: Seasonal Fluctuations in Zooplankton at Sampling Station A (2002-2004)

Table 5B.3: Quantitative Analysis of Zooplankton in Different Seasons of River Suswa at Sampling Station A (2002-2004)

Year	*Seasons*	*Protozoa*		*Rotifera*			*Cladocera*		*Copepod*	*Total l^{-1}*
		Arcella	*Amoeba*	*Keratella*	*Philodima*	*Notholca*	*Daphnia*	*Bosmina*	*Cyclops*	
2002-2003	Summer	60±15.50	42±10.18	92±8.24	78±6.11	85±16.14	62±17.50	3±0.50	45±3.55	467.00±2 8.67
	Monsoon	0±0.00	1±0.01	8±2.10	6±2.56	1±0.05	8±3.26	0±0.00	22±7.85	46.00±7.42
	Winter	45±1.98	52±2.38	20±1.10	36±2.96	48±3.33	82±12.48	55±16.33	60±9.17	398.00±18.03
	Average	35.00±31.22	31.66±27.02	40.00±45.43	40.00±36.16	44.66±42.09	50.66±38.27	19.33±30.92	42.33±19.13	303.61±9.48
2003-2004	Summer	50±12.14	72±18.00	90±3.87	30±4.96	45±12.11	75±7.58	25±2.39	4±0.75	391.00±28.94
	Monsoon	0±0.00	0±0.00	0±0.00	10±3.00	15.00±8.0	15±0.98	14±0.50	8±1.96	62.00±6.86
	Winter	58±3.96	65±2.78	55±3.85	85±4.96	15±1.05	52±3.50	95±4.44	108±8.48	533.00±29.14
	Average	36.00±31.43	45.66±39.70	48.33±45.36	41.66±38.83	25±17.32	47.33±30.27	44.66±43.93	40.00±58.92	328.64±7.66

±= Standard Deviation.

Table 5B.4: Comparitive Analysis of Seasonal Variation Among Phytoplankton (per liter) of River Suswa at Sampling Station A (2002-2004)

Year	*Seasons*	*Bacillariophyceae l^{-1}*	*Chlorophyceae l^{-1}*	*Myxophyceae l^{-1}*	*Total l^{-1}*
2002-2003	Summer	1169±80.48	451±30.03	995±70.23	2615±374.55
	Monsoon	794.0±82.23	49±6.57	319±105.79	1162±377.12
	Winter	1784±100.29	578±22.21	600±100.37	2962±690.02
	Average	1249±499.82	359.31±14.60	637.99±34.45	2246.30±455.07
2003-2004	Summer	583.0±43.46	205±26.86	328±52.50	1116±192.80
	Monsoon	462±33.91	24.0±8.71	250±21.93	736±219.03
	Winter	1343±47.28	419±25.70	1310±59.65	3072±524.20
	Average	796±477.56	215.97±14.72	185.33±11.05	1196.33±344.32

±= Standard Deviation.

± 14.15). In second year *i.e.* 2003–2004, *Amphora* (137.33 unit/l ± 50.36) was found to be dominating followed by *Diatoms* (123 unit/l ± 66.46), *Achnanthes* (103.33 unit/l 41.63), *Fragelaria* (84.33 unit/l ± 22.50), *Pinnularia* (79 unit/l ± 34.07), *Nitzschia* (64 unit/l ± 36.66), *Frustulia* (39.33 unit/l ± 7.57), *Cocconeis* (38.66 unit/l ± 47.25), *Cyclotella* (36.66 unit/l ± 63.50), *Cymbella* (34.33 unit/l ± 52.69), *Navicula* (31.33 unit/l ± 41.19) and *Gomphonema* (24.66 ± 28.58). Table 5B.5 and Figure 5B.6.

A great fluctuation among Bacillariophyceae was observed during seasonal study of Suswa river at sampling station A. In 2002–2003-summer season, *Gomphonema* was found maximum (252 unit/l ± 8.84) and *Cocconeis* was found minimum (1 unit/l ± 0.50), in monsoon season *Diatoms* were found highest (305 unit/l ± 11.67) while *Cocconeis* were found to be Nil. In winter again maximum concentration was observed for *Gomphonema* (290 unit/l ± 8.18) and *Cocconeis* was found to be minimum (25 unit/l ± 3.58). In 2003–2004 summer, *Amphora* was found maximum (115 unit/l ± 6.95) while *Cyclotella, Gomponema* and *Navicula* were recorded Nil. In monsoon season again *Amphora* was found highest (102 unit/l ± 5.05) while *Cymbella* and *Cyclotella* were found to be nil. In winter season *Amphora* and *Diatoms* were found maximum (195 unit/l ± 7.86), (195 unit/l ± 11.03) respectively, while *Frustulia* was found minimum (48 unit/l ± 4.09).

Among Chlorophyceae during 2002–2003 *Chlorella* was observed as dominating species (61 unit/l ± 52.84) followed by *Closterium* (56 unit/l ± 49.11), *Cladophora* (53 unit/l ± 45.17), *Schizogonium* (39.66 unit/l ± 32.19), *Spirogyra* (37 unit/l ± 15.58), *Zygnema* (35.66 unit/l ± 32.25), *Ulothrix* (32.66 unit/l ± 22.47), *Cosmerium* (30 unit/l ± 37.46) and *Oedogonium* (14.33 unit/l ± 14.01). During 2003–2004 *Schizogonium* and *Spirogyra* were found as dominant species (44 unit/l ± 36.49), (44 unit/l ± 39.39) respectively, followed by *Closterium* (36.66 unit/l ± 33.29), *Cladophora* (26.33 unit/l ± 42.19), *Ulothrix* (23.33 unit/l ± 35.34), *Chlorella* (14.66 unit/l ± 13.31), *Oedogonium* (9 unit/l ± 9.53) and *Cosmerium* (7.33 unit/l ± 9.45).

A great variation in seasonal values of Chlorophyceae was noted during the course of study at sampling station A. During first year 2002–2003 *Closterium* was found maximum (98 unit/l ± 2.48) and *oedogonium* was found recorded minimum (15 unit/l ± 2.31) in

Table 5B.5: Quantitative Analysis of Seasonal Variation Among Bacillariophyceae of River Suswa at Sampling station A (2002-2004)

	Seasons	*Achnanthes*	*Amphora*	*Cocconeis*	*Cymbella*	*Cyclotella*	*Diatoms*	*Fragelaria*
2002-2004	Summer	128±10.48	15.5±11.46	1±0.50	72±5.67	8±2.56	210±9.51	128±5.95
	Monsoon	68±8.88	56±1.98	0±0.00	65±8.89	2±0.00	305±11.67	72±6.76
	Winter	275±15.48	180±10.10	25±3.58	165±9.10	56±4.00	275±15.89	228±7.77
	Average	157.0±106.5	130.33±65.57	8.66±14.15	100.66±55.82	22.0±29.59	263.33±48.56	142.66±79.02
2003-2004	Summer	90±5.80	115±6.95	22±1.03	8±1.76	0.00±0.00	110±7.49	75±3.59
	Monsoon	70±4.97	102±5.05	2±0.03	0.00±0.00	0±0.00	64±6.60	68±2.45
	Winter	150±4.50	195±7.86	92±2.33	95±5.84	110±14.14	195±11.03	110±1.03
	Average	103.33±41.63	137.33±50.36	38.66±47.25	34.33±52.69	36.66±63.50	123.0±66.46	84.33±22.50
	Seasons	*Frustulia*	*Gomphonema*	*Navicula*	*Nitzschia*	*Pinnularia*	*Total I'¹*	
2002-2004	Summer	82±4.40	252±8.84	56±3.59	2±0.00	75±3.20	1169±80.48S	
	Monsoon	40±5.19	110±7.92	16±2.00	8±1.03	52±1.98	794±82.23	
	Winter	108±6.72	290±8.18	60±1.05	26±3.01	96±2.57	1784±100.29	
	Average	76.66±34.31	217.33± 94.87	44.00±24.33	12.00±12.48	74.33±22.00	1248.96±81.32	
2003-2004	Summer	36±2.10	0±0.00	0±0.00	72±11.00	55±3.26	583.00± 43.46	
	Monsoon	34±3.59	18±3.11	16±2.11	24±5.67	64±1.16	462±33.91	
	Winter	48±4.09	56±4.11	78±9.75	96±8.00	118±10.18	1343±47.28	
	Average	39.33±7.57	24.66±28.58	31.33±41.19	64.0±36.66	79±34.07	482.31±33.76	

± = Standard Deviation

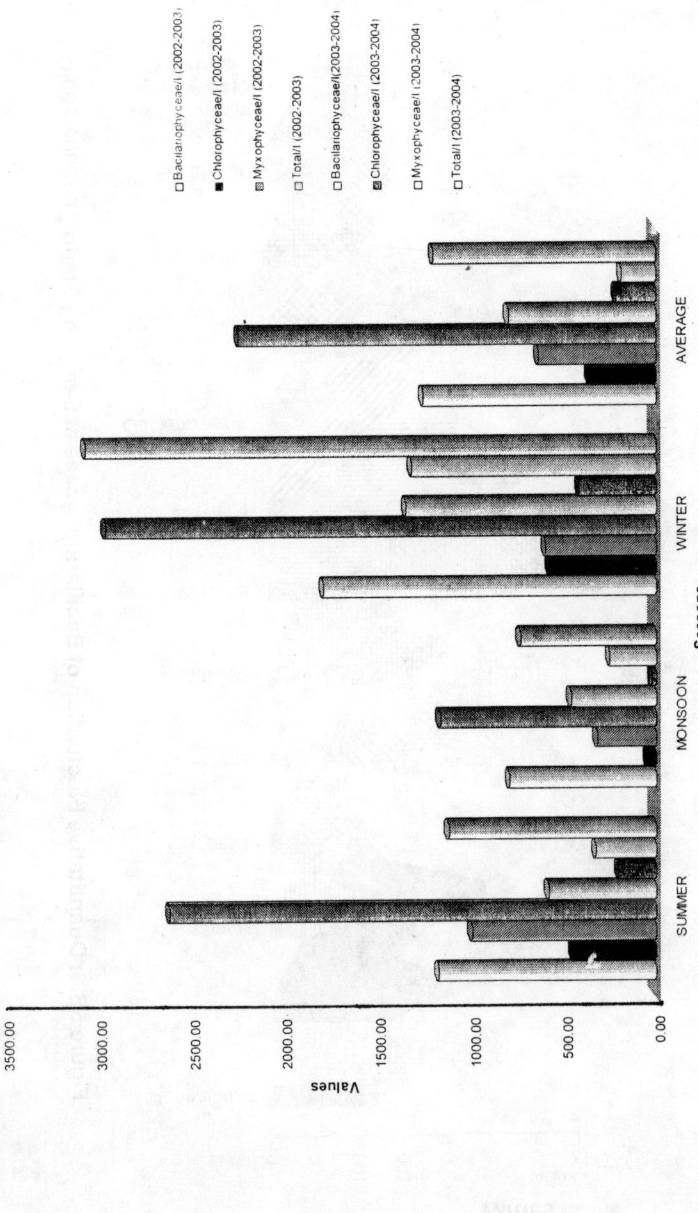

Figure 5B.5: Seasonal Fluctuations in Phytoplankton at Sampling Station A (2002-2004)

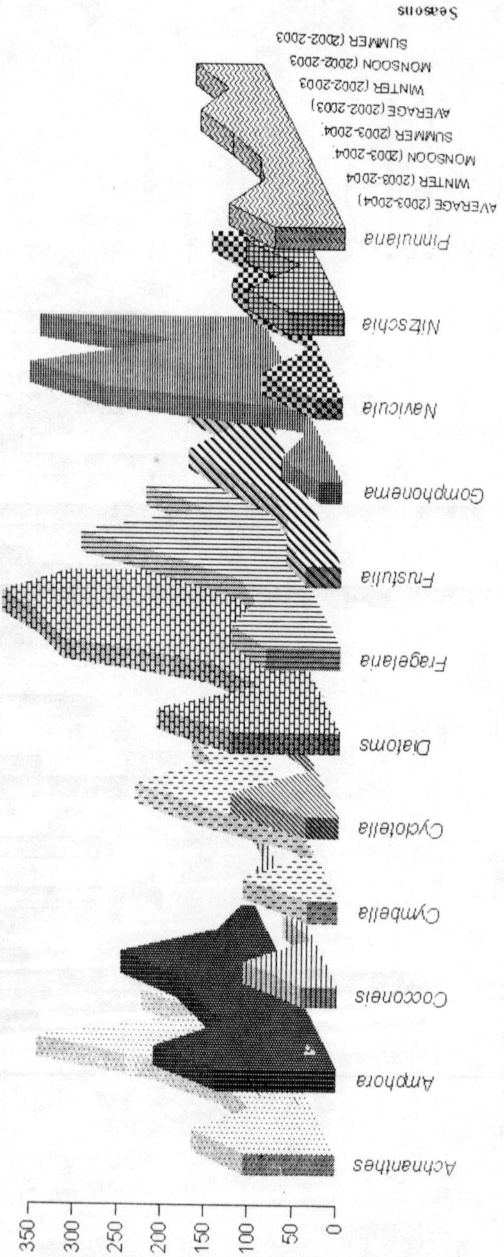

Figure 5B.6: Quantitative Fluctuation of Bacillariophyceae at Sampling Station A (2002-2004)

Table 5B.6: Quantitative Analysis of Seasonal Variation Among Chlorophyceae of River Suswa at Sampling Station A (2002-2004)

Year	Seasons	*Closterium*	*Cosmerium*	*Chlorella*	*Cladophora*	*Oedogonium*	*Schizogonium*	*Spirogyra*	*Ulothrix*	*Zygnema*	*Total* l^{-1}
2002-2003	Summer	98±2.48	98±2.22	90±8.48	69.00±14.11	15±2.31	32±8.80	46±1.76	52±3.98	31±2.22	451±30.03
	Monsoon	2±0.10	0±0.00	0.00±0.00	2±1.00	0±0.00	12±1.67	19±2.10	8±0.50	6±0.78	49±6.57
	Winter	68±2.86	72±4.95	93±11.00	88±4.46	28±12.64	75±4.46	46±4.14	38±3.25	70±2.98	578±22.21
	Average	56±49.11	30±37.46	61±52.84	53±45.17	14.33±14.01	39.66±32.19	37±15.58	32.66±22.47	35.66±32.25	359.31±14.60
2003-2004	Summer	15±2.00	4±1.10	18±3.16	4±0.50	8±1.79	62±8.72	76±4.87	6±0.78	12±0.98	205±26.86
	Monsoon	20±0.00	0±0.00	0±0.00	0±0.00	0.±0.00	2±0.10	0±0.00	0±0.00	2±0.00	24.0±8.71
	Winter	75±2.39	18±4.86	26±10.08	75±11.96	19±3.48	68±14.67	56±3.00	64±2.97	18±1.88	419±25.70
	Average	36.66±33.29	7.33±9.45	14.66±13.31	26.33±42.19	9±9.53	44±36.49	44±39.39	23.33±35.34	10.66±8.08	215.97±14.72

± = Standard Deviation.

summer season. While in monsoon season *Spirogyra* was found to be highest (19 unit/l ± 2.10) and *Cosmerium, Chlorella* and *Oedogonium* was recorded as nil. In winter season *Chlorella* was revealed maximum (93 unit/l ± 11.00) and *Oedogonium* was recorded minimum (28 unit/l ± 12.64). While in second year 2003–2004 *Spirogyra* was found maximum (76 unit/l ± 4.87) and *Cladophura* and *Cosmerium* was found minimum (4 unit/l ± 0.50), (4 unit/l ± 1.10) respectively in summer season. In monsoon season, *Closterium* was found maximum (20 unit/l ± 0.00) while *Cosmerium, Chlorella, Cladophora, Oedogonium, Spirogyra* and *Ulothrix* were nil. In winter season *Closterium* and *Cladophora* were found maximum (75 unit/l ± 2.39), (75 unit/l ± 11.96) respectively while *Cosmerium* and *Zygnema* were found minimum (18 unit/l ± 4.86), (18 unit/l ± 1.88) respectively. The total highest value of Chlorophyceae was recorded in winter (578 unit/l ± 22.21) and lowest in monsoon (49 unit/l ± 6.57) for first year (2002–2003) for second year (2003–2004) the highest total value of Chlorophyceae was recorded in winter (419 unit/l ± 25.70) and lowest in monsoon season (24 unit/l ± 8.71). Table 5B.6 and Figure 5B.7.

Among Myxophyceae, *Anabena* was recorded as dominant species, (245.33 unit/l ± 189.44) followed by *Oscillatoria* (216.0 unit/l ± 115.46) and *Anacystis* (176.66 unit/l ± 108.89) for first year (2002–2003). During second year *Anacystis* was found as dominating species (223.66 unit/l ± 151.28) followed by *Oscillatoria* (213 unit/l ± 252.88) and *Anabena* (192.66 unit/l ± 188.38).

For seasonal fluctuation of Myxophyceae it is revealed that in summer season of 2002–2003, *Anabena* existed in maximum (405 unit/l ± 16.69) while *Anacystis* was found minimum (265 unit/l ± 20.85). In monsoon season *Anacystis* was found maximum (55 unit/l ± 3.95) and *Oscillatiria* was found minimum (28 unit/l ± 2.26). In winter season, again *Anabena* was found maximum (295 unit/l ± 15.89) and *Oscillatoria* was least (95 unit/l ± 8.79). During second year (2003–2004), *Anacystis* was found maximum (168 unit/l ± 7.82) and *Oscillatoria* as minimum (68 unit/l ± 9.87) in summer season. In monsoon season again *Anacystis* was found maximum (108 unit/l ± 2.22) and *Oscillatoria* as minimum (66 unit ± 1.97). In winter season *Oscillatoria* was found maximum (505 unit/l ± 52.29) and *Anacystis* as minimum (395 unit/l ± 28.82). In total value of 2002-2004 the maximum Myxophyceae for 2002–2003 was recoded in summer season (995 unit/l ± 70.23) and minimum in monsoon season

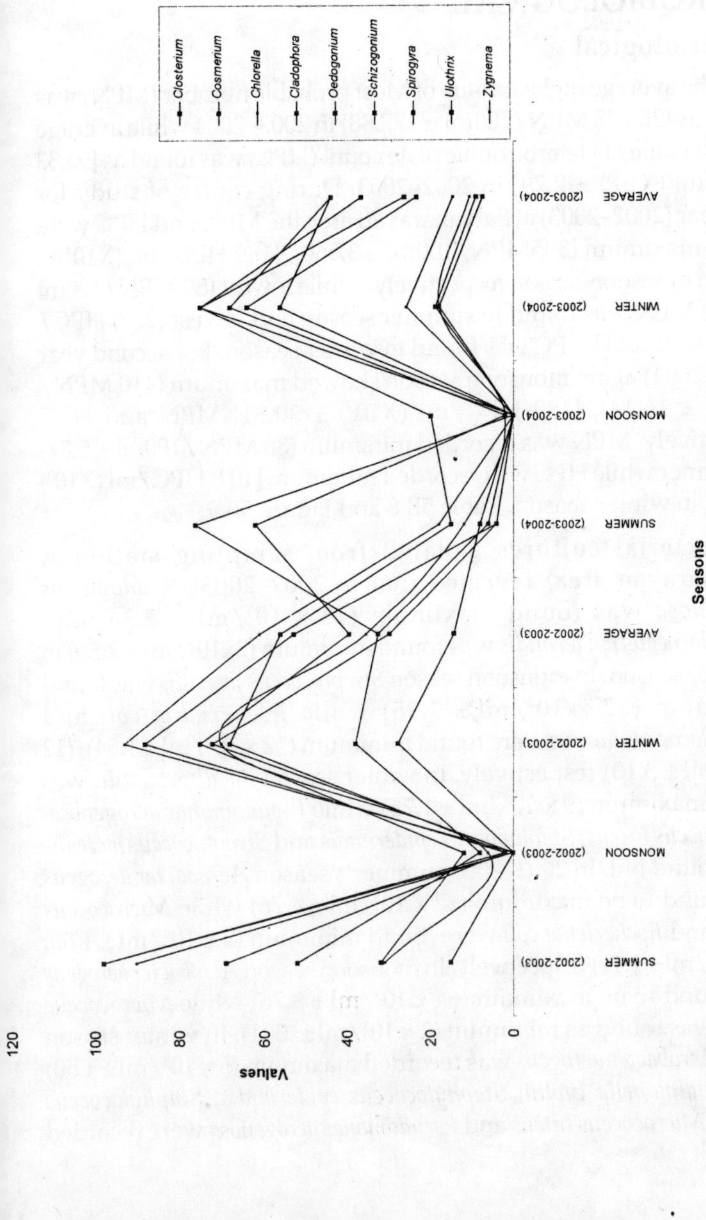

Figure 5B.7: Quantitative Fluctuation of Chlorophyceae at Sampling Station A (2002-2004)

(119 unit/l ± 105.79). In 2003–2004 the maximum Myxophyceae were recorded in winter season (1310 unit/l ± 59.65) and minimum in monsoon season (250 unit/l ± 21.93) Table 5B.7 and Figure 5B.8.

MICROBIOLOGICAL

Bacteriological

The average highest value of Most probable number (MPN) was found as (205.33 MPN/100ml ± 177.88) in 2003–2004 while average highest value of Heterotrophic plate count (HPC) was found as [93.33 HPC/ml ($X10^3$) ± 2.79] in 2002–2003. During course of study for first year (2002–2003) at Satyanarayan area the MPN and HPC were found maximum [395MPN/100ml ± 37.62], [189 HPC/ml ($X10^3$) ± 7.19] in monsoon season respectively. While lowest (80 MPN/100ml ± 8.62) MPN was found in summer season and lowest [26.0 HPC/ ml ($X10^3$) ± 3.51] HPC was found in winter season. For second year (2003–2004) again monsoon season showed maximum (410 MPN/ 100ml ± 16.14), [189 HPC/ml ($X10^3$) ± 20.31] MPN and HPC respectively. MPN was recorded minimum (88 MPN/100ml ± 5.37) in summer while HPC was recorded minimum [10.0 HPC/ml ($X10^3$) ± 1.69] in winter season. Table 5B.8 and Figure 5B.9.

Bacterial cultures isolated from sampling station A (Satynarayan area) revealed that in 2002–2003 *Pseudomonas aerogenosa* was found maximum (13 x 10^3/ml ± 2.36) and *Staphylococcus epidermidis* was found minimum (2x10^3/ml ± 2.50) in summer season. In monsoon season *Streptococcus facecalis* was found maximum (32 x 10^3/ml ± 2.95) while *Escherichia coli* and *Staphylococcus aureus* were found minimum (12 x 10^3/ml± 1.54), (12 x 10^3/ml± 3.10) respectively. In winter season *Bacillus subtilis* was found maximum (9 x 10^3/ml± 1.75) while *Pseudomonas aerogenosa, Micrococcus luteus, Staphyloccus epidermidis* and *Streptococcus facecalis* were found Nil. In 2003–2004 summer's season *Aerobacter aerogens* was found to be maximum (22 x 10^3/ml± 4.76) while *Micrococcus luteus* and *Escherichia coli* were found minimum (2 x 10^3/ml± 1.00, (2 x 10^3/ml± 1.11) respectively. In monsoon season *Aerobacter aerogens* was found to be maximum (64 x 10^3/ml± 8.76) while *Micrococcus luteus* was found as minimum (2 x 10^3/ml± .001). In winter season again *Aerobacter aerogens* was recorded maximum (5 x 10^3/ml± 1.50) while *Salmonella typhii, Staphylococcus epidermidis, Staphylococcus aureus, Micrococcus luteus* and *Pseudomonas aerogenosa* were recorded nil.

Table 5B.7: Quantitative Analysis of Seasonal Variation Among Myxophyceaee (per liter) of River Suswa at Sampling Station A (2002-2004)

Year	*Seasons*	*Anacystis*	*Anabena*	*Oscillatoria*	*Total l^{-1}*
2002-2003	Summer	265±20.85	405±16.69	325±24.86	995±70.23
	Monsoon	55±3.95	36±7.83	28±2.26	119±105.79
	Winter	210±11.86	295±15.89	95±8.79	600±100.37
	Average	176.66±108.89	245.33±189.44	216±115.46	637.99±34.45
2003-2004	Summer	168±7.82	92±5.95	68±9.87	328±52.20
	Monsoon	108±2.22	76±5.86	66±1.97	250±21.93
	Winter	395±28.82	410±32.18	505±52.29	1310±59.65
	Average	223.66±151.38	192.66±188.38	213±252.88	629.32±15.74

± = Standard Deviation.

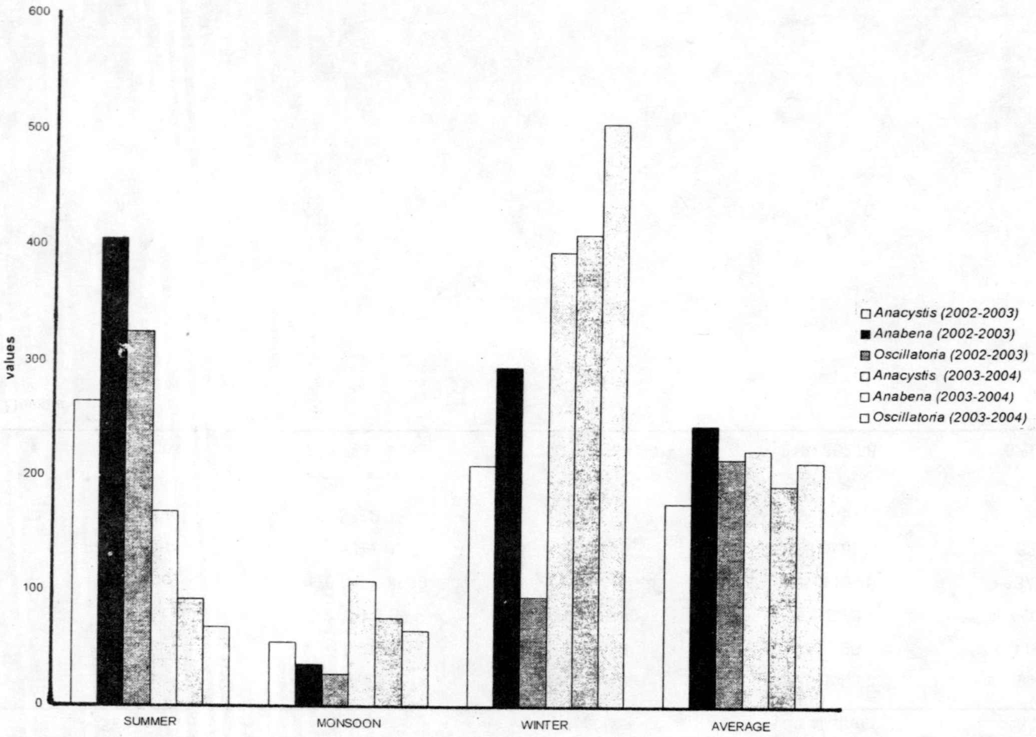

Figure 5R.8 : Quantitative Fluctuation of Myxophyceae at Sampling Station A (2002-2004)

Table 5B.8: Quantitative Analysis of Seasonal Variation in Bacteriological Parameters of River Suswa at Sampling station A (2002-2004)

Year	*Seasons*	*MPN/100 ml*	*HPC/ml ($X10^3$) ($\times 10^3$)*
2002-2003	Summer	80±8.62	65±3.63
	Monsoon	395±37.62	189±7.19
	Winter	125±75.48	26.0±3.51
	Average	200±170.36	93.33±2.79
2003-2004	Summer	88±5.37	63.0±6.10
	Monsoon	410±15.14	189.0±20.31
	Winter	118±20.12	10.0±1.69
	Average	205.33±177.88	87.33±8.82

± = Standard Deviation.

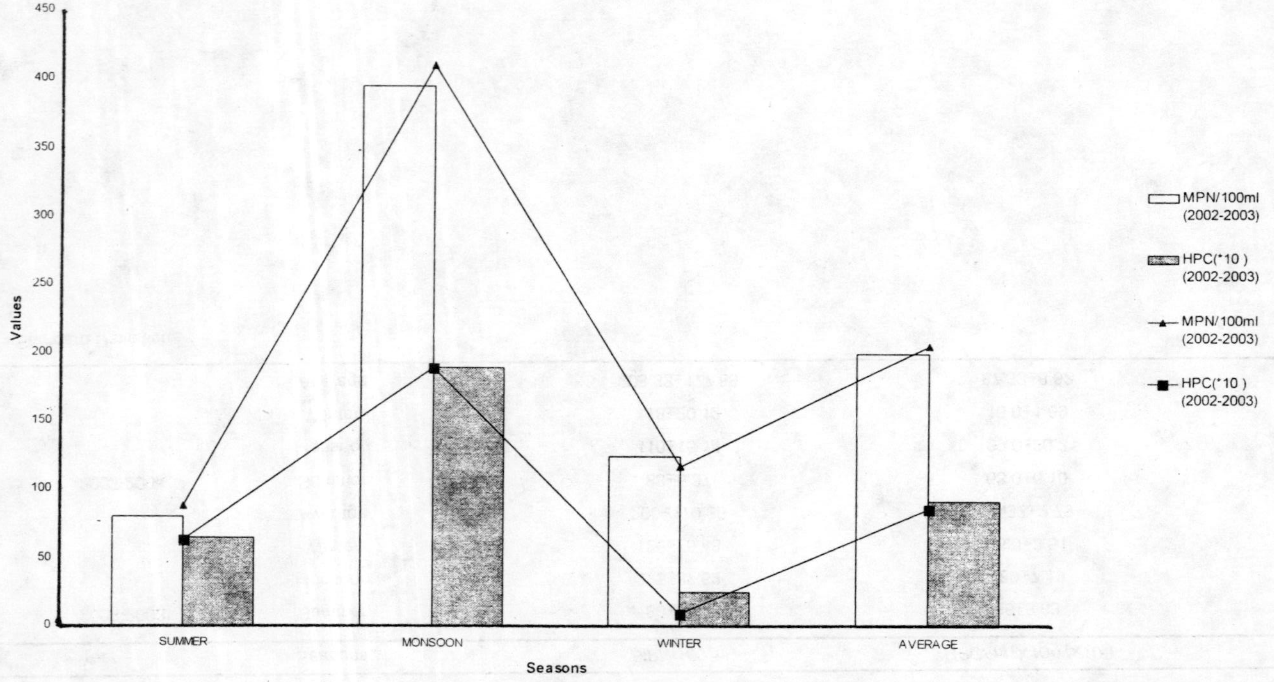

Figure 5B.9: Quantitative Fluctuation of Bacterial Parameters at Sampling Station A (2002-2004)

On an average calculation for 2002–2003 *Aerobacter aerogens* was observed as dominant species (14.33 x 10^3/ml ± 12.66) followed by *Streptococcus facecalis* (12.66 x 10^3/ml ± 17.0), *Salmonella typhii* (12.33 x 10^3/ml ± 11.15), *Micrococcus luteus* (11.66 x 10^3/ml ± 13.20), *Pseudomonas aeroginosa* (11.33 x 10^3/ml ± 10.59), *Bacillus subtilis* (10.0 x 10^3/ml ± 5.56), *Escherichia coli* (7.33 x 10^3/ml ± 4.16) *Staphylococcus aureus* (7.33 x 10^3/ml ± 5.03) and *Staphylococcus epidermidis* (6.33 x 10^3/ml ± 9.29). In 2003–2004 *Aerobacter aerogens* was noted maximum (30.33 x 10^3/ml ± 30.36) followed by *Streptococcus facecalis* (15.33 x 10^3/ml ± 21.38), *Escherichia coli* (11.66 x 10^3/ml ± 16.74), *Staphylococcus epidermidis* (8.0 x 10^3/ml ± 8.0), *Staphylococcus aureus* (6.66 x 10^3/ml ± 5.85), *Bacillus subtilis* (6 x 10^3/ml ± 5.56), *Salmonella typhii* (4.66 x 10^3/ml ± 4.16), *Pseudomonas aeroginosa* (3.33 x 10^3/ml ± 2.88) and *Micrococcus luteus* (1.33 x 10^3/ml ± 1.15). Table 5B.9 and Figure 5B.10.

AQUATIC FUNGI

During the course of study the average aquatic fungi at this sampling station was found highest (18.66 x 10^3/ml ± 2.33) in 2003–2004 and minimum (11.66 x 10^3/ml ± 0.83) in 2002–2003.

In seasonal study for first year (2002–2003) the maximum aquatic fungi was observed in monsoon season (14 x 10^3/ml ± 0.57) followed by winter (12 x 10^3/ml ± 1.0) and summer (9 x 10^3/ml^3 ± 1.0). In 2003–2004 maximum aquatic fungi was observed in monsoon season (25 x 10^3/ml ± 4.72) followed by summer (16 x 10^3/ml^3 ± 4.61) and winter season (15 x 10^3/ml ± 4.58). Table 5B.10 and Figure 5B.11.

In an average calculation for 2002–2003 *Aspergillus* was observed maximum (4.66 x 10^3/ml ± 0.57) followed by *Penicillium* (4 x 10^3/ml^3 ± 1.0) and *Fusarium* (3 x 10^3/ml ± 1.0). In 2003–2004, again *Aspergillus* was found as dominant species (8.66 x 10^3/ml ± 3.05) followed by *Fusarium* (6 x 10^3/ml ± 5.29) and *Penicillium* (4 × 10^3/ml ± 4.58). During 2002–2003 *Aspergillus* was found maximum (4 × 10^3/ml ± 3.56) and *Fusarium* was found minimum (2 x 10^3/ml ± 5.63) in summer season. Both *Aspergillus* and *Penicillium* were observed highest (5.0 x 10^3/ml ± 4.63) (5.0 x 10^3/ml ± 2.90) in monsoon season respectively while *Fusarium was* observed least (4 x 10^3/ml ± 2.0). In winter season *Aspergillus* was found maximum (5 x 10^3/ml ± 7.66) and *Fusarium* was minimum (3 x 10^3/ml ± 4.16). In

Table 5B.9: Isolation of Bacterial ($ml^{-1} \times 10^3$) Culture from Sampling station A (2002-2004)

Bacteria	*2002-2003*				*2003-2004*			
	Summer	*Monsoon*	*Winter*	*Average*	*Summer*	*Monsoon*	*Winter*	*Average*
*Salmonella typhii**	4±2.50	25±3..95	8±0.75	12.33±11.15	6±1.75	8±2.50	0±.00	4.66±4.16
*Streptococcus facecalis**	6±3.50	32±2.95	0.00±0.00	12.66±17.00	4±1.15	40±3.76	2±0.00	15.33±21.38
*Aerobacter aerogens**	12±4.87	28±2.53	3±0.50	14.33±12.66	22±4.76	64±8.76	5±1.50	30.33±30.36
*Staphylococcus epidermidis**	2±0.50	17±1.75	0±0.00	6.33±9.29	8±1.50	16±3..96	0±0.00	8.00±8.00
*Staphylococcus aureus**	8±0.75	12±3.10	2±1.00	7.33±5.03	9±0.75	11±3.13	0±0.00	6.66±5.85
*Micrococcus luteus***	9±1.50	26±2..95	0±0.00	11.66±13.20	2±2.00	2±1;.00	0±0.00	1.33±1.15
*Bacillus subtilis***	5±1.32	16±3..33	9±1.75	10.00±5.56	5±1.50	12±3.12	1±0.50	6.00±5.56
*Escherichia coli**	6±0.50	12±1.54	4±0.98	7.33±4.16	2±1.11	31±2..95	2±0.75	11.66±16.74
*Pseudomonas aerogenosa**	13±2.36	21±1.50	0±0.00	11.33±10.59	5±0.67	5±0.50	0±0.00	3.33±2.88
Total l^{-1}	**65±3.63**	**189±7.19**	**26.0±3.51**	**93.33±85.11**	**63±6.10**	**189±20.31**	**10.0±1.6 9**	**87.33±91.94**

* Pathogen; ** Non pathogen; ± = Standard Deviation.

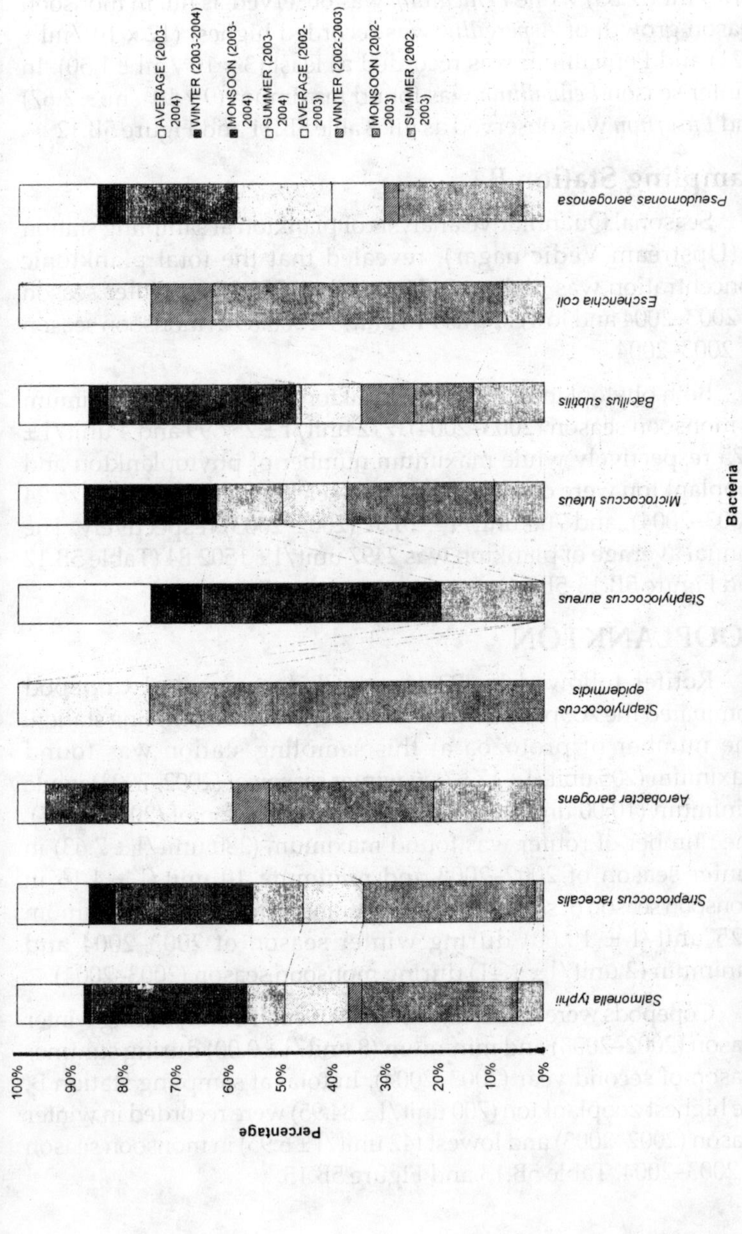

Figure 5B.10: Percentile Composition of Bacterial Culture at Sampling Station A (2002-2004)

2003–2004 summer's season observation revealed that growth of *Aspergillus* was optimum (8×10^3/ml ± 1.11) along with *Fusarium* (8×10^3/ml ± 7.53) while *Penicillium* was observed as nil. In monsoon season growth of *Aspergillus* was recorded highest (12×10^3/ml ± 4.21) and Penicillium was recorded as least (3×10^3/ml ± 1.50). In winter season *Penicillium* was found maximum (9×10^3/ml ± 3.67) and *Fusarium* was observed as nil. Table 5B.11 and Figure 5B.12

Sampling Station B

Seasonal Quantitative analysis of plankton at sampling station B (Upstream Vedic nagar), revealed that the total planktonic concentration was highest 5456 unit/l ± 3572.30 in winter season of 2003–2004 and lowest was 716 unit/l ± 500.63 in monsoon season of 2003–2004.

Both phytoplankton and zooplankton were observed minimum in monsoon season (2003–2004), 712 unit/l ± 257.99 and 4 unit/l ± 0.75 respectively while maximum number of phytoplankton and zooplankton were observed in winter season, 5254unit/l ± 1176.24 (2003–2004), and 700 unit/l ± 18.32 (2002–2003) respectively. The annual average of plankton was 2497 unit/l ± 1502.84 (Table 5B.12 and Figure 5B.13-5B.14).

ZOOPLANKTON

Rotifer followed by Protozoa, Cladocerans and Copepod dominated the zooplanktonic concentration at this sampling station. The number of protozoa at this sampling station was found maximum (205 unit/l ± 17.67) in winter season of (2002–2003) while minimum (10.00 unit/l ± 7.07) in monsoon season of (2003–2004). The number of rotifer was found maximum (280 unit/l ± 7.63) in winter season of 2002–2003 and minimum 10 unit/l ± 4.16 in monsoon season of same year. Cladocerans were observed maximum (125 unit/l ± 10.60) during winter season of 2003–2004 and minimum (2 unit/l ± 1.41) during monsoon season (2003–2004).

Copepods were found maximum (90 unit/l ± 3.11) during winter season (2002–2003) and minimum (8 unit/l ± 0.00) during summer season of second year (2003–2004). In total at sampling station B, the highest zooplankton (700 unit/l ± 84.95) were recorded in winter season (2002–2003) and lowest (42 unit/l ± 6.95) in monsoon season of 2003–2004. Table 5B.13 and Figure 5B.15.

Table 5B.10: Isolation of Fungus ($ml^{-1} \times 10^3$) from Sampling Station A (2002-2004)

Fungus	*2002-2003*				*2003-2004*			
	Summer	*Monsoon*	*Winter*	*Average*	*Summer*	*Monsoon*	*Winter*	*Average*
	9±1.0	14±0.57	12.0±1.0	11.66±0.83	16.0±4.61	25.0±4.72	15.0±4.58	18.66±2.33

± = Standard Deviation.

Table 5B.11: Isolation of Fungus ($ml^{-1} \times 10^3$) from Sampling Station A (2002-2004)

Fungus	*2002-2003*				*2003-2004*			
	Summer	*Monsoon*	*Winter*	*Average*	*Summer*	*Monsoon*	*Winter*	*Average*
Aspergillus	4.00±3.56	5.0±4.83	5.0±7.66	4.66±0.57	8.0±1.11	12±4.21	6±1.11	8.66±3.05
Penicillium	3.00±4.10	5.0±2.90	4.0±1.11	4.00±1.00	0±0.00	3±1.50	9.0±3.67	4.00±4.58
Fusarium	2.00±5.63	4.00±2.00	3.0±4.16	3.0±1.00	8±7.53	10±8.00	0±0.00	6±5.29
Total l^{-1}	9±1.0	14±0.57	12.0±1.0	11.66±2.51	16±4.61	25±4.72	15.0±4.58	18.66±5.50

± = Standard Deviation.

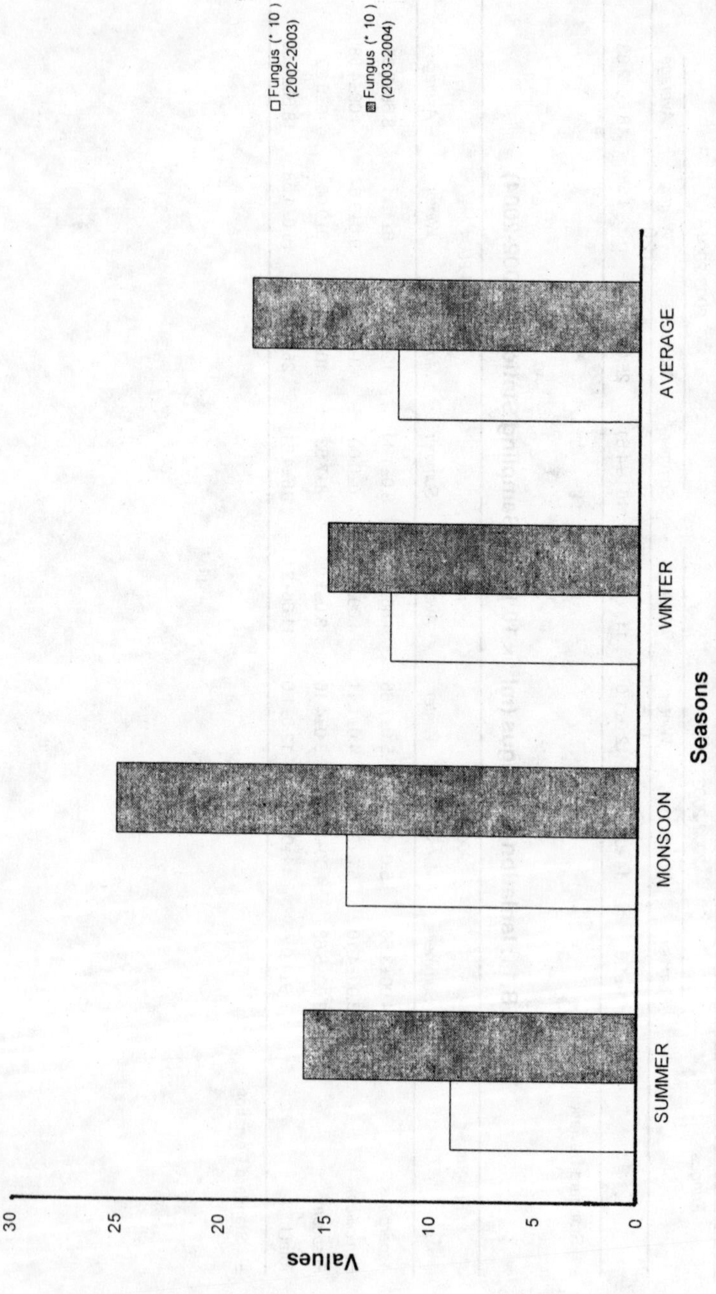

Fig 5B.11: Quantitative Fluctuation of Fungal Parameters at Sampling Station A (2002-2004)

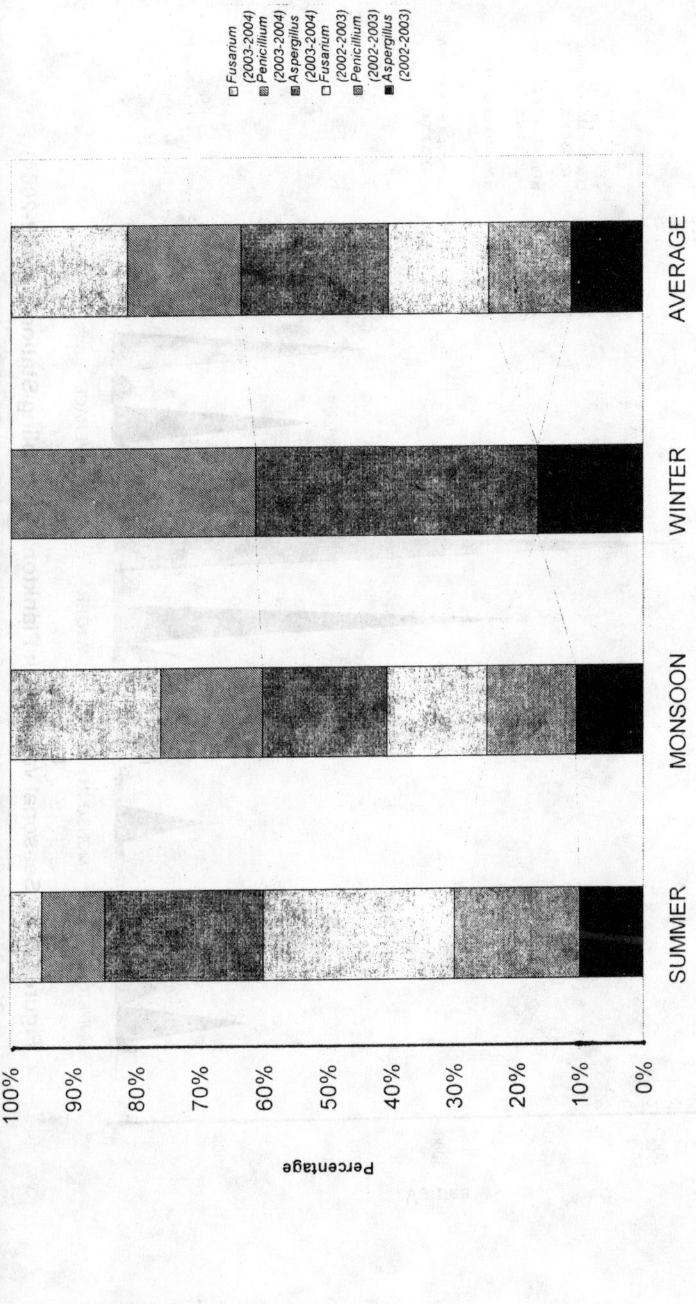

Figure 5B.12: Percentile Composition of Fungal Culture at Sampling Station A (2002-2004)

Figure 5B.13: Seasonal Variation in Plankton at Sampling Station B (2002-2004)

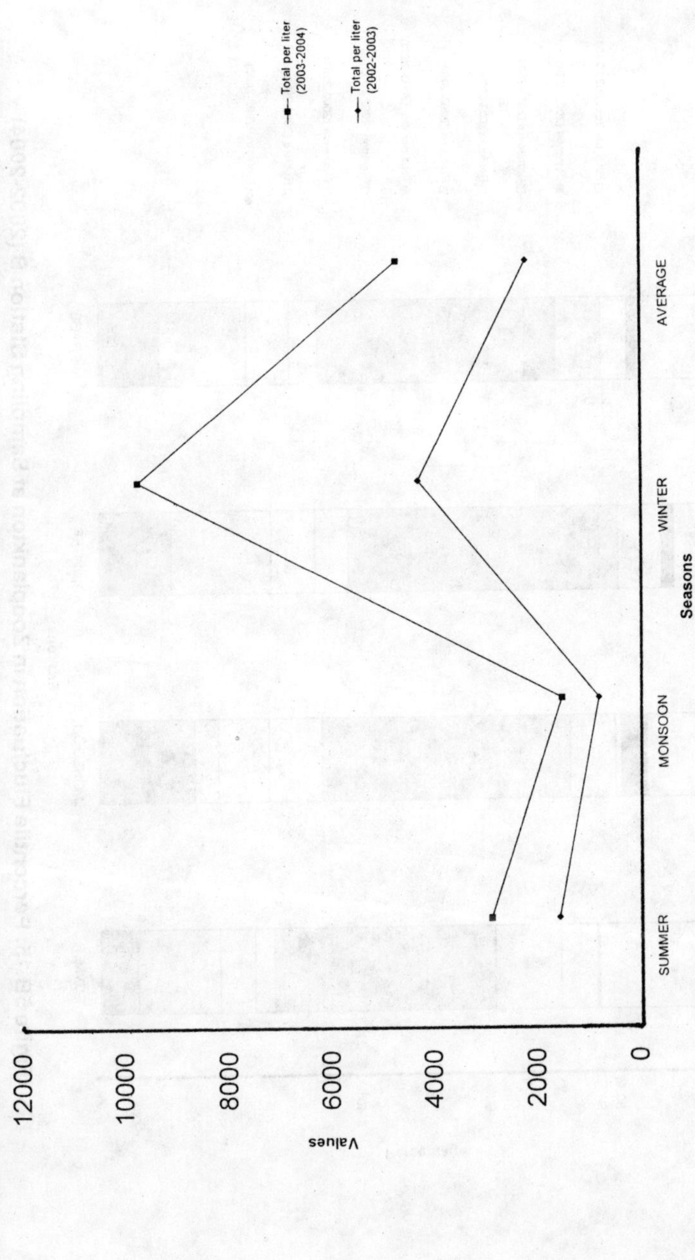

Figure 5B.14: Seasonal Variation in Total Plankton at Sampling Station B (2002-2004)

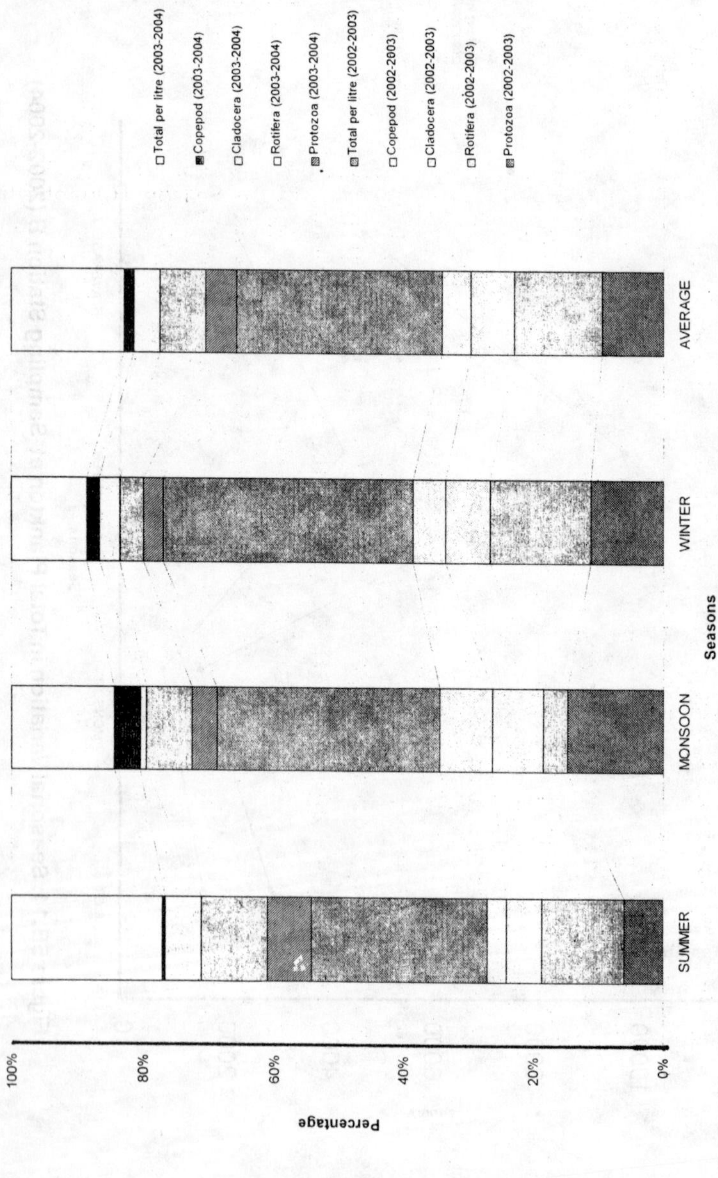

Figire 5B.15: Percentile Fluctuation in Zooplankton at Sampling Station B (2002-2004)

Table 5B.12: Seasonal Variations in Plankton Parameters (per liter) of River Suswa at Sampling Station B (2002-2004)

Plankton	2002-2003				2003-2004			
	Summer	*Monsoon*	*Winter*	*Average*	*Summer*	*Monsoon*	*Winter*	*Average*
Zooplankton	400.0±21.80	33±7.71	700±18.32	377.64±11.73	352±23.31	4±0.75	202±11.85	185.98±9.22
Phytoplankton	1167±197.27	771±154.94	3631±1091.24	1856.33±1549.60	968±143.96	712±257.99	5254±1176.24	2311.33±2551.63
Total	**1567±542.35**	**804±521.84**	**4331±2072.52**	**2233.97±1045.59**	**1320±435.57**	**716±500.63**	**5456±3572.30**	**2497±1502.84**

±= Standard deviation.

Table 5B.13: Quantitative Analysis of Zooplankton in Different Seasons of River Suswa at Sampling Station B (2002-2004)

Year	*Seasons*	*Protozoa*	*Rotifera*	*Cladocera*	*Copepod*	*Total l^{-1}*
2002-2003	Summer	95±10.60	198±9.64	86±18.38	48±2.95	427±64.15
	Monsoon	40.00±28.28	10.0±4.16	21±13.43	22±2.11	93±12.41
	Winter	205±17.67	280±7.63	125±10.60	90±3.11	700±84.95
	Average	113±84.01	162.66±138.48	77.33±52.53	53.33±34.31	377.64±49.83
2003-2004	Summer	107±12.02	160±25.16	85±3.53	8±0.00	360±63.08
	Monsoon	10±7.07	19±5.68	2±1.41	11±0.00	42±6.95
	Winter	53±12.02	65±12.74	55±10.60	35±3.54	208±12.48
	Average	56.66±48.60	81.33±71.90	47.33±42.02	18±14.79	203.32±26.16

±= Standard deviation.

Among average value *Arcella* was found dominating in the zooplankton, 2002–2003 (70 unit/l ± 34.68) followed by *Notholca* (59 unit/l ± 52.37), *Philodima* (55 unit/l ± 43.92), *Cyclops* (53.33 unit/l ± 34.31) *Keratella* (48.66 unit/l ± 42.45), *Amoeba* (43.33 unit/l ± 45.09), *Bosmina* (40 unit/l ± 26.45) and *Daphnia* (37.33 unit/l ± 31.46). While in second year 2003–2004, *Keratella* (40.33 unit/l ± 35.64) was found to be dominating followed by *Amoeba* (32.33 unit/l ± 31.08), *Bosmina* (26.66 unit/l ± 23.62), *Philodima* (26 unit/l ± 25.05), *Arcella* (24.33 unit/l ± 18.33), *Daphnia* (20.66 unit/l ± 19.00), *Cyclops* (18 unit/l ± 14.79), and *Notholca* (15 unit/l ± 13.00). Table 5B.14 and Figure 5B.16.

PHYTOPLANKTON

Among phytoplankton Bacillariophyceae was found dominating in followed by Chlorophyceae and Myxophyceae for first year (2002–2003) and Chlorophyceae followed by Bacillariophyceae and Myxophyceae in second year (2003–2004). In both the years Myxophyceae was found to be least in number. Bacillariophyceae was found maximum (2138 unit/l ± 62.50) in winter season (2002–2003) and minimum (22unit/l ± 2.91) in monsoon season of 2003–2004.Chlorophyceae was found maximum (2786 unit/l ± 19.85) in winter season of 2003–2004 and minimum (219 unit ± 12.32) in monsoon season of 2002–2003. Myxophyceae was found to be highest (486 unit/l ± 48.77) in summer season of 2002–2003 while minimum (8 unit/l ± 2.08) in winter season of same year *i.e.*, 2002 –2003 (Table 5B.15 and Figure 5B.17).

Among Bacillariophyceae *Diatoms* was found to be dominating (138 unit/l ± 165.05) in 2002–2003 followed by *Frustulia* (102.66 unit/l ± 5.75), *Cocconeis* (95 unit/l ± 86.65), *Fragelaria* (91 unit/l ± 69.15), *Cymbella* (83.66 unit/l ± 115.15), *Pinnularia* (78 unit/l ± 93.35), *Cyclotella* (76.66 unit/l ± 117.54), *Amphora* (67 unit/l ± 45.53), *Gomphonema* (59.66 unit/l ± 83.42), *Nitzschia* (57.33 unit/l ± 82.37), *Navicula* (53.33 unit/l ± 57.95) and *Achnanthes* (53.33 unit/l ± 46.36). In second year *i.e.* 2003–2004, *Diatoms* (106 unit/l ± 131.59) was found to be dominating followed by *Cyclotella* (80.33 unit/l ± 125.54), *Pinnularia* (76.33 unit/l ± 112.07), *Amphora* (73 unit/l ± 118.69), *Achnanthes* (67.66 unit/l ± 110.29), *Cymbella* (66.66 unit/l ± 86.93), *Cocconeis* (61.33 unit/l ± 102.78) *Gomphonema* (49.33 ± 83.72), *Frustulia* (48 unit/l ± 57.68), *Fragelaria* (46 unit/l ± 55.74), *Nitzschia*

Table 5B.14: Quantitative Analysis of Zooplankton in Different Seasons of River Suswa at Sampling Station B (2002-2004)

Year	*Seasons*	*Protozoa*		*Rotifera*			*Cladocera*		*Copepod*	*Total* l^{-1}
		Arcella	*Amoeba*	*Keratella*	*Philodima*	*Notholca*	*Daphnia*	*Bosmina*	*Cyclops*	
2002-2003	Summer	55±8.76	40±4.94	59±7.33	62±12.48	77±3.89	56±4.44	30±0.50	48±2.95	427±14.28
	Monsoon	40±0.00	0±0.00	2±1.00	8±2.13	0±0.00	1.0±0.00	20±0.00	22±2.11	93.0±14.50
	Winter	115±16.41	90±3.39	85±4.43	95±3.51	100±6.87	55±7.14	70±4.32	90±3.11	700±18.32
	Average	70±34.68	43.33±45.09	48.66±42.45	55.00±43.92	59.00±52.37	37.33±31.46	40±26.45	53.33±34.31	466.65±10.81
2003-2004	Summer	45±4.75	62±3.63	80±7.48	50±2.06	30±3.13	40±3.94	45±4.87	8±0.00	352±23.31
	Monsoon	10±0.00	0±0.00	11±0.00	0.0.00	8±0.00	2±0.00	0±0.00	11±0.00	42±5.20
	Winter	18±2.98	35±3.11	30±2.10	28±2.97	7±0.00	20±2.11	35±3.36	35±3.54	2.08±11.85
	Average	24.33±18.33	32.33±31.08	40.33±35.64	26.00±25.05	15±13.0	20.66±19.00	26.66±23.62	18±14.79	203.31±8.10

±= Standard Deviation.

Table 5B.15: Comparitive Analysis of Seasonal Variation among Phytoplankton of River Suswa at Sampling Station B (2002-2004)

Year	*Seasons*	*Bacillariophyceae* l^{-1}	*Chlorophyceae* l^{-1}	*Myxophyceae* l^{-1}	*Total* l^{-1}
2002-2003	Summer	519±21.05	162±16.09	486±48.77	1167±197.27
	Monsoon	210±22.15	219±12.32	430±31.64	771±154.94
	Winter	2138±62.50	885±39.28	8±2.08	3631±1091.24
	Average	955.63±24.80	515.31±25.0	307.99±25.27	1856.33±1549.60
2003-2004	Summer	225.0±16.25	788±37.71	255±27.73	968±143.96
	Monsoon	22±2.91	673±26.92	167±8.02	712±257.79
	Winter	1996±54.17	2786±19.85	472±81.05	5254±1176.24
	Average	747.64±20.42	1415.63±10.28	297.99±36.62	2311.33±2551.63

±= Standard Deviation.

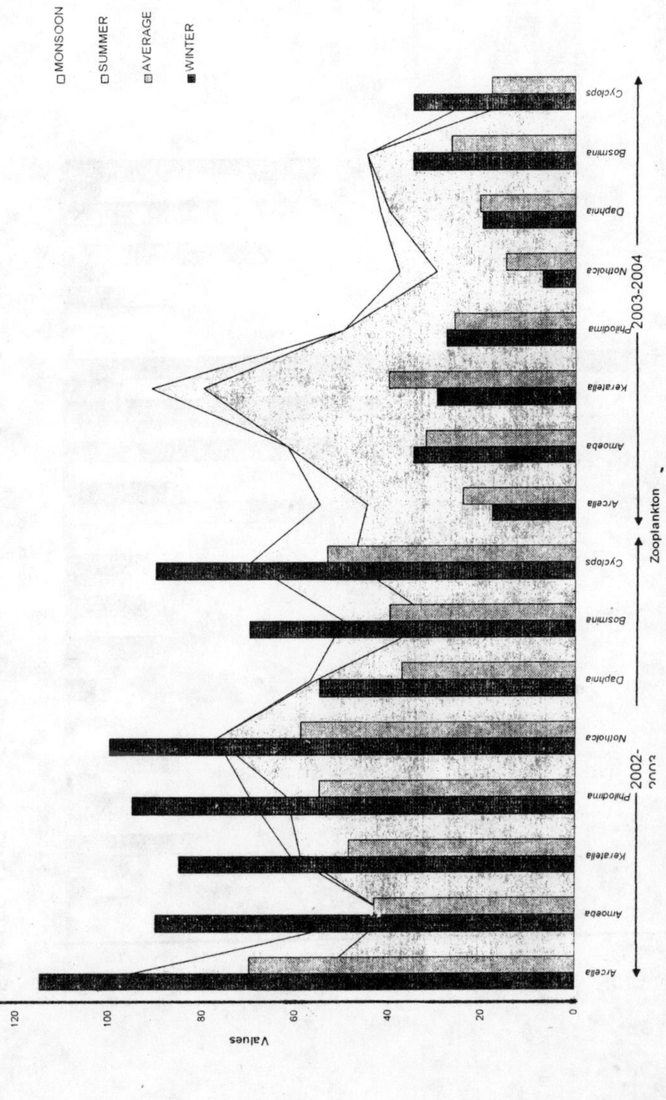

Figure 5B.16: Seasonal Fluctuations in Zooplankton at Sampling Station B (2002-2004)

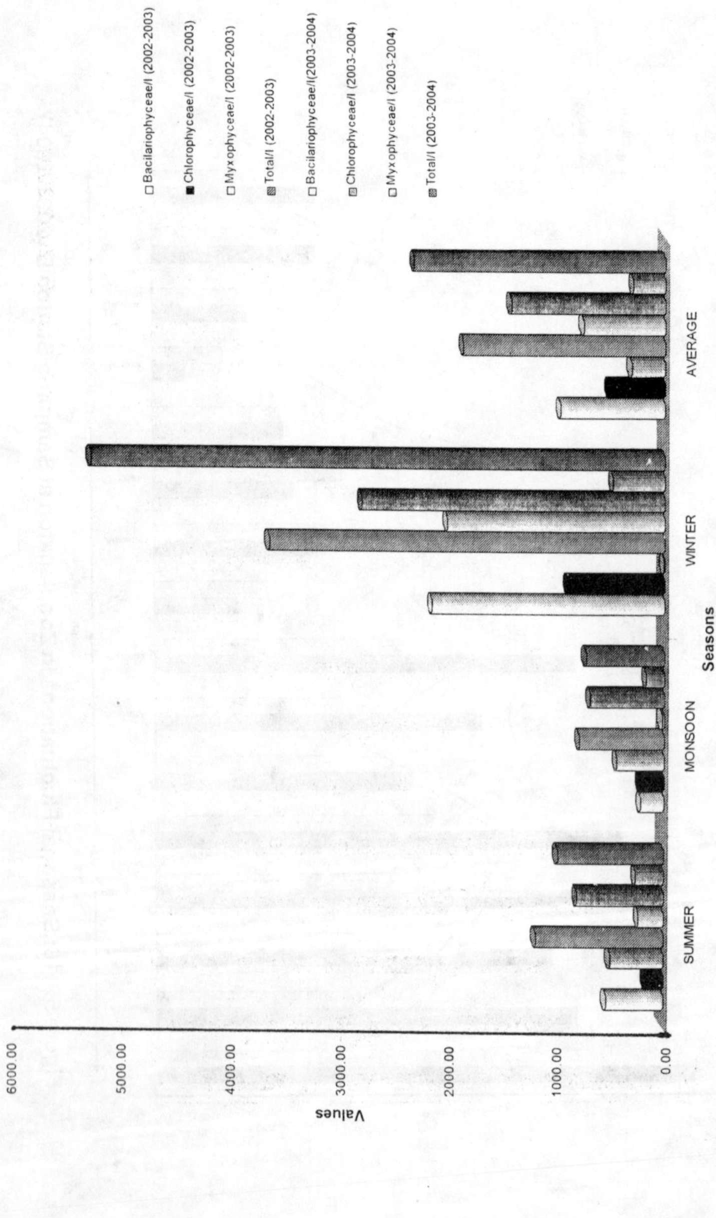

Figire 5B.17: Percentile Fluctuation in Phytoplankton at Sampling Station B (2002-2004)

(40 unit/l ± 50.71) and *Navicula* (33 unit/l ± 54.58) (Table 5B.16 and Figure 5B.18).

A great fluctuation among Bacillariophyceae was observed during seasonal study of Suswa river at sampling station B. In 2002–2003-summer season, *Fragelaria* was found maximum (80 unit/l ± 5.86) and *Cyclotella and Nitzschia* was found minimum (18 unit/l ± 2.11) and (18 unit/ltr ± 1.98) in monsoon season *Diatoms* were found highest (30 unit/l ± 2.96) while *Cymbella, Cyclotella and Gomphonema* were found to be nil. In winter again maximum concentration was observed for *Diatoms* (328 unit/l ± 28.08) and *Achnanthes* was found to be minimum (96 unit/l ± 5.67). In 2003–2004 summer, *Diatoms* was found maximum (52 unit/l ± 4.00) while *Gomponema* and *Navicula* were recorded nil. In monsoon season again *Diatoms* were found highest (10 unit/l ± 1.50) while *Cymbella, Cyclotella, Cocconeis, Fragelaria, Frustulia, and Pinnularia* were found to be nil. In winter season *Diatoms* were found maximum (256 unit/l ± 38.46), while *Navicula* was found minimum (96 unit/l ± 3.56).

Among Chlorophyceae during 2002–2003 *Zygnema* (96.33 unit/l ± 123.08), was observed as dominating species followed by *Spirogyra* (78 unit/l ± 98.07), *Schizogonium* (64.66 unit/l ± 95.70), *Ulothrix* (61.33 unit/l ± 50.29), *Closterium* (56.66 unit/l ± 48.75), *Chlorella* (56 unit/l ± 62.86), *Cosmerium* (50.33 unit/l ± 47.35), *Cladophora* (48 unit/l ± 47.28 and *Oedogonium* (4.00 unit/l ± 6.92). During 2003–2004 *Zygnema* (172.66 unit/l ± 143.19) were found as dominant species followed by *Cladophora* (168 unit/l ± 117.32), *Schizogonium* (163.66 unit/l ± 146.20), *Chlorella* (159.66 unit/l ± 144.31), *Oedogonium* (159.66 unit/l ± 128.72), *Cosmerium* (153 unit/l ± 114.4) *Ulothrix* (152 unit/l ± 160.36), *Closterium* (146.33 unit/l ± 130.29), *Spirogyra* (140.66 unit/l ± 129.71).

A great variation in seasonal values of Chlorophyceae was noted during the course of study at sampling station B, during first year 2002–2003 *Ulothrix* was found maximum (44 unit/l ± 5.88) and *Zygnema* was found as nil in summer season. While in monsoon season *Zygnema* was found to be highest (54 unit/l ± 6.68) and *Chlorella* was recorded as minimum (8 unit/l ± 0.00). In winter season *Zygnema* was revealed maximum (135 unit/l ± 21.24) and *Oedogonium* was recorded as nil. While in second year 2003–2004 *Chlorella* was found maximum (142 unit/l ± 3.20) and *Ulothrix* was found minimum (36 unit/l ± 5.66), in summer season. In monsoon

Table 5B.16: Quantitativeanalysis of Seasonal Variation Among Bacillariophyceae of River Suswa at Sampling Station B (2002-2004)

	Seasons	*Achnanthes*	*Amphora*	*Cocconeis*	*Cymbella*	*Cyclotella*	*Diatoms*	*Fragelaria*
2002-2003	Summer	60±2.01	75±6.11	48±7.46	36±3.19	18±2.11	56±1.05	80±5.86
	Monsoon	4±1.03	18±0.98	42±3.16	0±0.00	0±0.00	30±2.96	28±1.85
	Winter	96±5.67	108±14.11	195±20.19	215±12.62	212±14.97	328±28.08	165±15.97
	Average	53.33±46.36	67±45.53	95±86.65	83.66±115.15	76.66±117.54	138±165.05	91±69.15
2003-2004								
	Summer	6±1.19	8±0.78	4±0.50	35±3.01	16±2.98	52±4.00	30±6.56
	Monsoon	2±0.03	1±0.00	0±.00	0±0.00	0±0.00	10±1.50	0±0.00
	Winter	195±12.11	210±11.00	180±18.19	165±17.55	225±21.24	256±38.46	108±16.29
	Average	67.66±110.29	73±118.69	61.33±102.78	66.66±86.93	80.33±125.54	106±131.59	46±55.74

	Seasons	*Frustulia*	*Gomphonema*	*Navicula*	*Nitzschia*	*Pinnularia*	*Total l*$^{-1}$
2002-2003	Summer	26±6.76	24±3.21	36±4.11	18±1.98	42±3.18	519±21.05
	Monsoon	72±4.58	0±0.00	6±3.12	2±0.86	8±0.11	210±22.15
	Winter	210±16.00	155±24.01	118±13.11	152±8.87	184±6.34	2138±62.50
	Average	102.66±05.75	59.66±83.42	53.33±57.97	57.33±82.37	78±93.35	955.63±24.80
2003-2004	Summer	32±7.89	0±000	0±0.00	18±1.00	27±3.26	2256.0±16.25
	Monsoon	0±0.00	2±0.00	3±0.75	4±1.36	0±0.00	22±2.91
	Winter	112±8.89	146±6.56	96±3.56	98±4.80	205±13.92	1996±54.17
	Average	48±57.68	49.33±83.72	33±54.58	40±50.71	76.33±112.07	174.64±20.42

±= Standard Deviation.

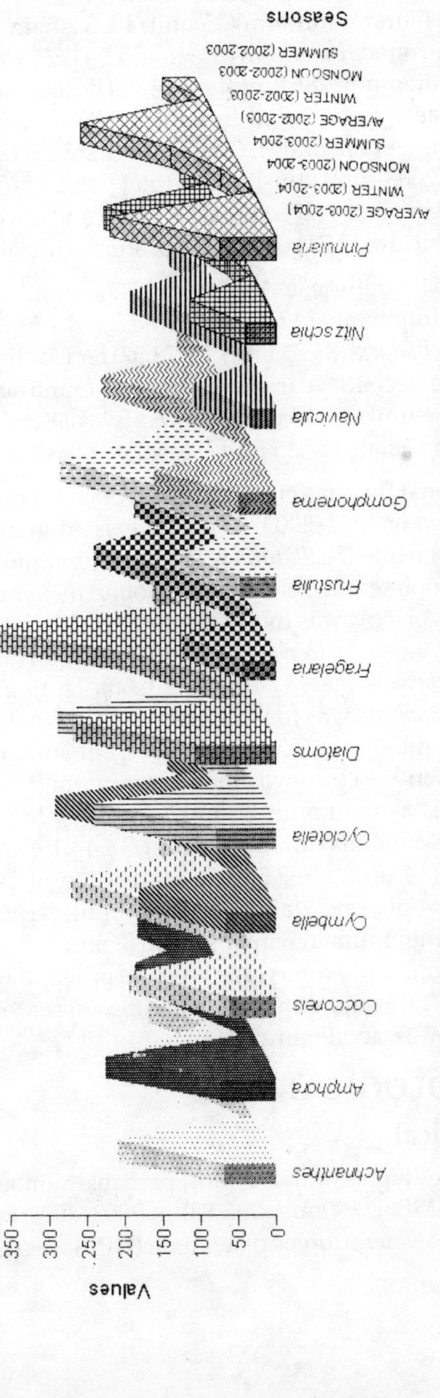

Figure 5B.18: Quantitative Fluctuation of Bacillariophyceae at Sampling Station B (2002-2004)

season, *Schizigonium* was found maximum (115 unit/l ± 12.64) while *Chlorella* was found minimum (25 unit/l ± 3.20). In winter season *Zygnema* were found maximum (338 unit/l ± 11.87) while *Cosmerium* were found minimum (285 unit/l ± 16.44). The total highest value of Chlorophyceae was recorded in winter (885 unit/l ± 39.28) and lowest in summer (162 unit/l ± 16.09) for first year (2002–2003) for second year (2003–2004) the highest total value of Chlorophyceae was recorded in winter (2786 unit/l ± 19.85) and lowest in summer season (788unit/l ± 37.71) (Table 5B.17 and Figure 5B.19).

Among Myxophyceae *Anacystis* (131.66 unit/l ± 113.80) was recorded as dominant species, followed by *Anabena* (91 unit/l ± 76.62) and *Oscillatoria* (85.33 unit/1 ± 73.52) and for first year (2002–2003). During second year *Anacystis* was found as dominating species (124.66 unit/l ± 76.06) followed by *Anabena* (116 unit/l ± 75.97) and *Oscillatoria* (57.33 unit/l ± 5.85).

For seasonal fluctuation of Myxophyceae it is revealed that in summer season of 2002–2003, *Anacystis* existed in maximum (215 unit/l ± 14.28) while *Oscillatoria* was found minimum (119unit/l ± 8.92). In monsoon season *Anacystis* was found maximum (178 unit/l ± 15.61) and *Anabena* was found minimum (116 unit/l ± 18.24). In winter season, again *Anabena* was found maximum (5 unit/l ± 0.00) and *Oscillatoria* was least (1 unit/l ± 0.30). During second year (2003–2004), *Anabena* was found maximum (102 unit/l ± 8.76) and *Oscillatoria* as minimum (53 unit/l ± 6.66) in summer season. In monsoon season *Anacystis* was found maximum (64 unit/l ± 3.59) and *Oscillatoria* as minimum (5 unit/l ± 12.99). In winter season *Anacystis* was found maximum (210 unit/l ± 14.16) and *Oscillatoria* as minimum (64 unit/l ± 7.59). In total value of 2002–2003 the maximum Myxophyceae was recoded in summer season (486 unit/l ± 48.77) and minimum in winter season (8 unit/l ± 2.08). In 2003–2004 the maximum Myxophyceae were recorded in winter season (472 unit/l ± 81.05) and minimum in monsoon season (167 unit/l ± 8.02 (Tabie 5B.18 and Figure 5B.20).

MICROBIOLOGICAL

Bacteriological

The average highest value of Most probable number (MPN) was found as (305 MPN/100ml ± 268.88) in 2003–2004 while average highest value of Heterotrophic plate count (HPC) was found as (64.33

Table 5B.17: Quantitative Analysis of Seasonal Variation Among Chlorophyceae of River Suswa at Sampling Station B (2002-2004)

Year	*Seasons*	*Closterium*	*Cosmerium*	*Chlorella*	*Cladophora*	*Oedogonium*	*Schizogonium*	*Spirogyra*	*Ulothrix*	*Zygnema*	*Total* l^{-1}
2002-2003	Summer	38±2.96	24±5.38	12±3.95	14±2.75	0±0.00	4±1.50	26±3.97	44±5.88	0±0.00	162±16.09
	Monsoon	10±0.00	12±0.50	8±0.00	28±1.67	12±4.69	15±3.96	18±2.54	22±1.77	54±6.68	219±12.32
	Winter	12±7.97	105±6.60	128±7.50	102±5.80	0±0.00	105±28.62	90±15.87	108±11.50	135±21.24	885±39.28
	Average	56.66±48.75	50.33±47.35	56.0±62.86	48±47.28	4±6.92	64.66±95.70	78±98.07	61.33±50.29	96.33±123.08	515.31±25.0
2003-2004	Summer	92±8.80	76±5.84	142±3.20	136±2.10	114±1.69	48±3.20	56±4.98	36±5.66	85±2.57	788±37.71
	Monsoon	52±2.59	98±3.66	25±3.20	70.00±0.00	60.00±0.00	115.0±12.64	76±4.08	85±5.21	92±3.11	673±26.92
	Winter	295±15.47	285±16.44	312±17.92	298±14.17	305±11.56	328±13.28	290±14.10	335±10.97	338±11.87	2786±19.85
	Average	146.33±130.29	153.0±114.4	159.66±144.31	168±117.32	159.66±128.72	163.66±146.20	140.66±129.71	152±160.36	172.66±143.19	1415.63±10.28

±= Standard Deviation.

Table 5B.18: Quantitative Analysis of Seasonal Variation Among Myxophyceaee of River Suswa at Sampling Station B (2002-2004)

Year	*Seasons*	*Anacystis*	*Anabena*	*Oscillatoria*	*Total* l^{-1}
2002-2003	Summer	215±14.28	152±12.11	119±8.92	486±48.77
	Monsoon	178±15.61	116±18.24	136±16.66	430±31.64
	Winter	2±0.50	5±0.00	1±0.30	8±2.08
	Average	131.66±113.80	91±76.62	85.33±73.52	307.99±25.27
2003-2004	Summer	100±10.69	102±8.76	53±6.66	255±27.73
	Monsoon	64±3.59	48±4.87	5±12.99	167±8.02
	Winter	210±14.16	198±7.59	64±7.59	472±81.05
	Average	124.66±76.06	116±75.97	57.33±5.85	297.99±36.62

±= Standard Deviation.

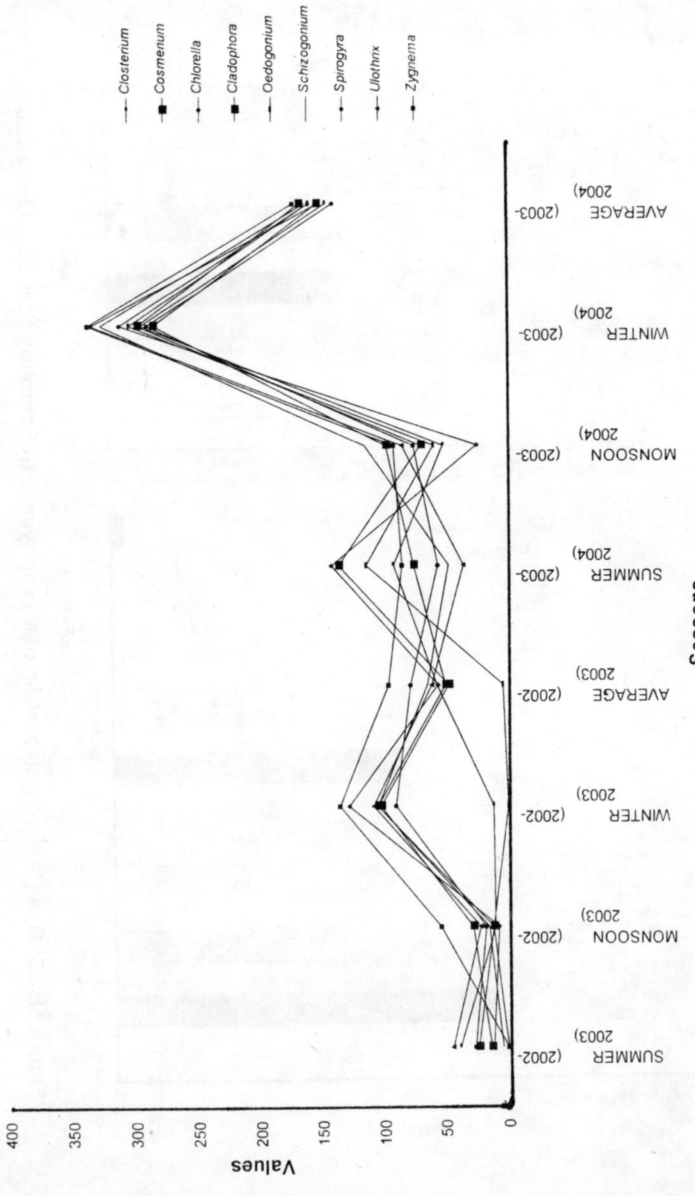

Figure 5B.19: Quantitative Fluctuation of Chlorophyceae at Sampling Station B (2002-2004)

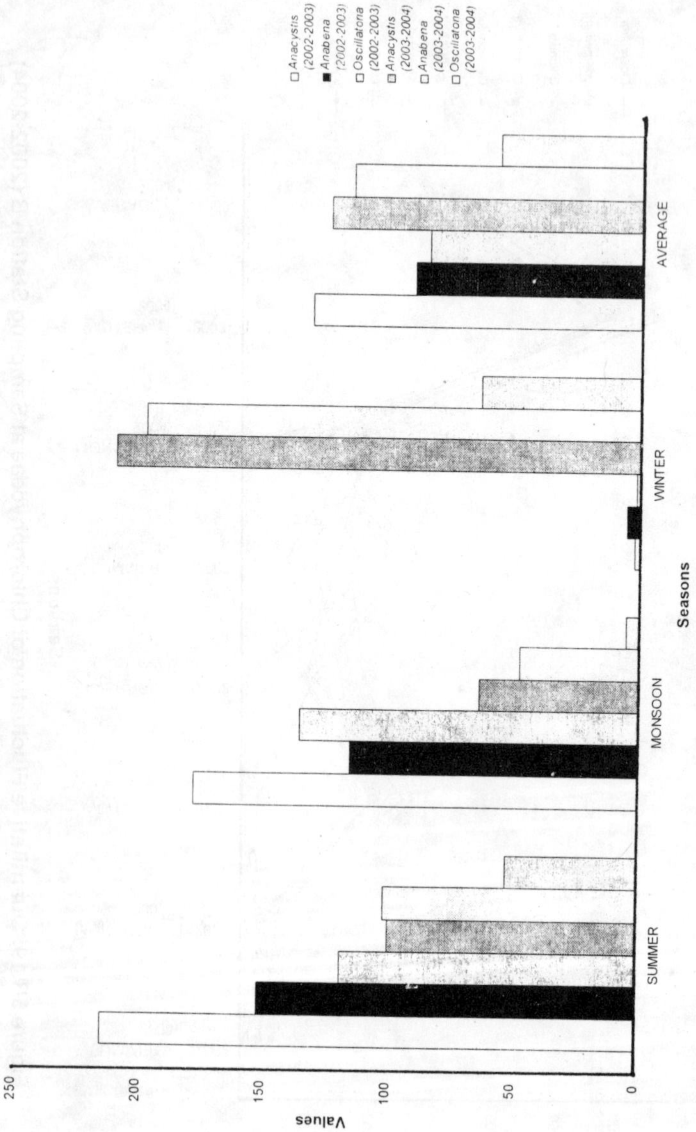

Figure 5B.20: Quantitative Fluctuation of Myxophyceae at Sampling Station B (2002-2004)

HPC/ml (x10^3) ± 5.57) in 2002–2003. During course of study for first year (2002–2003) at Upstream Vedic nagar the MPN and HPC were found maximum (280MPN/100ml ± 28.24), [131 HPC/ml (X10^3) ± 9.34] in monsoon season respectively. While lowest (65 MPN/100ml ± 7.76) MPN was found in summer season and lowest [23.0 HPC/ml (X10^3) ± 3.20] HPC was found in winter season. For second year (2003–2004) again monsoon season showed maximum (615MPN/100ml ± 38.76), [125 HPC/ml (X10^3) ± 12.45] MPN and HPC respectively. MPN was recorded minimum (135 MPN/100ml ± 42.48) in winter and HPC was recorded minimum [25.0 HPC/ml (X10^3) ± 2.86] in winter season. Table 5B.19 and Figure 5B.21.

Bacterial cultures isolated from sampling station B (Upstream Vedic nagar) revealed that in 2002–2003 *Aerobacter aerogens* and *Bacillus subtilis* were found maximum (12 x 10^3/ml ± 1.31), (12 x 10^3/ml ± 3.36) respectively and *Staphyloccus epidermidis* and *Staphylococcus aureus* was found as nil in summer season. In monsoon season *Escherichia coli* was found maximum (28 x 10^3/ml ± 5.76) while *Staphylococcus aureus* was found as nil. In winter season *Bacillus subtilis* was found maximum (9 x 10^3/ml ± 1.76) while *Streptocococcus facecalis, Staphylococcus aureus, Micrococcus luteus*, and *Staphyloccus epidermidis* and were found nil. In 2003–2004 summer's season *Staphylococcus aureus* was found to be maximum (12 x 10^3/ml ± 0.92) while *Staphyloccus epidermidis Escherichia coli*and *Aerobacter aerogens* were found as nil. In monsoon season *Bacillus subtilis* was found to be maximum (32 x 10^3/ml ± 3.36) while *Escherichia coli, Staphyloccus epidermidis, Escherichia coli and Micrococcus luteus* were found as minimum. In winter season *Micrococcus luteus* was recorded maximum (8 x 10^3/ml ± 1.73) while *Staphylococcus epidermidis, Escherichia coli* and *Aerobacter aerogens* were recorded nil.

On an average calculation for 2002–2003 *Escherichia coli* was observed as dominant species (12.66 x 10^3/ml ± 13.31) followed by *Aerobacter aerogens* (11.33 x 10^3/ml ± 7.20), *Bacillus subtilis* (10.33 x 10^3/ml ± 1.52), *Salmonella typhii* (10 x 10^3/ml ± 12.16), *Pseudomonas aeroginosa* (7.66 x 10^3/ml ± 8.96), *Streptococcus facecalis* (7.00 x 10^3/ml ± 11.26), *Micrococcus luteus* (4 x 10^3/ml ± 4.58), *Staphylococcus epidermidis* (1.33 x 10^3/ml ± 2.30) and *Staphylococcus aureus* (0 x 10^3/ml ± 0.00). In 2003–2004 *Staphylococcus aureus* (15.33 x 10^3/ml ± 11.37), was noted maximum followed by *Bacillus subtilis* (12 x 10^3/ml ± 17.34), *Pseudomonas aeroginosa* (11.33 x 10^3/ml ± 6.42), *Salmonella*

Table 5B.19: Quantitative Analysis of Seasonal Variation in Bacteriological Parameters of River Suswa at Sampling Station B (2002-2004)

Year	*Seasons*	*MPN/100 ml*	*HPC/ml* $(X10^3)$ $(x10^3)$
2002-2003	Summer	65±7.76	39±4.60
	Monsoon	280±28.24	131±9.34
	Winter	95±60.48	23±3.20
	Average	146.66±116.44	64.31±4.48
2003-2004	Summer	165±3.32	43±5.28
	Monsoon	615±38.76	125±12.45
	Winter	135±42.48	25±2.86
	Average	305±268.88	64.33±5.57

±= Standard Deviation.

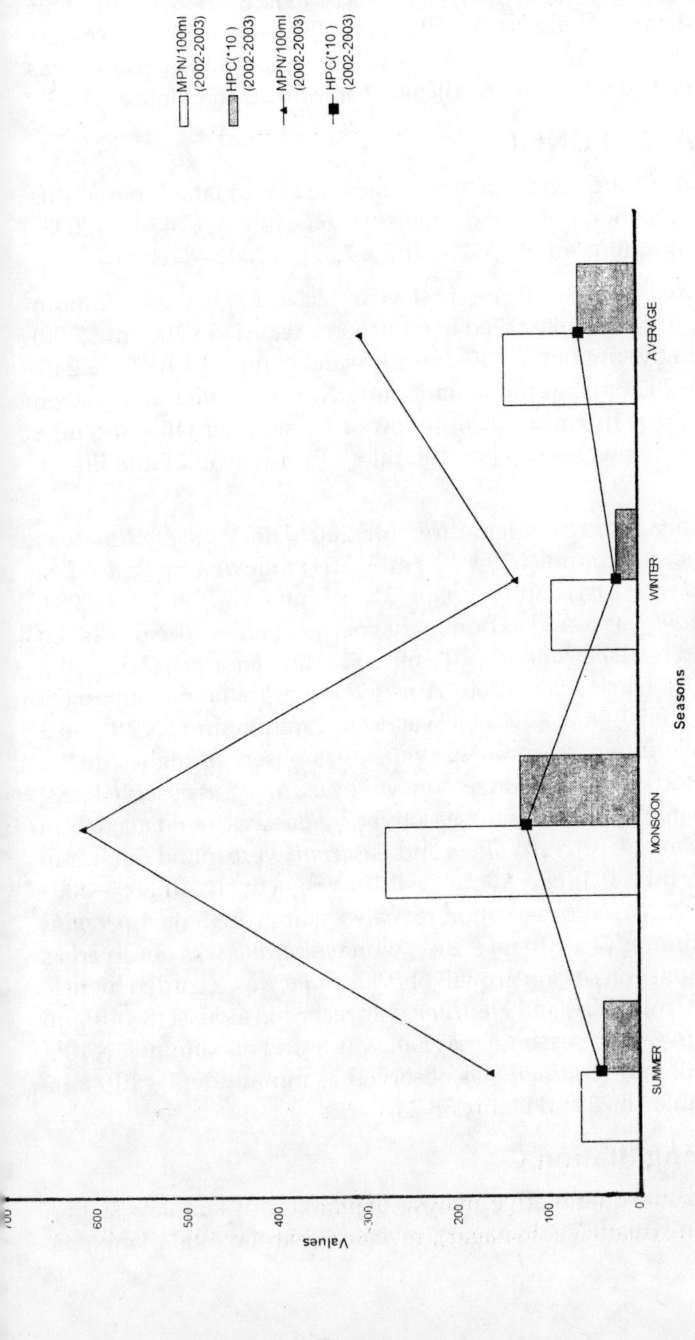

Figure 5B.21: Quantitative Fluctuation of Bacterial Parameters at Sampling Station B (2002-2004)

typhii (10.33×10^3/ml ± 12.09), *Streptococcus facecalis* (8.33×10^3/ml ± 6.80), *Micrococcus luteus* (4×10^3/ml ± 4.00), *Aerobacter aerogens* (3×10^3/ml ± 5.19), *Escherichia coli* (0×10^3/ml ± 0.00) and *Staphylococcus epidermidis* (0×10^3/ml ± 0.00), and Table 5B.20 and Figure 5B. 22

AQUATIC FUNGI

During the course of study the average aquatic fungi at this sampling station was found highest (23.66×10^3/ml ± 24.54) in 2003–2004 and minimum (9.33×10^3/ml ± 7.57) in 2002–2003.

In seasonal study for first year (2002–2003) the maximum aquatic fungi was observed in monsoon season (18×10^3/ml ± 2.00) followed by summer (6×10^3/ml ± 1.0) and winter (4×10^3/ml ± 2.0). In 2003–2004 maximum aquatic fungi was observed in monsoon season (52×10^3/ml ± 10.06) followed by summer (10×10^3/ml ± 3.51) and winter season (9×10^3/ml ± 1.0). Table 5B.21 and Figure 5B.23.

In an average calculation for 2002–2003 *Aspergillus* was observed maximum (4.33×10^3/ml ± 3.21) followed by *Penicillium* (3×10^3/ml ± 2.64) and *Fusarium* (2×10^3/ml ± 1.73). In 2003–2004, *Penicillium* was found as dominant species (11.33×10^3/ml ± 14.43) followed by *Aspergillus* (9×10^3/ml ± 6.24) and *Fusarium* (3.33×10^3/ml ± 4.16). During 2002–2003 *Aspergillus* was found maximum (3×10^3/ml ± 0.50) and *Fusarium* was found minimum (1×10^3/ml ± 0.00) in summer season. *Aspergillus* was observed highest (8.0×10^3/ml ± 2.31) in monsoon season while *Fusarium was* observed least (4×10^3/ml ± 2.11). In winter season *Aspergillus* was found maximum (2×10^3/ml ± 1.10), *Penicillium* and *Fusarium* were found minimum (1×10^3/ml ± 0.3) (1×10^3/ml ± 0.10) respectively. In 2003–2004 summer's season observation revealed that growth of *Aspergillus* was optimum (7×10^3/ml ± 2.61) while *Fusarium* was observed as nil. In monsoon season growth of *Penicillium* was recorded highest (28×10^3/ml ± 6.54) and *Fusarium* was recorded as least (8×10^3/ml ± 2.11). In winter season *Aspergillus* was found maximum (4×10^3/ml ± 1.10) and *Fusarium* was observed as minimum (2×10^3/ml ± 0.78). Table 5B.22 and Figure 5B.24.

Sampling Station C

Seasonal quantitative analysis of plankton at sampling station C (Down stream Vedic nagar), revealed that the total planktonic

Table 5B.20: Isolation of Bacterial ($ml^{-1} \times 10^3$) Culture from Sampling Station B (2002-2004)

Bacteria	*2002-2003*				*2003-2004*			
	Summer	*Monsoon*	*Winter*	*Average*	*Summer*	*Monsoon*	*Winter*	*Average*
*Salmonella typhii**	4±2.15	24±7.89	2±0.75	10.00±12.16	6±1.39	24±2.78	1±0.00	10.33±12.09
*Streptococcus facecalis**	1±0.00	20±2.33	0±0.00	7.00±11.26	6±0.65	16±4.15	3±1.55	8.33±6.80
*Aerobacter aerogens**	12±1. 31	18±2.10	4±1.30	11.33±7.20	0±0.00	9±1.50	0±0.00	3.0±5.19
*Staphylococcus epidermidis**	0±0.00	4±0.00	0±0.00	1.33±2.30	0±0.00	0±0.00	0±0.00	0±0.00
*Staphylococcus aureus**	0±0.00	0±0.00	0±0.00	0.00±0.00	12±0.92	28±6.36	6±1.37	15.33±11.37
*Micrococus luteus***	3±1.50	9±2.56	0±0.00	4.00±4.58	4±0.33	0±0.00	8±1.73	4±4.00
*Bacillus subtilis***	12±3.36	10±2.25	9±1.76	10.33±1.52	1±0.00	32±3.36	3±0.50	12.00±17.34
*Escherichia coli**	4.1±0.11	28±5.76	6±1.50	12.66±13.31	0±0.00	0±0.00	0±0.00	0.00±0.00
*Pseudomonas aerogenosa**	3±0.76	18±0.90	2±0.11	7.66±8.96	14±2.16	16±3.33	4±1.50	11.33±6.42
Total l^{-1}	39±4.60	131±9.34	23±3.20	64.31±4.48	43±5.28	125±12.45	25±2.86	64.33±5.57

*: Pathogen; **: Non pathogen; ±: Standard Deviation.

Table 5B.21: Isolation of fungus ($ml^{-1} \times 10^3$) from Sampling station B (2002-2004)

Fungus	2002-2003				2003-2004			
	Summer	*Monsoon*	*Winter*	*Average*	*Summer*	*Monsoon*	*Winter*	*Average*
	6.0±1.0	18±2.00	4±2.00	9.33±7.57	10.0±3.51	52±10.06	9±1.0	23.66±24.54

±: Standard Deviation.

Table 5B.22 : I solution of fungus ($ml^{-1} \times 10^3$) from Sampling station B (2002-2004)

Fungus	2002-2003				2003-2004			
	Summer	*Monsoon*	*Winter*	*Average*	*Summer*	*Monsoon*	*Winter*	*Average*
Aspergillus	3.00±0.50	8±2.31	2±1.10	4.33±3.21	7.0±2.61	16±3.97	4±1.10	9±6.24
Penicillium	2±0.76	6±3.63	1±0.30	3±2.64	3±1.03	28±6.54	3±1.03	11.33±14.43
Fusarium	1±0.00	4±2.11	1±0.10	2±1.73	0±0.00	8±2.11	2±0.78	3.33±4.16
Total I-1	**6±1.0**	**18±2.00**	**4±2.0**	**9.33±7.57**	**10±3.51**	**52±10.06**	**9±1.00**	**23.66±24.54**

±: Standard Deviation.

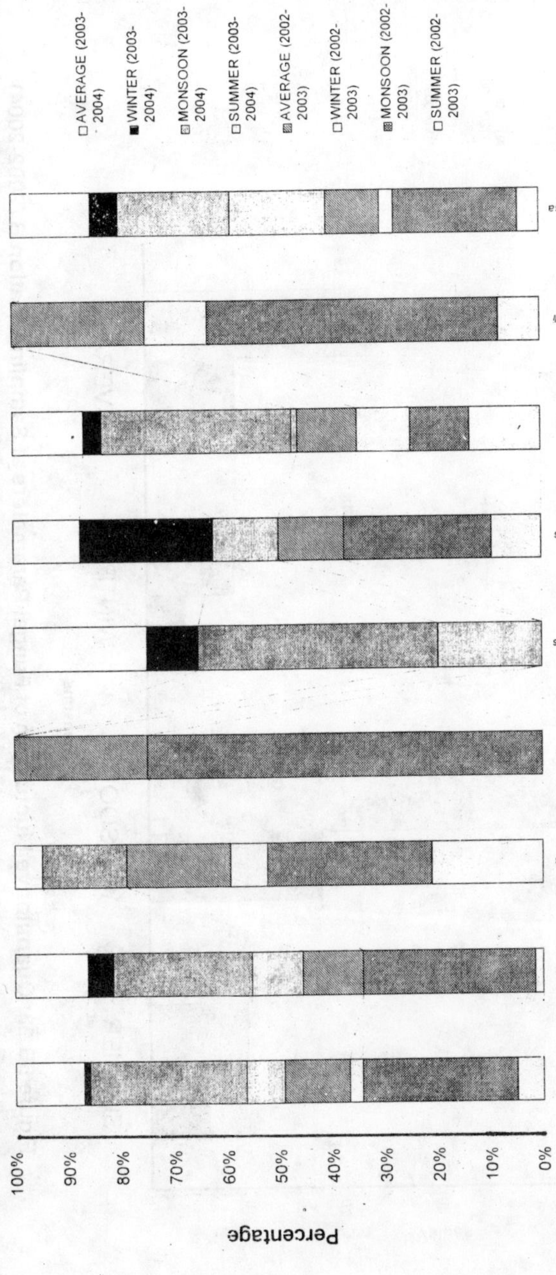

Figure 5B.22: Percentile Composition of Bacterial Culture at Sampling Station B (2002-2004)

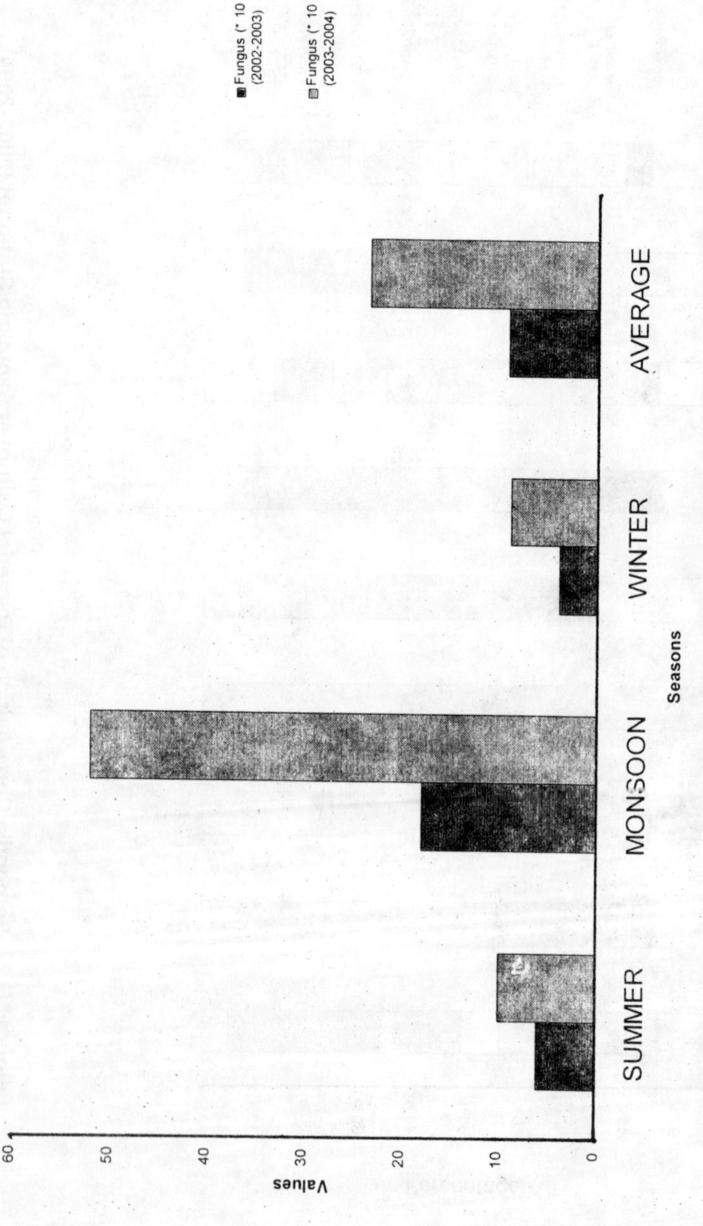

Figure 5B.23: Quantitative Fluctuation of Fungal Parameters at Sampling Station B (2002-2004)

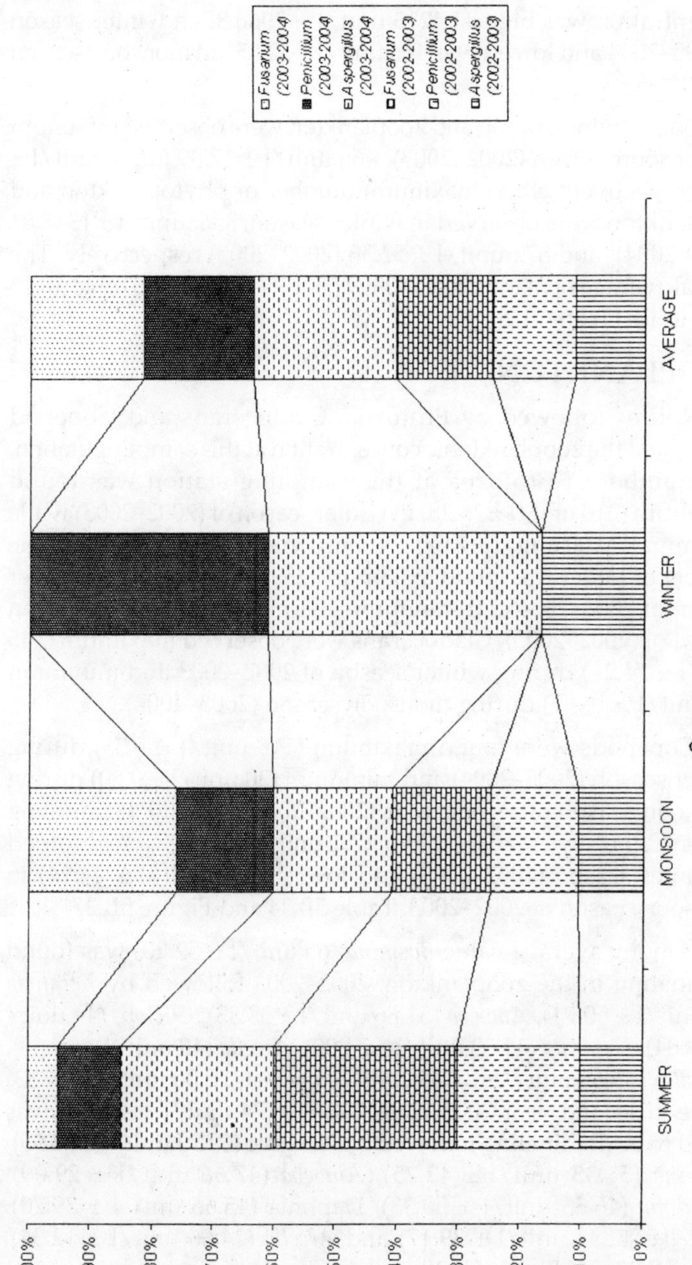

Figure 5B.24: Percentile Composition of Fungal Culture at Sampling Station B (2002-2004)

concentration was highest 4213 unit/l ± 2066.87 in winter season of 2003–2004 and lowest was 466 unit/l ± 329.51 in monsoon season of 2002–2003.

Both phytoplankton and zooplankton were observed minimum in monsoon season (2002–2003), 466 unit/l ± 17.89 and 0 unit/l ± 0.00 respectively while maximum number of phytoplankton and zooplankton were observed in winter season, 3568unit/l ± 1348.81 (2003–2004), and 872 unit/l ± 52.36 (2002–2003) respectively. The annual average of plankton was 2399.58unit/l ± 1180.62. Table 5B.23 and Figure 5B.25-5B.26.

ZOOPLANKTON

Rotifer followed by Protozoa, Cladocerans and Copepod dominated the zooplanktonic concentration at this sampling station. The number of protozoa at this sampling station was found maximum (210 unit/l ± 28.28) in winter season of (2002–2003) while minimum (30.00 unit/l ± 7.07) in monsoon season of same year. The number of rotifer was found maximum (259 unit/l ± 47.01) in winter season of 2003–2004 and minimum 18 unit/l ± 10.39 in monsoon season of (2002–2003). Cladocerans were observed maximum (245 unit/l ± 74.24) during winter season of 2002–2003 and minimum (24 unit/l ± 16.97) during monsoon season (2003–2004).

Copepods were found maximum (115 unit/l ± 5.33) during winter season (2003–2004) and minimum (20 unit/l ± 0.00) during monsoon season of second year (2002–2003). In total at sampling station C, the highest zooplankton (772 unit/l ± 70.13) were recorded in winter season (2002–2003) and lowest (138 unit/l ± 24.24) in monsoon season of 2002–2003. Table 5B.24 and Figure 5B.27.

Among average value *Bosmina* (65 unit/l ± 52.20) was found dominating in the zooplankton, 2002–2003 followed by *Keratella* (54 unit/l ± 50.71), *Amoeba* (51.66 unit/l ± 38.83), *Cyclops* (44 unit/l ± 39.84), *Daphnia* (42.33 unit/l ± 24.00), *Arcella* (40 unit/l ± 39.68), *Notholca* (35.66 unit/l ± 37.63), and *Philodima* (28.00 unit/l ± 24.33) While in second year 2003–2004, *Cyclops* (74 unit/l ± 40.03), was found to be dominating followed by *Notholca* (69.33 unit/l ± 48.95), *Bosmina* (51.33 unit/l ± 42.25), *Amoeba* (47.66 unit/l ± 29.09), *Philodima* (46.66 unit/l ± 50.33), Daphnia (45.66 unit/l ± 39.70), *Keratella* (42.33 unit/l ± 39.17) and *Arcella* (24.66 unit/l ± 12.34), Table 5B.25 and Figure 5B.28.

Table 5B.23: Seasonal Variations in Plankton (per liter) of River Suswa at Sampling Station C (2002-2004)

Plankion	*2002-2003*				*2003-2004*			
	Summer	*Monsoon*	*Winter*	*Average*	*Summer*	*Monsoon*	*Winter*	*Average*
Zooplankton	252±7.40	0±0.00	872±52.36	374.64±16.43	372±22.63	78±8.89	645±36.04	364.96±9.84
Phytoplankton	1137±154.28	466±17.89	2875±844.46	1492.61±266.56	1744±496.09	808±384.39	3568±1348.81	2034.62±573.08
Total	1389±625.78	466±329.51	3747±1416.33	1867.25±790.52	2116±970.15	886±516.18	4213±2066.87	2399.58±1180.62

±: Standard Deviation.

Table 5B.24: Quantitative Analysis for Zooplankton in Different Seasons of River Suswa at Sampling Station C (2002-2004)

Year	*Seasons*	*Protozoa*	*Rotifera*	*Cladocera*	*Copepod*	*Total* l^{-1}
2002–2003	Summer	65±10.60	108±6.92	57±2.12	22±3.33	252±35.33
	Monsoon	30.00±7.07	18.00±10.39	70.00±7.07	20±0.00	138±24.24
	Winter	210±28.28	227±36.004	245±74.24	90±16.69	772±70.13
	Average	101.66±95.43	117.66±104.83	124±104.99	44±39.84	387.32±36.45
2003–2004	Summer	80±7.07	175±23.62	102±29.69	35±1.19	392±58.41
	Monsoon	31±6.36	41±17.21	24±16.97	72±2.97	168±21.18
	Winter	106±35.35	259±47.01	165±24.74	115±5.33	645±70.14
	Average	72.33±38.08	148.33±126.13	97±70.63	47.33±58.62	369.99±43.12

Table 5B.25: Quantitative Analysis of Zooplankton in Different Seasons of River Suswa at Sampling Station C (2002-2004)

Year	*Seasons*	*Protozoa*		*Rotifera*			*Cladocera*		*Copepod*	*Total l^{-1}*
		Arcella	*Amoeba*	*Keratella*	*Philodima*	*Notholca*	*Daphnia*	*Bosmina*	*Cyclops*	
2002–2003	Summer	25±3.13	40±4.04	32±3.09	44±2.16	32±3.97	27±4.14	30±3.09	22±3.33	252±7.40
	Monsoon	10±0.00	20±0.00	18±0.00	0±0.00	0±0.00	30±0.00	40±0.00	20±0.00	138±13.85
	Winter	85±7.77	95±8.21	112±6.97	40±4.32	75±3.97	70±4.31	125±12.48	90±16.69	692±26.14
	Average	40±39.68	51.66±38.83	54±50.71	28.00±24.33	35.66±37.63	42.33±24.00	65±52.20	44±39.84	360.65±11.55
2003–2004	Summer	35±5.19	45±3.25	85±2.09	40±5.39	50±6.36	72±3.34	30±2.50	35±1.19	392±19.55
	Monsoon	11±2.97	20±4.86	8±1.17	0±0.00	33±0.75	0±0.00	24±4.83	72±2.97	168±23.62
	Winter	28±3.13	78±5.93	34±2.16	100±4.50	125±5.93	65±4.67	100±5.10	115±5.33	645±36.04
	Average	24.66±12.34	47.66±29.09	42.33±39.17	46.66±50.33	69.33±48.95	45.66±39.70	51.33±42.25	74±40.03	401.63±15.52

±: Standard Deviation.

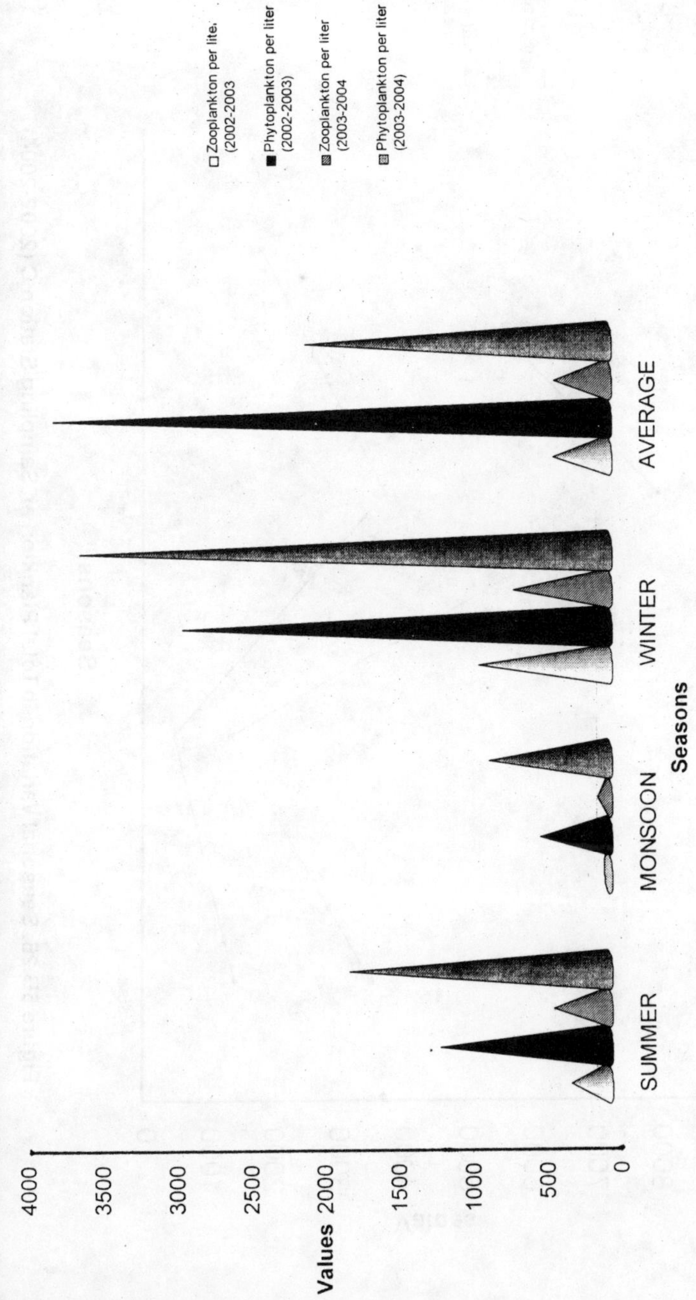

Figure 5B.25: Seasonal Variation in Plankton at Sampling Station C (2002-2004)

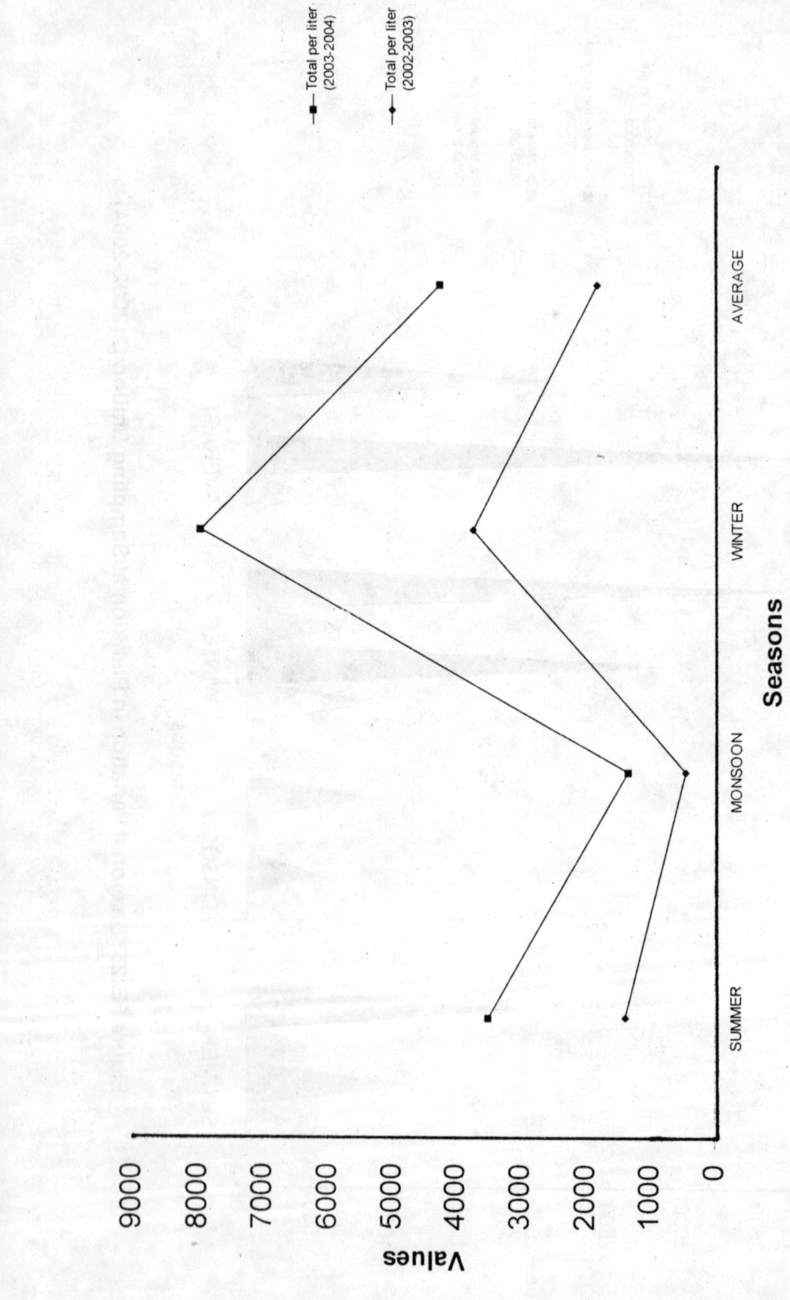

Figure 5B.26: Seasonal Variation in Total Plankton at Sampling Station C (2002-2004)

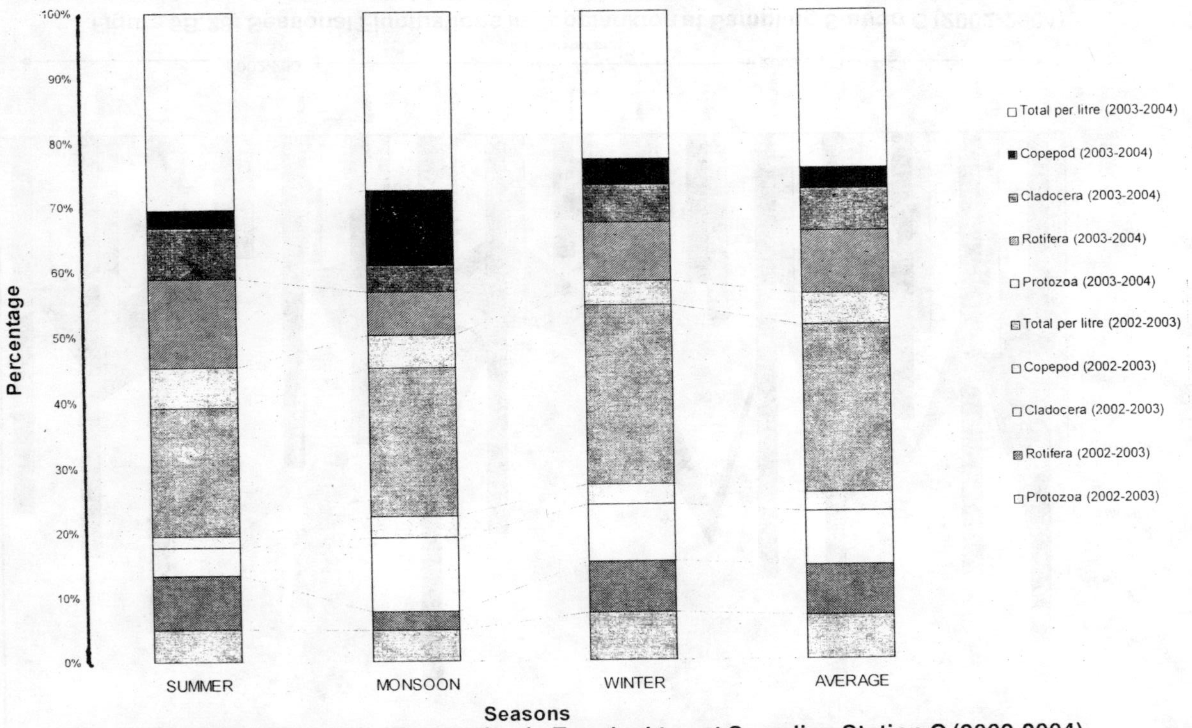

Figure 5B.27: Percentile Fluctuation in Zooplankton at Sampling Station C (2002-2004)

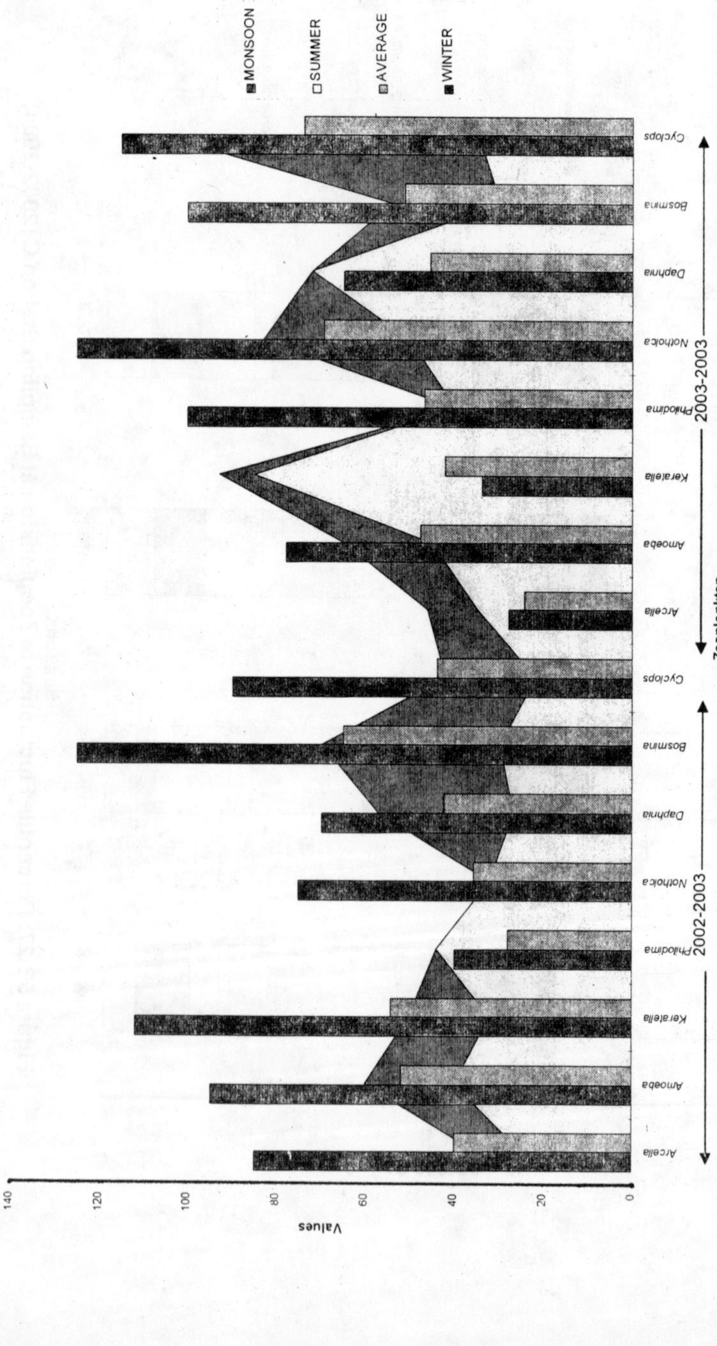

Figure 5B.28: Seasonal Fluctuations in Zooplankton at Sampling Station C (2002-2004)

PHYTOPLANKTON

Among phytoplankton Bacillariophyceae was found dominating followed by Chlorophyceae and Myxophyceae for first year (2002–2003) and Chlorophyceae followed by Bacillariophyceae and Myxophyceae in second year (2003–2004). In both the years Myxophyceae was found to be least in number. Bacillariophyceae was found maximum (1739 unit/l ± 57.50) in winter season (2002–2003) and minimum (36unit/l ± 4.84) in monsoon season of 2003–2004.Chlorophyceae was found maximum (2659 unit/l ± 49.57) in winter season of 2003–2004 and minimum (145 unit/l ± 19.49) in monsoon season of 2002–2003. Myxophyceae was found to be highest (518 unit/l ± 36.55) in summer season of 2002–2003 while minimum (59 unit/l ± 1.52) in monsoon season of. 2003–2004. Table 5B.26 and Figure 5B.29.

Among Bacillariophyceae *Diatoms* was found to be dominating (110.3 unit/l ± 108.2) in 2002–2003 followed by *Nitzschia* (95.33 unit/l ± 92.52), *Achnanthes* (84.33 unit/l ± 104.67). *Cymbella* (71.33 unit/l ± 118.39), *Amphora* (64 unit/l ± 97.07), *Navicula* (57.33 unit/l ± 69.86) *Gomphonema* (56.66 unit/l ± 60.87), *Pinnularia* (54.66 unit/l ± 40.46), *Frustulia* (53.33 unit/l ± 40.85), *Cocconeis* (46.66 unit/ ± 56.89), *Fragelaria* (40.33 unit/l ± 35.01) and *Cyclotella* (39.33 unit/l ± 60.50). In second year *i.e.* 2003–2004, Diatoms (91 unit/l ± 74.50), was found to be dominating followed by *Fragelaria* (78 unit/l ± 62.44), *Nitzschia* (71 unit/l ± 78.58), *Cocconeis* (66.33 unit/l ± 56.51), *Achnanthes* (63.33 unit/l ± 55.07), *Pinnularia* (62 unit/l ± 53.92), *Navicula* (52.66 unit/l ± 53.15), *Frustulia* (52.66 unit/l ± 62.68), *Amphora* (46.33 unit/l ± 40.50), *Cymbella* (46.16 unit/l ± 51.00), *Cyclotella* (37 unit/l ± 35.02) and *Gomphonema* (24 ± 41.56).

A great fluctuation among Bacillariophyceae was observed during seasonal study of Suswa river at sampling station C. In 2002–2003-summer season, *Pinnularia* was found maximum (80unit/l ± 7.66) and *Cymbella and* was found minimum (6 unit/l ± 0 88), in monsoon season *Diatoms* were found highest (40 unit/l ± 5.36) while *Cymbella, Cyclotella and Fragelaria* were found to be nil. In winter again maximum concentration was observed for *Diatoms* (235unit/l ± 16.48) and *Fragelaria* was found to be minimum (58unit/l ± 10.00). In 2003–2004 summer, *Diatoms* was found maximum (165 unit/l ± 5.97) while *Cyclotella*, was recorded minimum (30 unit/l ± 6.48. In monsoon season again *Diatoms* were found highest (16 unit/l ±

Table 5B.26: Comparitive Analysis of Seasonal Variation Among Phytoplankton of River Suswa at Sampling Station C (2002-2004)

Year	*Seasons*	*Bacillariophyceae l^{-1}*	*Chlorophyceae l^{-1}*	*Myxophyceae l^{-1}*	*Total l^{-1}*
2002–2003	Summer	406±27.85	213±32.08	518±36.55	1137±154.28
	Monsoon	176±13.05	145±19.49	145±14.29	466±17.89
	Winter	1739±57.50	1074±55.01	62.0±6.65	2875±844.46
	Average	773.64±22.07	477.31±23.55	241.66±19.01	1492.61±266.56
2003–2004	Summer	1149±41.10	364.0±28.45	231.0±10.81	1744±496.09
	Monsoon	36±4.84	713.0±43.66	59.0±1.52	808±384.39
	Winter	901±32.43	2659±49.57	78.0±3.61	3638±1318. 42
	Average	690.47±18.33	1245.3±25.36	122.66±2.14	2058.43±561.33

±: Standard Deviation.

Figure 5B.29: Seasonal Fluctuations in Phytoplankton at Sampling Station C (2002-2004)

0.02) while *Pinnularia, Frustulia, Achnanthes, Gomphonema* and *Amphora* were found to be nil. In winter season *Frustulia* were found maximum (122 unit/l ± 5.48), while *Gomphonema* was found as nil. Table 5B.27 and Figure 5B.30

Among Chlorophyceae during 2002–2003 *Spirogyra* (96 unit/l ± 83.86), was observed as dominating species followed by *Zygnema* (75 unit/l ± 112.65), *Ulothrix* (65.33 unit/l ± 50.21), *Cosmerium* (58.33 unit/l ± 85.00), *Closterium* (55 unit/l ± 65.33), *Chlorella* (39.33 unit/ l ± 61.32), *Cladophora* (39.33 unit/l ± 49.08 *Oedogonium* (32.33 unit/ l ± 30.56) and *Schizogonium* (22.66 unit/l ± 6.11). During 2003–2004 *Chlorella* (179.33 unit/l ± 191.77), was found as dominant species followed by *Cosmerium* (161.33 unit/l ± 124.54), *Ulothrix* (158.33 unit/l ± 106.92), *Closterium* (147.66unit/l ± 123.27), *Cladophora* (129.33unit/l ± 140.28), *Schizogonium* (128 unit/l ± 158.74), *Spirogyra* (122.66 unit/l ± 167.72), *Zygnema* (122.66 unit/l ± 83.52) and *Oedogonium* (96.33 unit/l ± 154.88).

A great variation in seasonal values of Chlorophyceae was noted during the course of study at sampling station C during first year 2002–2003 *Spirogyra* was found maximum (105 unit/l ± 7.77) and *Cladophora* was found as minimum (4 unit/l ± 1.11) in summer season. While in monsoon season *Ulothrix* was found to be highest (60 unit/l ± 5.87) and *Chlorella* was recorded as nil. In winter season *Zygnema* was revealed maximum (205 unit/l ± 32) and *Schizigonium* was recorded as minimum (28 unit/l ± 12.96). While in second year 2003–2004 *Cosmerium* was found maximum (84 unit/l ± 10.10) and *Schizigonium* was found minimum (8 unit/l ± 3.96), in summer season. In monsoon season, *Ulothrix* was found maximum (135 unit/ l ± 7.09) while *Oedogonium* was found as nil. In winter season *Chlorella* were found maximum (395 unit/l ± 15.00) while *Zygnema* were found minimum (205 unit/l ± 18.50). The total highest value of Chlorophyceae was recorded in winter (1074unit/l ± 55.01) and lowest in monsoon (145 unit/l ± 19.49) for first year (2002–2003) for second year (2003–2004) the highest total value of Chlorophyceae was recorded in winter (2659 unit/l ± 49.57) and lowest in summer season (364unit/l ± 28.45). Table 5B.28 and Figure 5B.31.

Among Myxophyceae *Anacystis* (100 unit/l ± 95.24) was recorded as dominant species, followed by *Anabena* (79.66 unit/l ± 83.57) and *Oscillatoria* (62 unit/1 ± 64.08 for first year (2002–2003). During second year *Anacystis* was found as dominating species

Table 5B.27: Quantitative Analysis of Seasonal Variation Among Bacillariophyceae of River Suswa at Sampling Station C (2002-2004)

	Seasons	*Achnanthes*	*Amphora*	*Cocconeis*	*Cymbella*	*Cyclotella*	*Diatoms*	*Fragelaria*
2002–2003	Summer	30±0.03	12±0.51	8±2.16	6±0.88	9±1.09	56±8.97	63±6.54
	Monsoon	18±0.59	4±0.78	20±1.08	0.00±0.00	0.±0.00	40±5.36	0±0.00
	Winter	205±12.00	76±11.04	112±9.99	208±6.76	109±5.84	235± 16.48	58±10.00
	Average	84.33±104.67	64.0±97.07	46.66±56.89	71.33±118.39	39.33±60.50	110.33±108.26	40.33±35.01
2003–2004	Summer	100±7.76	75±6.09	89±10.03	92±8.87	30±6.48	165± 5.97	128±6.36
	Monsoon	0±0.00	0±0.00	2±0.00	1±0.31	6±0.76	16±0.02	8±0.10
	Winter	90±2.02	64±1.69	108±3.24	60±1.03	75±5.67	92±7.81	98±6.66
	Average	63.33±55.07	46.33±40.50	66.33±56.51	46.16±51.00	37±35.02	91±74.50	78±62.44

	Seasons	*Frustulia*	*Gomphonema*	*Navicula*	*Nitzschia*	*Pinnularia*	*Total* l^{-1}
2002–2003	Summer	36±4.87	12±2.00	18±2.98	76±3.04	80±7.66	406±27.85
	Monsoon	24±2.58	32±4.19	16±3.66	14±1.76	8±0.90	176± 13.05
	Winter	100±9.57	126±8.88	138±7.62	196±6.86	76±4.98	1739±57.50
	Average	53.33±40.85	56.66±60.87	57.33±69.86	95.33±92.52	54.66±40.46	773.64±22.02
2003–2004	Summer	36±14.21	72±12.05	108±15.11	156±7.86	98±4.94	1149±41.10
	Monsoon	0±0.00	0±0.00	2±0.00	1±0.00	0±0.00	36±4.84
	Winter	122±5.48	0±0.00	48±4.12	56±3.96	88±11.78	901±32.43
	Average	52.66 ±62.68	24±41.56	52.66±53.15	71±78.58	62±53.92	690.47±18.33

±: Standard Deviation.

Table 5B.28: Quantitative Analysis of Seasonal Variation Among Chlorophyceae of River Suswa at Sampling Station C (2002-2004)

Year	*Seasons*	*Closterium*	*Cosmerium*	*Chlorella*	*Cladophora*	*Oedogonium*	*Schizogonium*	*Spirogyra*	*Ulothrix*	*Zygnema*	*Total* l^{-1}
2002–2003	Summer	35±3.98	18±4.40	8±2.96	4±1.11	3±0.78	16±3.48	105±7.77	18±4.10	6±2.00	213±32.08
	Monsoon	2±0.30	1±0.00	0±0.00	6±2.00	30±4.86	24±3.90	8±1.11	60±5.87	14±1.86	145±19.49
	Winter	128±11.11	156±8.79	110±7.80	90±5.97	64±4.88	28±12.96	175±32.88	118±49.68	205±32.00	1074±55.01
	Average	55±65.33	58.33±85.0	39.33±61.32	39.33±49.08	32.33±30.56	22.66±6.11	96±83.86	65.33±50.21	75±112.65	477.31±23.55
2003–2004	Summer	78±14.28	84±10.10	28±2.76	33±7.76	14±4.48	8±3.96	16±4.44	65±8.50	38±4.70	364±28.45
	Monsoon	75±4.44	95±3.96	115±2.22	64±1.59	0±0.00	68±7.90	36±8.88	135±7.09	125±6.39	713±43.66
	Winter	290±15.88	305±17.66	395±15.00	290±19.68	275±11.67	308±12.98	316±14.17	275±16.00	205±18.50	2659±49.57
	Average	147.66±123.27	161.33±124.54	179.33±191.77	129.33±140.28	96.33±154.88	128±158.74	122.66±167.72	158.33±106.92	122.66±83.52	1245.3±25.36

±: Standard Deviation.

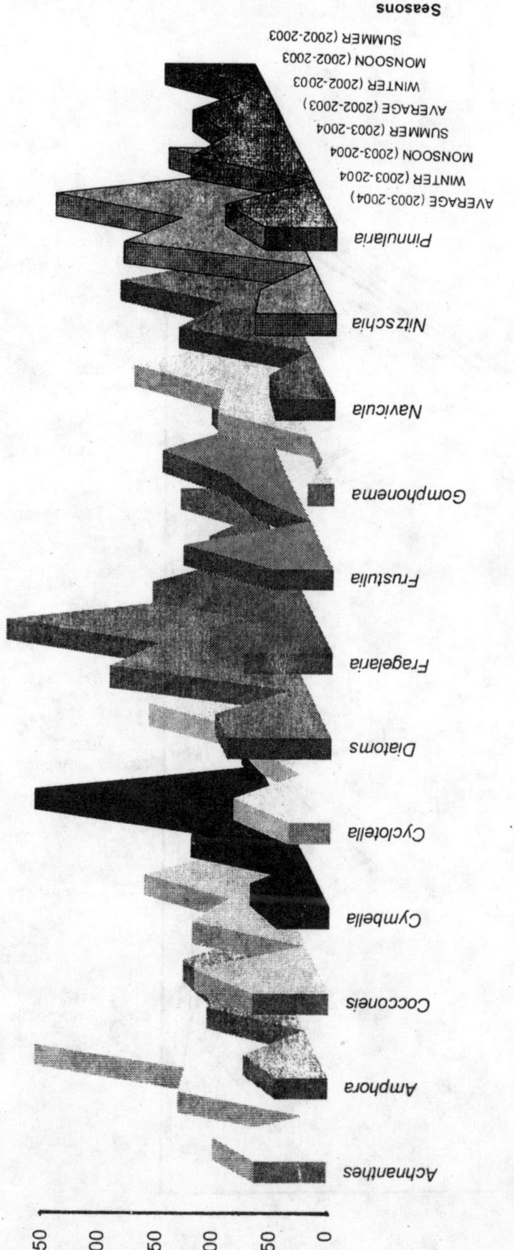

Figure 5B.30: Quantitative Fluctuation of Bacillariophyceae at Sampling Station C (2002-2004)

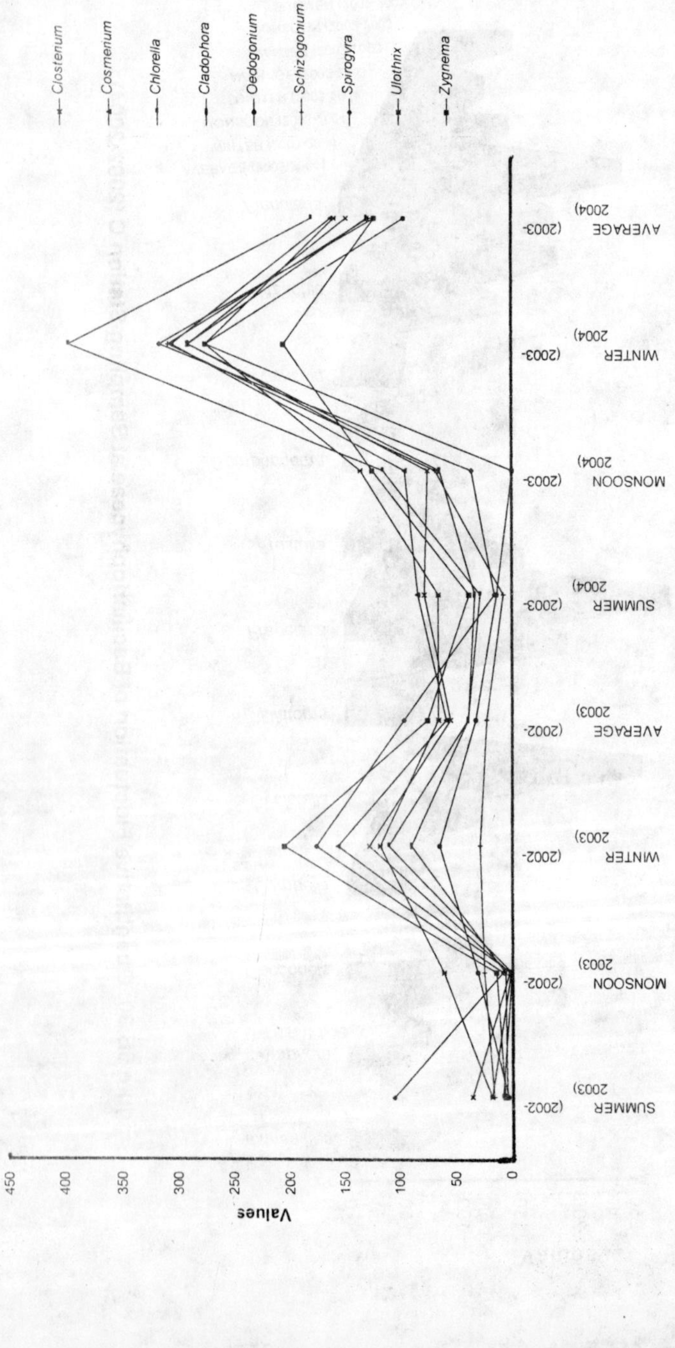

Figure 5B.31: Quantitative Fluctuation of Chlorophyceae at Sampling Station C (2002-2004)

(43.33 unit/l ± 39.62) followed by *Anabena* (40 unit/l ± 29.51) and *Oscillatoria* (39.33 unit/l ± 25.32).

For seasonal fluctuation of Myxophyceae it is revealed that in summer season of 2002–2003, *Anacystis* existed in maximum (208 unit/l ± 8.72) while *Oscillatoria* was found minimum (135unit/l ± 16.29). In monsoon season *Anacystis* was found maximum (64 unit/l ± 6.79) and *Oscillatoria* was found minimum (36 unit/l ± 3.77). In winter season, again *Anabena* was found maximum (28 unit/l ± 2.22) and *Oscillatoria* was least (15 unit/l ± 1.76). During second year (2003–2004), *Anabena* was found maximum (89 unit/l ± 9.97) and *Oscillatoria* as minimum (68 unit/l ± 3.76) in summer season. In monsoon season *Anabena* was found maximum (21 unit/l ± 3.10) and *Anacystis* as minimum (18 unit/l ± 2.00). In winter season *Oscillatoria* was found maximum (30 unit/l ± 0.00) and *Anacystis* as minimum (23 unit/l ± 1.50). In total value of 2002–2003 the maximum Myxophyceae was recorded maximum in summer season (518unit/l ± 36.55) and minimum in winter season (62 unit/l ± 6.65). In 2003–2004 the maximum Myxophyceae were recorded in summer season (231 unit/l ± 10.81) and minimum in monsoon season (59 unit/l ± 1.52) Table 5B.29 and Figure 5B.32.

MICROBIOLOGICAL

Bacteriological

The average highest value of Most probable number (MPN) was found as (253 MPN/100ml ± 186.97) in 2003–2004 while average highest value of Heterotrophic plate count (HPC) was found as [102.33 HPC/ml (X10^3) ± 6.35] in 2002–2003. During course of study for first year (2002–2003) at down stream Vedic nagar the MPN and HPC were found maximum (195 MPN/100ml ± 8.42), [216 HPC/ml (X10^3) ± 13.51] in monsoon season respectively. While lowest (70MPN/100ml ± 4.49) MPN was found in summer season and lowest [37.0 HPC/ml (X10^3) ± 2.80] HPC was found in winter season. For second year (2003–2004) again monsoon season showed maximum (428 MPN/100ml ± 24.24), [180HPC/ml (X10^3) ± 11.68] MPN and HPC respectively. MPN was recorded minimum (56 MPN/100ml ± 7.10) in summer and HPC was recorded minimum [47.0 HPC/ml (X10^3) ± 4.68] in winter season. Table 5B.30 and Figure 5B.33.

Table 5B.29: Quantitative Analysis of Seasonal Variation Among Myxophyceaee of River Suswa at Sampling Station C (2002-2004)

Year	*Seasons*	*Anacystis*	*Anabena*	*Oscillatoria*	*Total* l^{-1}
2002–2003	Summer	208±8.72	175±12.44	135±16.29	518±36.55
	Monsoon	64±6.79	45±2.89	36±3.77	145±14.29
	Winter	28±2.22	19±3.79	15±1.76	62±6.65
	Average	100±95.24	79.66±83.57	62±64.08	241.66±19.01
2003–2004	Summer	89±9.97	74±11.24	68±3.76	231±10.81
	Monsoon	18±2.00	21±3.10	20±2.06	59±1.52
	Winter	23±1.50	25±2.10	30±0.00	78±3.60
	Average	43.33±39.62	40±29.51	39.33±25.32	122.66±2.14

±: Standard Deviation.

Table 5B.30: Quantitative Analysis of Seasonal Variation in Bacteriological Parameters of River Suswa at Sampling Station C (2002-2004)

Year	*Seasons*	*MPN/100 ml*	*HPC/ml ($X10^3$) ($\times 10^3$)*
2002–2003	Summer	70±4.49	54±5.19
	Monsoon	195±8.42	216±13.51
	Winter	72±3.27	37.0±2.80
	Average	112.3±71.59	102.33±6.35
2003–2004	Summer	56±7.10	62.0±6.93
	Monsoon	428±24.24	180±11.68
	Winter	275±19.48	47±4.68
	Average	253±186.97	96.59±6.28

±: Standard Deviation.

Figure 5B.32: Quantitative Fluctuation of Myxophyceae at Sampling Station C (2002-2004)

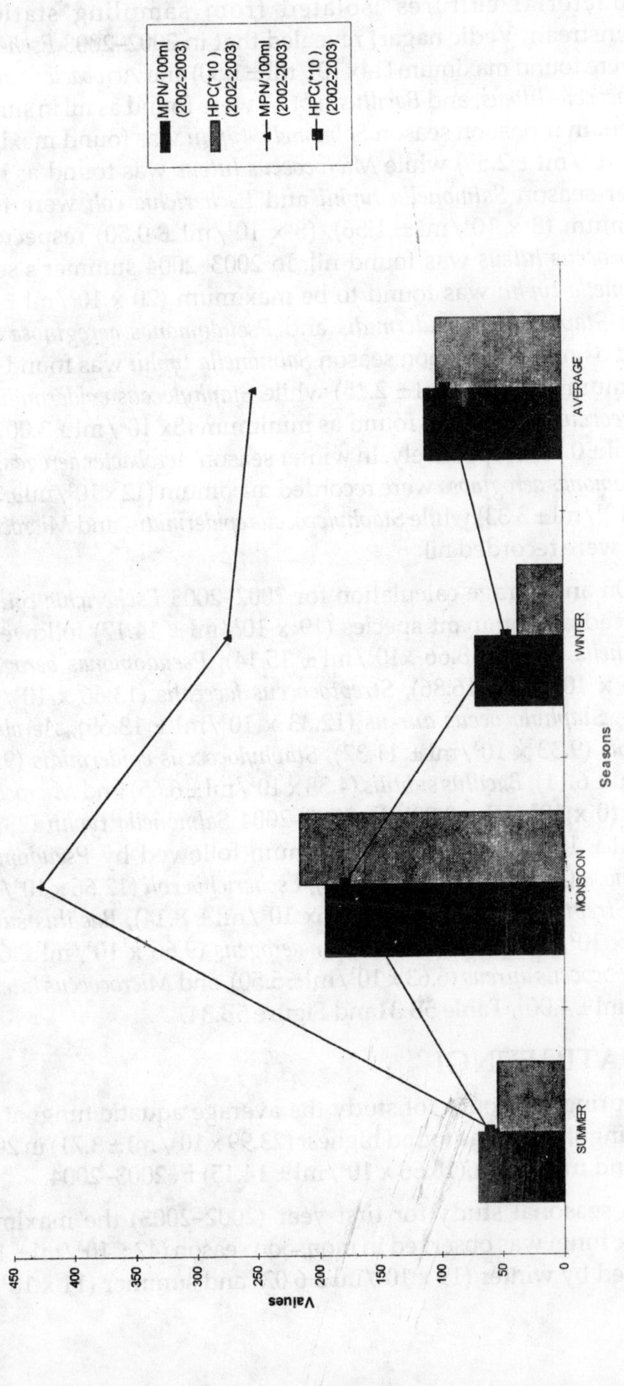

Figure 5B.33: Quantitative Fluctuation of Bacterial Parameters at Sampling Station C (2002-2004)

Bacterial cultures isolated from sampling station C (Downstream Vedic nagar) revealed that in 2002–2003 *Escherichia coli* were found maximum (14x 10^3/ml ± 1.50) and *Aerobacter aerogens, Micrococcus luteus*, and *Bacillus subtilis* were found as nil in summer season. In monsoon season *Salmonella typhii* was found maximum (36 x 10^3/ml ± 2.59) while *Micrococcus luteus* was found as nil. In winter season *Salmonella typhii* and *Escherichia coli* were found maximum (8 x 10^3/ml ± 1.56), (8 x 10^3/ml ± 0.50) respectively, *Micrococcus luteus* was found nil. In 2003–2004 summer's season *Salmonella typhii* was found to be maximum (20 x 10^3/ml ± 1.54) while *Staphyloccus epidermidis* and *Pseudomonas aeroginosa* were found as nil. In monsoon season *Salmonella typhii* was found to be maximum (42 x 10^3/ml ± 2.15) while *Staphyloccus epidermidis and Micrococcus luteus* were found as minimum (8x 10^3/ml ± 3.00), (8 x 10^3/ml ± 0.50) respectively. In winter season *Aerobacter aerogens* and *Pseudomonas aeroginosa* were recorded maximum (12 x 10^3/ml ± 2.00), (12 x 10^3/ml ± 3.33) while *Staphylococcus epidermidis*, and *Micrococcus luteus* were recorded nil.

On an average calculation for 2002–2003 *Escherichia coli* was observed as dominant species (19 x 10^3/ml ± 14.17) followed by *Salmonella typhii* (18.66 x10^3/ml ± 15.14), *Pseudomonas aeroginosa* (15.66 x 10^3/ml ± 16.86), *Streptococcus facecalis* (13.66 x 10^3/ml ± 15.94), *Staphylococcus aureus* (12.33 x 10^3/ml ± 13.65), *Aerobacter aerogens* (9.33 x 10^3/ml ± 11.37), *Staphylococcus epidermidis* (9.33 x 10^3/ml ± 6.11), *Bacillus subtilis* (4.33 x 10^3/ml ± 6.65) and *Micrococcus luteus* (0 x 10^3/ml ± 0.00), In 2003–2004 *Salmonella typhii* (23.33 x 10^3/ml ± 17.24), was noted maximum followed by *Pseudomonas aeroginosa* (15.66 x 10^3/ml ± 17.78), *Escherichia coli* (12.66 x 10^3/ml ± 7.57) *Streptococcus facecalis* (11.66x 10^3/ml ± 8.14), *Bacillus subtilis* (10.33x 10^3/ml ± 9.29), *Aerobacter aerogens* (9.66 x 10^3/ml ± 6.80), *Staphylococcus aureus* (6.63 x 10^3/ml ± 5.50), and *Micrococcus luteus* (4 x 10^3/ml ± 4.00), Table 5B.31and Figure 5B.34.

AQUATIC FUNGI

During the course of study the average aquatic fungi at this sampling station was found highest (23.99 x 10^3/ml ± 3.71) in 2002–2003 and minimum (18.66 x 10^3/ml ± 14.15) in 2003–2004.

In seasonal study for first year (2002–2003) the maximum aquatic fungi was observed in monsoon season (42 x 10^3/ml ± 4.00) followed by winter (19 x 10^3/ml ± 6.02) and summer (11 x 10^3/ml

Table 5B.31: Isolation of Bacterial ($ml^{-1} \times 10^3$) Culture from Sampling Station C (2002-2004)

Bacteria	*2002-2003*				*2003-2004*			
	Summer	*Monsoon*	*Winter*	*Average*	*Summer*	*Monsoon*	*Winter*	*Average*
*Salmonella typhii**	12±1.50	36±2.59	8±1.56	18.66±15.14	20±1.54	42±2.15	8±2.63	23.33±17.24
*Streptococcus facecalis**	6±0.50	32±2.76	3±0.75	13.66±15.94	8±3.12	21±1.79	6±0.50	11.66±8.14
*Aerobacter aerogens**	0±0 .00	22±3.75	6±1.75	9.33±11.37	2±0.65	15±1.50	12±2.00	9.66±6.80
*Staphylococcus epidermidis**	8±1.63	16±2.51	4±0.50	9.33±6.11	0±0.00	8±3.00	0±0.00	2.66±4.61
*Staphylococcus aurens**	6±3.16	28±6.78	3±0.66	12.33±13.65	6±0.73	12±1.59	1±0.00	6.63±5.50
*Micrococcus luteus***	0±0.00	0±0.00	0±0.00	0±0.00	4±0.50	8±0.50	0±0.00	4.00±4.00
*Bacillus subtilis***	0.0±0.00	12±2.39	1.00±0.00	4.33±6.65	6±3.13	21±2.59	4±1.50	10.33±9.29
*Escherichia coli**	14±1.50	35±1.59	8±0.50	19±14.17	16±2.16	18±3.89	4±0.50	12.66±7.57
*Pseudomonas aerogenosa**	8±0.50	35±7.96	4.0±3.22	15.66±16.86	0±0.00	35±4.79	12±3.33	15.66±17.78
Toial l^{-1}	54±5.19	216±13.51	37.0±2.80	102.33±6.35	62.0±6.95	180±11.68	47±4.68	96.59±6.28

*: Pathogens; **: Non pathogens; ±: Standard Deviation.

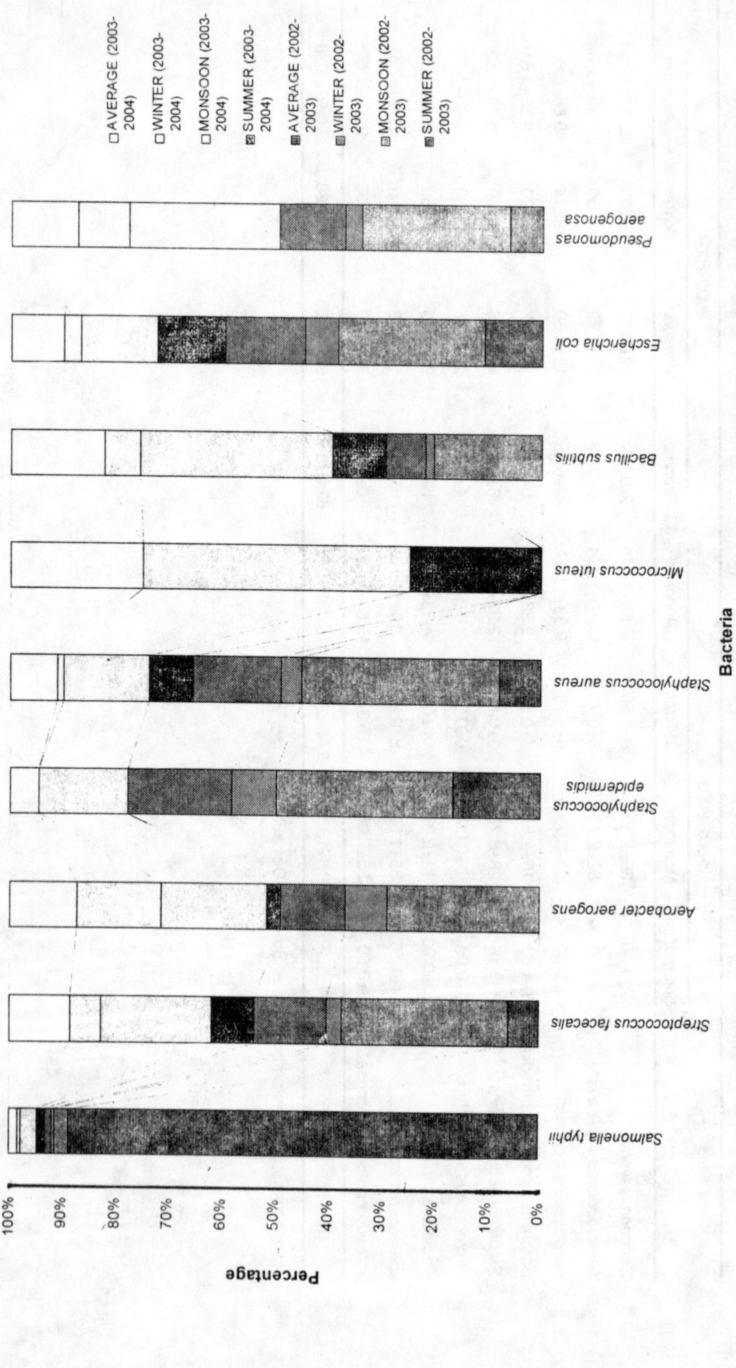

Figure 5B.34: Percentile Composition of Bacterial Culture at Sampling Station C (2002-2004)

± 2.51). In 2003–2004 maximum aquatic fungi was observed in monsoon season (35 x 10^3/ml ± 4.50) followed by summer (11 x 10^3/ml ± 4.04) and winter season (10 x 10^3/ml ± 3.05). Table 5B.32 and Figure 5B.35.

In an average calculation for 2002–2003 *Fusarium* was observed maximum (12 x 10^3/ml ± 6.00) followed by *Aspergillus* (7.33 x 10^3/ml ± 6.50) and *Penicillium* (4.66x 10^3/ml ± 5.03). In 2003–2004, *Aspergillus* was found as dominant species (7.00 x 10^3/ml ± 4.58) followed by *Penicillium* (6.66 x 10^3/ml ± 8.32) and *Fusarium* (5.0 x 10^3/ml ± 4.35). During 2002–2003 *Fusarium* was found maximum (6x 10^3/ml ± 2.51) and *Aspergillus* was found minimum (1 x 10^3/ml ± 0.00) in summer season. *Fusarium* was observed highest (18 x 10^3/ml ± 3.89) in monsoon season while *Penicillium* was observed least (10 x 10^3/ml ± 2.00). In winter season again *Fusarium* was found maximum (12 x 10^3/ml ± 5.86) and *Penicillium* was found as nil. In 2003–2004 summer's season observation revealed that growth of *Fusarium* was optimum (8 x 10^3/ml ± 3.97) and *Penicillium* was recorded as nil. In monsoon season growth of *Penicillium* was recorded highest (16 x 10^3/ml ± 2.76) and *Fusarium* was recorded as least (7 x 10^3/ml ± 1.10). In winter season *Aspergillus* was found maximum (6 x 10^3/ml ± 2.76) and *Fusarium* was observed nil. Table 5B.33 and Figure 5B.36.

Sampling Station D

Seasonal Quantitative analysis of plankton at sampling station D (Near water pumping station), revealed that the total planktonic concentration was highest 3334 unit/l ± 1096.01 in winter season of 2002–2003 and lowest was 476 unit/l ± 336.58 in monsoon season of 2002–2003.

Both phytoplankton and zooplankton were observed minimum in monsoon season (2002–2003), 476 unit/l ± 195.79 and 0 unit/l ± 0.00 respectively while maximum number of phytoplankton and zooplankton were observed in winter season, 2442unit/l ± 563.33 (2002–2003), and 892 unit/l ± 43.61 (2002–2003) respectively. The annual average of plankton was 1950.66 unit/l ± 857.96 Table 5B.34 and Figure 5B.37-5B.38.

ZOOPLANKTON

Rotifer followed by Protozoa, Cladocerans and Copepod dominated the zooplanktonic concentration at this sampling station.

Table 5B.32: Isolation of Fungus ($ml^{-1} \times 10^3$) from Sampling Station C (2002-2004)

	2002-2003				2003-2004			
	Summer	*Monsoon*	*Winter*	*Average*	*Summer*	*Monsoon*	*Winter*	*Average*
Fungus	11±2.51	42±4.0	19.0±6.02	23.99±3.71	11±4.04	35±4.50	10±3.05	18.66±14.15

±: Standard Deviation.

Table 5B.33: Isolation of Fungus ($ml^{-1} \times 10^3$) from Sampling Station C (2002-2004)

Fungus	2002-2003				2003-2004			
	Summer	*Monsoon*	*Winter*	*Average*	*Summer*	*Monsoon*	*Winter*	*Average*
Aspergillus	1.00±0.00	14±2.87	7±4.86	7.33±6.50	3±1.50	12±3.99	6±2.76	7.0±4.58
Penicillium	4.00±1.00	10.0±2.00	0.00±0.00	4.66±5.03	0.00±0.00	16±2.76	4.00±1.09	6.66±8.32
Fusarium	6±3.19	18±3.89	12±5.86	12±6.00	8±3.97	7±1.10	0±0.00	5.0±4.35
Total l^{-1}	11±2.51	42±4.0	19.0±6.02	23.99±3.71	11±4.04	35±4.50	10±3.05	18.66±14.15

±: Standard Deviation.

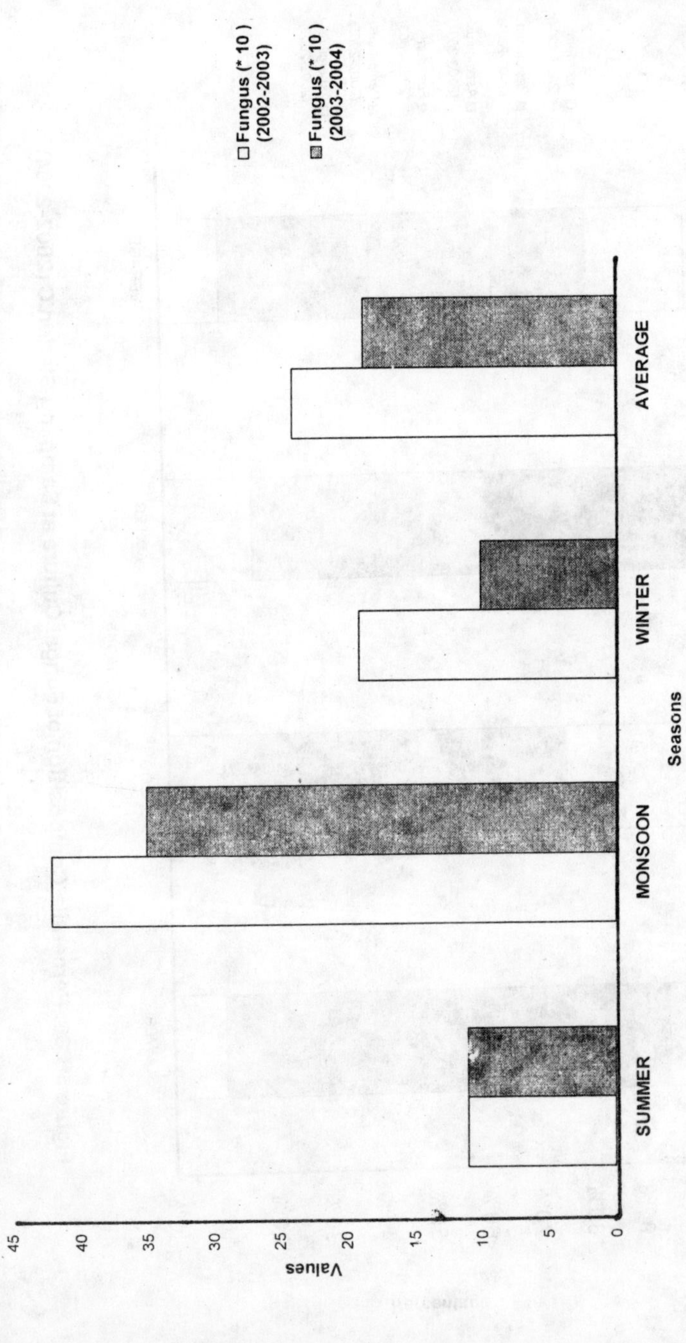

Figure 5B.35: Quantitative Fluctuation of Fungal Parameters at Sampling Station C (2002-2004)

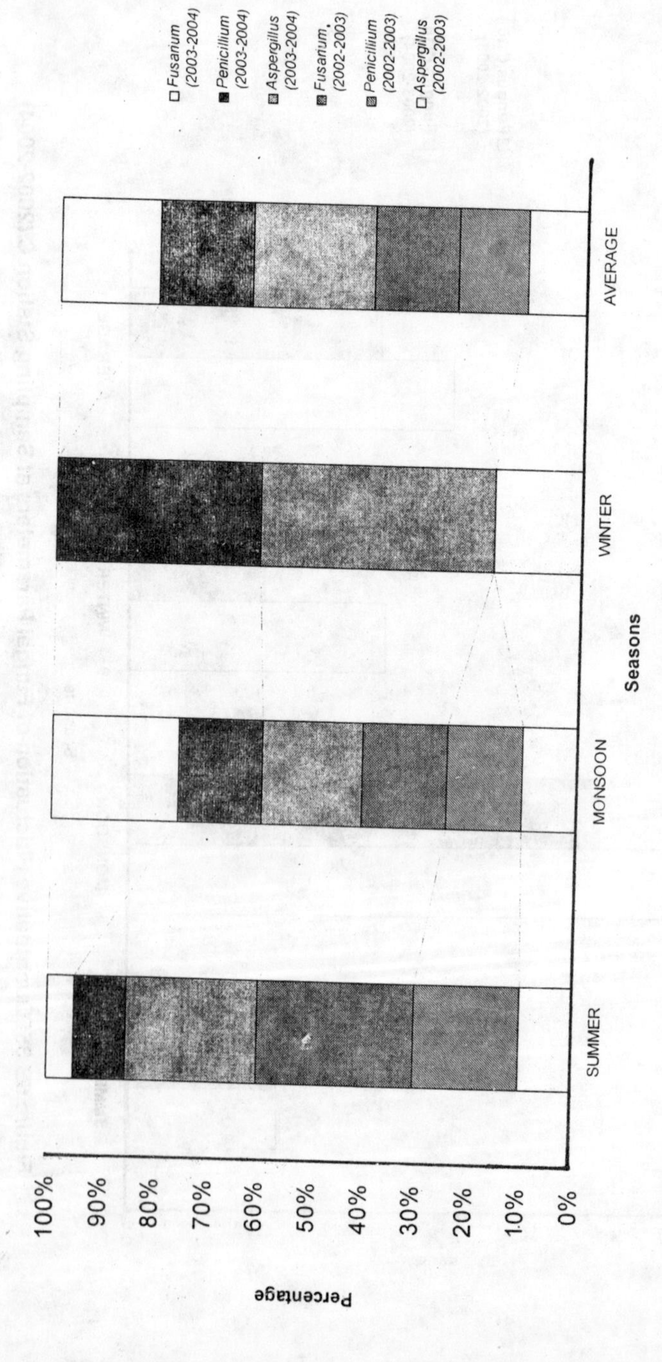

Figure 5B.36: Percentile Composition of Fungal Culture at Sampling Station C (2002-2004)

Table 5B.34: Seasonal Variations in Plankton (per liter) Parameters of River Suswa at Sampling Station D (2002-2004)

Plankton	*2002-2003*				*2003-2004*			
	Summer	*Monsoon*	*Winter*	*Average*	*Summer*	*Monsoon*	*Winter*	*Average*
Zooplankton	239±42.42	0.±0.00	892±43.61	377±461.73	371±67.75	80±12.02	655±55.50	368.66±287.50
Phytoplankton	1195±362.40	476±195.79	2442±563.33	1373.54±371.94	1344±353.16	1095±278.66	2337±821.26	1582..3±411..50
Total	1434±675.99	476±336.58	3334±1096.01	1750.54±704.66	1715±688.01	1175±717.71	2992±1189.35	1950.66±857.96

±: Standard Deviation.

Table 5A.35: Quantitative Analysis for Zooplankton in Different Seasons of River Suswa at Sampling Station D (2002-2004)

Year	*Seasons*	*Protozoa*	*Rotifera*	*Cladocera*	*Copepod*	*Total* l^{-1}
2002–2003	Summer	58±15.55	117±9.64	49±7.77	15±2.19	239±42.22
	Monsoon	48±8.48	28±16.16	30±21.21	40±8.0	146±9.29
	Winter	210±28.28	232±36.55	140±14.14	90±1.65	672±65.13
	Average	105.33±90.78	125.66±102.27	73.0±58.79	48.33±38.18	352.32±34.24
2003–2004	Summer	66±7.07	180±16.37	105±31.81	20±1.09	371±67.75
	Monsoon	23±4.94	44±5.03	33±2.12	30±1.90	130±8.73
	Winter	107±26.16	205±34.03	137±4.94	86±11.76	535±51.90
	Average	65.33±42.0	143±86.64	91.66±53.26	45.33±35.57	345.32±42.27

±: Standard Deviation.

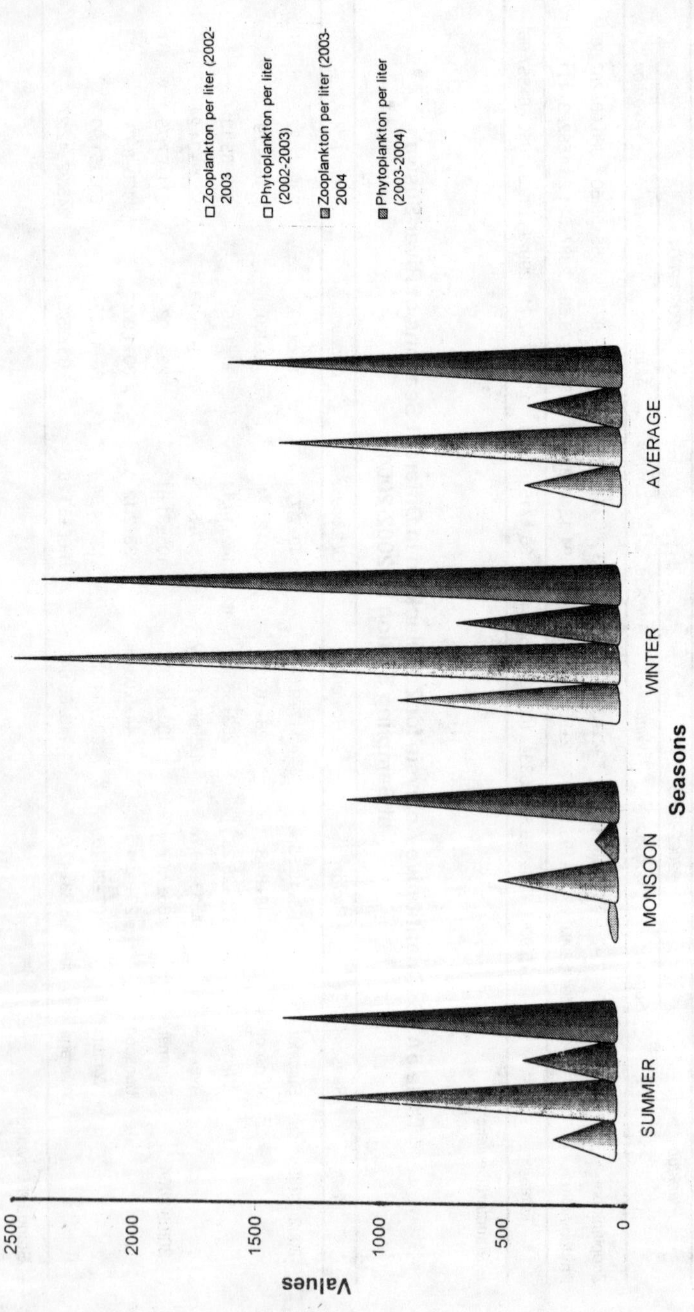

Figure 5B.37: Seasonal Variation in Plankton at Sampling Station D (2002-2004)

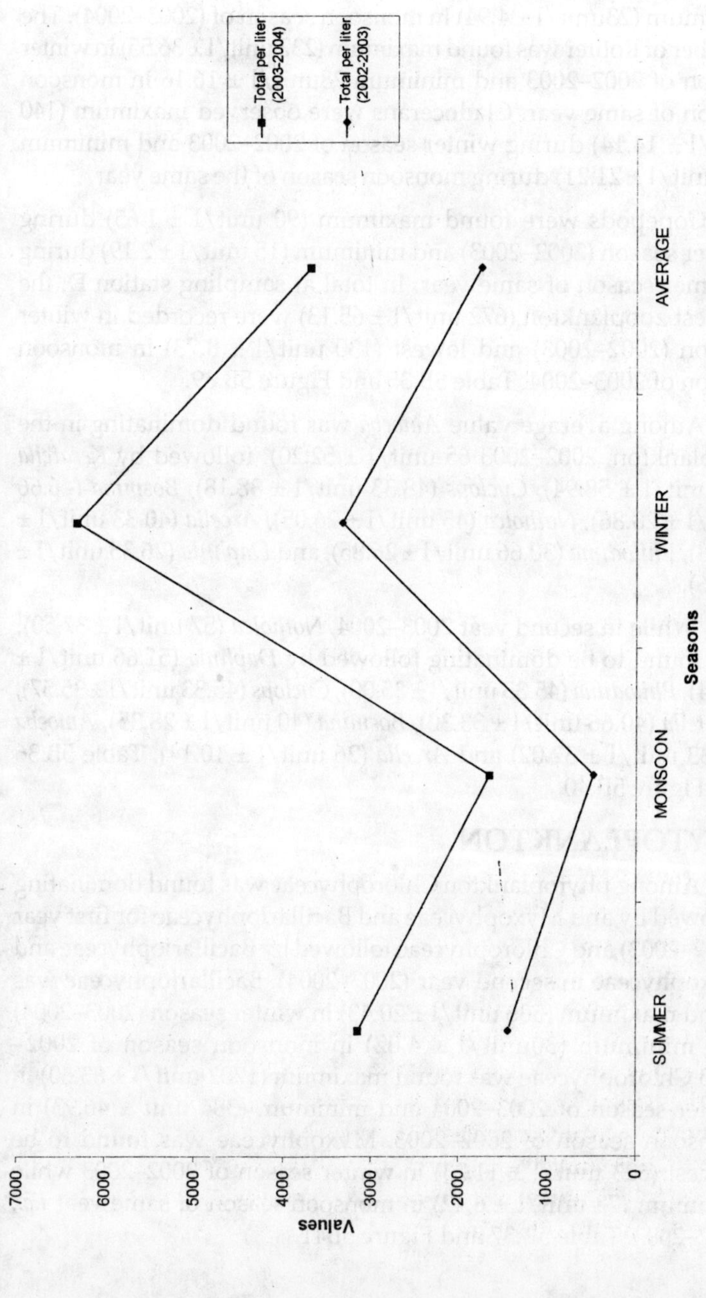

Figure 5B.38: Seasonal Variation in Total Plankton at Sampling Station D (2002-2004)

The number of protozoa at this sampling station was found maximum (210 unit/l ± 28.28) in winter season of (2002–2003) while minimum (23unit/l ± 4.94) in monsoon season of (2003–2004). The number of Rotifer was found maximum (232 unit/l ± 36.55) in winter season of 2002–2003 and minimum 28unit/l ± 16.16 in monsoon season of same year. Cladocerans were observed maximum (140 unit/l ± 14.14) during winter season of 2002–2003 and minimum (30 unit/l ± 21.21) during monsoon season of the same year.

Copepods were found maximum (90 unit/l ± 1.65) during winter season (2002–2003) and minimum (15 unit/l ± 2.19) during summer season of same year. In total at sampling station D, the highest zooplankton (672 unit/l ± 65.13) were recorded in winter season (2002–2003) and lowest (130 unit/l ± 8.73) in monsoon season of 2003–2004. Table 5B.35 and Figure 5B.39.

Among average value *Amoeba* was found dominating in the zooplankton, 2002–2003 65 unit/l ± 52.20), followed by *Keratella* (50 unit/l ± 58.94), *Cyclops* (48.33 unit/l ± 38.18), *Bosmina* (46.66 unit/l ± 28.86), *Notholca* (45 unit/l ± 26.05), *Arcella* (40.33 unit/l ± 38.68), *Philodima* (30.66 unit/l ± 26.85), and *Daphnia* (26.33 unit/l ± 30.66).

While in second year 2003–2004, *Notholca* (57 unit/l ± 37.50), was found to be dominating followed by *Daphnia* (51.66 unit/l ± 32.14), *Philodima* (45.33 unit/l ± 35.00), *Cyclops* (45.33 unit/l ± 35.57), *Keratella* (40.66 unit/l ± 33.30), *Bosmina* (40 unit/l ± 28.35), *Amoeba* (39.33 unit/l ± 32.02) and *Arcella* (26 unit/l ± 10.14), Table 5B.36 and Figure 5B.40.

PHYTOPLANKTON

Among phytoplankton Chlorophyceae was found dominating followed by and Myxophyceae and Bacillariophyceae for first year (2002–2003) and Chlorophyceae followed by Bacillariophyceae and Myxophyceae in second year (2003–2004). Bacillariophyceae was found maximum (506 unit/l ± 20.43) in winter season (2003–2004) and minimum (30unit/l ± 4.02) in monsoon season of 2002–2003.Chlorophyceae was found maximum (1702 unit/l ± 83.60) in winter season of 2003–2004 and minimum (384 unit ± 46.93) in monsoon season of 2002–2003. Myxophyceae was found to be highest (623 unit/l ± 11.23) in winter season of 2002–2003 while minimum (72 unit/l ± 6.42) in monsoon season of same year *i.e.*, 2002–2003. Table 5B.37 and Figure 5B41.

Table 5B.36: Quantitative Analysis of Zooplankton in Different Seasons of River Suswa at Sampling Station D (2002-2004)

Year	*Seasons*	*Protozoa*		*Rotifera*			*Cladocera*		*Copepod*	*Total l^{-1}*
		Arcella	*Amoeba*	*Keratella*	*Philodima*	*Notholca*	*Daphnia*	*Bosmina*	*Cyclops*	
2002–2003	Summer	18±2.19	40±3.24	35±1.97	50±3.09	32±2.06	19±3.75	30±3.08	15±2.19	239±12.06
	Monsoon	18±0.00	30±0.00	0±0.00	0±0.00	28±0.00	0±0.00	30±0.00	40±0.00	146±16.22
	Winter	85±7.13	125±9.30	115±8.37	42±6.56	75±5.59	60±4.32	80±8.76	90±9.15	672±27.03
	Average	40.33±38.68	65±52.20	50.0±58.94	30.66±26.85	45±26.05	26.33±30.66	46.66±28.86	48.33±38.18	352.31±11.99
2003–2004	Summer	28±5.26	38±4.97	78±3.13	46±2.09	56±3.73	75±3.34	30±7.77	20±1.09	371±21.65
	Monsoon	15±0.50	8±1.00	14±0.75	10±0.00	20±0.00	15±1.75	18±2.09	30±1.90	136±6.77
	Winter	35±2.39	72±5.73	30±3.19	80±12.73	95±11.59	65±4.73	72±9.27	86±11.76	535±23.17
	Average	26±10.14	39.33±32.02	40.66±33.30	45.33±35.00	57±37.50	51.66±32.14	40±28.35	45.33±35.57	345.31±9.24

±: Standard Deviation.

Table 5B.37: Comparitive Analysis of Seasonal Variation Among Phytoplankton of River Suswa at Sampling Station D (2002-2004)

Year	*Seasons*	*Bacillariophyceae l^{-1}*	*Chlorophyceae l^{-1}*	*Myxophyceae l^{-1}*	*Total l^{-1}*
2002-2003	Summer	167±9.80	816±33.23	212±5.13	1195±362.40
	Monsoon	30±4.02	384±46.93	72±6.42	486±193.40
	Winter	371±12.57	1448±73.13	623±11.23	2442±563.33
	Average	190.64±7.31	882.64±24.72	300.26±6.63	1373.54±371.94
2003–2004	Summer	423±18.51	813±26.79	118±8.08	1354±348.36
	Monsoon	46±6.45	488±32.63	561±18.24	1095±278.66
	Winter	506±20.43	1702±83.60	199±17.09	2407±794.11
	Average	324.97±11.32	1000.97±22.26	297.89±214.27	1582.3±411.50

±: Standard Deviation.

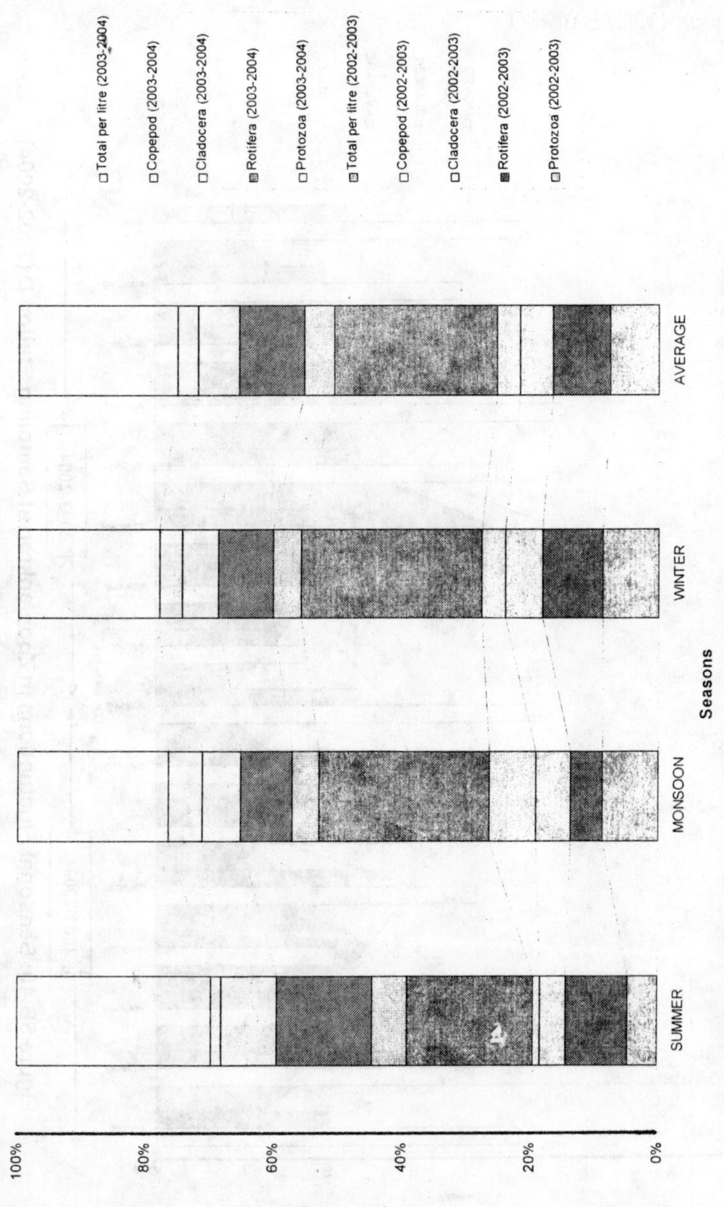

Figure 5B.39; Percentile Fluctuation in Zooplankton at Sampling Station D (2002-2004)

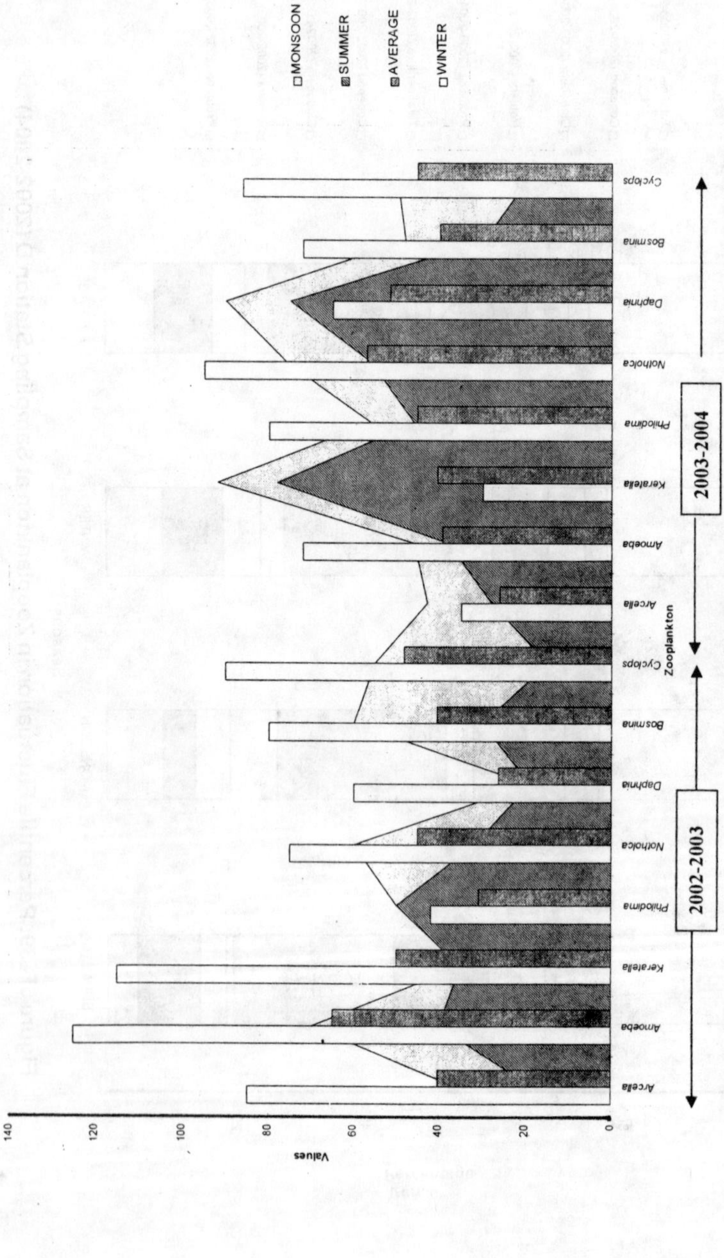

Figure 5B.40: Seasonal Fluctuations in Zooplankton at Sampling Station D (2002-2004)

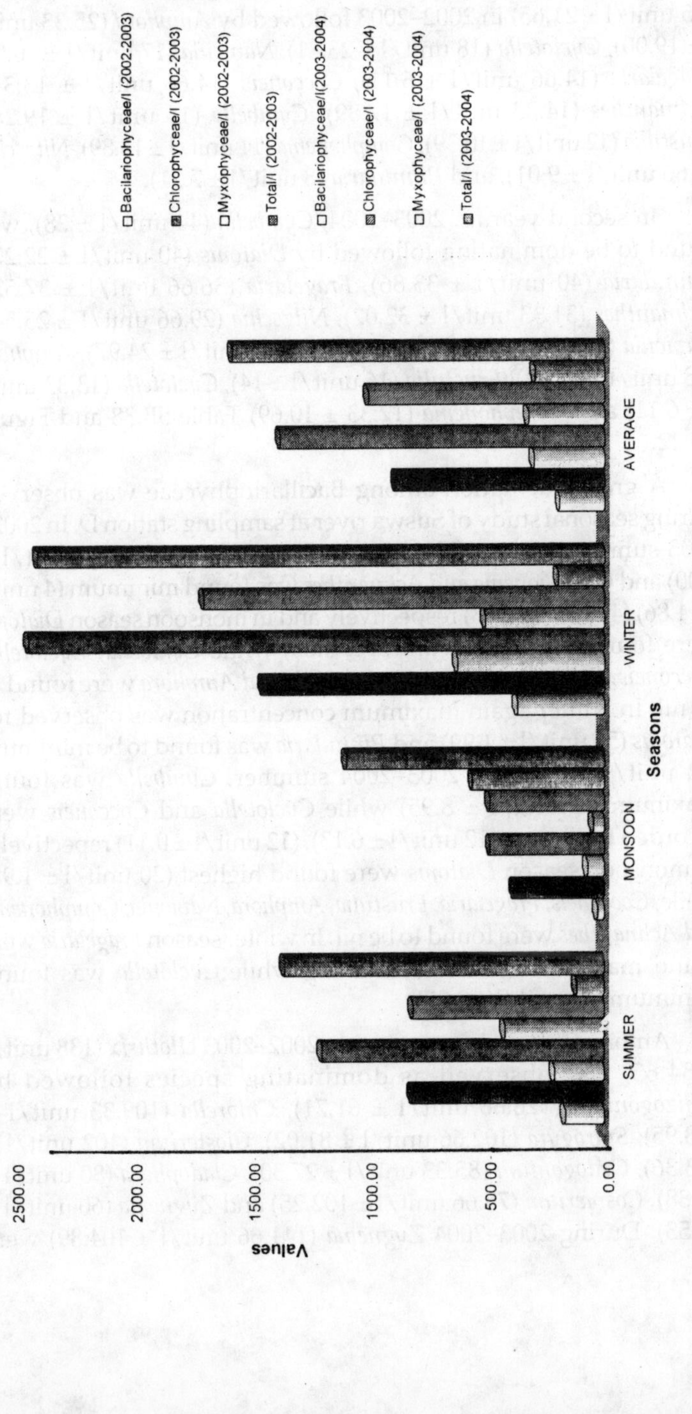

Figure 5B.41: Seasonal Fluctuations in Phytoplankton at Sampling Station D (2002-2004)

Among Bacillariophyceae *Diatoms* was found to be dominating (35 unit/l ± 21.65) in 2002–2003 followed by *Amphora* (25.33 unit/l ± 19.00), *Cyclotella* (18 unit/l ± 23.81), *Navicula* (17 unit/l ± 16.09, *Fragelaria* (14.66 unit/l ± 6.11), *Cocconeis* (14.66 unit/l ± 13.31), *Achnanthes* (14.33 unit/l ± 17.89), *Cymbella* (14 unit/l ± 19.28), *Frustulia* (12 unit/l ± 10.39), *Gomphonema* (11 unit/l ± 13.89), *Nitzschia* (8.66 unit/l ± 9.01), and *Pinnularia* (8 unit/l ± 7.21).

In second year *i.e.* 2003–2004, *Cymbella* (44 unit/l ± 28), was found to be dominating followed by *Diatoms* (40 unit/l ± 22.27), *Pinnularia* (40 unit/l ± 33.86), *Fragelaria* (36.66 unit/l ± 37.52), *Achnanthes* (31.33 unit/l ± 32.02), *Nitzschia* (29.66 unit/l ± 25.54), *Navicula* (23.66 unit/l ± 24), *Cocconeis* (20 unit/l ± 24.97), *Amphora* (18 unit/l ± 15.62), *Frustulia* (16 unit/l ± 14), *Cyclotella* (13.33 unit/l ± 6.11) and *Gomphonema* (12.33 ± 10.69) Table 5B.38 and Figure 5B.42.

A great fluctuation among Bacillariophyceae was observed during seasonal study of Suswa river at sampling station D. In 2002–2003-summer season, *Diatoms* was found maximum (38 unit/l ± 1.00) and *Gomphonema and Achnanthes* was found minimum (4 unit/l ± 1.86) (4 unit/l ± 0.03) respectively and in monsoon season *Diatoms* were found highest (12 unit/l ± 0.00) while *Cymbella, Cyclotella, Cocconeis, Frustulia, Pinnularia, Nitzshia and Amphora* were found to be nil. In winter again maximum concentration was observed for *Diatoms* (55 unit/l ± 1.99) and *Pinnularia* was found to be minimum (14 unit/l ± 0.26). In 2003–2004 summer, *Cymbella* was found maximum (64unit/l ± 8.95) while *Cyclotella* and *Cocconeis* were recorded minimum (12 unit/l ± 6.13), (12 unit/l ± 0.11) repectively. In monsoon season *Diatoms* were found highest (20 unit/l ± 1.98) while, *Cocconeis, Fragelaria, Frustulia, Amphora, Navicula, Gomphonema and Achnanthes* were found to be nil. In winter season *Fragelaria* were found maximum (75 unit/l ± 3.14), while *Cyclotella* was found minimum (20 unit/l ± 8.97).

Among Chlorophyceae during 2002–2003 *Ulothrix* (138 unit/l ± 84.65, was observed as dominating species followed by *Schizogonium* (126.66 unit/l ± 61.71), *Chlorella* (109.33 unit/l ± 118.95), *Spirogyra* (102.66 unit/l ± 81.02), *Closterium* (102 unit/l ± 103.36), *Oedogonium* (85.33 unit/l ± 27.30), *Cladophora* (80 unit/l ± 70.88), *Cosmerium* (78.66 unit/l ± 102.25) and *Zygnema* (60 unit/l ± 22.53). During 2003–2004 *Zygnema* (141.66 unit/l ± 104.89) were

Table 5B.38: Quantitative Analysis of Seasonal Variation Among Bacillariophyceae of River Suswa at Sampling Station D (2002-2004)

	Seasons	*Achnanthes*	*Amphora*	*Cocconeis*	*Cymbella*	*Cyclotella*	*Diatoms*	*Fragelaria*
2002–2003	Summer	4±0.03	24±0.73	18±1.16	6±0.05	9±1.10	38±1.00	16±2.00
	Monsoon	4±0.02	0±0.00	0±0.00	0±0.00	0±0.00	12±0.00	8±2.00
	Winter	35±2.15	42±2.90	26±3.66	36±4.88	45±1.09	55±1.99	20±3.96
	Average	14.33±17.89	25.33±19.00	14.66±13.31	14±19.28	18±23.81	35±21.65	14.66±6.11
	Summer	30±1.90	28±2.22	12±6.13	64±8.95	12±0.11	36±5.26	35±8.00
	Monsoon	0±0.00	0±0.00	0±0.00	12±0.50	8±0.76	20±1.98	0±0.00
	Winter	64±14.11	26±15.48	48±13.29	56±20.00	20±8.97	64±7.62	75±3.14
	Average	31.33±32.02	18±15.62	20±24.97	44±28	13.33±6.11	40.0±22.27	36.66±37.52
	Seasons	*Frustulia*	*Gomphonema*	*Navicula*	*Nitzschia*	*Pinnularia*	*Total l^{-1}*	
2003–2004	Summer	18±3.16	4±1.86	12±0.75	8±0.00	10±2.10	167±9.80	
	Monsoon	0±0.00	2±0.02	4±0.00	0±0.00	0±0.00	30±4.02	
	Winter	18±0.00	27±3.25	35±4.86	18±9.19	14±0.26	371±12.57	
	Average	12±10.39	11±13.89	17±16.09	8.66±9.01	8±7.21	190.69±7.31	
	Summer	22±7.11	18±6.32	48±5.05	56±4.18	62±8.78	432±18.51	
	Monsoon	0±0.00	0±0.00	0±0.00	5±2.15	1±0.00	46±6.45	
	Winter	26±2.15	19±16.00	23±11.91	28±8.00	57±7.79	506±20.43	
	Average	16.0±14.0	12.33±10.69	23.66±24.0	29.66±25.54	40±33.86	324.97±11.32	

±: Standard Deviation.

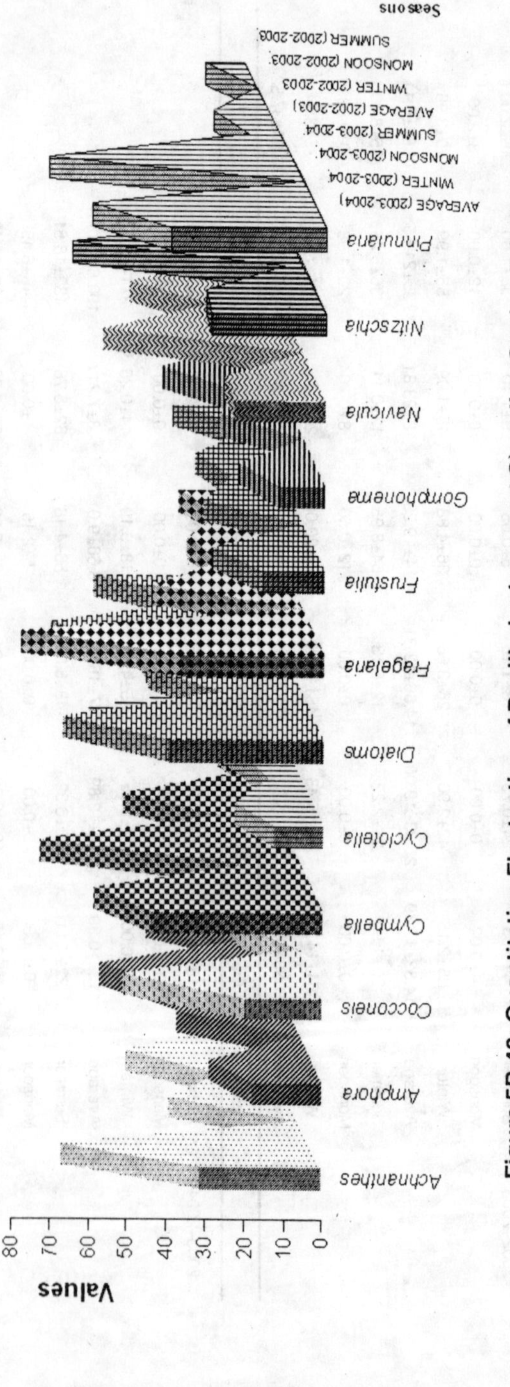

Figure 5B.42: Quantitative Fluctuation of Bacillariophyceae at Sampling Station D (2002-2004)

found as dominant species followed by *Closterium* (131.33 unit/l ± 131.97), *Ulothrix* (127.33 unit/l ± 76), *Cosmerium* (120.66 unit/l ± 80.62), *Cladophora* (110.66 unit/l ± 126.13), *Oedogonium* (107 unit/l ± 40.14), *Chlorella* (99 unit/l ± 86.81), *Spirogyra* (95.33 unit/l ± 55.86) and *Schizogonium* (68 unit/l ± 64.37).

A great variation in seasonal values of Chlorophyceae was noted during the course of study at sampling station D, during first year 2002–2003 *Cladophora* was found maximum (135unit/l ± 19.69) and *Cosmerium* was found as minimum (38 unit/l ± 4.44) in summer season. While in monsoon season *Schizigonium* was found to be highest (110unit/l ± 6.29) and *Chlorella and Cladophora were* recorded as nil. In winter season *Chlorella* was revealed maximum (236 unit/l ± 32.88) and *Cladophora* was recorded as minimum (10.5unit/l ± 8.79). While in second year 2003–2004 *Schizigonium* was found maximum (128 unit/l ± 5.49) and *Spirogyra* was found minimum (46unit/l ± 11.99), in summer season. In monsoon season, *Ulothrix* was found maximum (105 unit/l ± 7.23) while *Cladophora* was found as nil. In winter season *Closterium* were found maximum (280unit/l ± 12.00) while *Schizogonium* were found as nil. The total highest value of Chlorophyceae was recorded in winter (1448 unit/l ± 73.13) and lowest in monsoon (384 unit/l ± 46.93) for first year (2002–2003) for second year (2003–2004) the highest total value of Chlorophyceae was recorded in winter (1702 unit/l ± 83.60) and lowest in monsoon season (488unit/l ± 32.63). Table 5B.39 and Figure 5B.43.

Among Myxophyceae *Oscillatoria* (107.66 unit/l ± 100.08) was recorded as dominant species, followed by *Anacystis* (99.33 unit/l ± 93.36) and *Anabena* (95.33 unit/1 ± 93.21) for first year (2002–2003). During second year *Anabena* was found as dominating species (108.66 unit/l ± 90.16) followed by *Oscillatoria* (93.66 unit/l ± 73.11) and *Anacystis* (90.33 unit/l ± 74).

For seasonal fluctuation of Myxophyceae it is revealed that in summer season of 2002–2003, *Anabena* existed in maximum (72 unit/l ± 8.27) while *Oscillatoria* was found minimum (7.5unit/l ± 11.59). In monsoon season *Oscillatoria* and *Anacystis* was found maximum (28 unit/l ± 5.59), (28 unit/l ± 2.63), respectively and *Anabena* was found minimum (16unit/l ± 3.95). In winter season, again *Oscillatoria* was found maximum (220 unit/l ± 35.35) and *Anabena* was least (198 unit/l ± 20.33). During second year (2003–2004), *Oscillatoria*

Table 5B.39: Quantitative Analysis of Seasonal Variation Among Chlorophyceae of River Suswa at Sampling Station D (2002-2004)

Year	Seasons	*Closterium*	*Cosmerium*	*Chlorella*	*Cladophora*	*Oedogonium*	*Schizogonium*	*Spirogyra*	*Ulothrix*	*Zygnema*	Total l^{-1}
2002–2003	Summer	92±8.76	38±4.44	92±12.68	135±19.69	110±10.87	75±5.96	128±11.67	100±10.00	46±4.98	816±33.23
	Monsoon	4±1.11	3±1.09	0±0.00	0±0.00	90±3.26	110±6.29	12±0.50	79±7.66	86±8.93	384±46.93
	Winter	210±16.89	195±24.62	236±32.88	10.5±8.79	56±20.66	195±24 .66	168±3.96	235±11.87	48±2.00	1448±73.13
	Average	102±103.36	78.66±102.25	109.33±118.95	80±70.88	85.33±27.30	126.66±61.71	102.66±81.02	138±84.65	60±22.53	882.64±24.72
2003–2004	Summer	86±2.96	95±8.79	76±7.77	84±6.46	111±7.31	128±5.49	46±11.99	65±4.36	122±12.48	813±26.79
	Monsoon	28±6.66	56±4.87	26±2.87	0.0±0.00	65±8.49	76±10.41	84±8.88	105±7.23	48±6.56	488±32.63
	Winter	280±12.00	211±10.04	195±11.98	248±12.50	145±11.50	0.00±0.00	156±12.68	212±16.18	255±12.19	1702±83.60
	Average	131.33±131.97	120.66±80.62	99±86.81	110.66±126.13	107±40.14	68±64.37	95.33±55.86	127.33±76.00	141.66±104.89	1000.97±22.26

±: Standard Deviation.

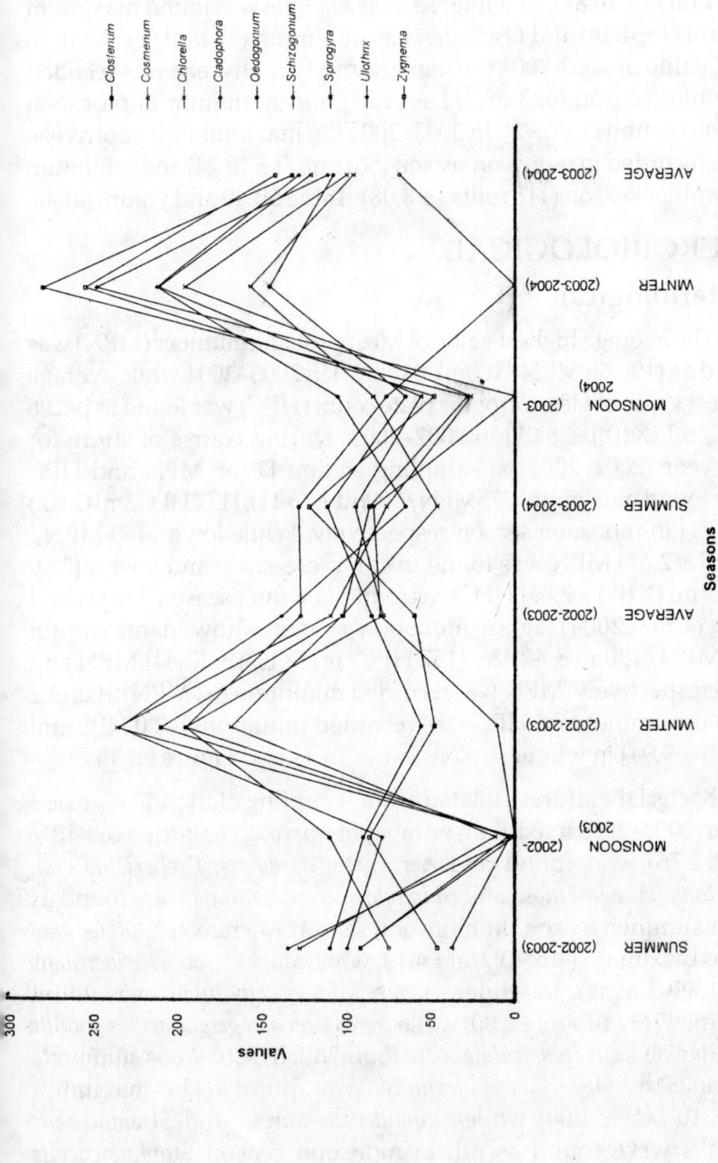

Figure 5B.43: Quantitative Fluctuation of Chlorophyceae at Sampling Station D (2002-2004)

was found maximum (48 unit/l ± 9.99) and *Anabena* as minimum (32 unit/l ± 6.98) in summer season. In monsoon season *Anabena* was found maximum (208 unit/l ± 12.62) and *Anacystis* as minimum (175 unit/l ± 16.88). In winter season *Anabena* was found maximum (86unit/l ± 4.49) and *Oscillatoria* as minimum (55 unit/l ± 2.38). In total value of 2002-2004 the maximum Myxophyceae was recoded in winter season (623 unit/l ± 11.23) and minimum in monsoon season (72unit/l ± 6.92). In 2003–2004 the maximum Myxophyceae were recorded in monsoon season (561unit/l ± 18.24) and minimum in summer season (118 unit/l ± 8.08). Table 5B.40 and Figure 5B.44.

MICROBIOLOGICAL

Bacteriological

The average highest value of Most probable number (MPN) was found as (190.66 MPN/100ml ± 178.93) in 2003–2004 while average highest value of Heterotrophic plate count (HPC) was found as [90.96 HPC/ml ($X10^3$) ± 8.05] in 2002–2003. During course of study for first year (2002–2003) at sampling station D the MPN and HPC were found maximum (275MPN/100ml ± 26.11), [177 HPC/ml ($X10^3$) ± 13.71] in monsoon season respectively. While lowest (50 MPN/100ml ± 2.41) MPN was found in summer season and lowest [28.0 HPC/ml ($X10^3$) ± 2.89] HPC was found in winter season. For second year (2003–2004) again monsoon season showed maximum (395MPN/100ml ± 42.48), [157 HPC/ml ($X10^3$) ± 12.84] MPN and HPC respectively. MPN was recorded minimum (62 MPN/100ml ± 7.86) in summer and HPC was recorded minimum [42.0 HPC/ml ($X10^3$) ± 9.94] in winter season. Table 5B.41 and Figure 5B.45.

Bacterial cultures isolated from sampling station D revealed that in 2002–2003 maximum number of *Micrococcus luteus* (26×10^3/ml ± 2.76), was found and *Aerobacter aerogens, Escherichia coli, Pseudomonas aeroginosa* and *Staphyloccus epidermidis* were found as nil in summer season. In monsoon season *Micrococcus luteus* was found maximum (40×10^3/ml ± 4.19) while *Staphylococcus epidermidis* was found as nil. In winter season *Micrococcus luteus* was found maximum (8×10^3/ml ± 2.00) while *Aerobacter aerogens, Bacillus subtilis* and *Staphyloccus epidermidis* were found nil. In 2003–2004 summer's season *Staphylococcus epidermidis* was found to be maximum (22×10^3/ml ± 1.00) while *Staphyloccus aureus* and *Streptococcus facecalis* were found as nil. In monsoon season *Staphylococcus*

Table 5B.40: Quantitative Analysis of Seasonal Variation Among Myxophyceaee of River Suswa at Sampling Station D (2002-2004)

Year	*Seasons*	*Anacystis*	*Anabena*	*Oscillatoria*	*Total* l^{-1}
2002–2003	Summer	65±5.96	72±8.27	7.5±11.59	212±5.13
	Monsoon	28±2.63	16±3.95	28±5.59	72±6.92
	Winter	205±16.89	198±20.33	220±35.35	623±11.23
	Average	99.33±93.36	95.33±93.21	107.66±100.08	300.26±6.63
2003–2004	Summer	38±3.95	32±6.98	48±9.99	118±8.08
	Monsoon	175±16.88	208±12.62	178±7.79	561±18.24
	Winter	58±8.00	86±4.49	55±2.38	199±17.09
	Average	90.33±74.0	108.66±90.16	93.66±73.11	256.66±7.99

±: Standard Deviation.

Table 5B.41: Quantitative Analysis of Seasonal Variation in Bacteriological Parameters of River Suswa at Sampling Station D (2002-2004)

Year	*Seasons*	*MPN/100 ml*	*HPC/ml ($X10^3$) ($\times 10^3$)*
2002–2003	Summer	50±2.41	68±9.04
	Monsoon	275±26.11	177±13.71
	Winter	95±16.49	28±2.89
	Average	140±119.05	90.96±8.05
2003–2004	Summer	62±7.86	62.0±7.67_
	Monsoon	395±42.48	157±12.84
	Winter	115±15.11	42±9.94
	Average	190.66±178.93	86.97±7.10

±: Standard Deviation.

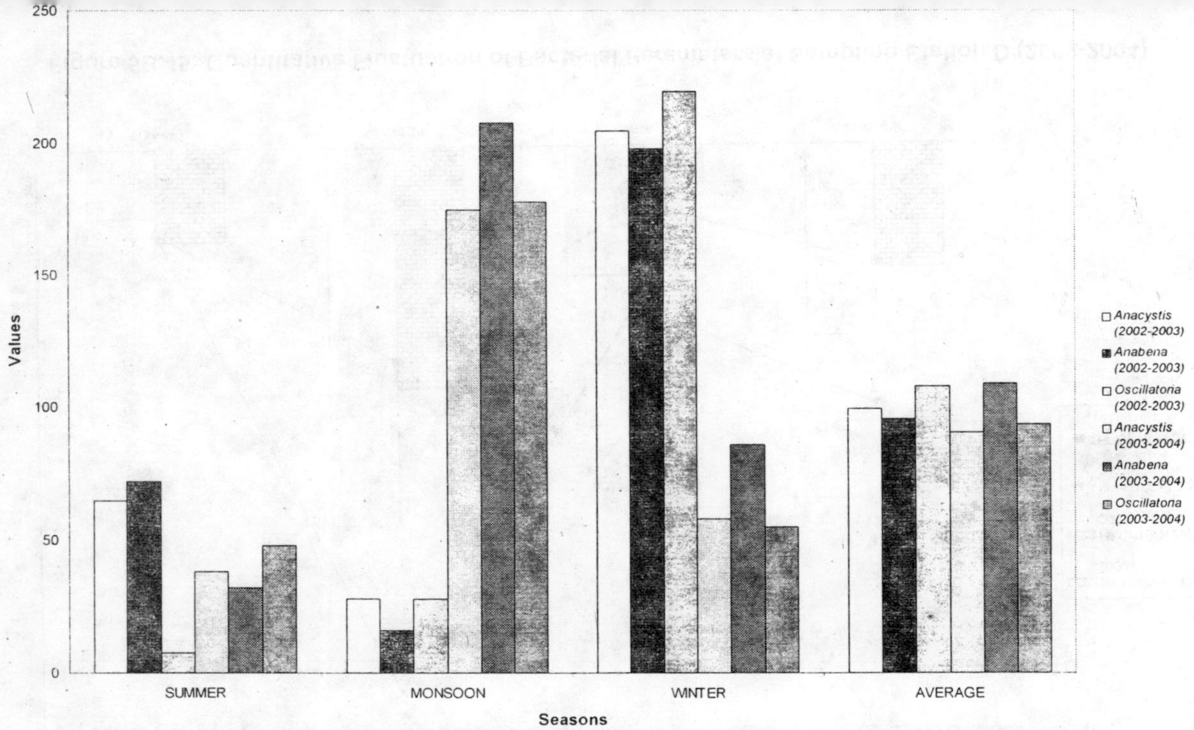

Figure 5B.44 : Quantitative Fluctuation of Myxophyceae at Sampling Station D (2002-2004)

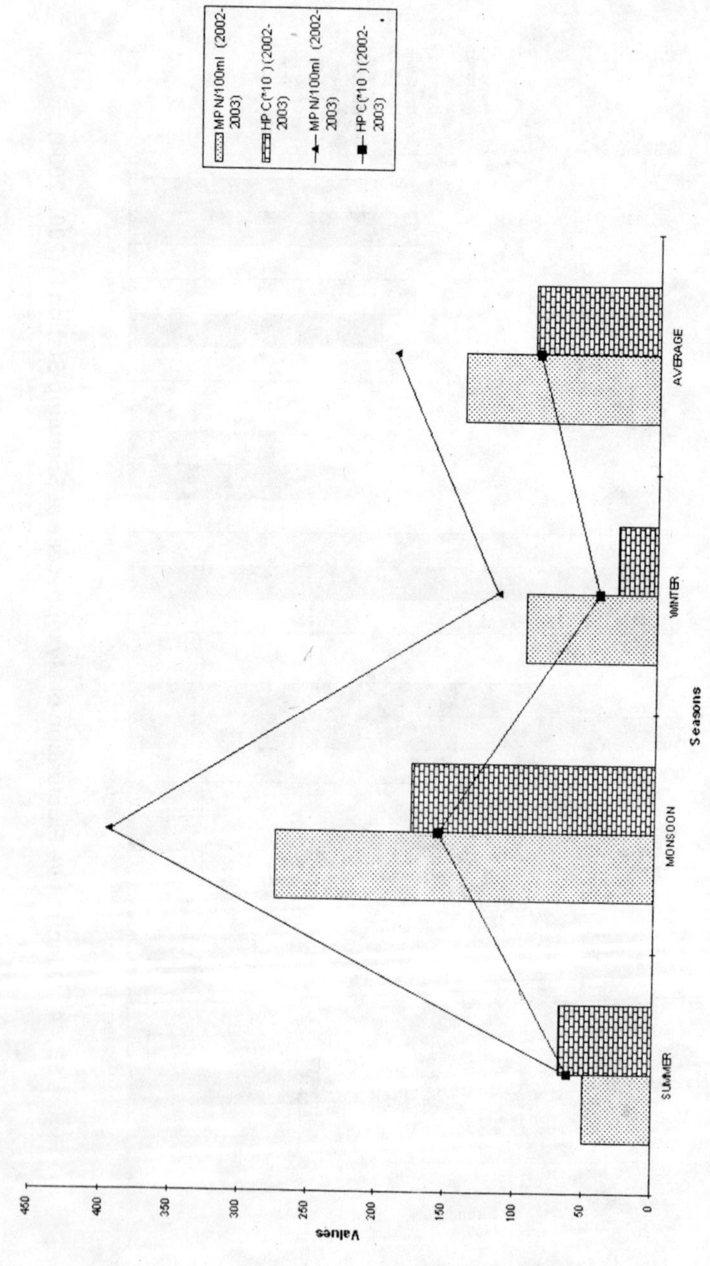

Figure 5B.45: Quantitative Fluctuation of Bacterial Parameters at Sampling Station D (2002-2004)

epidermidis was found to be maximum (42 x 10^3/ml ± 1.50) while *Streptococcus facecalis* was found as minimum. In winter season *Staphylococcus epidermidis and Salmonella typhii* were recorded maximum (12 x 10^3/ml ± 1.55) (12 x 10^3/ml ± 1.63) respectively while, *Streptococcus facecalis* and *Micrococcus luteus* were recorded nil.

On an average calculation for 2002–2003 *Micrococcus luteus* was observed as dominant species (24.66 x 10^3/ml ± 16.04) followed by *Streptococcus facecalis* (18 x 10^3/ml ± 17.08), *Salmonella typhii* (14.66 x 10^3/ml ± 11.71), *Bacillus subtilis* (11.66 x 10^3/ml ± 12.58) *Staphylococcus aureus* (9.66 x 10^3/ml ± 7.23), *Escherichia coli* (6.66 x 10^3/ml ± 8.32), *Pseudomonas aeroginosa* (3.66 x 10^3/ml ± 4.04), *Aerobacter aerogens* (2 x 10^3/ml ± 3.46) and *Staphylococcus epidermidis* (0 x 10^3/ml ± 0.00) and In 2003–2004 *Staphylococcus epidermidis* (25.33 x 10^3/ml ± 15.27was noted maximum followed by *Salmonella typhii* (13.0 x 10^3/ml ± 2.64), *Bacillus subtilis* (11.66 x 10^3/ml ± 5.50), *Pseudomonas aeroginosa* (11.33 x 10^3/ml ± 17.89), *Staphylococcus aureus* (8.33 x 10^3/ml ± 11.93), *Micrococcus luteus* (6.33 x 10^3/ml ± 5.68), *Aerobacter aerogens* (5.66 x 10^3/ml ± 4.04), *Escherichia coli* (5.33 x 10^3/ml ± 4.93) and *Streptococcus facecalis* (0x 10^3/ml ± 0.00), Table 5B.42 and Figure 5B.46.

AQUATIC FUNGI

During the course of study the average aquatic fungi at this sampling station was found highest (29.99 x 10^3/ml ± 1.44) in 2003–2004 and minimum (20.32 x 10^3/ml ± 1.17) in 2002–2003.

In seasonal study for first year (2002–2003) the maximum aquatic fungi was observed in monsoon season (46 x 10^3/ml ± 3.05) followed by summer (12 x 10^3/ml ± 2.0) and winter (3 x 10^3/ml ± 1.73). In 2003–2004 maximum aquatic fungi was observed in monsoon season (67 x 10^3/ml ± 4.50) followed by winter (15 x 10^3/ml ± 4.35) and summer season (8 x 10^3/ml ± 2.08). Table 5B.43 and Figure 5B.47.

In an average calculation for 2002–2003 *Fusarium* was observed maximum (8 x 10^3/ml ± 9.16) followed by *Penicillium* (6.66 x 10^3/ml ± 8.32) and *Aspergillus* (5.66 x 10^3/ml ± 5.50) In 2003–2004, *Aspergillus* was found as dominant species (11.66 x 10^3/ml ± 9.07) followed by *Fusarium* (9.33 x 10^3/ml ± 15.30) and *Penicillium* (9 x 10^3/ml ± 8.18). During 2002–2003 *Fusarium* was found maximum (6x 10^3/ml ± 1.11) and *Aspergillus* was found minimum (2 x 10^3/ml ± 0.30) in summer

Table 5B.42: Isolation of Bacterial (ml $^{-1}$× 10^3) Standard Deviation Culture from Sampling Station D (2002-2004)

Bacteria	*2002-2003*				*2003-2004*			
	Summer	*Monsoon*	*Winter*	*Average*	*Summer*	*Monsoon*	*Winter*	*Average*
*Salmonella typhii**	10±2.00	28±5.00	6±0.50	14.66±11.71	16±3.82	11±2.00	12±1.63	13.0±2.64
*Streptococcus facecalis**	16±4.16	36±4.44	2±1.50	18±17.08	0±0.00	0±0.00	0±0.00	0±0.00
*Aerobacter aerogens**	0±0.00	6±0.76	0±0.00	2.00±3.46	5±0.50	10±0.79	2±0.00	5.66±4.04
*Staphylococcus epidermidis**	0±0.00	0±0.00	0±0.00	0±0.00	22±1.00	42±1.50	12±1.55	25.33±15.27
*Staphylococcus aureus**	6±1.56	18±2.59	5±1.11	9.66±7.23	0±0.00	22±2.11	3±0.50	8.33±11.93
*Micrococcus luteus***	26±2.76	40±4.19	8±2.00	24.66±16.04	8±1.54	11±2.97	0.00±0.00	6.33±5.68
*Bacillus subtilis***	10±2.16	25±1.50	0±0.00	11.66±12.58	8±0.00	18±2.76	9±1.59	11.66±5.50
*Escherichia coli**	0±0.00	16±2.95	4±1.50	6.66±8.32	2±0.50	11±0.76	3±0.66	5.33±4.93
*Pseudomonas aerogenosa**	0±0.00	8±2.10	3±0.63	3.66±4.04	1±0.00	32±2.59	1±0.13	11.33±17.89
Total l^{-1}	68±9.04	177±13.71	28±2.89	90.96±8.05	62±7.67	157±12.84	42±9.94	86.97±7.10

*: Pathogens; **: Non pathogens; ±: Standard Deviation.

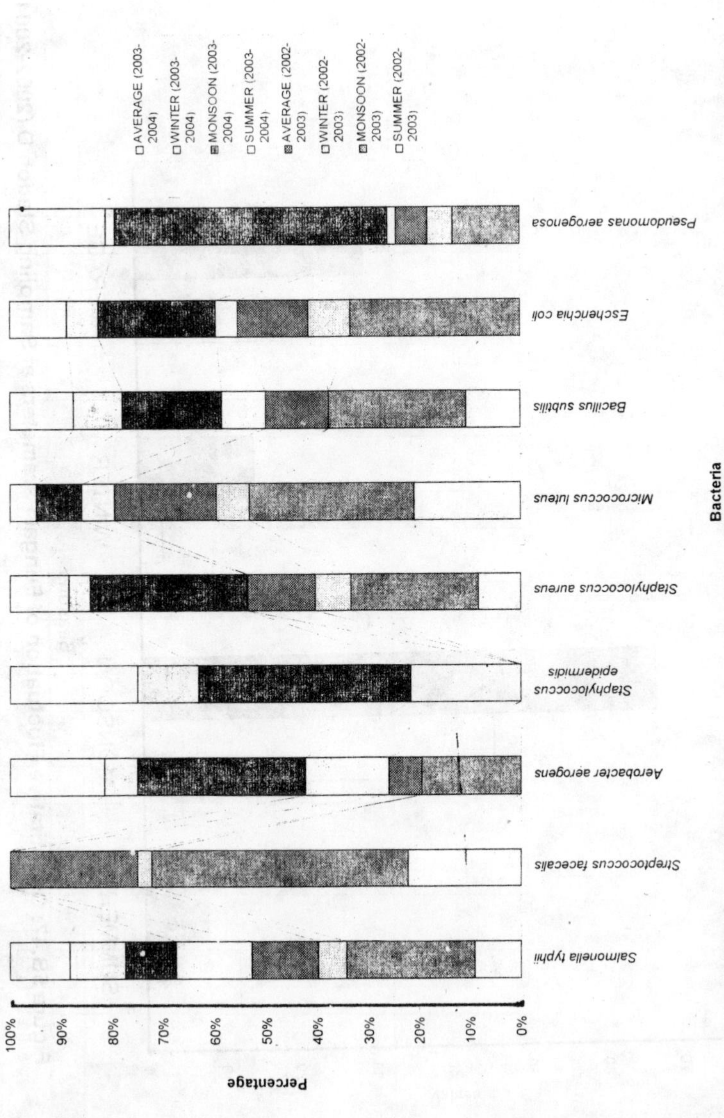

Figure 5B.46: Percentile Composition of Bacterial Culture at Sampling Station D (2002-2004)

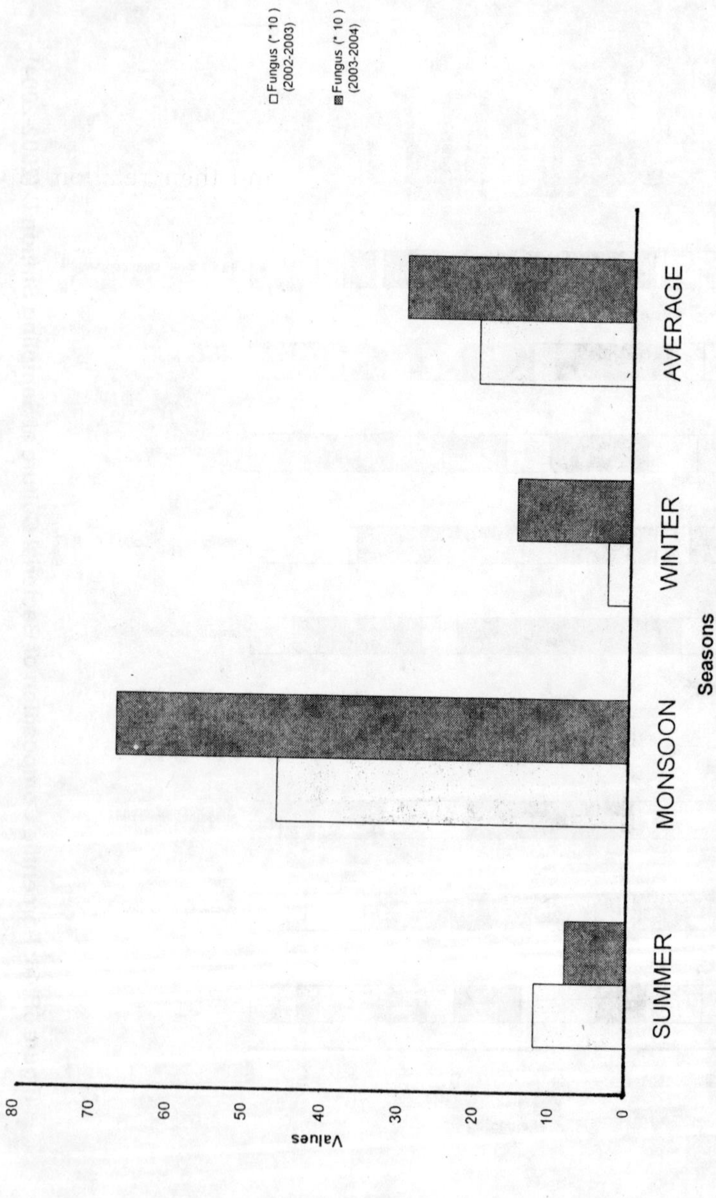

Figure 5B.47: Quantitative Fluctuation of Fungal Parameters at Sampling Station D (2002-2004)

Table 5B.43: Isolation of Fungus ($ml^{-1} \times 10^3$) from Sampling Station D (2002-2004)

Fungus	2002-2003				2003-2004			
	Summer	*Monsoon*	*Winter*	*Average*	*Summer*	*Monsoon*	*Winter*	*Average*
	12±2.0	46±3.05	3±1.73	20.32±1.17	8±2.08	67±4.50	15±4.35	29.99±1.44

±: Standard Deviation.

Table 5B.44: Isolation of Fungus ($ml^{-1} \times 10^3$) from Sampling Station D (2002-2004)

Fungus	2002-2003				2003-2004			
	Summer	*Monsoon*	*Winter*	*Average*	*Summer*	*Monsoon*	*Winter*	*Average*
Aspergillus	2±0.30	12±3.12	3±0.50	5.66±5.50	5±1.31	22±6.78	8±0.19	11.66±9.07
Penicillium	4±0.10	16±2.45	0±0.00	6.66±8.32	2±0.11	18±2.09	7±2.10	9±8.18
Fusarium	6±1.11	18±1.11	0±0.00	8±9.16	1±0.00	27±5.07	0±0.00	9.33±15.30
Total l^{-1}	**12±2.0**	**46±3.05**	**3±1.73**	**20.32±01.17**	**8±2.08**	**67±4.50**	**15±4.35**	**29.99±1.44**

±: Standard Deviation.

season. *Fusarium* was observed highest (18.0 x 10^3/ml ± 1.11) in monsoon season while *Aspergillus was* observed least (12 x 10^3/ml ± 3.12). In winter season *Aspergillus* was found maximum (3 x 10^3/ml ± 0.50), *Penicillium* and *Fusarium* were found as nil. In 2003–2004 summer's season observation revealed that growth of *Aspergillus* was optimum (5 x 10^3/ml ± 1.31) while *Fusarium* was observed as least (1 x 10^3/ml ± 0.00). In monsoon season growth of *Fusarium* was recorded highest (27 x 10^3/ml ± 5.07) and *Penicillium* was recorded as least (18 x 10^3/ml ± 2.09). In winter season *Aspergillus* was found maximum (8 x 10^3/ml ± 0.19) and *Fusarium* was observed as nil. Table 5B.44 and Figure 5B.48.

C) Mathematical Modeling

Sampling Station B

The value of DO is obtained as 7.35mg/l for the monsoon season of year 2002 and 7.74 mg/l for the monsoon season of year 2003. While the value of BOD is obtained as 0.46 mg/l for the monsoon season of year 2002 and 0.50 mg/l for the monsoon season of year 2003 (here monsoon season stands for the period July–August) by applying the given model:

DO: for the year 2002 (monsoon season)

$$\lambda_1 (S) = C_1 \lambda_1 (S\text{-}1) + C_2 U_1 (S\text{-}1) + C_3 e_1 (S)$$

$$\lambda_1 (S) = 0.715 (7.93) + 0.174 (8.08) + 0.554 (0.53)$$

$$\lambda_1 (S) = 5.66 + 1.40 + 0.29$$

$$\lambda_1 (S) = 7.35 \text{ mg/l}$$

DO: for the year 2003–2004

$$\lambda_1 (S) = C_1 \lambda_1 (S\text{-}1) + C_2 U_1 (S\text{-}1) + C_3 e_1 (S)$$

$$\lambda_1 (S) = 0.715 (8.55) + 0.174 (8.37) + 0.554 (0.33)$$

$$\lambda_1 (S) = 6.11 + 1.45 + 0.18$$

$$\lambda_1 (S) = 7.74 \text{ mg/l}$$

BOD: for the year 2002–2003

$$\lambda_2 (S) = C_4 \lambda_1 (S\text{-}1) + C_5 U_1 (S\text{-}1) - C_6 e_1 (S)$$

$$\lambda_2 (S) = 0.751 (0.69) + 0.102 (0.52) - 0.313 (0.35)$$

$$\lambda_2 (S) = 0.518 + 0.05 - 0.10$$

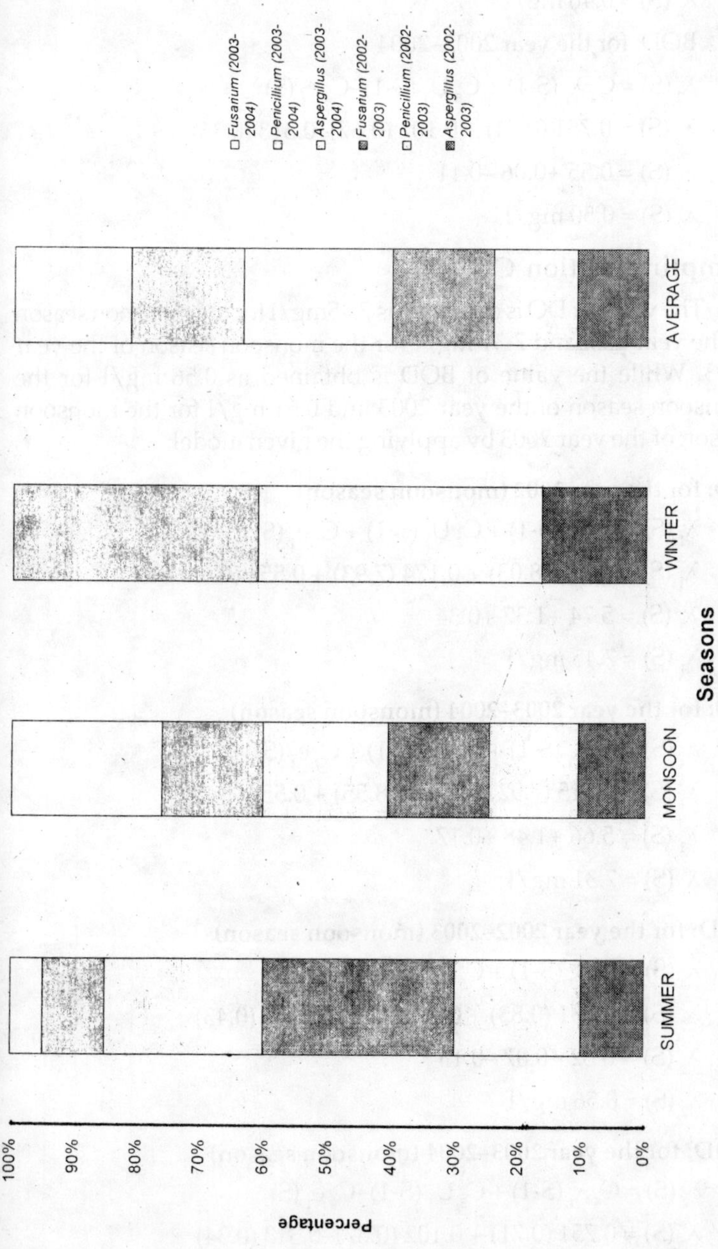

Figure 5B.48: Percentile Composition of Fungal Culture at Sampling Station D (2002-2004)

$\lambda_2 (S) = 0.46$ mg/l

BOD: for the year 2003–2004

$\lambda_2 (S) = C_4 \lambda_1 (S-1) + C_5 U_1 (S-1) - C_6 e_1 (S)$

$\lambda_2 (S) = 0.751 (0.74) + 0.102 (0.67) - 0.313 (0.36)$

$\lambda_2 (S) = 0.55 + 0.06 - 0.11$

$\lambda_2 (S) = 0.50$ mg/l

Sampling Station C

The value of DO is obtained as 7.45mg/l for the monsoon season of the year 2002and 7.31 mg/l for the monsoon season of the year 2003. While the value of BOD is obtained as 0.56 mg/l for the monsoon season of the year 2003 and 0.51 mg/l for the monsoon season of the year 2003 by applying the given model:

DO: for the year 2002 (monsoon season)

$\lambda_1 (S) = C_1 \lambda_1 (S-1) + C_2 U_1 (S-1) + C_3 e_1 (S)$

$\lambda_1 (S) = 0.715 (8.03) + 0.174 (7.93) + 0.554 (0.63)$

$\lambda_1 (S) = 5.74 + 1.37 + 0.34$

$\lambda_1 (S) = 7.45$ mg/l

DO: for the year 2003–2004 (monsoon season)

$\lambda_1 (S) = C_1 \lambda_1 (S-1) + C_2 U_1 (S-1) + C_3 e_1 (S)$

$\lambda_1 (S) = 0.715 (7.92) + 0.174 (8.55) + 0.554 (0.32)$

$\lambda_1 (S) = 5.66 + 1.48 + 0.17$

$\lambda_1 (S) = 7.31$ mg/l

BOD: for the year 2002–2003 (monsoon season)

$\lambda_2 (S) = C_4 \lambda_1 (S-1) + C_5 U_1 (S-1) - C_6 e_1 (S)$

$\lambda_2 (S) = 0.751 (0.83) + 0.102 (0.69) - 0.313 (0.43)$

$\lambda_2 (S) = 0.62 + 0.07 - 0.13$

$\lambda_2 (S) = 0.56$ mg/l

BOD: for the year 2003–2004 (monsoon season)

$\lambda_2 (S) = C_4 \lambda_1 (S-1) + C_5 U_1 (S-1) - C_6 e_1 (S)$

$\lambda_2 (S) = 0.751 (0.71) + 0.102 (0.87) - 0.313 (0.34)$

λ_2 (S) = 0.53 +0.08 –0.10

λ_2 (S) = 0.51 mg/l

Sampling Station D

The Value of DO is obtained as 7.37 mg/l for the monsoon season of the yearr 2002and 7.20 mg/l for the monsoon season of the year 2003. While the value of BOD is obtained as 0.51 mg/l for the monsoon season of the year 2002and 0.65mg/l for the monsoon season of the year 2003 by applying the given model:

DO: for the year 2002 (monsoon season)

λ_1 (S) = C_1 λ_1 (S-1) + C_2 U_1 (S-1) + C_3 e_1 (S)

λ_1 (S) = 0.715 (7.97) + 0.174 (8.03) + 0.554 (0.53)

λ_1 (S) = 5.69 +1.39 +0.28

λ_1 (S) = 7.37 mg/l

DO: for the year 2003 (monsoon season)

λ_1 (S) = C_1 λ_1 (S-1) + C_2 U_1 (S-1) + C_3 e_1 (S)

λ_1 (S) = 0.715 (7.90) + 0.174 (7.92) + 0.554 (0.35)

λ_1 (S) = 5.64 +1.37 +0.19

λ_1 (S) = 7.20 mg/l

BOD: for the year 2002 (monsoon season)

λ_2 (S) = C_4 λ_1 (S-1) + C_5 U_1 (S-1)–C_6 e_1 (S)

λ_2 (S) = 0.751 (0.68) + 0.102 (0.83)–0.313 (0.27)

λ_2 (S) = 0.51 +0.08 –0.08

λ_2 (S) = 0.51 mg/l

BOD: for the year 2003 (monsoon season)

λ_2 (S) = C_4 λ_1 (S-1) + C_5 U_1 (S-1)–C_6 e_1 (S)

λ_2 (S) = 0.751 (0.87) + 0.102 (0.71)–0.313 (0.23)

λ_2 (S) = 0.65 +0.07 –0.07

λ_2 (S) = 0.65 mg/l

The values obtained from the model are given in the Table 5.46 and the original values of DO and BOD are given in Table 5.47.A look of the various values given in Table 5.46 and Table 5.47 shows that expected values (of Table 5.46) and actual values based on the samples (Table 5.47) showsgood agreement between two values. This observation is also in agreement with standard deviation calculated in these values. (Table 5A.1, 5A.3, 5A.5, and 5A.7). Also it is observed that the values obtained from model are quite effective and their relationship confirms our previous findings. The relationship between the values as obtained by model is shown in Figure 5.C.1–Figure 5.C.3.The graph clearly indicates that there is a negative relationship between DO and BOD.

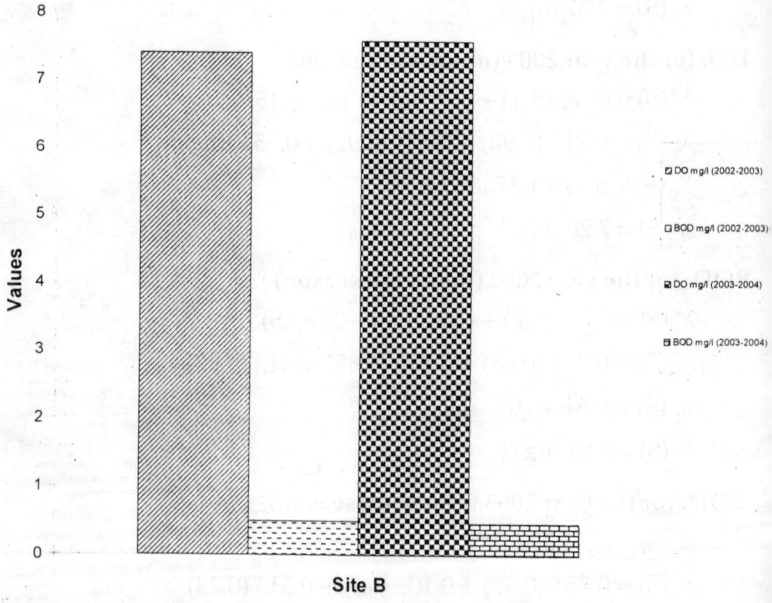

Figure 5 C.1: Graph Showing Negative Relationship Between DO and BOD at Sampling Station B

Table 5B.45: Systematic List of Fish Found in Suswa River

Present Scientific Name	*Name According to Day*	*Name According to Hamilton*	*Local Name*
	Phylum	Vertebrata	
	Sub phylum	Craniata	
	Super class	Gnathostomata	
	Series	Pisces	
	Class	Teleostomi	
	Sub class	Aetinopterygii	
	Order	Cyprinoidei	
	Suborder	Cyprinoidei	
	Family	**Cyprinidae**	
Barilius bendelisis (Ham)	*Barilius bendelisis*	*Cyprinus bendelisis*	Chal
Barilius barna	—	—	Pota
Raimas bola (Endangered)	*Barilius bola*	*Cyprinus bola*	Bola
Garra gotyla gotyla (Gray)	*Discognathus lamta*	*Cyprinus lamta*	Gunthala
Labeo gonius (Ham)	*Labeo gonius*	*Cyprinus gonius* *Cyprinus curchia* Cyprinus cursa	Bata
Labeo dero (Ham)	*Labeo dero*	*Cyprinus dero*	Aragi
Labeo boga (Bloch)	*Labeo boga*	*Cyprinus boga*	Bhagan
Oxygastor bacaila (Ham)	*Chela bacaila*	*Cyprinus bacaila*	Chalhawa
Puntius conchonius (Ham)	*Barbus conchonius*	*Cyprinus conchonius*	Sidhari
Puntius chola (Ham)	*Barbus chola*	*Cyprinus chola*	Sidhari.
Puntius sarna (Ham)	*Barbus sarana*	*Cyprinus sarana*	Darahee
Puntius sophore (Ham)	*Barbus stigma*	*Cyprinus sophore*	Sidhari
Puntius ticto (Ham)	*Barbus ticto*	*Cyprinus ticto*	Puthi Sidhari
Tor-putitora (Ham) (Endangered)	*Barbus tor*	—	Mahaseer
Rasbora daniconius (Ham)	*Rasbora daniconius*	*Cyprinus* daniconius	Dendua
	Family	**Cobitidae**	
Botia dario (Ham)	*Botia dario*	*Cobitus geto*	Baghaua
Lepidocephalichthys guntea (Ham)	*Lepidocephalichthys guntea*	*Cobitus guntea*	Nakati
Nemacheilus botia (Ham buch)	*Nemacheilus botia*	*Cobitus botia*	Natwa
Nemacheilus montanus (McClelland)	*Nemacheilus denisoni*	—	Natwa

Contd...

Table 5B.45–Contd...

Present Scientific Name	*Name According to Day*	*Name According to Hamilton*	*Local Name*
Nemacheilus rupicola (McClelland)	*Nemacheilus rupicola*	—	Natwa
Nemacheilus savona (Ham)	*Nemacheilus savona*	*Cobitus turio*	Sona
	Family	**Bagridae**	
Mystus bleekeri (Day)	*Macrones bleekari*	—	Tenger
Mystus Seenghala (Sykes)	*Macrones Seenghala*	—	Dariai Tenger
Mystus tengara (Ham)	*Macrones tengara*	*Pimelodus tengara*	Tengra
	Family	**Claridae**	
Clarias batrachus (Linn)	*Silurus batrachus*	—	Mangur
	Family	**Belonidae**	
Xenentodon cancila (Ham)	*Belone cancila*	*Esox cancila*	Kauwa
	Family	**Mastacembelidae**	
Mastacembelus armatus (lacepedi)	*Mastacembelus armatus*	*Macrognathus armatus*	Baam
	Family	**Ophiocephalidae**	
Channa punctatus (Bloch)	*Ophiocephalus punctatus*	—	Girai
	Family	**Anabantidae**	
Colisa fasciatus (Bloch & schn.)	*Trichogaster fasciatus*	*Trichopodius colisa* *Trichopodius bejeus* *Trichopodius cotra*	Khosti
	Family	**Nandidae**	
Nandus nandus (Ham.)	*Nandus marmoratus*	*Gobius nandus*	Dhebari

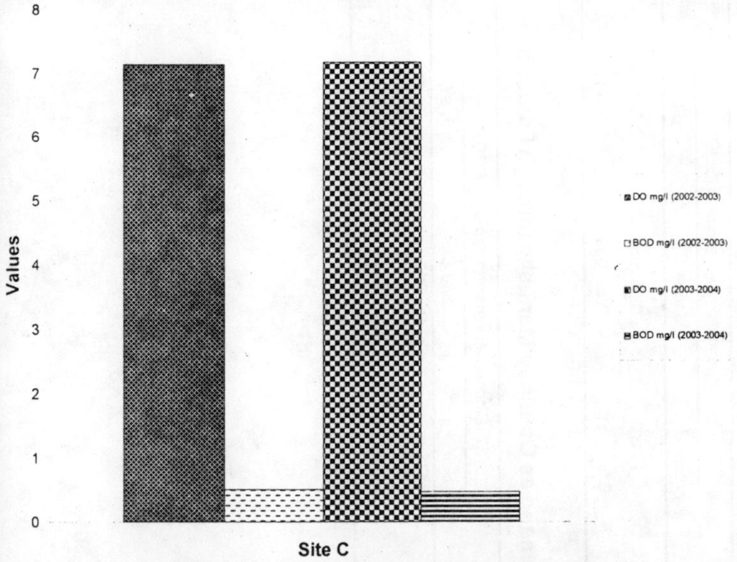

Figure 5C.2: Graph Showing Negative Relationship Between DO and BOD at Sampling Station C

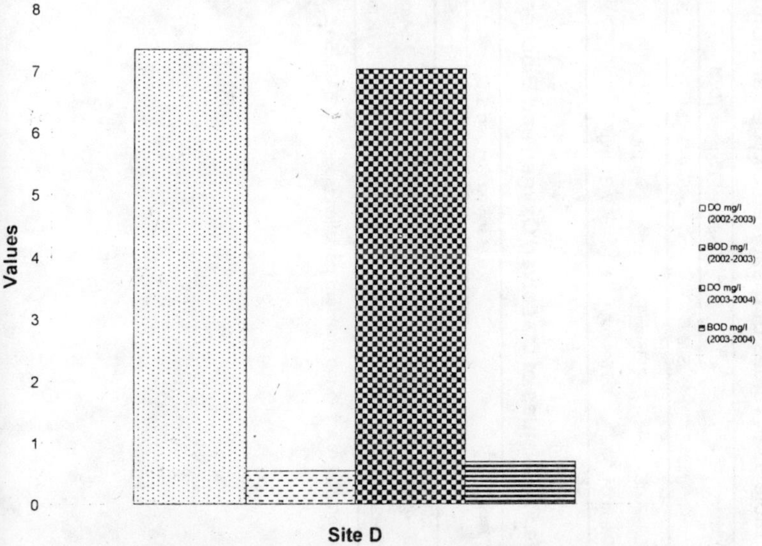

Figure 5C.3: Graph Showing Negative Relationship Between DO and BOD at Sampling Station D

Table 5.46: Values of Dissolved Oxygen and Biochemical Demand as Obtained from BMKB Model

Year	*Dissolved Oxygen (DO)*			*Biochemical oxygen demand (BOD)*		
	Site B	*Site C*	*Site D*	*Site B*	*Site C*	*Site D*
2002–2003	7.35mg/l	7.45 mg/l	7.37mg/l	0.46mg/l	0.56 mg/l	0.51mg/l
2003–2004	7.74 mg/l	7.31 mg/l	7.20 mg/l	0.50 mg/l	0.51 mg/l	0.65 mg/l

Table 5.47: Values of Dissolved Oxygen and Biochemical Demand as Obtained Manually through Fitration

Year	*Dissolved Oxygen (DO)*			*Biochemical oxygen demand (BOD)*		
	Site B	*Site C*	*Site D*	*Site B*	*Site C*	*Site D*
2002–2003	8.25mg/l±(0.93)	7.94 mg/l±(1.00)	7.54mg/l±(0.62)	0.74mg/l±(0.72)	0.81 mg/l±(0.57)	0.50mg/l±(0.12)
2003–2004	7.05 mg/l±(0.58)	7.00 mg/l±(1.74)	7.72 mg/l±(0.57)	0.89 mg/l±(0.15)	1.13 mg/l±(0.60)	0.62 mg/l±(0.17)

The figures in bracket refers to the standard deviation (see 5A.1, 5A.3, 5A.5, 5A.7)

Chapter 6
Discussion

Increasing demand for water develops the need to define the quality of water for specific uses. The most fundamental need is for water suitable for drinking, personal hygiene and food preparation and that poses no risk to human health. Increasing development and its associated industrialization have in addition introduced the need for water quality with specific physical, chemical or biological characteristics.

Accurate assessment of water quality, whether in relation to the requirements of intended water uses or in order to determine the impacts of an activity on the water resources, depends on the results generated by specific monitoring activities, which defines the physical, chemical and/or biological condition of the resource.

The average annual values of physico-chemical, heavy metals, and biological parameters are given in Tables 6.1-6.5.

Temperature measurements are useful in indicating the trends of biochemical and biological activities in water body. Biological activities are enhanced by higher temperature. The rate of oxidation of organic matter is much greater during summer than in winter. In the Suswa river at Raiwala, a difference in the fluctuation of water temperature was maximum (25.61°C ± 0.76) observed in monsoon and minimum (17.70°C ± 1.11) in winter. The water temperature showed an upward trend from winter season to summer season followed by a downward trend from monsoon season onwards. A more or less similar trend has been observed in the river Yamuna by Chakrabarty *et al.* (1959) and in the Kallayi (John, 1976). Badola and Singh (1981) reported similar trend in river Alaknanda. The fluctuation of temperature was well within the limit for survival of fishes. Similar types of fluctuations were reported by Dwivedi *et al.* (1995) in two ponds at Patna.

The temperature showed negative relationship with the dissolved oxygen almost throughout the study as also reported by Das and Srivastava (1956a), Das and Pathani (1978), Dobriyal (1985), Khanna *et al.* (1993) and Chugh (2000). The dissolved oxygen in water is often attributed to the fact that the oxygen is dissolved more during the period of active photosynthesis. According to Hutchinson (1957), colder water has greater capacity for holding dissolved gases.

The dissolution of oxygen from the atmosphere is the major source of oxygen in any water body. The rate at which the oxygen diffuses into the water from the atmosphere increases as the water turbulence increase. Although, the dissolution of oxygen from the atmosphere occurs at the surface, its downward movement into water body requires mechanical mixing or mass flow of water.

Maximum dissolved oxygen was recorded (9.11 mg/l ± 0.77) in winter season and minimum (7.00 mg/l ± 1.74) in monsoon season. This trend was also reported by Singh *et al.* (1982) in the river Brahamputra of Guwahati. The dissolved oxygen reduced gradually from summer to monsoon season due to turbidity, which retarded the photosynthetic activity of aquatic flora. Again the dissolved oxygen increases from monsoon to winter season it was due to the activity of plankton in water, which are found more active when temperature was not too high. Similar trend was also reported by Badola and Singh (1981) in the river Alaknanda, Khanna (1993) in the river Ganga, and Chugh (2000) in river Ganga. During winters low temperature conditions and high aeration rate was responsible for increased amount of dissolved oxygen. In warm water the rate of respiration and decomposition of organic matter increases, which in turn decreases, the dissolved oxygen content of the water and increases the risk of suffocation and high killing.

It has been recommended that a minimum of 4 mg/l of dissolved oxygen should be maintained in water for healthy growth of fish

Table 6.1: Average Annual Value of Physico-Chemical Parameters

Physico-Chemical Parameters	Sampling Station A		Sampling Station B		Sampling Station C		Sampling Station D		Average
	2002–2003	2003–2004	2002–2003	2003–2004	2002–2003	2003–2004	2002–2003	2003–2004	2002-2004
Temperature (°C)	22.27±2.02	22.64±2.72	23.17±2.57	22.46±2.93	22.67±3.32	22.80±2.19	21.41±3.27	21.82±3.57	22.40±0.56
Conductivity Siemens/cm	0.21±0.002	0.04±0.03	0.017±0.003	0.23±0.005	0.02±0.005	0.02±0.006	0.023±0.007	0.02±0.004	0.07±0.09
Turbidity (JTU)	8.33±14.43	10.00±17.32	8.33±14.43	11.66±20.20	13.33±23.09	11.66±20.20	13.33±23.09	8.33±14.43	10.62±2.17
Total Solids (mg/l)	889.58±204.83	751.0±2.40	958.3±72.16	791.66±260.20	1125±.125	1000±375.0	916.66±260.20	1125±433.01	944.65±137.85
Velocity (m/s)	0.27±0.06	0.26±0.03	0.31±0.02	0.35±0.02	0.30.±0.04.	0.30±0.04	0.39±0.08	0.38±0.07	0.32±0.04
pH	7.45±0.21	7.42±0.10	7.35±0.12	7.30±0.06	7.37±0.15	7.41±0.03	7.35±0.14	7.48±0.05	7.39±0.05
BOD (mg/l)	0.64±0.10	0.68±0.12	0.72±0.02	0.77±0.17	0.69±0.21	0.75±0.35	0.76±0.30	0.79±0.14	0.72±0.05
COD (mg/l)	2.35±0.65	3.45±0.61	3.06±0.16	3.00±0.78	3.30±0.30	3.14±1.46	3.08±1.33	3.20±0.22	3.07±0.32
DO (mg/l)	8.22±0.13	8.07±0.47	8.43±0.61	8.04±0.86	8.14±0.27	7.96±0.98	7.75±0.21	7.70±0.20	8.03±0.23
O.R.I	28.66.±0.28	28.14±0.24	28.17±0.36	27.97±1.00	28.12±0.09	27.90±0.16	28.0±0.31	28.45±0.15	28.17±0.25
O.R.P	0.36±0.01	0.40±0.02	0.38±0.02	0.38±0.02	0.37±0.02	0.36±0.02	0.35±0.005	0.37±0.02	0.37±0.01
Free CO_2 (mg/l)	3.11±1.05	2.20±0.74	3.08±1.91	2.99±1.87	2.68±2.08	2.98±2.15	3.26±1.97	2.67±2.10	2.87±0.33
Acidity (mg/l)	53.90±3.18	57.46±10.52	50.94±7.18	51.57±5.00	56.58±4.67	59.87±9.38	57.89±8.54	62.44±9.74	56.33±3.98
Alkalinity (mg/l)	255.55±5.91	289.16±28.24	254.29±13.34	279.16±23.92	262.21±21.22	294.09±21.24	265.27±11.97	285.92±20.26	273.20±15.77
Total hardness (mg/l)	237.43±11.33	242.46±3.33	228.80±8.88	246.52±3.69	239.91±8.94	250.26±8.67	236.41±3.00	243.50±9.30	240.66±6.62
Chlorides (mg/l)	17.68±1.49	17.60±2.17	19.28±2.22	19.21±4.53	16.82±0.64	18.87±2.27	18.09±3.22	18.98±3.44	18.31±0.90
Magnesium (mg/l)	42.20±3.17	44.58±4.83	39.79±3.06	39.34±0.74	39.33±3.59	46.51±6.65	48.40±5.07	45.77±6.37	43.24±3.56
Phosphates (mg/l)	0.07±0.04	0.06±0.07	0.06±0.04	0.06±0.02	0.07±0.04	0.08±0.05	0.05±0.04	0.05±0.02	0.06±0.01
Calcium (mg/l)	59.42±3.26	63.97±6.09	60.24±1.62	60.72±6.53	63.50±2.79	61.70±4.36	63.19±4.52	65.63±11.26	62.29±2.12

±: Standard Deviation.

Table 6.2: Average Annual Value of Heavy Metals

Parameters	Sampling Station A		Sampling Station B		Sampling Station C		Sampling Station D		Average
	2002–2003	2003–2004	2002–2003	2003–2004	2002–2003	2003–2004	2002–2003	2003–2004	2002-2004
Lead (Pb) (mg/l)	0.067±0.00	0.064±0.005	0.07±0.003	0.076±0.003	0.076±0.003	0.076±0.001	0.076±0.002	0.076±0.001	0.071±0.004
Copper (Cu) (mg/l)	0.017±0.0005	0.05±0.001	0.021±0.002	0.020±0.002	0.020±0.003	0.019±0.003	0.016±0.004	0.014±0.003	0.022±0.011
Iron (Fe) (mg/l)	5.43±0.21	5.41±0.44	5.35±0.15	5.71±0.49	5.64±0.08	5.35±16.07	5.26±0.25	5.42±0.40	5.44±0.15
Manganese (Mn) (mg/l)	0.0020±0.0005	0.003±0.0005	0.007±0.001	0.002±0.001	0.005±0.01	0.005±0.016	0.002±0.0005	0.003±0.0005	0.003±0.001
Zinc (Zn) (mg/l)	3.52±0.33	3.70±0.22	3.8±0.10	3.64.±015	3.77±0.12	3.77±0.07	3.70±0.04	3.73±0.04	3.70±0.08
Cobalt (Ca) (mg/l)	0.006±0.003	0.006±0.004	0.007±0.001	0.028±0.035	0.005±0.002	0.08±0.0005	0.007±0.001	0.007±0.0005	0.018±0.026

±: Standard Deviation.

Table 6.3: Average annual value of Plankton (per liter)

Plankton	Sampling Station A		Sampling Station B		Sampling Station C		Sampling Station D		Average
	2002–2003	2003–2004	2002–2003	2003–2004	2002–2003	2003–2004	2002–2003	2003–2004	2002-2004
Zooplankton	303.61±9.46	317.31±8.95	377.64±11.73	185.98±9.22	374.64±16.43	364.96±9.84	377.0±461.73	368.66±287.50	333.72±66.19
Phytoplankton	2295.99±448.89	1190±345.85	1856.33±1549.60	2311.33±2551.63	1492.61±266.56	2034.62±573.08	1373.54±371.94	1582.30±411.50	1767.09±423.06

±: Standard Deviation.

Table 6.4: Average annual value of Bacteriology

Bacteriology		*MPN/100ml*	*HPC/100ml*
Sampling station A	2002–2003	200.0±170.36	93.33±2.79
	2003–2004	205.33±177.88	87.33±8.82
Sampling station B	2002–2003	146.66±116.44	64.31±4.48
	2003–2004	305.0±268.88	64.33±5.57
Sampling station C	2002–2003	112.30±71.59	102.33±6.35
	2003–2004	253.00±186.97	96.59±6.28
Sampling station D	2002–2003	140.00±119.05	90.96±8.05
	2003–2004	190.66±178.93	86.97±7.10
Average		194.11±63.02	85.76±14.13

±: Standard Deviation.

and other microbial population. Adebisi (1981) observed high levels of dissolved oxygen on Ogun river in Nigeria during flood due to aeration of river waters. Highest values of dissolved oxygen were recorded in river Cauvery by Somashekar *et al.* (1984), and in river Kosi by Bhatt *et al.* (1984).

Table 6.5: Average Annual Value of Fungi (ml $^{-1}$ × 10^3)

Sampling Stations	*Year*	*Fungi*
Sampling station A	2002–2003	11.66±0.83
	2003–2004	18.66±2.33
Sampling station B	2002–2003	9.33±7.57
	2003–2004	23.66±24.54
Sampling station C	2002–2003	23.99±3.71
	2003–2004	18.66±14.15
Sampling station D	2002–2003	20.32±1.17
	2003–2004	29.99±1.44
Average		19.53±6.70

±: Standard Deviation.

The maximum velocity was recorded (0.49 m/s ± 0.08) in summer season and minimum (0.22 m/s ± 0.05) in winter. The velocity started increasing after winter season and beyond monsoon season, the velocity started decreasing in winter. In the present study it has been observed that the velocity and the total solids showed positive relationship. Total solids may be in the form of coarse, floating, settleable, fine or colloidal particles as a floating film. Most of Indian rivers showed a similar tendency with respect to fluctuations of total solids (Kudesia and Verma, 1985; and Reddy and Venkateshwarlu, 1987). The maximum total solids were noted (1375 mg/l ± 478.71) in monsoon season and minimum (500 mg/l ± 0.00) in winter season. The total solids were recorded minimum in winter due to gradual sedimentation of the filterable residue, at the bottom and also due to the minimum velocity of the river, which favored effective sedimentation. The total solids were maximum in monsoon season due to increased velocity, which favored soil-erosion. Similar condition was also reported by David (1956) in Bhadra river and Verma and Shukla (1967) in their studies. The residues when present in excess in water may create an imbalance to the aquatic life, but when the filterable residues are present in a

Table 6.6A(): Correlation Coefficient of Different Parameters

Parameters	Physical				Chemical				
	Temperature °C	Conductivity siemens/cm	Turbidity in JTU	Total Solids in mg/l	pH	BOD in mg/l	COD in mg/l	Dissolve Oxygen in mg/l	Oxidation Reduction Index (rH2
Temperature°C		+0.26	+0.71	+0.35	+0.65	+0.22	-0.26	-0.64	+0.41
Conductivity siemens/cm			-0.30	-0.20	-0.17	-0.30	-0.14	+0.32	+0.06
Turbidity in JTU				+0.52	+0.89	+0.68	+0.09	-0.72	+0.12
Total Solids in mg/l					+0.83	-0.02	-0.65	+0.11	+0.71
pH						+0.41	-0.24	-0.36	+0.39
BOD in mg/l							+0.60	-0.58	-0.40
COD in mg/l								-0.37	-0.97
Dissolve Oxygen in mg/l									+0.18
O R i (rH2)									
O R P (Eh)									
Free Carbon Dioxide in mg/l									
Acidity in mg/l									
Alkalinity in mg/l									
Total Hardness in mg/l									
Chlorides in mg/l									
Magnesium in mg/l									
Phosphates in mg/l									
Calcium mg/l									

Contd...

Table 6.6A Contd....

Parameters	Chemical								
	Oxidation Reduction Potential (Eh)	Free Carbon Dioxide in mg/l	Acidity in mg/l	Alkalinity in mg/l	Total Hardness in mg/l	Chlorides in mg/l	Magnesium in mg/l	Phosphates in mg/l	Calcium in mg/l
Temperature°C	+0.31	+0.73	-0.32	+0.54	-0.35	+0.76	-0.83	+0.51	+0.57
Conductivity siemens/cm	+0.32	-0.23	+0.80	+0.22	+0.31	-0.28	+0.25	-0.41	+0.29
Turbidity in JTU	+0.31	+0.68	-0.63	+0.45	-0.43	+0.99	-0.76	+0.86	+0.61
Total Solids in mg/l	-0.55	+0.79	-0.20	-0.46	-0.84	+0.51	-0.49	+0.34	-0.13
pH	-0.01	+0.77	-0.38	+0.10	-0.67	+0.86	+0.66	+0.67	+0.39
BOD in mg/l	+0.64	+0.05	-0.40	+0.57	+0.29	+0.67	-0.27	+0.86	+0.79
COD in mg/l	+0.76	-0.64	-0.08	+0.64	+0.61	+0.01	+0.36	+0.16	+0.47
Dissolve Oxygen in mg/l	-0.55	-0.39	+0.77	-0.78	+0.04	-0.74	+0.71	-0.67	-0.58
O R i (rH2)	-0.66	+0.78	-0.08	-0.51	-0.60	+0.21	-0.55	+0.09	-0.30
O R P (Eh)		-0.34	+0.04	+0.93	+0.61	+0.30	+0.01	+0.34	+0.87
Free Carbon Dioxide in mg/l			-0.56	-0.08	-0.76	+0.73	-0.91	+0.54	+0.06
Acidity in mg/l				-0.22	+0.38	-0.65	+0.72	-0.64	-0.06
Alkalinity in mg/l					+0.39	+0.45	-0.28	+0.40	+0.82
Total Hardness in mg/l						+0.39	+0.51	-0.09	+0.37
Chlorides in mg/l							-0.84	+0.90	+0.63
Magnesium in mg/l								-0.69	-0.31
Phosphates in mg/l									+0.66
Calcium mg/l									

Table 6.6B: Correlation Coefficient of Different Parameters

Parameters	Heavy Metals						Biological			
	Lead (Pb) mg/l	Copper (Cu) l mg/	Iron (Fe) mg/l	Manganese (Mn) mg/l	Zinc (Zn) mg/l	Cobalt (Co) mg/l	Zooplankton l^{-1}	Phytoplankton l^{-1}	MPN/100ml	HPC ($X 10^3$)
Temperature °C	+0.54	+0.29	-0.60	+0.25	0.05	+0.97	-0.75	-0.91	+0.63	+0.86
Conductivity siemens/cm	-0.36	+0.58	-0.83	-0.13	+0.43	+0.40	+0.16	-0.36	-0.35	-0.14
Turbidity in JTU	+0.72	-0.08	+0.00	+0.39	-0.44	+0.54	-0.97	-0.77	+0.99	+0.96
Total Solids in mg/l	+0.29	+0.55	-0.24	-0.12	-0.22	+0.38	-0.57	-0.30	+0.58	+0.61
pH	+0.52	+0.28	-0.21	+0.23	-0.33	+0.56	-0.90	-0.71	+0.91	+0.91
BOD in mg/l	+0.70	-0.37	+0.38	+0.14	-0.79	-0.00	-0.68	-0.45	+0.70	+0.50
COD in mg/l	-0.04	-0.80	+0.58	+0.51	-0.19	-0.44	+0.04	-0.00	+0.08	-0.16
Dissolve Oxygen in mg/l	-0.65	+0.52	-0.16	-0.53	+0.18	-0.46	+0.62	+0.57	-0.64	-0.67
O. R. I (rH2)	+0.29	+0.77	-0.56	-0.52	+0.00	+0.56	-0.25	-0.15	+0.12	+0.35
O. R. P. (Eh)	+0.21	-0.38	-0.02	+0.42	-0.14	+0.16	-0.30	0.55	+0.25	+0.21
Free CO_2 mg/l	+0.61	+0.39	-0.33	-0.04	-0.15	+0.73	-0.71	-0.52	+0.66	+0.82
Acidity in mg/l	-0.65	+0.52	-0.49	-0.31	+0.32	-0.16	+0.50	+0.13	-0.61	-0.55
Alkalinity in mg/l	+0.32	-0.43	-0.07	+0.56	-0.01	+0.39	-0.40	-0.65	+0.36	+0.39
Total Hardness in mg/l	-0.04	-0.27	0.15	-0.24	-0.21	-0.38	+0.37	+0.18	-0.45	-0.52
Chlorides in mg/l	+0.81	-0.02	-0.06	+0.28	-0.47	+0.61	-0.98	-0.78	+0.97	+0.97
Magnesium in mg/l	-0.78	-0.12	+0.24	-0.09	+0.21	-0.77	+0.77	+0.62	-0.70	-0.87
Phosphates in mg/l	+0.94	-0.12	+0.18	+0.01	-0.79	+0.33	-0.89	-0.57	+0.87	+0.79
Calcium mg/l	+0.55	-0.06	-0.20	+0.20	-0.42	+0.42	-0.67	-0.80	+0.57	+0.56
Lead (Pb) mg/l		+1.93	+0.07	-0.21	-0.74	+0.42	-0.79	-0.50	+0.71	+0.72
Copper (Cu) mg/l			-0.81	-0.59	+0.05	+0.47	-0.13	-0.26	-0.06	+0.15
Iron (Fe) mg/l				+0.19	-0.40	-0.77	+0.15	+0.55	+0.06	-0.25
Manganese (Mn) mg/l					+0.41	+0.12	+0.18	-0.31	+0.34	+0.28
Zinc (Zn) mg/l						+0.18	+0.52	+0.11	-0.51	-0.32
Cobalt (Co) mg/l							-0.62	-0.83	+0.46	+0.75
Zooplankton l^{-1}								+0.82	-0.96	-0.97
Phytoplankton l^{-1}									-0.71	-0.84
MPN/100ml										+0.93
HPC ($X 10^3$)										

proper concentration, a good fish crop can be expected (Hart *et al.*, 1945).

The BOD (Biochemical oxygen demand) was observed maximum (1.13 mg/l ± 0.60) in monsoon season and minimum (0.42 mg/l ± 0.08) in winter season. A negative relationship has been observed between BOD and DO contents. A similar pattern has been reported by Khanna (1993), Chugh (2000). BOD determination is a most useful technique to assess the level of organic pollution in river system.

COD (Chemical oxygen demand) represents chemically oxidizable load of organic matter in water. The maximum value of COD was observed (4.67 mg/l ± 0.50) in monsoon season and minimum (1.75 mg/l ± 0.05) in winter season. A negative relationship has been observed between COD and water temperature (r =–0.26).

Free carbon dioxide (free CO_2) is about 200 times more soluble in the water than is the oxygen. The carbon dioxide content of the water depends upon the temperature of water, depth of water, rate of respiration, decomposition of organic matter, chemical nature of the bottom and the geographical and physiological features of the terrain surrounding the water. The carbon dioxide content of the water increases with increase in temperature.

Free Carbon dioxide was observed maximum (5.00 mg/l ± 2.97) in monsoon season due to high temperature, and minimum (0.5 mg/l ± 0.01) in winter season when temperature was decreased and turbidity was lowest. Pahwa and Mehrotra (1966) have reported that the Ganga river contains maximum free carbon dioxide in monsoon season at Allahabad. Chakrabarty *et al.* (1959) also recorded the maximum free CO_2 in Jamuna during monsoon at Allahabad. Free Carbon dioxide is released during the decomposition of certain substances and metabolic activity of the living organism. Since higher temperature accelerates the decomposition of organic substances as well as the respiratory activity of the biota, a direct relationship was established between the water temperature and free carbon dioxide.

The dissolved oxygen and free carbon dioxide are usually inversely related to one another because of the photosynthetic and respiratory activities of the biota (Hynes, 1970). The fluctuations in the dissolved oxygen content were mainly influenced by the factors like plankton and microbial activity.

Conductivity determines the total amount of ionisable salts in water. It is due to ionization of dissolved inorganic solids. Seasonal fluctuations in this factor were caused mainly by variations in the ionic precipitations and the diluting effect of rains (Welch, 1948).

In the present study maximum conductivity was observed (0.085 siemens/cm ± 0.12) in summer this may be due to evaporation of water, which is in confirmation with the observations of Meshram, (1996). According to Ellis (1937) the conductivity of the inland water should range between 150-450 μ mhos/cm to flourish good flora & fauna.

The maximum turbidity was found (40.0 JTU ± 5.60) in monsoon season. In winter and summer season the turbidity was found nil. The turbidity and total solids were closely interrelated with one another and cause common effect upon the river and aquatic life as also stated by Verma *et al.* (1984). Bhatt *et al.* (1984) attributed that during monsoon months, the river water contained large amount of silt, fine sand particles, organic matter and clay. Bilgrami and Duttamunshi, (1985) observed minimum values of turbidity in winter and summer seasons while, maximum in monsoon period.

pH (Hydrogen ion Concentration) expresses the intensity of acidity and alkalinity of water. It plays a limiting role in the growth of flora and fauna of aquatic body. The pH (hydrogen ion concentration) increases with active decomposition of organic matter. Zinc, copper and manganese become growth limiting in alkaline waters but never in acidic waters. According to Basu *et al.* (1973), the measurement of pH has great importance because chemical and biochemical reactions in an aquatic body take place at a particular pH. In the present study the pH was always found slightly alkaline in nature. The maximum pH was recorded (7.70 ± 0.28) in monsoon season, which might be due to increased chemical load in the river. The minimum pH was observed (7.19 ± 0.13) in winter season. Similar observations were reported by Sangu and Sharma (1985) in river Yamuna. Meshram (1996) reported lower pH values during summer and higher pH during rainy season. Das (1961) reported that pH of water has an important behavior on both plankton and microbial production. He found that a pH ranging between 7.2-8.5 was favorable for the growth of plankton and higher values were detrimental to plankton production, microbial production and there by,to the fish production also.

The oxidation-reduction potential (Eh) and oxidation-reduction index (rH_2) showed its higher values during summer and monsoon, while lower during winters. This variation in Eh and rH_2 values could be explained by the addition of biodegradable material throughout the year from sewage and other sources. Low values during winter might be due to increased biodegradable material in water. Similar observations were also reported by Gautam (1990):

The term alkalinity is defined as the quality of ions in water, which react to neutralize hydrogen ions. It is measured as carbonates, bicarbonates and total alkalinity. The maximum value of alkalinity was observed (319.58 mg/l ± 35.39) in monsoon season and minimum (241.24 mg/l ± 33.86) in summer season. The cause of increasing alkalinity was the decomposition of the organic matter. Similar types of findings were observed by Venkateshwarlu and Jayanti (1968) in the river Sabarmati. Total alkalinity of water is usually caused by the carbonates, bicarbonates, and hydroxyl ions and less frequently by borates, silicates and phosphates (APHA, 1998). pH and alkalinity showed a positive correlation with one another as suggested by Freiser and Fernando (1966) in the ionic equilibria in analytical chemistry. According to Hay and Anthony (1958), the decomposition of organic matter leads to the high alkalinity of the waters.

The presence of total hardness is governed by the contents of calcium and magnesium salts, largely combined with bicarbonate, carbonate sulphate and chloride. According to Barrett (1953) hard water is more productive than soft water. The maximum and minimum values of hardness were recorded (257.74 mg/l ± 21.73) and (219 mg/l ± 19.02) in monsoon season respectively. Hardness showed a negative relationship with chloride Chopra and Patrick (1994) observed positive relationship between chloride and hardness in river Ganga at Rishikesh. Hardness showed a positive relationship with alkalinity while Chopra and Patrick (1994) observed negative relationship in river Ganga at Rishikesh.

In the present study, total hardness showed a significant positive correlation with magnesium hardness at almost all the sampling spots indicating that magnesium salts are the main cause of such high hardness of water.

Calcium is one of the most abundant substance of natural waters. Being present in high quantities in the rocks, it is leached from there to contaminate the water. Calcium is essential for metabolic processes in all-living organisms. Lund (1965) suggested calcium, main effect on phytoplankton by buffering pH of water. The maximum amount of calcium in Suswa was found as (76.89 mg/l ± 13.73) in monsoon season and minimum (54.37 mg/l ± 7.73) in winter season. pH and calcium showed positive relationship to one another. Atkin and Harris (1924) and Mohanty (1981) reported negative relationship between pH and calcium in dried water ponds in some water bodies of Bhubaneswar.

The demand of magnesium in metabolism is minor in comparison to quantities generally available in fresh water. The value of magnesium was observed maximum (53.87 mg/l ± 4.17) in winter season and minimum (35.50 mg/l ± 3.82) in winter season. Singhai (1986) reported a positive correlation between magnesium and total hardness as also observed in present study. The magnesium hardness was always observed lower than calcium hardness.

Chlorides occur in most water as the salts of sodium and calcium. Maximum value of chlorides was observed (24.33 mg/l ± 6.58) in monsoon season and minimum (15.02 mg/l ± 1.35) in winter season. Chloride is one of the important chemical indicator of pollution. Chlorides are present in sewage, sewage effluents and farm discharges and remain unaltered during the purification of sewages. Sengar *et al.* (1985), Reddy and Venkateshwarlu (1987), Govindan and Sundaresan (1979), Raina *et al.* (1984) and Mishra and Saxena (1984) also showed significant levels of chloride content.

The role of phosphorus for the phytoplankton production in tropical ponds (Heper, 1962; Subbamma and Ramasarma, 1992) is well known. The observed low value of phosphorus are not to be taken as indication of low productivity.

In the present study all the heavy metals as Lead, Copper, Iron, Manganese, Zinc and Cobalt were taken for observation and revealed that all heavy metals are having partial or some how positive relation with velocity and negative relation with plankton life. Concentrations of all the heavy metals in different seasons were quite favorable for the biota and not in favorable to the water quality as suggested by Mathur (1982). Heavy metals get contaminated into aquatic systems as a result of various natural activities (weathering of soils and rocks from volcanic eruptions) and from a variety of human activities involving the mining, processing or use of metals or substances.

Various metals like iron, copper, zinc, manganese are essential micronutrients while other such as mercury, cadmium and lead are not required even in small amount by any organisms. Virtually all metals, including the essential metal micronutrients, are toxic if exposure levels are sufficiently high. Cadmium, chromium, copper, lead, mercury, nickel and zinc are of particular relevance in fresh waters.

The effects of metals in water and wastewater range from beneficial through trouble some to dangerously toxic. Some metals are essential to plant and animal growth while others may adversely affect water consumers, wastewater treatment system, and receiving waters. The benefits versus toxicity of some metals depend on their concentrations in waters. The increased circulation of toxic metals in recent times resulted in the unavoidable build up of such toxic substances in the human food chain.

Since heavy metals are rapidly absorbed to particulate materials (*e.g.*, detritus, plankton, suspended sediments) and assimilated by living organisms. The concentration of metals dissolved in the water may give a highly misleading picture of the degree of metal pollution. Andren (1974) reported that about 67 per cent of the mercury in the Mississippi river water is associated with suspended sediments. Metals adhering particulate materials could be absorbed by an organisms in the process of pumping water over its gills or in the process of filtering water to obtain food. Lloyd (1961) found that suspended zinc was indeed toxic to Rainbow trout. There is paucity of information on the toxicity of suspended metals to most aquatic organisms.

The term 'plankton' coined by Hensen in 1887 and originated from Greek (literally that which wonders about) is a collective term for all organisms that floats in the water and do not executive individual movement of any importance. The majorities of phytoplankton are non-motile and are therefore at the mercy of water turbulence within the upper water mass. Phytoplankton are very sensitive to change in the environmental conditions and their bloom (burst of growth) being of only few weeks duration and their species replacement takes place in a matter of month or less. Khanna (1993) emphasized the need for monitoring of a river system continuously at least for ten years to assess the importance of various chemical parameters in the growth and distribution of plankton. According to Moss (1982) the plankton are the heterogeneous assemblage of minute organisms, which occur in the natural water and float about by the wave action and movement of water.

The total planktonic concentration was recorded maximum (5456 unit/l ± 3572.30) in winter and minimum (466 unit/l ± 329.51) in monsoon season. It was due to the blanketing effect caused by the velocity. Allen (1920) was also of the view that the water current above the moderate speed is usually directly inhibitory to plankton development. The abundance and quality of life and species richness are influenced by current velocity as stated by Crayton and Summerfield (1979), in tributaries of Colorado rivers. Chakraborty *et al.* (1959) obtained peak values of total plankton during summer and minimum during monsoon. Roy (1955) and Venkateshwarlu (1969) reported maximum values during winter and minimum in monsoon season as also observed in the present study.

Phytoplankton dominated over zooplankton during the course of study (Table 6.3). The maximum number of phytoplankton and zooplankton was observed (5254 unit/l ± 1176.24) and (892 unit/l ± 43.61) in winter season while minimum number of phytoplankton was observed (466 unit/l ± 329.51) and zooplankton were nil in monsoon season. The same conclusion was supported by Pahwa and Mehrotra (1966) in the Ganga river. Singh *et al.* (1982) reported high values of plankton during January to March.

The numbers of plankton were also affected by the turbidity. The increased turbidity reduces the plankton production as also reported by Das and Pathani (1978).

The phytoplankton production was maximum in winter season when the temperature was low. It shows negative relationship between water temperature and plankton as also reported by Das and Srivastava (1956) and Chugh (2000). Griffith (1955) and Sharma (1985) could not establish any pronounced effect of temperature upon plankton.

According to Eddy (1934) the plankton production is mainly influenced by temperature. Kofoid (1908), Chakraborty *et al.* (1959) observed that in the warmer month the plankton production was medium. According to Bhowmick and Singh (1985), maximum density of phytoplankton was recorded in summer and lowest in monsoon. According to Holden and Green (1960), the temperature, when compared with certain other factors, has less significance in influencing the abundance of plankton.

The results indicated that the plankton were maximum in winter months probably due to low temperature, high content of dissolved oxygen and low velocity.

It was observed that as soon as the water level, velocity and turbidity decreases, the water becomes clear. The diatoms and green algae appear on the surface of stones, gravel and other substratum. Although during winter season the water temperature was lowest, even then the microbial life flourishes very well because they receive maximum solar energy due to high transparency of water.

Carpenter (1928) reported that the plankton are sparse in swift running water.

A negative relationship was found between phytoplankton and BOD (r =–0.45) and zooplankton and BOD (r =–0.68). A negative correlation was observed between pH and phytoplankton (r =–0.71) and zooplankton (r =–0.90).

Free carbon dioxide shows a negative relationship with the phytoplankton (r =–0.52) and zooplankton (r =–0.71) and positive relationship between dissolved oxygen and phytoplankton (r = +0.57) and zooplankton (r = +0.62) was observed.

The physico-chemical and biological parameters of all the four sampling stations were almost similar.

Study reveals that the value of most probable number (MPN) Coliforms bacteria increase from summer season, maximum value was observed (615 MPN/100 ml ± 138.76) in monsoon season and minimum (50 MPN/100 ml ± 2.41) in summer season. At relatively higher temperature microbial activity increase and this results in increasing microbial population and biochemical oxygen demand.

Since MPN and HPC (Hetrotrophic plate count) have positive relationship, the higher value of HPC was recorded [189 x 10^3 HPC/ml (X10^3) ± 20.31] in monsoon season and minimum [10 x10^3 HPC/ml (X10^3) ± 1.69] in winter season.

So it is concluded that HPC, MPN and BOD are directly proportional to temperature.

Bissonnete *et al.* (1975), showed influence of environmental stress on enumeration or indicator bacteria from natural water. Bonde (1977) reported *Escherichia coli* as bacterial indicator of water pollution. Dutka (1973), Dutka and Bell (1973) and Borrego *et al.* (1990) also reported that coliphages as an indicator of pollution. Borrego *et al.* (1990) revealed that *Escherichia coli, Salmonella sp.* and *Pseudomonas sp.* are indicator of fecal pollution in water source, similar type of pollution indicators were found at all sampling stations and it revealed the river Suswa at Raiwala is polluted due to Coliforms bacteria.

Cherry *et al.* (1972) reported *Salmonella* as index of pollution of surface water. Kanner and Clarke (1924) detected *Salmonella* and *Pseudomonas* in surface water. Goyal *et al.* (1977) noted occurrence and distribution of bacterial indicators and pathogens in canal communities along the Texas coast. Sukumaran (2002) reported Coliforms bacteria an index of aquatic pollution.

The dominating bacteria of river Suswa at Raiwala are *Salmonella typhii, Streptococcus facecalis, Aerobacter aerogens, Bacillus subtilis, Pseudomonas aerogenosa, Escherichia coli, Staphylococcus aureus, Micrococcus luteus* and *Staphylococcus epidermidis*

Among 9 isolated and identified bacteria (Photo Plate 5.8) some are noted pathogenic and others as non-pathogenic *Streptococcus facecalis, Salmonella typhii, Aerobacter aerogens, Pseudomonas aerogenosa, Escherichia coli, Staphylococcus aureus* and *Staphylococcus epidermidis* were found in river Suswa as pathogens, where as the non-pathogenic bacteria are *Bacillus subtilis* and *Micrococcus luteus.*

The maximum number of fungus was observed (67×10^3/ml ± 4.50) in monsoon season and minimum (3×10^3/ml ± 1.73) in winter season, similar observation was also given by Klinch and Tiffney (1985). Slightly alkaline pH and moderate water temperature favored the growth of the water molds. Alabi (1971) also reported fewer water molds during summer and flooded rainy seasons. Winter season did not favor most of the water molds, which might be due to very low temperature in temperate region.

The differences and fluctuations in fungal members may be due to surface run-off, washing of cloths and other such activities.

Quantitatively among the three isolated and identified fungi (Photo Plate 6.9) the dominant fungi was *Aspergillus* followed by *Penicillium* and *Fusarium*.

The value of Correlation Coefficient(r) between different parameters *viz.* physical-physical, physical-chemical, physical heavy metals, physical-microbiological, chemical-chemical, chemical-heavy metals, chemical-microbiological, heavy metal–heavy metals, heavy metals-microbiological and in between microbiological-microbiological are given in Tables 6.6.A-6.6.B.

By the analysis for correlation coefficient of parameters, it is extracted that there are highly significant correlation (r = > + 0.80), between Conductivity and Acidity (r = + 0.80), Turbidity and pH (r = +0.89), Turbidity and Chloride (r = + 0.99), Turbidity and Phosphates (r = + 0.86), Total Solids and Velocity (r = + 0.83), Total solids and pH (r = + 0.83), pH and Chloride (r = + 0.86), Biochemical oxygen demand and Phosphates (r = +0.86), Oxidation reduction potential and Calcium (r = + 0.87), Alkalinity and Calcium (r = + 0.82), Chlorides and Phosphates (r = + 0.90),Temperature and Cobalt (r = + 0.97), Temperature and HPC (r = +0.86), Turbidity and MPN (r = + 0.99), Turbidity and HPC (r = + 0.96),pH and MPN (r = + 0.91), pH and HPC (r = + 0.91), Free CO_2 and HPC (r = + 0.82), Chlorides and Lead (r = + 0.81),Chlorides and MPN (r = + 0.97),Chlorides and HPC (r = + 0.97), Phosphates and Lead (r = + 0.94), Phosphates and MPN (r = + 0.87),Lead andCopper (r = + 1.93), Zooplankton and Phytoplankton (r = + 0.82) and MPN and HPC (r = + 0.93).

In the present study the highly non-significant (r >–0.70) were noted between Temperature and Magnesium (r =–0.83), Turbidity and Dissolved Oxygen (r =–0.72), Turbidity and Magnesium (r =–0.76), Total solids and Total hardness (r =–0.84), Chemical Oxygen demand and Oxidation reduction index (r =–0.97), Dissolved Oxygen and Alkalinity (r =–0.78), Dissolved Oxygen and Chloride (r =–0.74), Free CO_2 and Total hardness (r =–0.76), Free CO_2 and Magnesium (r =–0.91), Chlorides and Magnesium (r =–0.84), Temperature and Zooplankton (r =–0.75), Temperature and Phytoplankton (r =–0.91), Conductivity and Iron (r =–0.83),Turbidity and Zooplankton (r =–0.97), Turbidity and Phytoplankton (r =–0.77), pH and Zooplankton (r =–0.90), pH and Phytoplankton (r =–0.71), Biochemical oxygen demand and Zinc (r =–0.79), Free CO_2 and Zooplankton (r =–0.71), Chlorides and Zooplankton (r =–0.98),

Chlorides and Phytoplankton (r =–0.78), Magnesium and Lead (r =–0.78), Magnesium and Cobalt (r =–0.77), Magnesium and MPN (r =–0.70), Magnesium and HPC (r =–0.87), Phosphates and Zinc (r =–0.79), Phosphates and Zooplankton (r =–0.89), Calcium and Phytoplankton (r =–0.80), Lead and Zinc (r =–0.74), Lead and Zooplankton (r =–0.79),Copper and Iron (r =–0.81), Iron and Cobalt (r =–0.77), Cobalt and Phytoplankton (r =–0.83),Zooplankton and MPN (r =–0.96), Zooplankton and HPC (r =–0.97), Phytoplankton and MPN (r =–0.71) and Phytoplankton and HPC (r =–0.84).

Rests of the parameters were observed some how positive and Negative relationship (r = < +0.80 or r = <–0.70), which shows insignificant correlation according to Table 6.6.A-6.7.A.

Few observations were noted about Zero, which shows no correlation between those parameters, *e.g.*, Total solids and Biochemical oxygen demand (r =–0.02), pH and Oxidation reduction potential (r =–0.01), Chemical oxygen demand and Chlorides (r = 0.01), Oxidation reduction potential and Magnesium (r = 0.01), Biochemical oxygen demand and Cobalt (r =–0.00), Chemical oxygen demand and Phytoplankton (r = 0.00), Oxidation reduction and Zinc (r = 0.00), Alkalinity and Zinc (r =–0.01) and Phosphates and Manganese (r = 0.01).

Mathematical modeling aims at defining quantitatively alternative course of action. It provides a useful means in evaluating the pollution problem in an appropriate fashion. Indeed, the idea of comprehensive analysis is not entirely new but it is an approach to the usage of better quality water that the recent years have witnessed and recognised the importance of mathematical and computational analysis.

Recall that various DO models have been developed based on the classical Streeter-Phelphs approach, including models which incorporate oxygen demands by sediments and oxygen supply by photosynthesis. In addition there are lake and reservoir models as well as models of surface water quality are in Biswas (1981), Grimsrud, Finemore and Owen (1976), and U.S. Army corps of Engineers (1987) a state –of-the-art book on water quality modeling is James (1993).

The simplest type of a model is a "Black box model", mainly because it assumes no priori knowledge of the system's characteristics.

We have developed two models for DO and BOD with multiple input and single output after Beck (1974). Our model gives the seasonal value on the basis of previously taken upstream and downstream observations/concentrations of DO and BOD. The model given by Beck (1974) uses light intensity while our model fits when light intensity is very less or negligible in monsoon season or in cloudy days. Our model is considerably in agreement with our findings at all the four sampling sites, the minor variations in results may be due to manual errors while finding the concentrations of DO and BOD *i.e.*, while using titration method or due to error in chemical preparation during the course of study. It is impossible to have mathematical models, which totally confirms the nature and problem arising in physical situations. Thus the BMKB model may be characterised as 'white box' model.

Of course we should always remember that no model of a real system is perfect: if it were we might call it a "White box" model.

The DO model has a good potential for control applications, in the first instance, it is a very simple model, and in the second instance it does not require any information on BOD conditions in the reach as also mentioned by Beck (1974).

Chapter 7
Summary

The thesis embodies the findings of study conducted on *"Limnological status of river Suswa with reference to its mathematical modeling"* during 2002-2004 and consists of 6 chapters The text is supported by 62 tables, 96 figures, including one map, and 13 photo plates.

For this study, the water samples were collected from four spots.

1. Sampling station A (Satyanarayan area)
2. Sampling Station B (Upstream Vedic nagar)
3. Sampling station C (Downstream Vedic nagar)
4. Sampling station D (Near water pumping station)

The sampling stations were selected on the basis of accessibility and uniformity of concentration across the river implying well mixed conditions. The riverbed at all the four sampling stations has stones and gravel covered by sand. The four spots were selected for this study due to difference in their physiogeography and other conditions.

Suswa is a spring fed river and immediately after crossing Raiwala it assimilates in to river Ganga. The parameters of river water were analyzed by the methods outlined in Welch (1948), Mathur (1982), Trivedi and Goel (1984), APHA (1998), Khanna (1993),

Jhingran (1975), Badola (1979), Shrivastava (1986) and Das (1989) and Mathematical modeling was done according to Giordano *et al.* (1997), Beck (1974) and Rutherford *et al.* (2000).

The results, which were observed during the present investigation, may be summarized as below:

1. The water temperature of the Suswa river at Raiwala (Dehradun) fluctuated between 17.70°C ± 1.11 to 25.61°C ± 0.76. The water temperature showed an upward trend from winter season to summer season followed by a downward trend from monsoon season onwards.
2. Most of the salts dissolved in water are in ionic forms by which water is capable to conduct electricity. The conductivity of Suswa water at Raiwala (Dehradun) was observed maximum (0.085 siemens/cm ± 0.12) in summer season this may be due to evaporation of water, generally, natural water possess low conductivity but contamination increase its level.
3. The turbidity of river Suswa was found maximum (40 JTU ± 5.60) in monsoon season. In winter and summer season the turbidity was found nil. The turbidity was found maximum in monsoon season due to silt, clay, sand, microscopic biota, organic matter etc.
4. A total solid is a measure of dissolved and suspended impurities of water. Higher concentrations of these are much harmful to the biota of the water body and also to man when he uses it for various purposes. The maximum (1375 mg/l ± 478.71) total solids were recorded in monsoon season and minimum (500 mg/l ± 0.00) in winter season. The minimum concentration in winter season was due to gradual sedimentation of the filterable residue at the bottom.
5. The velocity was found to be directly proportional to the flood level and also with gradient of the river stretch. The maximum velocity was recorded (0.49 m/s ± 0.08) in summer season and minimum (0.22 m/s ± 0.05) in winter season.
6. pH expresses the intensity of acidity or alkalinity of an aqueous solution, and represents hydrogen ion

concentration. The pH of river Suswa was slightly alkaline. It fluctuates from 7.70 ± 0.28 to 7.19 ± 0.13.

7. BOD is value of DO used by microorganisms in decomposing the organic matter. BOD was observed maximum (1.13 mg/l ± 0.60) in monsoon season and minimum (0.42 mg/l ± 0.08) in winter season.
8. The test for COD is designed to measure the oxygen required for the oxidation of organic matter in the sample by strong oxidant. The maximum value of COD was observed (4.67 mg/l ± 0.50) in monsoon season and minimum (1.75 mg/l ± 0.05) in winter season.
9. The determination of DO is vital for ensuring aerobic conditions in water. For the control of river pollution it is necessary to maintain conditions satisfactory for the growth and reproduction of fish and other biota. Maximum (9.11 mg/l ± 0.77) oxygen content of water was recorded in winter season and minimum (7.00 mg/l ± 1.74) in monsoon season. The dissolved oxygen reduced gradually from summer to monsoon season due to turbidity, which retarded the photosynthetic activity of aquatic flora. In winters low temperature conditions and high aeration rate was responsible for increased amount of dissolved oxygen.
10. The oxidation-reduction index (rH_2) was found maximum (28.90 ± 0.16) in monsoon season while minimum (26.85 ± 0.54) in winter season.
11. The redox potential is an indication of the 'energy' state of water system, governed by the presence of oxidized and reduced chemical substances or their biological activities. The maximum (1.35 ± 0.01) oxidation-reduction potential was observed in monsoon season while minimum (0.35 ± 0.02) in winter season.
12. Free carbon dioxide of Suswa water fluctuated between (5.00 mg/l ± 2.97) to (0.5 mg/l ± 0.01). The carbon dioxide content of the water increases with increase in temperature.
13. The acidity of water ranges from (73.18 mg/l ± 6.85) to (44.58 mg/l ± 8.53) maximum acidity was recorded in winter season and minimum in summer season.

14. The capacity of water to neutralize a strong acid is known as alkalinity. The alkalinity was present throughout the year. The maximum (319.58-mg/l ± 35.29) alkalinity was found in monsoon season while minimum (241.24-mg/l ± 33.86 in summer season.
15. The carbonates and bicarbonates of calcium and magnesium mainly cause hardness of the natural water. The total hardness fluctuates between (257.74 mg/l ± 21.73) to (219 mg/l ± 19.02).
16. Natural water generally contains low concentration of chloride; higher concentration is harmful and produces salty taste. The maximum (76.89 mg/l ± 13.73) calcium was observed in monsoon season and minimum (54.37 mg/l ± 7.75) in winter season.
17. The magnesium in Suswa water was observed maximum (53.87 mg/l ± 4.17) in winter season and minimum (35.50 mg/l ± 3.82) in winter season.
18. The prominent sources of phosphorus in natural water are sewage, agricultural runoff, detergents etc. The phosphates were highest in monsoon season (0.15 mg/l ± 0.03) and minimum (0.01 mg/l ± 0.03) in winter season.
19. The maximum amount of calcium in Suswa was found as (76.89 mg/l ± 13.73) in monsoon season and minimum (54.37 mg/l ± 7.73) in winter season.
20. Among heavy metals, the concentration of lead (Pb) fluctuated between 0.08 mg/l ± 0.00 to 0.062 mg/l ± 0.011, concentration of copper fluctuated between 0.024 mg/l ± 0.0014 to 0.012 mg/l ± 0.00, concentration of Iron fluctuated between 6.10 mg/l ± 0.16 to 4.92 mg/l ± 0.33, concentration of manganese fluctuated between 0.008 mg/l ± 0.001 to 0.002 mg/l ± 0.001, concentration of Zinc fluctuated between 3.92 mg/l ± 0.05 to 3.22 mg/l ± 0.06 and the concentration of cobalt fluctuated between 0.009 mg/l ± 0.01 to 0.002 mg/l ± 0.0008.
21. The total planktonic concentration was found maximum (5456 units/l ± 3572.30) in winter season and minimum (466 unit/l ± 329.51) in monsoon season. The plankton showed a positive relationship with dissolved oxygen

while showed a negative relationship with pH, temperature, and free CO_2.

22. The genera of zooplankton and phytoplankton of the river Suswa at Raiwala (Dehradun) at different study points are listed in the text.

    Total 8 genera of zooplankton were recorded. Rotifera group dominated among zooplankton. Total 24 genera of phytoplankton were observed. Among different groups of phytoplankton the diatoms were found dominating.

23. The coefficient correlation among zooplankton and phytoplankton were found highly positive. The correlation of different parameters is given in the text.

24. Bacteria were found minimum in winters due to low temperature, much dissolved oxygen, low velocity, low turbidity and maximum zooplankton of water. Bacteria were recorded maximum in monsoon season.

25. Total 9 species of bacteria were recorded in the water of river Suswa at Raiwala (Dehradun). Among these species 7 were recorded pathogens (bio-indicators) and rest are non-pathogenic.

26. Fungus was found minimum in winter and maximum in monsoon season.

27. Total 3 fungus were isolated during the course of study.

28. The fish fauna of the river Suswa at Raiwala (Dehradun) was surveyed. As a result of this survey 30 species, belonging to 9 families have been reported. The list of fish fauna is given in the text.

29. The Value of DO at site B is obtained as 7.35mg/l for the year 2002–2003 and 7.74 mg/l for the year 2003–2004. While the value of BOD is obtained as 0.46 mg/l for the year 2002–2003 and 0.50 mg/l for the year 2003–2004 by applying the given model, The Value of DO at site C is obtained as 7.45mg/l for the year 2002–2003 and 7.31 mg/l for the year 2003–2004. While the value of BOD is obtained as 0.56 mg/l for the year 2002–2003 and 0.51 mg/l for the year 2003–2004 by applying the given model, The Value of DO at site D is obtained as 7.37 mg/l for the year 2002–2003 and 7.20 mg/l for the year 2003–2004. While the

value of BOD is obtained as 0.51 mg/l for the year 2002–2003 and 0.65mg/l for the year 2003–2004 by applying the given model:

30. From the present study it may be concluded that:–
    (a) There were only minor differences in physical, chemical, heavy metals and biological parameters of all the four sampling stations selected for the study.
    (b) All the bacterial and fungal species especially pathogens were not found in large number, but their presence in Suswa water is an alarm for increasing pollution of river Suswa.
    (c) Various DO and BOD models had been developed so far but with the help of our BMKB model, we have calculated DO and BOD concentrations without using light intensity. All the models developed so far use light intensity, but in cloudy day or in monsoon season when light intensity is zero, this model provides good data. As we know that there is a negative relationship between DO and BOD. This is also proved by graphic representation of data obtained from the mathematical model.

References

Abraham, Beena T. Anirudhan, T.S. and Sumesh Kumar, K.S. (2002): Distribution of hydrographic parameters and heavy metal ions in river Periyar, *J.Nat. Env. & Poll. Tech.*, Vol. 1(3): 161-163.

Adebisi, A.A. (1981): The physico-chemical hydrology of a tropical seasonal river–Upper Ogun river (Nigeria), *Hydrobiologia*, 79(2): 157-165.

Adoni, A.D. (1985): Eutrophication and production studies of some lentic ecosystem around Sagar (M.P) Ann. Rept.,*MBA Proj.*, 100-108.

Adoni, A.D. (1975): Studies on microbiology of Sagar lake,. *Ph.D. Thesis*, Univ. Sagar, M.P.

Aggarwal, D.K, Gaur, S.D., Tiwari, I.C., Narayanaswami, M.S. and Marwali, S.M. (1976): Physico-chemical characters of the Ganga at Varanasi, *Indian J. Environ. Health*, 18:201-206.

Ahmed, K. and Begum, J. (2002): Bacteriological quality of water in hill stream of Khanapara during different seasons, *J.Nat. Env. & Poll. Tech.*, Vol. 1(3): 171-173.

Akan, A.O., Schafran, G.C., Pommerenk, P. and Harrell, L.J. (2000): Modeling storm water run off quantity and quality from Marine drydocks, *J.Env. Eng.*, 126(1): 5-11.

Alabi, R.O. (1971): Factors affecting seasonal occurrence of Saprolegniaceae in Nigeria., *Trans. Br. Mycol. Soc.*, 56:289-299.

Alexander, W.B., Southgate, B.A. and Bassumdale, R. (1935): Survey of the river Tees. II the estuary chemical and biology Tech. pap, *Wat. Poll. Res.*, No. 5 HM S0 London.

Allen, W.E. (1920): A quantitative and statistical study of the plankton of the San Joaquin River and its tributaries in a near Stockton California, 1913, *Univ. Calf. Publ. Zool.*, 22 (1): 1-24.

Andren, A.W. (1974): Ph.D. Dissertation, Florida state university, Oceanography Department, Tallahassee, Fla.

APHA, AWWA, WPCF (1998): Standard methods for the examination of water and wastewater, 20th ed., Washington D.C., New York.

Arjariya, Amita (2003): Physico-chemical profile and plankton diversity of Ranital lake, Chhatarpur, M.P., *J.Nat. Env. & Poll. Tech.*, Vol. 2(3): 327-328.

Asaeda, Takashi, Trung, Vukien, and Mangtunge, Jagath (2000): Modeling the effects of macrophyte growth and decomposition on the nutrient budget in Shallow lakes, *Aquatic Botany*, 68:217-237.

Asaeda, Takashi and Karunaratne, Shiromi (2000): Dynamic modeling of the growth of *Phragmites australis*: model description, *Aquatic Botany*, 67:301-318.

Asaeda, Takashi, Pham, H.S., Priyantha, D.G.N., Manatunge, J. and Hocking, G.C. (2001): Control of algal blooms in reservoirs with a Curtain: a numerical approach, *Ecological Engineering*, 16: 395-404.

Asaeda, Takashi, Trung, Vukein, Manatunge, Jagath and Bon Truong van (2001): Modeling macrophyte-nutrient–phytoplankton interaction in shallow eutrophic lakes and the evaluation of environmental impacts, *Ecological Engineering*, 16: 341-357.

Atkin, W.R.G. and Harris, G.T. (1924): Seasonal changes in the water and Heleoplankton of fresh water ponds, *Proc. Roly. Dub. Soc.*, VIII (N.S): 1-21.

Awatramani, G.M. (1980): Limnological studies of Sagar lake, *Ph.D. Thesis*, Univ. of Sagar, M.P.

Babu, Narendra, G. and Manoharachary (1992): Studies on the extra aquatic fungi associated with two polluted water bodies, Andhra Pradesh, India, *J. Indian bot. Soc.*, Vol.71:129-132.

Badola, S.P. (1979): Ecological studies on the Ichythofauna of some freshwater resources of Garhwal Region, *D.Phil Thesis*, Garhwal University.

Badola, S.P. and Badola, Smita (1999): Observations on destructive fishing methods and recommendations to protect fish fauna in Garhwal Himalaya, *Sus. Eco. SysEnv. &*, Ed. By D.R. Khanna, A.Gautam and A.Gautam pp-99-104.

Badola, S.P. and Singh, H.R. (1981): Hydrobiology of the river Alaknanda of Garhwal Himalaya, *Indian J. Ecol.*, 8(2): 269-276.

Bale, E. Andrew (2000): Modeling aquatic mercury fate in clear lake, Calif.,*J. Env. Eng.*, 126 (2): 153-163.

Baloni, M.C. and Sarkar, H.L. (1965): Some on the pollution of Yamuna river at Okhla water works intake Delhi., *Indian J. environ. Health*, 7: 84-86.

Barrett, P.H. (1953): Relationship between alkalinity and absorption and regeneration of added phosphorus in fertilized trout lakes. *Trans. Amer. Fish. Soc.*, 82: 78-90.

Bartholow, J., Hanna, R.B., Saito, L., Lieberman, D. and Horn, M. (2001): Simulated limnological effects of the Shasta lake temperature control device., *Environmental management*, 27(4): 609-626.

Basu M. and Mitra, A.K. (2002): Studies on the pollution of river Damodar at Burdwan with special reference to metals, COD and pH, *J. Nat Env.& Poll Tech.*, Vol. 1(4): 397-399

Basu, A.K. Rao, C.G.S., Dhaneshwar, G, Mukherjee, M.K.A., Kutty, D., Ray and Trivedi, R.C. (1973): Study on Hooghly estuaries pollution in the vicinity of tissue mill. *Proc. Symp. On Environ. Poll*, 24-46.

Beck, M.B. (1974): Maximum likelihood identification applied to DO-BOD-algae models for a fresh water stream, *Report 7431(C), Lund Institute of Technology*, Division of automatic control, Sweden.

Berner, L.M. (1951): Limnology at the lower Missouri River, *Ecology*, 32: 1-12.

Bhatnagar, Babita and Garg, A.P. (1990): Qualitative and Quantitative analysis of microfungi colonising leaf-litter of *Oryza Sativa*. L., *J..Indian bot. Soc*, Vol. 69:81-87.

Bhatt, S.D., Bisht, Y. and Negi, U. (1984): Ecology of Limniflora in river Koshi of the Kumaun Himalaya (U.P.). *Proc. Indian Natu. S.C.*, 50(4): 395-405.

Bhowmick, B.N. and Singh, A.K. (1985): Phytoplankton Population in relation to physico-chemical factors of River Ganga at Patna., *Indian J. Ecol.*,12(2): 360-364.

Bilgrami, K.S. and Duttamunshi, J.S. (1985): Ecology of river Ganges (Patna Farrakka). *Technical report, CSIR*.

Birge, E.A. and Judey, C. (1911): The inland lake of Wisconsis, the dissolved gases and their biological significance., *Bull. Wis. Geat Nat. Hist. Surv*, 22-259.

Bissonnette, G.K., Jezeski, J.J., McFeters, G.A. and Stuart, D.G. (1975): Influence of environmental stress on enumeration of indicator bacteria from natural waters. *Appl. Microbiol.*, 29, 186-194.

Biswas, A.K. (1970): History of hydrology, North–Holland, Amsterdam.

Biswas, A.K. (1981): Models for water quality management, McGraw-Hill Book Company, New York.

Biswas, Asit K. (1998): Water resources: Environmental Planning, management and development., *Tata Mc. Graw Hill Publishing company limited*, New Delhi. Pp 1-737.

Blois, C.J. de, Wind, H.G., Kok, L. de and Koppeschoar, K. (2003): Robustness of river basin water quality models, *J. WaterResources planning and management*, May/June 129 (3): 189-199.

Bonde, G.J. (1977): Bacterial indication of water pollution. In Advances in Aquatic Microbiology (Edited by Droop M.R. and Jannash H.W.). Vol. 1 *Academic press*, London.

Borrego, J.J., Cornax, R., Morninigo, M.A., Manzanares, E.M. and Romero, P. (1990): Colliphages as an indicator of fecal pollution in water. Their survival and productive infectivity in natural aquatic environments. *Water Res.*, 24(1): 111-116.

Brezonik, P.L. and Stadelmann, T.H. (2002): Analysis and predictive models of storm water runoff volumes, loads and pollutant concentration from watersheds in the Twin cities metropolitan area, Minnesota, USA., *Water Research*, 36: 1743-1757.

Canter, Larry W. (1996): Environmental impact assessment, *Mc Graw–Hill Inc. New York.*, Pp 1–660.

Carpenter, K.E. (1928): Life in inland waters with special reference to animals. *Sidwick and Jackson*, London, 1-15:1-267.

Chacko, P.I. and Srinivasan, R. (1955): Observations on the hydrobiology of the major rivers of Madras state, south India, *Fresh Biol. Stn.* Madras, 13: 1-14.

Chakarbarty, R.D., Ray, P and Singh, S.B. (1959): A quantitative survey of plankton and physiological conditions of the river Jamuna at Allahabad I 1954-1955., *Indian J. Fish*, 6(1): 186-203.

Chandler, D.S. (1940): Limnological studies of western Eric I: Plankton and certain physico–chemical data of Bass island region from September 1938 to November 1939, Ohio., *J. Sc*; 40:291-336.

Chandra shekhar, T. and Kodarkar, M.S {1994}: Biodiversity of zooplankton in Saroornagar lake, Hyderabad, *J.Aqua Bio, l9* {1 & 2}: 30-33.

Chandramouli, V. and Raman, H. (2001): Multi reservoir modeling with dynamic programming and neural networks., *Journal of water resources planning and management*, 127 (2): 89-98.

Chapman, Deborah. V. (1998): Water Quality monitoring: In water resources a book edited by Asit K. Biswas, *Tata Mc. Graw Hill Publishing house*, New Delhi. pp: 209-248.

Chapra, Steven C. (2003): Engineering water quality models and TMDLs, *J. water Resources planning and management*, July/August: 247-256.

Chatterjee, Ranjan Pinaki and Raziuddin, M. (2003): A case study on evolution of water quality of lakes by pollution index method., *J.Nat. Env. & Poll. Tech.*, Vol. 2(2): 171-172.

Chattopadhya, S.N., Routh, T., Sharma, V.P., Arora, H.C. and Gupta, R.K. (1984): A short-term study on the pollution status of Ganga river in Kanpur Region., *Indian J. Environmental Hlth.*, 26(3): 244-257.

Chau, K.W. and Jiang, Y.W. (2002): Three dimensional pollutant transport model for the Pearl river estuary., *Water Research*, 36: 2029-2039.

Cherry, W.B., Hanks, J. B., Thomason, B.M., Murlin, A.M., Biddle, J.W. and Croom, J.W. (1972): Salmonellae as an index of pollution of surface water. *Appl. Microbiol.*, 24: 334-340.

Chopra, A.K. and Patrick, Nirmal. J. (1994): Effect of domestic sewage on self purification of Ganga water at Rishikesh I. Physico Chemical parameters, *Ad. Bios*, Vol., 13 (11): 75-82.

Chopra, A.K. and Rehman, A. (1995): A study on self-publication of physico–Chemical properties of Ganga Canal water at Jwalapur, Haridwar, *Him. J. Env–Zoo*, Vol.9: 11-13.

Choubey, U. (1997):Observations on community analysis of zooplankton from Gandhisagar reservoir, Mandsaur {M.P}. India, *Recent advances in fresh water Biol.*, 2:21-48.

Chugh, Tarun (2000): Seasonal variation in the microbial ecology of River Ganga at Hardwar, *Ph. D. thesis* submitted to Gurukul Kangri University Haridwar.

Clark, R.M. and Sivaganesan, M. (2002): Predicting chlorine residuals in drinking water: Second order model, *J.Wat. Res. Pla. & Man.*, 128(2): 152-161.

Clarke, F.W (1924): The data Geochemistry., Sthed–Bull *U.S Goel. Surv*, P– 770.

Comin, Francisco, A., Silveira, J.A.H. and Ramirez, J. R. (2000): Limnology and aquatic Birds: Monitoring, modeling and management,.*Proc. of second international symposium on limnology and aquatic birds*, pp 1-262.

Crayton, W.M. and Sommerfield, M.R. (1979): Composition and abundance of phytoplankton in tributaries of the lower Colorado River, Canyon region., *Hydrobiologia*, 66(1): 81-93.

Crowder, D.W. and Diplas, P. (2000): Using two –dimensional hydrodynamic models of scales of ecological importance,*Journal of Hydrology*, 230:172-191.

Das, S. M. (1961): Hydrogen ion concentration, plankton and fish in fresh water Eutrophic lakes of India, *Nature*, 191(4787): 511-512.

Das, S.M. (1989): In: Handbook of limnology and water pollution, *South Asian Publishers*, New Delhi 1-174.

Das, S.M. and Pathani, S.S. (1978): A study on the effect of lake ecology on productivity of Mahaseer (*Tor tor* and *Tor putitora*) in Kumaon lakes, India, *Matsya*, 4:25-31.

Das, S.M. and Srivastava, V.K. (1956 a): Some new observations on fresh water plankton Pt. I, plankton of fish tanks of Lucknow *Sci. and Cult*, 21(8): 466-467.

Das, S.M. and Srivastava, V.K. (1956 b): Quantitative studies on fresh water plankton, Part II. Correlation between plankton and hydrological factors. *Proc. Nat. Acad. Sci.* India, 26B: 243-254.

David, A. (1956): Studies on the pollution of the Bhadra river at Badrawati fisheries effluents. *Proc. Nat. Inst. Set. India*, 93(3): 132-160.

Dobriyal, A.K. (1985): Ecology of Limnofauna in the small streams and their importance to the village life in Garhwal Himalaya. *Uttar Pradesh J. Zool.*, 5(2): 139-144.

Dorris, T.C. (1963): Limnology of the middle Mississippi river IV physical and chemical limnology of river and chute., *Limnol. Oceanogr*, 8:79–99.

Dutka, B.J. (1973) and Bell, J.B. (1973): Isolation of Salmonellae from moderately waters. *J. Wat. Pollut. Cont. Fed*, 45: 316-323.

Dutka, B.J. (1973): Coliforms are an inadequate index of water quality. *J. Envir. Hlth.*, 36:39-46.

Dwivedi, H.N., Pandey, B.N., Manoj, Kumar and Naushad Alam (1995): Limnological studies in relation to fish production of two ponds of Patna, *Him. J. Env–zool.*, Vol.9: 7-10.

Eddy, S. (1934): A study of the fresh water plankton communities Illinois, *Biol. Monogr*, 12(4): 1-93.

Ellis, M.N. (1937): Detection and measurement of stream pollution *Bull. V.S. Bur. Fish*, 48: 356-437.

Fokmare, Anil, K. and Musaddiq, Mohmmad. (2002): A study on Physico-chemical characteristics of Kapshi lake and Purna river water in Akola district of Maharastra (India)., *J. Nat. Env. & Poli.Tech.*, Vol. 1(3): 261-263.

Freiser, H. and Fernando, Q. (1966): Ionic equilibria in analytical chemistry, *Willey and sons*, New York.

Galtsoff, P.S. (1924): Limnological observation in the upper Mississippi, 1921. *Fish Bull. V.S.*, 39: 347-438.

Gandhe, R.V. and Gandhe, Kanchanganga. (2000): Occurence of riverine water molds in relation to hydrogen ion concentration, *J.Indian bot.Soc.*, Vol. 79: 149-153.

Gangji, Zhen, Hamrick, J.H. and Pagenkopf, James (2002): Sediment and metals modeling in shallow river, *J. Env. Eng.*, 128 (2): 105-119.

Ganpati, S.V. and Chacko, P.I. (1951): An investigation on the river Godavari and effect of paper mills pollution at Rajahmundry,*Proc. Pacific fish Comm.*,:70.

Garner, J.H., Brown, F.W. and Lovett, M. (1936): Chemical and biological survey of the river Holme., *Rep. W. riding Riv. Bd.*

Gautam, Ashutosh. (1990): Ecology and pollution of mountain waters, Ashish publishing house, New Delhi, 1-209.

Gautam, Ashutosh, Sarkar, Praveen and Khanna, D.R. (2001): Quality deterioration in aquatic environment of the Ganges: A growing problem for future, *Ind J. Env. Sc.*, 5 (2): 113-117.

Gelda, R.K., Effler, S.W. and Donnell, S.M.O. (2001): Probabilistic model of ammonia and toxicity status for urban lake, *Journal of water resources planning and management*, 127 (5): 337-347.

Ghousuddin, M. (1934): Notes on the algal flora of the river Mossi, Hyderabad. (Deccan), *J. Qsm. Univ.*, 1-3.

Giordano, F.R., Weir, M.D., Fox, W.P. (1997): A first course in mathematical Modeling, 2nd ed. *Brooks/Cole Publishing company*, 1-525.

Govindan, V.S. and Sundaresan, B.B. (1979): Seasonal succession of algal flora in polluted region of Adyar river. *Indian J. Env. Hlth*, 21(2): 131-142.

Goyal, S.M., Gebra, C.P. and Melnick J.L. (1977): Occurrence and distribution of bacterial indicators and pathogens in canal communities along the Texas coast. *Appl. Envir. Microbiol*, 34: 139-149.

Greenfield, R.E. (1925); Comparison of chemical and bacteriological examination made on the Illinois river during a season of low and season of high water 1923–24 Illinois State, *Wat. Surv. Bull*, 10; 9-33.

Griffith, R.S. (1955): Analysis of plankton yield in relation to certain physical and chemical factors of lake Michigan, *Ecology*,36(4); 543-552.

Grimsrud, G.P., Finnemore, E.J. and Owen, H.J.,(1976): Evaluation of water quality models–*A management guide for planners*, EPA 600/ 5-76-004, U.S. Environmental Protection Agency,Washington, D.C. pp. 21-35.

Hanna, R.Blair, Saito, Laurel, Bartholow, M. John and Sandelin Jeff (1999): Results of simulated temperature control device operations on in-reservoir and discharge water temperatures using CE-QUAL-W2., *Journal of lake and Reservoir management*, 15(2): 87-102.

Hart, W.B., Doudroff, P. and Greenbank, J. (1945): The evaluation of the toxicity of the industrial wastes, chemicals and other substances to fresh water fishes. *Atlantic Refining Company*, Philadelphia, 317-331.

Hays, E.R. and Anthony, E.H. (1958): *Limnol. Oceanogr*, 3(3): 297-307.

Heper, B. (1962): Primary production in the fishpond and its application to fertilization experiments. *Limnol. Oceanogr*, 7(2): 131-136.

Holden, S.M. and Green, J. (1960): Hydrology and Plankton at river Sokoto, *J. Anim. Ecol.*, 29 (I): 65-84.

Hutchinson, G.C. (1957): A treatise on Limnology, Geography, Physical and chemical, Vol. I New York: *John Wiley and Sons*, Inc., 1-1015.

Hynes, H.B.N. (1970): The ecology of running waters. *Liver Pool University Press* Liverpool, 4th impression, 1–555.

Jain, Renu and Sharma, Dushyant, (2000): Water quality of Rampur reservoir of Guna District (Madhya Pradesh, India), *Env.Cons.J*, 1 (2&3): 99-102.

James, A. (1993): Ed. An introduction to water quality modeling, *John wiley and sons*, west sussex, England,

Jaya Devi, M. (1985): Ecological Studies of the limnoplankton of three freshwater bodies of Hyderabad., *Ph.D Thesis*,Osmania University, Hyderabad.

Jayachandran, M., Samuvel, D.J., Ahmed, A.N and Mushtha, M. (1995): Seasonal variation in physico-chemical parameters and plankton analysis Periakulum Pond, *Environ.and Ecol.*, 13{3}: 542-544.

Jena, B., Sudarshana, R. and Chaudhary, S.B. (2003): Studies on water quality parameters around sagar island, sunderbans, *J.Nat env. & Poll. Tech.*, Vol. 2(3): 329-332.

Jha, Ramakar, Ojha, C.S.P and Bhatia, K.K.S. (2001): Two-dimensional river modeling using finite element technique, Proc. Of International Conf. On mathematical modeling, published by, *Tata Mc Graw hill Publishing Company Limited*, pp: 579-584.

Jhajhria, Anita (2002): Limnobiotic studies of Shekwat Pond, Jodhpur with Special reference to plankton., *J.Nat. Con.*, Vol. 14 (2): 215-224.

Jhingran, V.G (1975): Fish and fisheries of India, *Hindustan Publishing Corporation*, (India): 1-954.

Jindal, R. and Ghezta, R. (1998): Pollution Status of water bodies of Chandigarh., *Abs. Nat Con. Sus. Eco. Env*, 68.

John, V. (1976): Hydro biological studies of the river Kallayi in Kerala. *Indian J. Fish*, 23: 72-85.

Johnson, O. Kathryn (1996): Geochemical model of water quality in Pit lake in oxidized Tuff, A report prepared for *Morrison-Maierle Environmental Corporation* Helena, MT., pp: 1-34.

Jokiel, Christian and Loucks, Daniel, P. (1998): Water Quality prediction and management.In water resources a book edited by Asit,K. Biswas, *Tata Mc Graw hill publication*, New Delhi. Pp: 249-296.

Joshi, B.D., Bisht, R.C.S., Joshi, Namita and Singh, Rajendra (1996): A study of planktonic and benthic components of three selected tributaries of river Ganga between Devprayag and Rishikesh., *Him. J. Env–zool.*, Vol.10 pp 23-26.

Joshi, B.D., Pathak, J.K., Singh, Y.N., Bisht, R.C.S. and Joshi, P.C. (1993): On the physico-chemical characterstics of river Bhagirathi in uplands at Garhwal Himalaya., *Him.J.Env. Zool.*, 7: 64-75.

Joshi, C.B. (1996): Hydrobiological profile of river Sutlej in its middle stretch in western Himalaya, *U.P.J.Zool*, 16(2): 9-103.

Juang, R.S. and Shao, Huey, Jen (2002): A simplified equilibrium model for sorption of heavy metal ions from aqueous solution on Chitosan, *Water Research*, 36: 2999-3008.

Kala, Rakhee and Sharma, R.C. (2002): Effect of Physico-chemical factors on phytoplankton population in lotic environment of Alaknanda river, Garhwal Himalaya, Indian *J. Ecol.*, 29(2): 221-226.

Kant, S. and Anand, V.K. (1978): Interrelationship of phytoplankton and physical factors in Mansar lake, Jammu, (J&K), *Indian J.Ecol.*, 5 (2): 134-140.

Kapur, J.N. (2000): Mathematical Modeling, *New age international (P) Limited Publishers,* New Delhi, PP 1-255.

Karunaratne, Shiromi and Asaeda, Takashi (2002): Mathematical modeling as a tool in aquatic ecosystem management., *J. Env. Eng.*, 128(4): 352–359.

Kaul, V. (1977): Limnological survey at Kashmir Lakes with references to trophic status and conservation, *Intl. J. Ecol. Environ. Sc.*, 3: 29-44.

Kaur, Rajendra and Khulbe, R.D. (1998) Occurrence, Distribution and ecology of watermolds in Nanaksagar reservoir Kamaun Himalaya Nainital, Uttarpradesh, India, J. *Indian bot. Soc.,* Vol 17: 111-116.

Kaur, Surender and Joshi, B.D. (2003): Seasonal variation in some physico-chemical parameters of river Ganga in and around Haridwar., *Him. J. Env. & Zoo.*, Vol. 17(1): 45-55.

Keinath, Thomas, M. and Wanielista, Martin P. (1975): Mathematical modeling for water pollution Control processes., *Ann Arbor Science Publishers*,INC. Mich, pp. 1 –446.

Kelly, R.A. (1975): The Delaware Estuary Model. Ecological modeling in a resource management frame work, ed. C.S. Russell resources for the future working paper QE-1, (Baltimore, MD: *Johns Hopkins University Press*), pp: 103-134.

Khanna, D.R. (1993): Ecology and pollution of Ganga River, *Ashish Publication House, Delhi*, 1-241.

Khanna, D.R. and Bhutiani, R. (2003): Limnological characteristic of the river Ganga at Haridwar (Uttaranchal), *U.P.J.Zool.*, Vol. 23(3): 179-183.

Khanna, D.R. and Bhutiani, R. (2003): Limnological status of Satikund pond at Hardwar (U.A.), *Indian J. Env. Sc.*, Vol.7 (2): 131-136.

Khanna, D.R. and Bhutiani, R. (2004): Fish and their ecology of River Ganga at Gohri Ghat Garhwal (Uttaranchal), *Proc. Nat. Sem,* Fish diversity in protected habitats, Ed. By S. Ayyappan, D.S. Malik, Rani Dhanze and R.S. Chauhan pp. 291-298

Khanna, D.R. and Singh R.K. (2000): Seasonal fluctuations in the plankton of Suswa river at Raiwala (Dehradun)., *Env. Cons. J.*, Vol. 1 (2&3): 89-92.

Khanna, D.R. and Singh, S. (2002): Pond fish Ecology and Economics, *Daya Publishing House*, Delhi 1-816

Khanna, D.R. and Singh, Shekhraj. (1999): Diurnal variation in microbial ecology of Narkewala Pond at Ferupur, Hardwar, *Sus. Eco. Sys. & Env.*, Ed. By D.R. Khanna, A.Gautam and A.Gautam pp-99-104.

Khanna, D.R. Chugh, Tarun and Sarkar Praveen (2001): Fluctuation in the population density of Macro-invertebrates of river Ganga At Pashulok barrage, Rishikesh (Uttaranchal, India), *Env. Cons. J.*, 2(1): 37-39.

Khanna, D.R. Malik, D.S. and Rana, D.S. (1997): Phytoplanktonic communities in relation to certain physico–chemical parameter of Ganga canal at Hardwar., *Him. J.Env–Zool.*, 12; 193-197.

Khanna, D.R., Badola, S.P. and Dobriyal, A.K. (1993): Plankton ecology of the river Ganga at Chandighat, Haridwar, *Advances in limnology,* Ed. By H.R. Singh, Narendra Publishing house, New Delhi. 171-174.

Khanna, D.R., Gautam, Ashutosh, Chugh, Tarun, and Sarkar, Praveen (2000): Impact of abiotic factors on the phytoplanktonic population of a pond, *Env. Con. J.*, 1(1): 41-46.

Khanna, D.R., Malik, D.S., Seth, T.R. and Rupendra (1999): Correlation Between abiotic factors and planktonic population in river Ganga at Rishikesh (U.P), *Sus. Eco Sys. & Env*, Ed. by D.R.Khanna

A Gautam and A. Gautam, Published by ASEA, Rishikesh pp. 69-76.

Khanna, D.R., Seth, T.R., Malik, D.S. and Singh, R.K. (1999); Fishes and their ecology of river Suswa at Raiwala (Dehradun), *Sus. Eco. Sys. & Env.*, Ed. By D.R. Khanna, A.Gautam and A.Gautam pp-105-110.

Khulbe, R.D., Bisht, G.S. and Joshi, Chandra (1995): An ecological Study on water molds of some rivers of Kamaun Himalayas, *J. Indian bot. Soc.*, Vol. 74 61-64.

Klich, M.A. and Tiffney, L.H. (1985): Distribution and seasonal occurrence of aquatic Saprolegniaceae in Northwest lowa.

KodarKar, M.S. {1994}: Conservation of Saroornagar lake Hyderabad, Bachao, 3{9}.

Kofoid, C.A. (1908): The plankton of the Illinois river 1894 1899, with introductory notes upon the Illinois rivers and its basin Part III. Constituent organisms and their seasonal distribution, *Bull–Ili. State Lab. Nat. Hist.*, 8; 1-354.

Krishna, D., Bhavani, T. and Sarma, P. N. (2001): Prediction of Treatment concentrations for the reduction of COD of the effluents of pesticide plant by LOGIT model., *Ind J. Env. Prot.*, 21(2): 105-109.

Kudesia, V.P. and Verma, S.P. (1985): A study of industrial pollution on Kali river, *J. Env. Sc.*, 1(2): 41-49.

Kumar, Neeraj and Sharma, R.C. (2002): Water quality of river Krishni {Part-I Physico-chemical characteristics], *J.Nat.Con.*, Vol. 14(2): 273-297.

Kumar, Neeraj and Sharma, R.C. (2002): Water quality of river Krishni {Part-II Physico-chemical characteristics], *J.Nat.Con.*, Vol. 14(2): 299-333.

Lazaras, Asha, D. and Mishra, P.K. (2002); Physico–chemical analysis of Machna river water and related fish ecology at Betul, M.P., India, *Env. Cons. J.*, 3(3): 75-76.

Li, Bin and Fleming, Chris, A (2003): Three–dimensional hydrodynamic model for free surface flow, *J. Hydraulic research*, and 41(4): 367-377.

Lickens, G.E. (1961): Primary production of aquatic ecosystems. In: The primary productivity of the Biosphere, edited by H. Lieth and R.H. Wittakar, *Springer verlgg*, New York.

Lloyd, R. (1961): The toxicity of mixture of zinc and copper sulphate to rain bow trout (*Salmo gaidnerii*) Richardson. Ann *Appl. Biol.*, 49:535-538.

Lund, J.W.B. (1965): The ecology of freshwater phytoplankton. *Biol. Rev.*, 40: 231-293.

Mahajan, S.K, Garde, Yogesh, Bhawsar, Rakesh and Sharma Sharad (2002): Physico-chemical and Biological Characterization of the river Kunda at downstream of Khargone (Madhya Pradesh), India, *Env. Cons. J*, 3(2): 53-55.

Marsh, M.C. (1907): The effect of some industrial wastes on fishes. Wat. Supp. & irrig. Paper no, 192 US *Goel. Surv*, 337–348.

Maruthanayagam, C., Sasikumar, M. and Senthilkumar, C. (2003): Studies on Zoo plankton population in Thirukkulam pond during summer and rainy seasons., *J. Nat. Env. & Poll. Tech.*, Vol. 2(1): 13-19.

Masch, F.D. and Associates (1970): QUALI, Simulation of water quality in streams and canals, program documentation and user's manual., *Report to Texas water development Board, Austin, Tx.*

Mathur, R.P. (1982): Water and waste water testing, *Neemchand and Bros. Publishers*, Roorkee, 1-54.

Mc Bean, E, A, Seth, S, M, Bhatia, K, K.S, and Tyagi, A. (1999): The role of modeling and monitoring data in intrinsic remediation assessments, *Hydrology Journal*, 22(1-4):27-35

Meixner, T. (2002): Multi criteria parameter estimation for models of stream chemical composition., *Water Resources research*, 38(3): 1-9.

Meshram, C.B. (1996): Limnological studies of Wadali lake, Amravati, Maharashtra, *Ph.D. Thesis*, Amravati University, Amravati.

Mir, A.M. and Kachroo, P. (1990): Limnological studies in Kashmir lakes VIII Dynamics of phytoplankton in Dal Lake; *J. Indian bot. Soc*, Vol. 69:435-441.

Misra, N. and Saxena, A.B. (1984): The effect of sewage with special reference to aquatic insects in the river Kshipra (India). *Int. J. Environ. Studies*, 23: 191-208.

Mohanty, R.C. (1981): Water quality studies of some water bodies of Bhubaneshwar, *Ph.D. Thesis*, Utkal University, pp. 1-240.

Monichan, K.K. and Sharma, R.K. (2003): Study on the distribution status of fish fauna in Etawah district, U.P., *Indian J. Env. Sc.*, Vol. 7(2): 115-117.

Morley, Donald A. (1979): Mathematical modeling in water and wastewater treatment. *Applied Science Publishers Ltd.*, London, pp 1–366.

Moss, Brain (1982): Ecology of fresh waters. *Blackwell Scientific Publications*, Oxford, 1-332.

Mruthunjaya, T.B. and Hosmani, S.P. (2002): Comparative account of physico-chemical parameters, enzymatic activity and plankton population in three water bodies of Mysore city., *J.Nat. Env. & Poll.Tech.*, Vol. 1(3): 165-169.

Munawar, M. (1970): Limnological studies on freshwater Pond of Hyderabad–I] Biotape, *Hydrobiologia*, 35: 127-162.

Naito, W. Miyamoto, K.I, Nakanishi, J., Masunaga, S. and Bartell, S.M. (2002): Application of an ecosystem model for aquatic ecological risk assessment of Chemical for a Japanese Lake, *Water Research*, 36:1-14.

Nautiyal, P. (1990): Ecology of the Ganga river system in the upland of Himalaya environment., *Resource and development*, 69-73.

Nayak, T.R., Iyer, S.J. and Jaish, S.C. (1982): Seasonal variations of rotifers and certain physico-chemical factors Matyatal Panna (M.P), India., *Comp. Physiol. Ecol.*, 7(3): 165-169.

Naz, Sabrina, Shah, M. Alam, and Das Tapoti (2002): Aquatic fungi as indicator organisms., *J.Nat. Env. & Poll. Tech.*, Vol. 1(3): 207-211.

Needham, J.G. and Needham, P.R. (1972): A guide to the study of freshwater Biology. Holden-Day I.N.C. San Francisco, *Calif*, 94(3): 1-108.

Oliff, W.O. (1959): Hydrological studies on the Tugela river system. Part I the main Tugela River, *Hydrobiologia*, 14: 281-370.

Olsen, N.R.B., Hedger, R.D. and George, D.G.(2000): 3D Numerical modeling of *Microcystic* distribution in a water reservoir, *J. Env. Eng.*, 126(10): 949-953.

Orlob, G.T. (1983): Mathematical modeling of water quality: Streams, lakes and reservoirs., *John Wiley & Sons*, pp: 1-518.

Pahwa, D.V. and Mehrotra, S.M. (1966): Observations on fluctuations in abundance of plankton in relation to certain hydrological conditions of river Ganga. *Proc. Nat. Acad. Sci.* 36B(2): 157-189.

Pandey, A. K., Siddique, S. Z. and Ramarao, K. V. (1993): Physico-chemical and biological characteristics of Hussain Sagar, an industrially polluted lake Hyderabad.

Pandey, B.N., Kumar, K., Lala, A. and Das, P.K.L. (1993): A preliminary Study on the physico-chemical quality of water of the river Kosi., *J. Ecobiol*, 5:237-339.

Parashar, Nagendra Bhushan, Kaushik, Purroshottam and Pandey shachindra (2003): Physico–Chemical and microbiological studies of Ganga Canal at Haridwar during Kumbh period–1998, *Him. J. Env. Zoo.*, Vol. 17(2): 167–171.

Patel, Pushpa, Mahajan, S.K. Pathak, S.K. (2002): Hydrobiological observations on Virlal reservoir at Khargone (Madhya. Pradesh), India, *Env. Con. J.*, 3(2): 57-59.

Pathak, J.K. (1991): Some aspects of the ecology of river Sarju and Gomti of Kumaun Himalaya, *Ph.D. Thesis*, Kumaun Univertisty Nainital.

Patnik, K.C. and Nayak, L. (2003): Study on diurnal variation of some physico-chemical properties of Gopalpur coastal water of Orissa during the monsoon period., J. *Nat. Env. & Poll. Tech.*, Vol. 2(4): 437-440.

Peenak, R.W. (1962): Quantitative zooplankton sampling in littoral Vegetation areas., *Limnol. Oceanogr*, 7:487-489.

Pinault, J.L, Plagnes, V.and Aquilina, L. (2001): Inverse modeling of the hydrological and the hydrochemical behaviour of hydrosystems: Characterization of Karst system functioning., *J. Wat. Res. Research*, 37(8): 2191 –2204.

Prasad, B.Guru (2003): Physico-chemical and bacteriological quality of ground water at Tadepalli Mandal of Guntur district, Andhra Pradesh, J. *Nat. Env. & Poll. Tech.*, Vol. 2(2): 173-178.

Prasad, Bijay Bhushan, and Singh, R.B. (2003): Composition, abundance and distribution of phytoplankton and zoobenthos in a tropical water body., *J. Nat Env. & Poll. Tech.*, Vol. 2(3): 255-258.

Pruthi, H.S. (1933): Studies on the bionomics of freshwater of India I seasonal changes in the Indian Museum compound Int. Rev., *Hydrobiologia*, 28: 46-67.

Radwan, Mona, Willems, Patrick and Berlamont, Jean (2004): Sensitivity and uncertainty analysis for river quality modeling, *J. Hydro informatics*, and 06.2: 83-99.

Raghavaendra and Hosmani, S.P. (2002): Hydrobiological study of Mandakally lake, a polluted water body of Mysore, *J.Nat. Env. & Poll. Tech*, Vol. 1(3): 291-293.

Raina, V., Saha, A.R. and Ahmed, S.R. (1984): Pollution Studies on river Jhelum–I: An assessment at water quality,*Indian J. env. Hlth.*, 26: 187-210.

Rao, D.S. and Govind, B.V. (1964): Hydrobiology of Tungbhadra reservoir, *Indian J. Fish*. 2(1): 321-344.

Rao, K.S. and Shrivastava, S. (1989): Studies on biological monitoring of water quality in Chambal and Khan rivers of Central India, *Geobios*, 16:78-82.

Rao, K.S., Kartha, K.N., Gupta, D.R., Pandya, S.S. and Iyer, H.K. (1988): Studies on morphometry and hydrology of Gandhi sagar reservoir with special reference to its fisheries, *J. Fish Tech.*, 25(1): 21-28.

Ray, H. K. (1955): Plankton ecology of the river Hoogly at Patna. Ecology, 36(2): 169-175

Reddy, P.M. and Venkateshwarlu, V. (1987): Assessment of water quality and pollution in the river Tungbhadra near Kurnool, (A.P.), *J. Environ. Biol.*, 8(2): 109-119.

Richardson, R.E (1921); Changes in bottom and shore fauna of the middle Illinois river and its connecting lakes Since1913–1915, as a result of the increased southward of sewage pollution Illinois, *Nat Hist. Surv. Bull*, 14:33-75.

Robinson, J.M. and Kaller, E.C. (1976): A comparison of the water characteristics of four northern West Virginia rivers. *Jr. Proc. W.Va. Acad. Sci.*, 48(1): 1-67.

Rutherford, J.C, Scarsbrook, M, R, and Broekhuizen, N. (2000): Grazer control of stream algae: modeling temperature and flood effects., *Journal of Environment Eng*, 331-339.

Saito, L., Fontane, G., Johnson, B.M., Bartholow, J.M (2001): Interdisciplinary modeling to assess ecosystem effects of reservoirs operation., *Integrated water resources management*, Proc. of a Symposium,. Pp. 373-377.

Saito, Laurel, Johnson, B.M., Bartholow, John and Hanna, R. Blair (2001): Assessing ecosystem effects at reservoir operations using food web–energy transfer and water quality models., *Ecosystems*, 4:105-125.

Sangu, R.P.S. and Sharma, K.D. (1985): Studies on water pollution on Yamuna river at Agra. *Indian J. Env. Hlth.*, 27(3): 257-261.

Sarkar, J.P. and Chaudary, S. (1993): Fungi of wastewater environment in relation to pollution of the Hooghly river, *J. Mycopathol. Res.*, 31(1): 5-12.

Saxena, K.K. and Chauhan, R.R.S. (1993): Physico-chemical aspects of pollution studies of river Ganga near Kanpur, *Indian J.Env. Health*, 8: 270-385.

Saxena, K.L., Chakaraborty, R.N., Khan, A.Q. and Chattopadhay, S.N. (1966): Pollution studies of river Ganga near Kanpur, *Indian J. Env. Health*, 8:270-385.

Schnoor, J.L. (1996): Environmental Modeling, *Inter Sc. Publication.*

Schumann, A.H., Funke, R. and Schultz, G.A. (20002): Application of a geographic information system for conceptual rainfall run off modeling., *Journal of Hydrology*, 240:45-61

Sedamkar, Eshwarlal and Angadi, S.B. (2002): Primary Productivity of two fresh water bodies of Gulbarga, India., *J.Nat. Env. & Poll. Tech.*, Vol. 1(3): 151-157.

Seenayya, G. and Zafar, A.R. (1979): An ecological study of the Mir. Alam Lake, Hyderabad, *India. Ind. J. Bot.*, 2:214-220.

Sehgal, K.L. (1983): Planktonic copepods of freshwater ecosystem, Environ. *Sc.*, Series Interprint New Delhi, 1-169.

Selva Raj, D, Jeyaraj Thampi, C. and Chithra, G. (2003): Studies on hydrology and fish species diversity of Thamiraparani river in Kanyakumari district.

Sengar, R.M.S., Sharma, K.D. and Pathak, P.D. (1985): Studies on distribution of algal flora in polluted and non polluted regions in Yamuna river at Agra (U.P.), *J. Indian Bot. Soc.*, 64: 365-376.

Shaikh, Nisar and Yeragi, S.G. (2003): Biodiversity of plankton in Tansa river of Thane district, Maharashtra., *J.Nat. Con.*, Vol. 15 (2): 361-366.

Shanthi, K. Ramasamy, K. and Lakshmanaperumalsamy, P. (2002): Hydrobiological study of Singanallur lake at Coimbatore, India., *J.Nat.Env.&Poll. Tech.*, Vol. 1(2): 97-101.

Sharma, Dushyant and Jain, Renu (2001): Diurnal variation in some aspects of limnology of Gopalpura tank of district Guna (Madhya Pradesh, India), *Env. Cons. J.*, 2(1): 41-44.

Sharma, R.C. (1985): Seasonal abundance of phytoplankton in the Bhagirathi river, Garhwal Himalaya. *Indian J. Ecol.*, 12(1): 157-160.

Sharma, S.D. and Pandey, K.S. (1998): Pollution status of Ramganga river at Moradabad, *Poll. Res.*, 17(2); 201-209.

Shreenivasan, A. (1970): Limnology of a tropical impoundment: A Comparative study of the major reservoirs in Madras State, India,*Hydrobiologia*, 36 (3&4): 443–469.

Shreenivasan, A. (1974): Limnology features of a tropical impoundment, Bhavanisagar reservoir (Tamil nadu), India, Intl. Revue ges., *Hydrobiologia*, 53(3): 327-342.

Shrivastava, G.L. (1986): Fishes of Eastern Uttar Pradesh *Vishwavidyalaya Prakashan*, Varanasi, 1-63.

Shrivasttava, V.S. and Patil, P.R. (2002): Tapti river water pollution by industrial wastes: A statistical approach, *J.Nat. Env. & Poll. Tech.*, Vol. 1(3): 279-283.

Siddiqui, S.Z. (1990): Ecolgical. Studies on the distribution, species composition and seasonal and dial variations in the lake plankton and associated pond–marsh biosis in some lakes and ponds in India., *Ph.D. Thesis*, Meerut university Meerut.

Singh, A.K. and Ahmad, S.H. (1990): A comparative study of the phytoplankton of the River Ganga and Pond of Patna (BIHAR), India, J. *Indian bot. Soc.*, Vol. 69:153-158.

Singh, H.P., Choudhry, M. and Kalekaur, V. (1982): Seasonal and diurnal changes in physico-chemical features of the river Brahamputra at Guwahati, *Ind. J. Zool.*, 2(82): 77-84.

Singh, H.R. (1991): Advances in limnology, *Narendra Publ. House*, New Delhi, p.322.

Singh, K.P. (1960): The chlorophyceae of Kumaon Hills, U.P. India I, Agra *Univ. J. Res.*, (Science), 9(2): 211.216.

Singh, R.K. (1999): A study on seasonal fluctuations in the limnological status at Suswa River at Raiwala (Dehradun), *Dissertation report*, submitted to Gurukula Kangri Vishwavidyalaya Haridwar.

Singhai, S. (1986): Hydro biological and ecological studies of newly made Tawa reservoir at Ranipur. H.S. Gaur University Sagar, *Ph.D. Thesis*.

Sivakumar, A.A., Arunadevi, P. and Aruchami, M. (2003): Studies on water quality of the river Ambarampalayam, Coimbatore, distirict, Tamilnadu., *J. Nat. env. & Poll. Tech.*, Vol.2 (3). 305-308.

Somashekhar, R.K. (1984): Phytoplankton constituents as indicator of water quality. A study of the river Cauvery. *Int. J. Env. Studies*, 24: 115-123.

Son, Duong Hong and Fujino, Takashi (2003): Modeling approach to periphyton and nutrient interaction in a stream, *J. Env. Eng.*, 129 (9): 834-843.

Sorenson, S. (1909): Uber die Messung und dies Bedeutung der w asserstoff ionen Konzentration bei enzymatischen Proozessen, *Biochem. Z.*, 21:131.

Stehfest, H. (1977): Mathematical modeling of self-purification of rivers., *Professional Paper*, pp-77-11 (Laxenburg, Austria International Institute for applied Systems analysis).

Stiff, M.J. (1980): River pollution Control, *Ellis Harwood limited Publisher*, Chichester, Pp 1-423.

Streeter, H.W., and Phelps, E.B. (1925): A study of the pollution and natural purification of the Ohio river, *Bulletin No. 146*. U.S. Public Health Service.

Subbamma, D.V. and Ramasarma, D.V. (1992): Studies on the water quality characteristics of a temple pond near Machilipatnam, Andhra Pradesh., *J. Aqua. Biol.*, Vol. (1 & 2): 22-27.

Subramanyam, B. and Subrahmanya Kumar, C.S.V. (2003): A case study on evaluation of water quality of lakes by pollution index method., *J. Nat. Env. & Poll. Tech.* Vol. 2(1): 69-72.

Sukumaran, S.K. (2002): Coliform bacteria on index of aquatic Pollution, *Trends in Life Sciences*, Vol.17 (1): 19-24.

Texas water development board (1970): DOSAG-I Simulation of water quality in streams and canals., *Program documentation and user's manual*.

The Euro press encyclopedia (1999): Taking action on the environment, *Webster Publishing/Contributors*, (CD–ROM), pp–141-143.

Thomann, R.V. (1963): Mathematical model for dissolved oxygen, *Proc. of American Society of civil engineers, Journal of Sanitary Engineering Division*, 89(SA5): 1-30

Thomann, R.V. and Muller, J.A. (1987): Principles of surface water quality modeling and control, *Harper international edition*, New Delhi.

Thomas, J.F.J. (1958): Churchill River and Mississippi river drainage Basin in Canada, *Ottawa ont. Wat. Surv. Rep.*, 9:53

Tirath, R. and Bhargawa, D.S. (1982): Water quality in Gomti River at Lucknow (U.P.), *J.Ind. Water works Assoc.*, 14: 299-304.

Trivedi, R.K. and Goel, P.K. (1984): Chemical and biological methods for water pollution studies, Karad: *Environmental Publication*, 1-251.

Unni, K.S. (1982): Limnological studies on Sumpna reservoir, Betul, M.P., *Proc. Nat. Sci. Acad.*, India 52(B), IV.

Unni, K.S. (1983): Comparative limnology of several reservoirs in Central India Int. Rev., *Hydrobiologia*, 70 (6), 845–856.

Varshney, C.K. (1981): Macrophytes as indicators of water quality, WHO workshop on biological indicators and indices of environmental pollution.,*Cent. Bd. Prev.Cont. Water poll.*, Osmania University. Hyderabad, India 53-59.

Vasisht, H.S. and Dhir, S.C. (1970): Seasonal distribution of freshwater zooplankton of four tanks, Chandigarh (India),*Ichthyologica*, 110: 44-56.

Venkateshwarlu, T. (1969): An ecological study of the algae of the river Moosi Hyderabad (India) with special reference to the effect of *Microcystis aeruginosa* (kutza) bloom on fish production and suggestions for the improvement of the tank fishery. *Ichthyologica*, 3: 37-46.

Venkateshwarlu, T. and Jayanti, T.V. (1968): Hydrobiological studies of the river Sabarmati to evaluate water quality, *Hydrobiologia*, 33 (3-4): 442-448.

Verma, M. (1967): Diurnal variation in a fishpond in Seoni, India, *Hydrobiologia*, 30: 129-137.

Verma, S.R. and Shukla, G.R. (1969): Pollution in a perennial stream Khala, by the sugar factory effluent near Laksar (Dist. Saharanpur). U.P., *India. J. Env. Hlth.*, 11: 145-162.

Verma, S.R., Sharma, P., Tyagi, A., Rani, S., Gupta, A.K. and Dalela, R.C. (1984): Pollution and saprobic status of eastern Kalinadi, *Limnologica*, 15(1): 69-133.

Viney, N.R., Sivapalam, M. and Deelay, D. (2000): A Conceptual model of nutrient mobilization and transport applicable at large catchment Scales., *Journal of Hydrology*,240:23-44

Vogler, E.T. and Scherfig, J.S. (2000): Modeling BOD removal in constructed wetlands with mixing cell method., *J. Env. Eng*, 125 (1): 782-785.

Wang, Hong, Appan, Adhityan and Gulliver, John S. (2003): Modeling of phosphorous dynamics in aquatic sediments, I – model development, *Water research*, 37: 3928-3938.

Water Resources engineers, Inc. (1973): Computer program documentation for the stream quality model QUAL II., *Report to US environmental protection agency*,pp. 90.

Welch, P.S. (1948): Limnological methods, *The Blakiston. Co. Philadelphia*, 1-381.

Whitton, B.A. (1985): Biological monitoring of heavy metal in flowing waters., *Symp. Biomonitoring state of Environment*, 50-55.

Zafar, A.R. (1959): Taxonomy of lakes, *Hydrobiologia*, 13 (3): 187-299.

Zafar, A.R. (1966): Limnology of the Hussain Sagar Lake, Hyderabad, India, *Phykos*, 5(1&2): 115-126.

Zafer, A.R. (1964): On the ecology of algae in certain fishponds of Hyderabad. India I Physico-chemical Complexes, *Hydrobiologia*, 23:179-195.

Zafer, A.R. (1968); Certain aspects of distribution pattern of phytoplankton in the lakes of Hyderabad. In Symposium on " Recent advances in Tropical Ecology", *Internal. Soc. Trop. Ecol.*, Varanasi, India.

Zafer, A.R. (1986): Seasonality of phytoplankton in some south Indian lakes, *Hydrobiologia*, 138: 177-187.

Index

U

W

Z